A

B O O K

The Philip E. Lilienthal imprint
honors special books
in commemoration of a man whose work
at University of California Press from 1954 to 1979
was marked by dedication to young authors
and to high standards in the field of Asian Studies.
Friends, family, authors, and foundations have together
endowed the Lilienthal Fund, which enables UC Press
to publish under this imprint selected books
in a way that reflects the taste and judgment
of a great and beloved editor.

The publisher gratefully acknowledges the generous support of the Philip E. Lilienthal Asian Studies Endowment Fund of the University of California Press Foundation, which was established by a major gift from Sally Lilienthal.

Paisanos Chinos

Paisanos Chinos

Transpacific Politics among
Chinese Immigrants in Mexico

Fredy González

UNIVERSITY OF CALIFORNIA PRESS

University of California Press, one of the most
distinguished university presses in the United States,
enriches lives around the world by advancing scholarship
in the humanities, social sciences, and natural sciences. Its
activities are supported by the UC Press Foundation and
by philanthropic contributions from individuals and
institutions. For more information, visit www.ucpress.edu.

University of California Press
Oakland, California

Library of Congress Cataloging-in-Publication Data

Names: González, Fredy, 1984– author.
Title: Paisanos Chinos : transpacific politics among
    Chinese immigrants in Mexico / Fredy González.
Description: Oakland, California : University of
    California Press, [2017] | Includes bibliographical
    references and index.
Identifiers: LCCN 2016049873 (print) | LCCN 2016052200
    (ebook) | ISBN 9780520290198 (cloth : alk. paper) |
    ISBN 9780520290204 (pbk. : alk. paper) | ISBN
    9780520964488 (Epub)
Subjects: LCSH: Chinese—Mexico—History. |
    Immigrants—Mexico—History. | Chinese—Mexico—
    Social conditions—20th century.
Classification: LCC F1392.C45 G67 2017 (print) |
    LCC F1392.C45 (ebook) | DDC 972/.004951—dc23
LC record available at https://lccn.loc.gov/2016049873

Manufactured in the United States of America

25 24 23 22 21 20 19 18 17
10 9 8 7 6 5 4 3 2 1

Contents

Illustrations

MAPS

Acknowledgments

I am incredibly grateful to Chinese Mexicans for their help and support, particularly Monica Cinco Basurto and Ignacio Chiu. They and their group Inmigraciones Chinas a México have served as an important vehicle for preserving the community's history, including a conference dedicated to Chinese Mexican history and a commemoration of the 1960 repatriation of Chinese Mexicans. Monica was truly an inspiration, having done so much not only for me but also for other scholars who work on the history of Chinese Mexicans. Despite the fact that I was a community outsider, both were incredibly welcoming and supportive, and their thoughts helped improve parts of this book and made me think about Chinese Mexican history in a more complete way. I also received considerable assistance from Cristina Jolie Lau, Mariana Ming Sze Cheng Leung, and Pilar Chen.

Sources for this project are scattered across several archives in five countries, and thus I am incredibly grateful to the librarians and archivists who helped me quickly and efficiently find the documentation I needed. This especially included the archivists at the Archivo General de la Nación and the Acervo Histórico Diplomático de la Secretaría de Relaciones Exteriores (Mexico) and Academia Historica and the Institute of Modern History at Academia Sinica (Taiwan). I am also grateful for the pools of funding that made this project possible. A Richard U. Light fellowship from Yale provided language training in Beijing and Harbin, while funding was also provided by Yale's Council on East Asian Studies and Fox Fellowship. An IIE Graduate Fellowship for International Study allowed me to conduct research in Mexico. At the University of Colorado, I received funding from the A&S Fund for Excellence, IMPART, GCAH, and the Hazel Barnes Flat. Part of chapter 2 was first published as "Chinese Dragon and Eagle of Anáhuac: The Local, National, and International Implications of the Ensenada Anti-Chinese Campaign of 1934," *Western Historical Quarterly* 44, no. 1 (2013): 48–68.

Kate Marshall and Bradley Depew at University of California Press have truly been a joy to work with, quickly and efficiently moving the project forward from advance contract to publication. Many thanks to the scholars who provided careful and thorough feedback on the manuscript—including Erika Lee, Evelyn Hu-DeHart, Jason Chang, and two anonymous readers. Their support and helpful criticism helped me refine the argument of the book, be more assertive, and consider its true significance. Roger Waldinger's NEH Summer Seminar encouraged me to think about wider migratory trends, and I appreciate the useful questions posed by members of the seminar. Thanks also to the friends and colleagues who work on Asians in the Americas, including Julia Maria Schiavone Camacho, Jason Chang, Ana María Candela, and Kathleen López.

The University of Colorado has been a wonderful place to work, supporting my research and conference travel to several countries. Several colleagues generously spent a considerable amount of time reading multiple chapter drafts and pushing me to refine my ideas. Elizabeth Fenn was an amazing chair who spent so much time supporting my work at Colorado and never failed to provide encouragement and advice. My brilliant friend and colleague Miriam Kingsberg read the entire manuscript and provided feedback. Elissa Guralnick provided amazingly insightful editing on three chapters during her "Well Argued? Well Written!" seminars. The Department of History's Junior Faculty Reading Group—Mithi Mukherjee, Marjorie McIntosh, Céline Dauverd, John Willis, Kwangmin Kim, Liora Halperin, Sungyun Lim and Samanthis Smalls—generously discussed several drafts and didn't mince words when they had questions or concerns. Many thanks to the rest of the history department who took time out of their busy schedules to provide advice, answer questions, and offer encouragement and congratulations (often over a coffee or beer).

My friends from graduate school are now scattered across the globe, but it has been a joy to see them at conferences and at joyful occasions. Andre Deckrow wrote a review of my dissertation and provided helpful feedback. Romeo Guzmán often dropped everything to read a last-minute chapter or article draft, for which I'm incredibly grateful. Lisa Ubelaker Andrade and Marian Schlotterbeck helped me set clear goals as we met week after week with the target of publishing our work. Gil Joseph has continued to be a wonderful mentor even years after graduation, taking time to strategize with me and write letters on my behalf.

It's overwhelming to think about the incredible kindness that people showed me in the course of this project. Several people graciously opened their homes to me either repeatedly or over an extended period of time, or took time to show me around the city or even the island. They took a deep breath and explained things again in simpler Chinese and Spanish. They told me my work was interesting even when it wasn't. They pointed out helpful archives and resources and introduced me to gatekeepers who made all the difference. Others took me under their wing without knowing much about me and invited me to participate in conferences and symposia, or introduced me to editors. I didn't deserve any of this and thus feel incredibly grateful. I particularly would like to thank Xander Woolverton and Marie Barnett, J. C. Kollmorgen, Javier Pérez Espinoza and Rogelio Maya, Stone and Carol Chen, Austin Paichun Cheng, Benjamin Paske, Nancy and Norma González Gómez, Peter Liu Hanzhong, and the Cai family.

Thanks to my family for all the love and support through the many years it took to complete this project. My siblings, Carlos, Nancy, Evelyn, and Brian, and my nephew, Mathew, were always there for me no matter what part of the world I found myself in. Several times they came out and kept me company, or welcomed me back to Los Angeles. My parents, Carlos González Arellano and Imelda Alvarado Ríos, encouraged me, from the time I was very young, to read extensively and to be curious about the world outside of South Central. I owe my life path to them.

Taipei, Taiwan
August 22, 2016

Note on Language and Usage

Chinese-language names, documents, and phrases are transliterated using the Hanyu Pinyin system. If extant documents reveal that Chinese migrants, diplomats, and politicians spelled their names differently, or used a Spanish- or English-language name, I use that name to refer to them, although where possible I include their name in Hanyu Pinyin on first mention. I record the Chinese names of migrants and diplomats using the surname first. In Spanish, some Chinese migrants followed the Mexican practice of using both their paternal and maternal last name after their given name.

Some Chinese-language books include English- or Spanish-language titles (even if they don't have any text in Spanish or English). Where those are available, I have provided them in the text and notes.

Even as I recognize the troublesome nature of the word *huaqiao* (overseas Chinese), I have retained it when translating from Chinese-language sources. *Moguo huaqiao* was often translated as "Chinese Mexicans."

Introduction

Two celebrations carried out by Chinese Mexicans just a week apart—
one featuring Mexican dance in Taipei, the other performing Chinese
dance in Mexico City—allowed a small and seemingly insignificant
community to demonstrate before a transpacific audience their understanding of home and belonging in a world sharply divided by the politics of the Cold War. On October 20, 1961, a visiting Chinese Mexican
dance group performed before a packed house at the International
House in Taipei, Republic of China (located on Taiwan after 1949).
Wearing traditional costumes like the *china poblana* and the *traje de
charro*, they performed Mexican folkloric dances including the *jarabe
tapatío* and other regional dances from the Mexican states of Jalisco,
Oaxaca, and Veracruz. In this way they introduced the Taiwanese audience, likely for the first time, to their Mexican culture.[1] On October 29,
over eight thousand miles away in Mexico City, members of the same
community donned *qipao* dresses, carried Mexican and Republic of
China flags as well as banners of the Virgin of Guadalupe, and performed lion and dragon dances on the pilgrimage route to the Basílica
de Nuestra Señora de Guadalupe, Mexico's holiest Catholic shrine.

Because images of the Chinese as the literal standard-bearers of Mexican culture are largely absent from Mexican archives, historians of the
Chinese community in Mexico have not had access to these brief but
telling moments about belonging and nationhood. The lack of Mexican
sources that document the presence of Chinese Mexicans in the country

at midcentury seems to suggest the community's absence, as if they had been completely driven out of the country thirty years prior. In the aftermath of the Mexican Revolution, a nationalist backlash focused squarely on the "Chinese problem," one that, anti-Chinese activists argued, required urgent and dramatic solutions.[2] They formed associations, particularly in the northwestern states of Sonora and Sinaloa, that lobbied for hateful legislation targeting the Chinese, boycotted Chinese-owned businesses, and eventually placed the Chinese, against their will, on trucks and boats that carted them away from the country. Over four thousand Chinese were forced, some at gunpoint, to cross into the United States, from which they were deported to China. Many more, horrified at what was happening in Sonora and Sinaloa, left the country on their own. From a height of over sixty thousand, the Chinese population fell dramatically to just over twelve thousand, the vast majority of those who were expelled never to return.[3] The Chinese presence declined to the extent that most anti-Chinese associations languished or disbanded, convinced that they had definitively eliminated the Chinese. Although scholars have examined the fate of the refugees from the anti-Chinese campaigns, it is particularly difficult to reconstruct the histories of those who remained after the anti-Chinese movement by using only Mexican sources.

In addition to their simple absence from the archive, the twin celebrations demonstrate that the Mexican sources that do exist present a distorted view of Chinese immigrants and their associations. During the 1930s anti-Chinese activists, obsessed with groups like the Guomindang and the Chee Kung Tong, derided them as "*maffias*" and "secret societies with suspicious ends," infamous for their use of opium and their recurrence to violence.[4] They cited these associations as evidence that the Chinese were self-segregating and unwilling to assimilate into Mexican society. These negative images, used to call for the expulsion of the Chinese during the 1930s, have also influenced the scholarship on Chinese associations in Mexico. Yet the twin celebrations present a radically different picture of these groups—not as secret societies and criminal gangs, but rather as civic organizations enmeshed in Mexican society. For example, in contrast to racist depictions of Chinese associations as "bands of Buddhist criminals," by 1961 Chinese Mexicans could publicly present themselves as faithful and pious Catholics.[5]

In addition to documenting their permanence in the country and disproving allegations of their sinister nature, the 1961 celebrations further discredit a particularly destructive idea propagated in the aftermath of the Mexican Revolution: that the Chinese, no matter how hard they tried, would never fit into the Mexican nation. As the revolution began to give rise to a one-party state, intellectuals such as José Vasconcelos and Manuel Gamio conceived of the Mexican nation as a racial mixture of Europeans, Africans, and Indians.[6] Even as they celebrated miscegenation, Vasconcelos and Gamio decried the potential integration and racial mixture of other groups, such as the Arabs and the Chinese, which they believed would degenerate the racial composition of the country. Anti-Chinese activists concurred, arguing that, while the Mexican was formed of racial mixture, the Chinese were so racially different as to be unassimilable: "[I]t is well known," argued Espinoza, "that the racial spirit [of the Chinese] never dies and if some acquire Mexican nationality, it is simply a question of self-interest."[7] These ideas were crucial to the anti-Chinese campaigns of the 1930s, which were predicated upon the community's marginality.[8] So, too, surprisingly, were the 1961 celebrations. Whereas during the 1930s Chinese ethnic and cultural differences made the community vulnerable to expulsion from the country, by the 1960s it made their message more visible. For this reason, they dressed as outsiders—as Mexicans in Taipei, and as Chinese in Mexico City. Rather than expressing their "racial spirit," however, the twin celebrations demonstrate that, in spite of the violence propagated against them during the 1930s, by the 1960s Chinese Mexicans claimed to belong to Mexico as much as China: by then, Mexico had become home as well.

The dramatically different representations of the Chinese during the 1930s and the 1960s point not only to differences in the source material, but also to important changes affecting the community in the intervening thirty years. During the 1930s, language barriers prevented the Chinese from challenging the racist depictions of their community and hindered them from entering the historical record. Sources in which Chinese migrants contest Mexican racism are overshadowed by the much more numerous racist screeds written by anti-Chinese activists, government officials, and outside observers presenting an unflattering image of the community. Yet the two celebrations also suggest that by 1961 Chinese communities had taken a more proactive role in Mexican society. Despite the fact that the anti-Chinese campaigns might have encouraged the community to remain hidden and quiet, prominent community leaders believed that such open demonstrations were not only logical, but indispensable.

Chinese Mexicans believed public activities to be necessary because by the 1960s there were not one but two Chinese governments seeking international legitimacy and the loyalty of Chinese around the world. The twin celebrations described above were both implicit statements of support for one of these governments: the Republic of China (ROC) on Taiwan. They demonstrated that, although the People's Republic of China (PRC) ruled over mainland China, including the group's home province of Guangdong, Chinese Mexicans nonetheless stood with the ROC. When Chinese groups visited Taipei, they described it as "visiting China" (*fanghua*) even though no Chinese Mexicans traced their ancestry to the island. The Catholic pilgrimage, too, served as an argument against the People's Republic of China: it drew attention to conflicts between the Catholic Church and the Communist government, as well as to the alleged persecution of Catholics in mainland China.

Chinese participation in transnational political issues was the legacy of their exclusion from the Mexican nation during the 1930s. Sources written by these migrants allow us to understand the motivations and aspirations behind their participation in political activities. By focusing on those who through bravery, pluck, or good fortune persevered in the country after the anti-Chinese campaigns, the book traces the racial formation and political participation of Chinese Mexicans through the Second World War and the Cold War. Scholars of immigration to Mexico have contended that extensive ties between immigrants and foreign diplomats erected barriers to immigrants' integration into the host society. They argue that by maintaining transnational ties to foreign diplomats and institutions, immigrant associations helped keep foreigners separate from Mexican society and encouraged the retention of a separate national identity.[9] In contrast, this book contends that transnational ties did not prevent integration, but rather forged an alternative path to achieve it: their links to China helped the Chinese make themselves at home in Mexico.

Chinese integration into Mexico could never have followed the traditional route of assimilation, resulting in a loss of ties to the sending country. This route was foreclosed by the anti-Chinese campaigns, which denied the Chinese a place in the Mexican nation. For the rest of the century, the community saw guarding against another anti-Chinese campaign as essential to their survival. But appeals to the Mexican government would not guarantee their safety. After the success of the anti-Chinese campaigns demonstrated that Mexican citizenship provided little protection from harm, few Chinese sought Mexican nationality or continued to assert their rights as Mexican nationals. Instead, they strengthened their attachments to China, particularly by joining Chinese associations, which first allowed them to guard against anti-Chinese violence and then helped them develop a sense of community among their countrymen.[10] Migrants were convinced that greater cooperation with Chinese diplomats in Mexico would help them respond to anti-Chinese racism, guard against another anti-Chinese movement, and obtain greater stability in the country.

Rather than keeping them separate from Mexican society, Chinese Mexicans' participation in transnational politics made Chinese migrants visible and brought them into contact with Mexican neighbors, other Mexican civic associations, and local and federal politicians. These public demonstrations began as early as 1943, just ten years after the anti-Chinese movement. Despite their small numbers, their activities were regularly featured in newspaper articles and newsreel clips in both Mexico and the Republic of China. Government celebrations and diplomatic functions included Chinese Mexicans as special guests. State and local officials often met with them, particularly in cities and towns where Chinese migrants were numerous. These events enabled the community to demonstrate belonging to both Mexico and China without causing shock, rejection, or ridicule. The ability of Chinese Mexicans to "make themselves 'at home'" despite the exclusionary tendencies of Mexican nationhood is thus similar to Yen Le Espiritu's concept of differential inclusion: they eventually experienced inclusion into the Mexican nation, even if not on the basis of equality with other Mexicans.[11] This book thus helps bring the study of transnational politics among immigrants in Mexico in line with a general pattern observed around the world: that transnational politics makes immigrants more likely to integrate into the host community.[12]

This book offers the history of a generation of migrants and their children who searched for inclusion in Mexican society. Most Mexicans referred to all members of the community, whether first-generation or second-, of full or mixed parentage, as *chinos* or, using the diminutive, *chinitos*—which marked them as foreign and excluded from Mexican society.[13] Yet first-generation migrants referred to themselves by using the Spanish word *paisanos,* or "countrymen."[14] Subsequent generations, which tended to be of mixed Chinese and Mexican heritage, usually referred to themselves instead as *chinos mestizos*. In striking contrast to other foreign diasporas in Mexico, which "reproduced the culture of the sending state" even into the third and fourth generation, *mestizos* showed near-universal rates of full assimilation to Mexican culture by the second generation.[15] Throughout the text, I will refer to the community collectively as "Chinese Mexican" since, regardless of citizenship, migration status, or length of residency, the community and its associations slowly began to demonstrate belonging to both Mexico and China. The title of this book, *Paisanos Chinos,* represents the ways in which Chinese migrants forged their own path to integration in Mexico even in the face of the racist and exclusionary mind-set of the host society.

Despite continued racial animosity toward it, the community became more rooted in Mexico during its long separation from mainland China. After the 1920s, few Chinese migrants arrived in Mexico. From 1937 until 1971, most *paisanos* and their children were largely unable to travel to China and were thus cut off from parents, spouses, and friends on the other side of the Pacific. Unable to return, they increasingly set down roots in Mexico; the men married Mexican wives and fathered Chinese Mexican children. *Mestizo* children demonstrated affective attachments to both countries, but few spoke Cantonese or ever traveled to mainland China. Because of this long separation, in spite of racial ideologies like *mestizaje,* which excluded foreigners from the Mexican nation, by the 1940s the Chinese began to integrate.[16] As the decades passed, many Chinese Mexicans responded to their long separation by claiming to belong to Mexico. Over time they became more likely to adopt symbols like the Mexican flag and the banner of the Virgin of Guadalupe, write to the Mexican president and other government officials like other Mexicans, and express pride in their longtime residency in the country. They did this even as they no longer felt pressured to assimilate to Mexican ways or cut off their ties to their ancestral country. This slow, but significant, integration helps explain why, even after the anti-Chinese campaigns, Chinese immigrants chose to remain in Mexico rather than return to China or migrate elsewhere. In looking at Chinese Mexican political and ethnic identity in the context of local, national, and international forces, this book follows Jeffrey Lesser's assertion that identity "is multifaceted and simultaneously global and local."[17]

Nether China nor Taiwan perceived the increasing integration of Chinese immigrants into Mexican society as a loss, but rather as a potential opportunity to engage in public diplomacy. Both sought to use Chinese Mexicans as interlocutors in the relationship between Mexico and their ancestral country. They viewed Chinese associations as potential lobbying groups that spoke openly to Mexicans, in their own language, about political issues of importance to them. During the Second World War and the Cold War, *paisanos* discussed the impact of those global conflicts on East Asia, and tried to convince the Mexican public and government to sympathize with and support the Republic of China. Because *paisanos* were so useful to the diplomatic relationship, even as they slowly integrated, they didn't shed their ties to the Chinese government, but rather intensified them. Their utility also explains why both the Republic of China and the People's Republic of China were so eager to compete for the loyalty of Chinese Mexicans, even if they were so few in number.

Paisanos primarily engaged in these homeland political activities through two competing associations—the Guomindang (Chinese Nationalist Party) and the Chee Kung Tong (later called the Hongmen Minzhidang and sometimes translated as the "Chinese Freemasons"). By discussing their rivalry, this book will illustrate the ways in which political differences in mainland China reverberated locally in Mexico, even affecting Chinese who were not members of either organization. During the 1920s, armed conflict between the two groups, poorly understood by Mexican observers, was used by anti-Chinese activists to justify expelling Chinese residents from the country. During the Second World War, when the Guomindang tried to raise funds for the war effort, the Chee Kung Tong withdrew for several years and raised funds separately. Finally, during the Cold War, while the Guomindang tried to engage in public activities in support of the Republic of China, the Chee Kung Tong was considered to be sympathetic to the Chinese Communist Party and the People's Republic of China. The differences between them remain powerful into the present. While the Guomindang held uncontested power in Taiwan until the end of the twentieth century, the Chee Kung Tong is tied to one of the few legally recognized opposition parties in mainland China.

Beyond political affairs, the book will show that the Guomindang and the Chee Kung Tong were important pillars of community life. Their activities reached the community at large despite the fact that the leadership of both organizations was composed exclusively of *paisano* men. No woman ever served in the leadership in either organization, nor did many Mexican-born Chinese. Yet both associations served multiple functions for the community as a whole, helping integrate women and Chinese Mexican descendants into the country after the anti-Chinese campaigns. They served as mutual-aid associations, helping take care of migrants as they faced unemployment and old age; they acted as civic associations, contributing to the development of Mexican cities and towns that they inhabited; and they were social organizations, celebrating important Mexican and Chinese holidays and commemorations. Together, these functions helped build community among Chinese migrants.[18]

The fact that these associations were exclusively male and almost entirely composed of *paisanos* meant that they would weaken as their membership dwindled. By 1971, when Mexico ended its diplomatic relationship with the Republic of China, many members of the first wave of Chinese migrants to Mexico had passed away or withdrawn from participation in political organizations because of their advanced age. Their children grew up with the memory of their parents' political activities, but also saw a less hostile environment for the Chinese community in the country, and as a result thought it less pressing to participate in Chinese associations. Additionally, a second large wave of Chinese migrants arrived after 1971, much more tied to the ROC's rival, the People's Republic of China. Because of the absence of *paisanos* from Mexican society today, the memory of their political and mutual-aid activities has proved difficult to maintain.

ASIAN MIGRATION DURING THE NINETEENTH AND TWENTIETH CENTURIES

Chinese migrants to Mexico were part of a much larger wave of Asian migration from China, Japan, and the former Ottoman Empire to destinations around the Pacific Rim and throughout the Western Hemisphere. Beginning in the 1840s, Cantonese migrants departed Guangdong Province for work in the United States and Canada, but also toiled in free and unfree forms of labor in Latin America. This included the railroad construction workers in Panama and Costa Rica, as well as the coolies who worked the sugar and cotton plantations and the guano pits of Cuba and Peru.[19] Japanese colonists also began to arrive, settling particularly in Peru and Brazil. These early coolies, laborers, and settlers who arrived in much of Latin America set the stage for further waves of migration in the twentieth century.

For much of the nineteenth and twentieth centuries, these migrants continued to face questions of belonging and nationhood—the same kinds of questions that would challenge Chinese Mexicans. Experiments with Chinese labor in Cuba and Peru "prompt[ed] decades of international debate on 'coolie' labor and the suitability of Asians for settlement in the New World."[20] Animosity against these immigrants led the United States and Canada to limit Asian migration. In the United States, the Chinese Exclusion Act (1882) and Gentlemen's Agreement (1907) sharply curtailed Chinese and Japanese migration to the country. These exclusions led the Chinese to seek out new routes of transit, such as through northern Mexico, which would allow them to circumvent Chinese exclusion. Eventually, the Chinese would choose Mexico as a place of settlement.

Into the twentieth century, Asians continued to face charges that they didn't belong or that their presence was inconvenient, threatening, or subversive. Throughout Latin America, national leaders who believed that their nations were composed of the racial mixture of Indigenous peoples with the descendants of Europeans and Africans nonetheless asserted that Asians were unwelcome.[21] These concerns encouraged countries around the Americas, including Canada and Mexico and even countries without Asian populations, to sharply limit or prohibit Asian immigration.[22] During this period, Asian immigrants were also targets for harassment and mob violence. Though Mexico's anti-Chinese campaigns were among the most destructive, other countries, including Cuba and Peru, also experienced periodic backlashes against Chinese migrants. Several countries, including Canada, the United States, and Peru, interned Japanese migrants during the Second World War, while Brazil, Mexico, and others forced Japanese migrants to move farther inland or to specifically designated areas.

Despite the material and societal differences between Chinese Mexicans and their counterparts in the United States, Canada, and Southeast Asia, they nonetheless have faced similar challenges in defining their relationship to China over the course of the twentieth century. Across all of these regions, international and domestic changes would impose similar pressure on Chinese migrants, although they would not always react in the same fashion. For example, the activities Chinese Mexicans engaged in during the Second World War also took place in such faraway countries as Canada and Singapore, and some of these efforts would also be hampered by internal factionalism.[23] The Cold War cut off Chinese Mexicans from mainland China and encouraged their integration into Mexico—a phenomenon that similarly occurred in communities as disparate as those of New Zealand and the Philippines.[24] Finally, the resurgence of Chinese migration to Mexico described in this work also happened in multiple countries, including Peru and Canada, and in those places put pressure on old community associations and activities.[25] These examples demonstrate that, despite their small numbers, the Chinese of Mexico were far from alone, but rather could look to other diasporic communities as potential models. Although there were important differences between Chinese Mexicans and their counterparts around the world, the ways in which Chinese Mexicans similarly experienced racism and barriers to integration demonstrate the utility of including the experiences of Chinese Mexicans in the study of Asian migrants in the Americas and around the world.

POSTREVOLUTIONARY MEXICO

The increasing integration of Chinese immigrants in Mexico could take place only at midcentury. A few decades after the end of the anti-Chinese movement, Mexico emerged from its long revolution and embarked on a course of political stability, economic development, and diplomatic outreach. As John Womack Jr. noted, after the social-justice mission of the revolution gave way to unfettered capitalism, "the business of the Mexican Revolution is now business."[26] As revolutionary nationalism declined and the country became more receptive to foreign, particularly U.S., capital, the result was greater stability for the Chinese and other foreign communities in the country. Political stability came in the form of the Institutional Revolutionary Party (PRI), which perpetuated itself in power from 1929 to 2000. The Chinese, like other residents of Mexico, benefitted from increased economic development in the course of the mid–twentieth century, particularly during the period of rapid economic growth and increasing prosperity known as the Mexican Miracle. Additionally, the party's desire to improve its relationship with countries in the Third World in an effort to burnish its image at home strongly diminished the likelihood of violence against Chinese and other migrants. Thus, Mexican postrevolutionary political and economic developments helped protect Chinese migrants from further harm.

Despite a more stable environment for *paisanos,* few Chinese Mexicans participated in the Mexican political system. Unlike Chinese immigrants to the United States, who were ineligible for citizenship until 1943, *paisanos* were able to naturalize throughout the twentieth century. But the experience of the anti-Chinese movement suggested that citizenship would not protect them from expulsion from the nation. Moreover, the PRI's domination of the political system through electoral fraud and violence meant that Mexican citizenship provided few avenues for democratic participation for Chinese migrants.[27] Chinese associations could not pressure even local politicians with the threat of pursuing their concerns at the ballot box. Unsurprisingly, then, after 1940 few Chinese Mexicans became citizens. Even fewer Chinese joined the PRI, and for Chinese the best option was to strengthen Chinese associations with transnational connections in hopes of obtaining the support of local and state officials.[28]

Even as Chinese were largely shut out of the political process, they nonetheless witnessed considerable benefits during the Mexican Miracle. Economic growth, which averaged 6 percent per year between 1940 and 1970, helped diffuse the pressure on the Chinese community brought by the economic nationalism of the Mexican Revolution. Furthermore, since this growth was built in part on foreign investment, the imperatives of economic development encouraged an environment increasingly amicable to foreigners and immigrants. Though the Chinese did not provide a significant share of foreign trade and investment (although not, as chapters 4 through 6 will show, because the Mexican government didn't seek it), Mexico's openness to foreign trade nonetheless led to a less hostile environment for Chinese immigrant associations.[29] Even during the Cold War, some Mexicans continued to question the loyalty and good morals of the Chinese—as late as the sixties, there were occasional articles on Chinese gambling and opium smuggling—but there were also several articles that provided a more neutral or even a positive impression.

Expanded Mexican diplomacy also encouraged better protection of its foreign resident communities. As part of its drive to develop Mexico's economy, the PRI sought out diplomatic relations with countries around the world, including Cuba, the Soviet Union, and several countries in the Eastern Bloc. In contrast to other countries in the Americas, Mexico enjoyed the autonomy to build a relationship with Communist countries.[30] During the Cold War, Mexico's left and right wings argued extensively about diplomatic recognition for the People's Republic of China—a diplomatic tie that the PRC believed was crucial to its obtaining a seat in the United Nations. The dispute over whether to recognize the People's Republic of China or continue relations with the ROC (Taiwan) led to the public diplomacy activities that gave Chinese Mexicans new prominence.

SOURCES AND ORGANIZATION

This book recovers the experiences of Chinese immigrants in Mexico through the use of diplomatic and community sources scattered on both sides of the Pacific Ocean, primarily in the United States, Mexico, China, and the ROC (Taiwan). It uncovers the histories of Chinese communities that have been understudied, particularly those of the Soconusco region of Chiapas, the Gulf Coast city of Tampico, and Mexico City. Diplomatic sources provide crucial qualitative data about the Chinese Mexicans at midcentury, including where they lived, where they worked, and what associations they belonged to. Community directories and the memoirs of Chinese ambassadors and government officials provided critical information not only on prominent Chinese Mexican merchants, but also on the issues facing the community at midcentury. The Chinese in Mexico did not have the flourishing newspaper culture that has proven so fruitful to historians of Chinese America, Cuba, Canada, and Peru, but surviving issues of two newspapers—*Moguo Gongbao,* published by the Chee Kung Tong; and *Qiaosheng Yuekan,* published primarily by the Guomindang—give insight into how Chinese understood transpacific politics in a global and local context. Local archives, particularly from cities where the Chinese had a presence such as Tampico, Tapachula, Mexico City, and Mérida, also hold sources on local associations. The *testimonios* of second-generation Chinese Mexicans have also given insight into the lives and identity formation of the descendants of *paisanos.*[31]

The sources presented here from five different countries offer different perspectives on Chinese Mexicans and their political and emotional attachments. U.S., Mexican, and U.K. sources present analyses of *paisanos* whose tone shifts between tentative acceptance and occasional suspicion. In contrast, the PRC and ROC sources both tend to claim the allegiance of Chinese Mexicans, and can be quick to criticize them if they fail to maintain their loyalty. Few English- or Spanish-language sources document Chinese transnational connections, either because the Chinese didn't share them or because foreign observers deemed them unimportant. Moreover, only Chinese-language sources are able to provide insight into the motivations behind Chinese Mexican political activities. Thus, putting these sources together reveals the different subjecthoods of Chinese Mexicans and their attempts to navigate these competing claims.

Because sources written from the United States, Mexico, and the United Kingdom are relatively few, the vast majority of sources used in this study are Chinese-language sources, especially those reflecting the history of the Republic of China and the Chinese Nationalist Party in Mexico. Of the sources used to tell the history of Chinese Mexicans, a majority come from the archives of the Ministry of Foreign Affairs of the Republic of China and the Guomindang. Their rivals, the numerically superior Chee Kung Tong and government of the People's Republic of China, did not preserve as many historical sources and have made fewer of them publicly available. The same applies to clan and native-place organizations, some of whose members also formed part of the Guomindang. Although Guomindang and ROC sources have noted biases against the PRC and the Chee Kung Tong, these sources also reflect the fact that the Guomindang also felt the need to attract the support of the Chee Kung Tong during major political campaigns. As a result, that organization reported on and studied Chee Kung Tong chapters and activities with surprising regularity. Additionally, Guomindang members tended to head Chinese Mexican community associations around the country, and had a more open working relationship with Mexican and Chinese government officials; they participated more actively in the transpacific politics that are the focus of this study.

To understand the political activity of a Chinese community thousands of miles from East Asia, this book follows a generation of Chinese immigrants from the widespread violence against them during the anti-Chinese campaigns to the present. The first two chapters track the reaction of the community to the anti-Chinese movements. In response to increasing anti-Chinese activity, *paisanos* formed and strengthened Chinese associations around Mexico. In their attempt to end widespread violence to protect the status of the Chinese in the country, these associations appealed to both Mexican and Chinese officials. In spite of these activities, the anti-Chinese movement was overwhelmingly disastrous for Mexico's Chinese. Chapter 1 follows the cases of Sonora and Sinaloa, where political pressure from Mexico's former president trumped any attempt to protect their presence in the country, resulting in the exodus from the country of thousands of Chinese. Chapter 2 follows cases in which Chinese associations were able to beat back anti-Chinese aggression, particularly in the states of Tamaulipas, Baja California, and Chiapas. Thus, while anti-Chinese activists declared a victory over the Chinese in northwestern Mexico, other areas of the country quietly maintained Chinese communities for the rest of the twentieth century.

In response to the violence against them, *paisanos* asserted the need for a strong and consolidated Chinese government. As a result, Chinese Mexicans between 1937 and 1945 engaged in donation drives and public diplomacy activities to increase popular sympathy for the Chinese government during the Second Sino-Japanese War. Chapter 3 argues that, while some *paisanos* believed that the Chinese victory in the Second World War improved local perceptions of Chinese immigrants, their activities during the war were the true transformative force, helping integrate Chinese into Mexican society. By the end of the war, *paisanos* around the country held widespread victory celebrations alongside Mexicans, suggesting that they felt increased acceptance in Mexican society.

Although the end of the war might have provided *paisanos* with the opportunity to quietly live out the rest of their lives in Mexico, the beginning of the Cold War provided a new impetus for political activity. In 1949, civil war between Chinese Communists and Chinese Nationalists ended with the proclamation of the People's Republic of China in Beijing and the retrocession of the government of the Republic of China to the island of Taiwan. Both governments claimed to represent China, and both sought the support of overseas Chinese communities like the Chinese Mexicans. Chapters 4 and 5 illustrate the consequences of this diplomatic struggle for Chinese Mexicans between 1949 and 1972. Most Chinese Mexicans continued to embrace the Republic of China, the government to which they had appealed during the anti-Chinese movement and the one they had supported during the Second Sino-Japanese War. In continuing to cooperate with the government of the Republic of China, the subject of chapter 4, they created public diplomacy activities, like the annual pilgrimage, which persist into the present. A minority of Chinese Mexicans, noting the incongruity of supporting a Chinese government that no longer governed their home province, began to quietly support the People's Republic of China. Chapter 5 examines the backlash against these individuals, who were ostracized as subversives and surveilled by the ROC and the Mexican and U.S. governments.

Mexican diplomatic recognition of the People's Republic of China, which came in 1972, fundamentally changed the Chinese Mexican community and the associations that *paisanos* created. As demonstrated in chapter 6, Chinese Mexicans abruptly lost their partnership with the Republic of China as the embassy hastily closed and left the country. Additionally, a new wave of immigrants began to enter Mexico in 1979, loyal to the ROC's rival. This chapter thus captures the considerable demographic changes brought about in part by shifts in international politics and the rise of the People's Republic of China.

During the twentieth century, then, local conditions encouraged *paisanos* to participate in transpacific politics, while distant political changes had local repercussions. This dynamic had begun during the anti-Chinese movement, a traumatic memory for Chinese Mexicans and a reference point for the community throughout the twentieth century.

CHAPTER I

Mexico for the Mexicans, China for the Chinese

*Political Upheaval and
the Anti-Chinese Campaigns in
Postrevolutionary Sonora and Sinaloa*

After arriving in Mexico, Cantonese immigrants underwent two proc-esses that tied them more closely to political activities in China and encouraged them to identify as Chinese. The first was the formation of Chinese social and political associations. Tension between Mexico's two largest Chinese associations, the Guomindang and the Chee Kung Tong, led to open violence in the 1920s and lasting enmity throughout the twentieth century. The second was the anti-Chinese campaigns. Between 1931 and 1934, anti-Chinese associations in the northwestern states of Sonora and Sinaloa (see map 1), sheltered by the support of the state and federal government, increased pressure on Chinese immigrants until ultimately carrying out their expulsion from those states. While wealthy Chinese fled to other parts of the country or paid for their own passage to China, those without means were forced to cross into the United States, from where immigration authorities deported them to China. Both processes, which occurred in the context of the Chinese and Mexican revolutions, led to appeals to Chinese officials and contin-ued engagement with Chinese politics.

A new wave of studies has uncovered the history of Mexico's Chinese immigrant population and the anti-Chinese movement that drove the vast majority from the country. This chapter will emphasize the role of politics both in organizing the community and in fostering postrevolu-tionary xenophobia. Few Chinese could escape the political upheaval of the early twentieth century, whether it was the anarchy of the Mexican

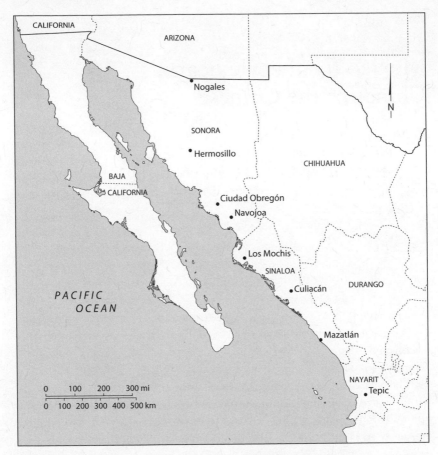

MAP 1. Northwestern Mexico, including the states of Sonora and Sinaloa.

Revolution, the internecine chaos of the Tong Wars, or the xenophobic violence of the anti-Chinese campaigns. The sober analyses contained in Chinese-language sources demonstrate that diplomats and associations had a sophisticated understanding of each, including the political and economic causes behind the anti-Chinese campaigns. Moreover, they show that migrants tried to appeal both to Mexico and to China to end xenophobic attacks, yet ultimately found that appealing to domestic officials was not an effective strategy. The anti-Chinese campaigns thus proved the utility of transnational ties to China.

Although the anti-Chinese campaigns were organized and backed by lower- and middle-class anti-Chinese activists around the country, crucial was the role of the Mexican government, particularly during the Maxi-

mato (1928–34). That period saw former president Plutarco Elías Calles
wield more power behind the scenes than the three presidents he had
helped bring into power. Indeed, crucial was the relative weakness of the
office of the presidency during the Maximato, particularly during the
presidency of Pascual Ortiz Rubio (1930–32), the peak of Calles's political power during this six-year period. The Maximato also witnessed the
creation of a national political party that incorporated anti-Chinese activists and supported their message. The partnership between anti-Chinese
associations and Mexico's emerging one-party state thus illustrates the
crucial role of xenophobia in Mexican postrevolutionary state formation.

The support the Mexican government accorded to anti-Chinese
activists led not only to new legislation primarily targeting the Chinese,
but also to anti-Chinese associations being granted a wide latitude to go
beyond the law in persecuting the Chinese. In turn, the anti-Chinese
campaigns distracted from a grueling depression and served to increase
popular support for the government. Government support for anti-
Chinese campaigns was most notable in the areas in which Calles had
the most control, particularly in Sonora and Sinaloa, the two states in
northwestern Mexico where the expulsion of Chinese was most successful. In all, the anti-Chinese campaigns conducted during this three-year
period saw the departure of three-quarters of the Chinese population of
the country. Even for those who remained, the expulsion of Chinese
from the state of Sonora represented a lasting trauma and a reference
point for the community through the rest of the twentieth century.[1]

This chapter will begin by examining the arrival of Chinese migrants
in the country and the economic activities that brought them success.
Whereas earlier scholarship has examined the emergence of violence
among Chinese migrants and the role of such violence in spurring the
anti-Chinese campaigns, this chapter will link such violence to Chinese
political associations tied to mainland Chinese political currents. After
examining the tactics employed by anti-Chinese activists to help encourage Chinese migrants to leave the country, it will examine the expulsion
of Chinese migrants from the states of Sonora and Sinaloa, dispossess-
ing Chinese migrants of the fruits of decades of hard work.

EARLY CHINESE IMMIGRATION TO MEXICO

Chinese immigrants to Mexico, almost all of whom came from the Pearl
River delta of Guangdong Province, formed part of a large wave of
Cantonese immigration to the Americas.[2] The Chinese of the Americas

made a small but rapidly growing fraction of the eight million Chinese who had settled outside of mainland China by 1922. Coming from the same province and speaking similar dialects, these Chinese migrants could organize for mutual aid as well as respond to the anti-Chinese immigration restrictions and xenophobia that swept the Americas. For example, after the enactment of the Chinese Exclusion Act in the United States in 1882, networks involving Chinese migrants residing along several points of the Pacific Rim collaborated to help overcome exclusion laws and smuggle Chinese migrants to the United States. These networks first brought Chinese migrants to Mexico and soon after smuggled them across the U.S.–Mexico border, "invent[ing] undocumented emigration from Latin America."[3]

Despite the initial impulse to find a circuitous path to the United States, many migrants chose to remain in Mexico.[4] Though small groups of Chinese settled during the nineteenth century, the vast majority arrived after the 1899 Treaty of Amity and Commerce between the Mexican and Chinese governments.[5] Chinese immigrants arrived in a Mexico that had just begun to exercise control over its borders, and found that the migration service was understaffed, underpaid, and easily corruptible. As a result, foreigners like the Chinese often paid bribes to enter Mexico without proper authorization.[6] From 1915 to 1920, the governor of Baja California, Esteban Cantú, alone brought in thousands of Chinese migrants to help develop the lands of the Mexicali Valley. Many of the migrants entered without documentation, and, according to the U.S. consul, paid up to $140 to enter the territory to work.[7] After arriving, Chinese migrants were welcomed by representatives of Chinese organizations, "taught . . . basic Spanish, and familiarized . . . with the fundamentals of Mexican culture."[8]

Chinese migrants took part in a variety of industries around the country. For example, many Chinese settled in the Mexicali Valley of northwestern Mexico and worked the lands of the Colorado River Land Company. Their toil helped irrigate the arid territory and turned the valley into a bountiful area for Mexican agriculture, particularly cotton.[9] In Torreón, in the northeastern state of Coahuila, Chinese arrivals worked in the mines and on the railroad. In Monterrey, the earliest migrants worked in the construction of municipal public-works projects.[10] On the Yucatán Peninsula, Chinese and other migrants worked the henequen plantations before moving on to the cities.[11] By the 1920s, many migrants had remained in the country after the termination of their labor contracts and become small-business owners, largely divided among general stores, laundries, and cafés.[12] The transition to small businesses was relatively easy, since they required little start-up capital. Moreover, because there was a need for their services, Chinese quickly found an eager clientele.[13] Once they found success, some migrants began to send for family members to join them.

One of the most notable Chinese settlements in the first decade of the twentieth century was the city of Torreón, Coahuila—a city Chinese immigrants called "cai yuan," or vegetable garden. Chinese formed the largest foreign group in Torreón at the beginning of the twentieth century, with over five hundred residents. In addition to establishing grocery stores and laundries, wealthy Chinese residents bought large tracts of land for agricultural work (giving the town its Chinese name). Torreón's wealthiest resident was Wong Foon Chuck, who owned the Hotel del Ferrocarril in the city and five other hotels nearby, and who served as director of the Mexico-China Banking Company.[14] Chinese reformer Kang Youwei took an interest and visited the city, which had formed a chapter of the reformist organization the Baohuanghui.

Much of the city's economic and political life was devastated during the Torreón massacre of 1911. After forces loyal to Mexican revolutionary Francisco Madero took control of Torreón, the city was sacked and over three hundred Chinese men and five Japanese were killed. The men had been "stripped, robbed, and mutilated while their homes and stores were ransacked and burned."[15] The destruction of Torreón represented the worst act of violence ever committed against the Chinese in North America.[16] Even after the Torreón massacre, a reduced Chinese community remained in the city for much of the twentieth century, and many worked the surrounding Chinese farms until the 1930s. But sophisticated Chinese commercial, social, and political activities would take decades to recover.

Even during the chaos of the Mexican Revolution, when Chinese and other foreigners were targeted for robbery or worse, Chinese continued to arrive in the country. Whereas there were only 1,023 Chinese in the country in 1895—before the Treaty of Amity and Commerce between the Mexican and Chinese governments—by 1910 the number had grown more than tenfold, to 13,000. About one-third of the population lived in Sonora, where they formed the largest group of foreign residents in the state.[17] During the Mexican Revolution, the number of Chinese migrants in the country would almost double, reaching 24,000 by 1926, "the second-largest immigrant group in all of Mexico."[18]

Chinese migrants to Mexico were mostly men, a fact that partially explains the prevalence of Chinese-Mexican interracial romantic relationships. Of 15,976 Chinese recorded by the Mexican census in 1930, only 412 were women—a figure that would have included Mexican spouses of Chinese men.[19] Reasons to explain these unions are numerous, and of course include romantic affection. Frequent interaction between Chinese business owners and female customers and employees often led to courtship and marriage.[20] For Chinese laborers unable to return to China to marry, seeking a spouse in Mexico may have been a more feasible option.[21] Others may have been attracted by the possibility of "claim[ing] a place in [Mexican] society." Having opened businesses and started families, many Chinese migrants before the anti-Chinese campaigns acquired Mexican citizenship.[22]

THE FORMATION OF CHINESE ASSOCIATIONS: THE GUOMINDANG AND THE CHEE KUNG TONG

Following the example set by Chinese migrants in Southeast Asia and the United States, as well as that of other communities of foreigners in Mexico, Chinese migrants established associations for mutual aid and assistance, facilitating the arrival and settlement of new migrants and advocating for their interests.[23] Native-place associations, including the Haiyan Gongsuo, Zhongshan Huiguan, and Sanyi Huiguan, linked Chinese migrants from the same towns; surname and clan associations brought together Chinese of similar family backgrounds; and general associations served as umbrella organizations for Chinese migrants.[24] These latter organizations were frequently named Zhonghua Huiguan, Zhonghua Shanghui, or Huaqiao Tuantihui and often called, in Spanish, *asociaciones chinas* ("Chinese associations") or *cámaras de comercio chinas* ("Chinese chambers of commerce").[25] The functions of these associations were numerous: they provided migrants a place to sleep once they arrived in the country; they collected funds to remit to migrants' sending regions; they arbitrated disputes between migrants; they took care of elderly Chinese; and they helped negotiate conflicts between Chinese and native Mexican residents. More important, they also provided a vehicle for Chinese migrants to resist anti-Chinese racism, particularly during the anti-Chinese campaigns.[26]

One of the largest organizations to precede the advent of the Republic of China was a fraternal organization known as the Chee Kung Tong (CKT), colloquially known as the Chinese Freemasons. Before the 1911 Xinhai revolution, it advocated the overthrow of the Qing dynasty and the restoration of the Ming dynasty (*fanqing fuming*), by which it meant a return to a Han Chinese monarchy. Although their visions for the future of China were different, the Guomindang and societies like the Chee Kung Tong were, before the 1911 revolution, allies in the struggle against the Qing dynasty. In much of northern Mexico, CKT branches were founded well before branches of the Guomindang. In the first decade of the twentieth century, for example, Tampico and Torreón both established CKT branches, and a branch was established in Mexicali in 1914.[27] Eventually, the Chee Kung Tong would establish a headquarters in Mexico City, which coordinated the activities of its branches around the country.[28] In Spanish-language correspondence and publications, the CKT identified itself as a Masonic order and used Masonic symbols, but it was not strictly speaking a secret society, nor was it affiliated with other Masonic groups.[29]

The formation of these Chinese associations took place in the context of increased contact between Chinese around the Pacific Rim and the Chinese government. Chinese migration to the region was a crucial factor behind the establishment of Chinese–Mexican relations in 1899, and the treaty the two countries signed promised Chinese subjects "free and voluntary" migration to Mexico.[30] In the aftermath of the Xinhai revolution, the Chinese Republican government would strengthen its links with Chinese communities around the world. Seeing the Chinese communities of Southeast Asia and the Americas as instrumental to the revolution, the Republic of China established a government body, the Overseas Chinese Affairs Commission, to keep Chinese overseas firmly tied to the government—representing Chinese migrants in times of trouble, asking them for contributions, and even claiming a responsibility for their education. In Mexico, the Republic of China opened consulates in areas with large Chinese populations far from Mexico City. By the mid-1920s, Nogales, Tampico, and Mexicali all had Chinese consulates, and Mazatlán and Tapachula had opened vice consulates by the following decade.[31]

After the foundation of the Republic of China, cities across Mexico established chapters of the Guomindang (the Chinese Nationalist Party), the party established by Sun Yat-sen and the ruling party in China for much of the first half of the twentieth century. Cananea, Sonora, which had earlier established a branch of the Tongmenghui, opened Mexico's first Guomindang chapter. From there, the party spread to Mazatlán and Tampico during the 1910s, with a branch following in Tapachula in 1924 and Mérida in 1927.[32] A national headquarters in Nogales, Sonora, organized the different party branches until the anti-Chinese movement; afterward, five main branches around the country coordinated party activities.[33]

Even as, years later, anti-Chinese activists would describe the two organizations as secretive "*maffias*" that primarily engaged in illicit activities, during the 1920s both maintained regular contact with Mexican society as well as with local and national government officials. Both, for example, registered their associations in compliance with Mexican law. In different cities around the country, the Guomindang shared with Mexican officials the names of its officials and even agendas for high-level meetings.[34] When, in 1928, Plutarco Elías Calles announced his refusal to extend his presidential term after the assassination of president-elect Álvaro Obregón, among the organizations to send their congratulations were two chapters of the CKT.[35] In their openness and active participation in Mexican society, they resembled other kinds of Mexican civic associations, even those composed of foreigners.

Tensions between the Guomindang and the Chee Kung Tong began to emerge after the 1911 Xinhai revolution, particularly during the 1920s. These tensions had Mexican domestic as well as transpacific causes. As both organizations expanded, they began to struggle for members and control of illicit activities.[36] Throughout the twentieth century, the CKT had more members than the GMD; this consistently unnerved the latter organization, whose members tended to be wealthier and thought of themselves as better educated and more civilized.[37] Both groups also competed for control over illicit activities such as opium and gambling. Robert Chao Romero notes that "both Chinese and Mexican observers of the early twentieth century depict the Chee Kung Tong as a source of various forms of vice, including opium and gambling." Although GMD members denounced the activities of the CKT, its members also engaged in the same activities, especially members of the Lung Sing Tong, a subgroup of the GMD "allegedly founded by members of the Mexican Guomindang to counteract the financial power of their Chee Kung Tong rivals through organized participation in the trafficking of opium and the management of casinos."[38]

The causes of their growing antagonism were not merely local. The Tong Wars also took place as the government of mainland China was beginning to consolidate control following the 1911 revolution. Members of the Mexican Guomindang supported its counterpart established in southern China, which was fighting to wrest control of much of the rest of the country. Members of the Chee Kung Tong, in contrast, supported the Beiyang government in northern China.[39] As Lisa Rose Mar and Elliott Young point out, this political transformation divided not only Chinese Mexicans, but also Chinese around the world. Skirmishes between the Guomindang and Chinese Freemason organizations like the Chee Kung Tong also took place in the United States, Canada, and Cuba during the 1920s. Mexican president Álvaro Obregón, for example, received a newspaper clipping in which the World Order of Chinese Freemasons expressed its resolute opposition to the Guomindang, which it considered to be "bolshevist."[40] Among Chinese Mexicans, these differences manifested themselves just before the outbreak of violence in 1922. While the CKT raised funds for the construction of a new consulate in Nogales, Sonora, the GMD, conscious of the fact that the Chinese diplomatic corps during the 1920s was biased against them, tried to stymie the project. At the same time, the GMD raised funds for its counterpart in mainland China.[41]

Initially, disagreements between the two groups were limited to print. The early GMD in Mexico published the *Xinghua Zazhi* ("Revive China Journal"), while the CKT published a monthly periodical called the *Gongbao* ("Bulletin"). Each periodical was a propaganda instrument of each faction, spreading its political ideology among its members. The *Xinghua Zazhi,* for example, frequently criticized the anti-Guomindang Chinese diplomatic corps, which unnerved CKT members.[42] Eventually, differences between the newspapers escalated to the point where they were directly antagonizing one another. Finally, the CKT offered a reward of 10,000 Chinese Yuan for the death of the leader of the GMD, Francisco Yuen, causing Yuen to flee to the United States. One Guomindang member later remarked that the organization felt it had to respond with violence, lest the Chinese community in Mexico consider it weak.[43] Thus began the Tong Wars of the mid-1920s. During the first period of violence in the summer of 1922, twenty-five Chinese were killed, including the leaders of the local GMD and CKT.[44] The second Tong War began in July 1924 as shots were fired toward the Mexicali CKT branch, the war then expanding beyond Baja California to the states of Chihuahua, Coahuila, Chiapas, and Tampico. During the course of the war, national Guomindang leader Yuen was assassinated "in broad daylight on a railroad platform."[45]

The episodes of violence were what Evelyn Hu-Dehart refers to as "self-inflicted wounds," not only for the Chinese who were deported for taking part, but also for the larger community.[46] The violence made headlines across the country and added to perceptions that Chinese were pernicious foreigners, a threat to postrevolutionary Mexican stability and, because of the presence of opium and gambling among Chinese, a corrupting force in Mexican society.[47] Indeed, since most Mexicans were unaware of the political and economic differences among Chinese, many chose to understand these conflicts as clashes between Chinese groups over the opium trade.[48] Marches and petitions demanded that the president deport all Chinese involved in the Tong Wars.[49] President Obregón, who was biased in favor of the Guomindang and generally more sanguine about the Chinese presence in the country, initially modified the order to deport only CKT members, and eventually set all of the detained free. Obregón's perceived lenience toward the Chinese even after the Tong Wars incensed anti-Chinese activists in Sonora, who "denounced the central state authorities and their failure to respect the wishes of the Sonoran people."[50] Much of the violence of the second Tong War occurred during the presidential campaign of Plutarco Elías Calles, and the future president may have been influenced by the violence to oppose the Chinese presence in the country and thus differentiate himself from Obregón.[51] Ultimately, the Tong Wars served as ammunition for those who advocated restrictions against Chinese immigration in the country, and were a motivating factor in the growth of anti-Chinese organizations in northern Mexico.

THE RISE OF MEXICAN ANTI-CHINESE ASSOCIATIONS

Despite the fact that early episodes of anti-Chinese activity had already demonstrated considerable resentment toward Chinese success—the massacre of Torreón in 1911 is the most salient example—such resentment did not crystallize into an organized network until 1916.[52] The ideological leader of these campaigns was José Ángel Espinoza, whose volumes *El problema chino en México* and *El ejemplo de Sonora* combined a strong economic nationalism with concerns that the Chinese would lead to the degeneration of the Mexican mestizo nation, inspiring anti-Chinese activists across the country. The two books argued that Chinese merchants succeeded only because they engaged in deceitful business practices that allowed them to undersell Mexican merchants. Their success didn't benefit Mexicans, since they repatriated their profits to China. As a result, they argued, the Mexican government needed to expel Chinese immigrants from the country to allow Mexicans to regain control over the country's commerce.

Anti-Chinese intellectuals like Espinoza were certainly influenced by Mexican postrevolutionary notions of *mestizaje*—the idea that the racial mixture of Europeans, indigenous Mexicans, and Africans would produce a new, vibrant race. Such notions allowed them to argue that the Chinese, by intermixing with Mexicans, were weakening the country's racial stock. The fact that the Chinese had settled in cities and towns across the republic for decades, married Mexican women, and had native-born children alarmed nativists, who accused them of changing the ethnic makeup of the mestizo nation—for the worse. But they also liberally borrowed their rhetoric from the mid-nineteenth-century anti-Chinese labor movement in the United States, which had no such racial ideology.[53] From their point of view, the anti-Chinese campaigns were their attempt to change the makeup of the Mexican periphery on their own terms, and to alter the elements of the mestizo nation through violence. Where they could not obtain the support of federal government officials, they deeply resented any federal government attempts to restrain their actions.[54]

Anti-Chinese activists often pointed to the conflict between the Guo-mindang and the Chee Kung Tong to illustrate the danger that Chinese migrants represented to Mexican society. Espinoza derided these organizations as "*maffias*" and repeated the accusation that the Tong Wars were merely fought over the control of immigrant smuggling, gambling, and the opium trade—accusations that ignored Chinese political divisions. In this view, the Tong Wars demonstrated "Asian ferocity, slyness, and perfidy," a viewpoint that was widely reproduced in the Mexican press. The conflicts between the GMD and the CKT, then, confirmed anti-Chinese activists' stereotyped assumptions and fears about the Chinese, and allowed them to portray the Chinese not only as an abstract threat to Mexican mestizo nationalism, but also as an immediate threat to Mexican bystanders.[55]

Instead of physically attacking Chinese migrants, anti-Chinese activists tried to persuade Mexican officials to deport Chinese migrants as well as encourage Chinese migrants to deport themselves.[56] Their campaigns attacked the rights that the Chinese were entitled to as foreign nationals or naturalized citizens in Mexico—in particular, their right to settle, manage their businesses, and marry freely. The goal of anti-Chinese activists was to increase restrictions on the Chinese community until residency became so burdensome that they would leave. Although the tactics had changed, the effects were similar: anti-Chinese activists "in effect resort[ed] to a different kind of violence" to remove Chinese from the country.[57]

An early priority was removing the legal protections that shielded Chinese migrants from the activist associations' attacks, in particular the 1899 Treaty of Amity and Commerce. As Sonora proposed discriminatory legislation against Chinese immigrants and proposed barring Chinese immigrants from entering the country, Chinese consuls and ministers frequently reminded the executive that Chinese had the "right to travel and conduct business in all parts of Mexico under the same conditions as nationals from all other nations."[58] Anti-Chinese organizations made abrogating the treaty with China a priority, believing it would enable them to enact harsher legislation against the Chinese. As governor of Sonora, Adolfo de la Huerta supported abrogating the treaty as early as 1919, and by 1921 President Obregón sought to amend the treaty to prohibit Chinese workers, similar to the Chinese Exclusion Act in the United States.[59] Calles would finally abrogate the treaty in July 1927.[60] Although the two countries maintained diplomatic relations, they would not conclude another treaty until 1943. The abrogation of the Treaty of Amity and Commerce was a harbinger of coming anti-Chinese violence, an indication that the federal government would be more permissive toward anti-Chinese legislation and extralegal attacks.

Anti-Chinese activity specifically targeted naturalized Mexicans in addition to Chinese nationals.[61] Although the constitution of 1917 and subsequent legislation theoretically differentiated the rights of natural-born Mexicans from naturalized citizens, how their rights were different in practice was still unclear.[62] Xenophobic activists complained that the Chinese had no interest in forming part of the Mexican nation and naturalized only so that they would be exempt from Mexican legislation targeting foreigners. José Ángel Espinoza doubted that any Chinese sincerely wished to become part of the nation. He contrasted naturalized Europeans and Americans, who "know how to be[come] Mexican," with the Chinese—who, he argued, did not obtain Mexican nationality "in response to an intimate sense of gratitude to our hospitality. . . . [W]hen nationalizing they only look for advantages under our laws offered to Mexican citizens." Even if a Chinese obtained Mexican nationality, argued Espinoza, he would never become truly Mexican: "the government may judge him as Mexican, the Secretaría of Foreign Relations may judge him as Mexican, but to the people he continues to be Chinese; a doubly dangerous Chinese exploiter," a wolf in sheep's clothing.[63] Instead of encouraging Chinese to nationalize and assimilate to Mexican ways, the federal government should, Espinoza recommended, prevent them from nationalizing altogether.

Anti-Chinese activists commonly advocated for the deportation of Chinese immigrants regardless of immigration and naturalization status. Most frequently, they called for the use of Article 33 under the Mexican Constitution of 1917 to remove undesirable Chinese from the country. Article 33 empowered the president to remove any foreigner without trial "whose presence is considered to be inconvenient." Because of the ambiguity of the word "inconvenient," anti-Chinese activists seized upon Article 33 a quick and easy solution to the Chinese problem. During a march in Gusave, Sonora, one protester displayed a placard simply reading "33," which, the caption from Espinoza clarified, was intended for "the infamous traders from Asia."[64]

Anti-Chinese associations accused Chinese of many different violations in order to argue for their deportation under Article 33. Probably the most egregious request for the application of Article 33 came from the city of Durango, Durango, in 1930. Authorities stumbled upon a gambling house where 23 Chinese were allegedly discovered "smoking opium and gambling." The governor of the state, José Ramón Valdez, suggested to the Secretary of Gobernación that they be deported as "pernicious foreigners."[65] Once he had gotten the attention of the Secretaría, the governor added another 76 Chinese, none of whom had been accused of any crime but whom Valdez described as "in their majority pernicious elements, because of which it would benefit the state to expel as many as possible." The 99 Chinese, probably the entire Chinese male population of the state capital, were apprehended, photographed, fingerprinted, and investigated the following month. Ultimately, the Secretaría declined to expel all of the Chinese from Durango, sending away only those with prior criminal records.[66] Anti-Chinese activists' call for the use of Article 33 was not often successful; Pablo Yankelevich notes that between 1911 and 1940, only 149 Chinese were expelled and very few naturalized Mexicans were deported. However, the threat of Article 33 must have proved very unsettling to Chinese migrants in Mexico, whose shops could be closed and who could be transferred to distant jails while awaiting deportation proceedings.[67]

When anti-Chinese activists could not deport Chinese immigrants outright, they tried to increase restrictions on Chinese migrants in hopes of encouraging them to leave on their own. Some of the restrictions proposed included special ghettos for Chinese; preventing Chinese from living at their place of business; preventing Chinese from obtaining Mexican citizenship; and outlawing relationships between Chinese men and Mexican women. These restrictions would target all Chinese in the country regardless of how long they had been there or whether they had Mexican wives and children.

One of the recurring restrictions on Chinese was legislation prohibiting marriages or free unions between Chinese men and Mexican women, which were common throughout northern Mexico. Large numbers of Chinese men had married or cohabited with Mexican women, and fathered many Mexican-born children.[68] The state of Sonora passed such legislation in December 1923; a second piece of legislation, signed in October 1930, specifically mentioned naturalized Mexicans.[69] Francisco Gin, a naturalized Mexican in Naco, Sonora, sued to overturn this racist legislation. Gin had been fined 200 pesos for living with and attempting to marry a Mexican woman. His appeal, which eventually went before the Mexican Supreme Court, was based partially on the fact that the fine violated his rights as a Mexican citizen. Gin's lawsuit, if successful, could have set a precedent that reaffirmed basic civil rights for naturalized Mexicans. But this entailed "a redefinition of who the Chinese were . . . from a state of existence so immutable that neither naturalization nor birth in Mexico could alter that identity." In deciding Gin's case on procedural grounds, the supreme court declined to rule on the constitutionality of the Sonora law, which presented "'complex issues' about race that they could not then consider."[70] Anti-Chinese activists could not but feel encouraged that the highest levels of the Mexican judiciary declined to uphold the basic rights of naturalized Mexican citizens, and the ruling likely pushed them to seek more restrictions on naturalized Chinese.

ANTI-CHINESE ACTIVISTS, THE MAXIMATO, AND THE NATIONAL REVOLUTIONARY PARTY

The anti-Chinese campaigns took place just as Mexico was emerging from the Mexican Revolution, a large social and political upheaval initially sparked in reaction to the long presidency of Porfirio Díaz. During the subsequent decade, Mexican military leaders—some of whom merely advocated political change, others of whom sought deeper reforms that would address the plight of Mexico's dispossessed masses—fought each other for control of the country. During the 1910s, roughly 10 percent of the population died, either directly from the violence or due to hunger and disease. In addition, hundreds of thousands of Mexicans sought refuge from the revolution in the United States.

The year 1920 witnessed the rise to power of a group of political leaders, hailing from the northwestern state of Sonora and known as the Sonoran Triangle, who would implement reforms that brought political stability to the country. The Sonoran Triangle incorporated Adolfo de la Huerta (interim president, 1920), Álvaro Obregón (president, 1920–

24), and Plutarco Elías Calles (president, 1924–28). Through the 1920s, these three political figures would make their mark on Mexican politics by centralizing power, obtaining the diplomatic recognition of the United States, and creating a political party that governed the country through the rest of the twentieth century. They also took advantage of the idea of racial mixing, or *mestizaje,* as a political project to paper over substantial differences among Mexicans and help build the one-party state.[71]

The rise of the Sonoran triangle coincided with the rise in anti-Chinese organized activity, which Obregón discouraged but de la Huerta and Calles backed. As governor of Sonora, Calles had rolled back aggressive measures against the Chinese.[72] Obregón, needing the diplomatic backing of the United States, judged the campaigns and legislation spawned by anti-Chinese activists to be potentially harmful for Mexico's relationship with its northern neighbor. Calles, however, enacted a much more populist agenda, and gave explicit approval to anti-Chinese campaigns. Although Calles's presidential term expired in 1928, his influence would be magnified by events outside of his control. In 1928, Obregón won reelection, but was assassinated by a Catholic activist before taking office. During the ensuing political crisis, which threatened the stability that the Sonoran Triangle brought to national politics, Calles declined to remain in the presidency but nevertheless dominated Mexican politics in a period known as the Maximato (1928–34). Although three presidents were installed during the six-year period, Calles was considered to be the country's strongman.

During the Maximato, anti-Chinese activists often wrote to or quoted Calles to legitimize their message. During an interview in Villa Juárez, as the Calles family attempted to evict Chinese residents from that town, Calles expressed his belief "that the anti-Chinese campaign should intensify" and that judges should stop protecting Chinese from their inevitable expulsion. The quote was printed in Espinoza's anti-Chinese work *El problema chino en México.*[73] In the midst of the Chinese expulsion in Sonora, the cover of Espinoza's second book, *El ejemplo de Sonora,* appears to show Calles, clutching the anti-Chinese labor law, kicking out a Chinese immigrant carrying gold and opium.[74] Calles never led an anti-Chinese campaign on his own, but his vocal support led anti-Chinese activists to believe that they would not be hindered, and it encouraged more locals to participate in aggression against the Chinese.

In addition to obtaining the approval of Calles himself, anti-Chinese activists were an important element of Calles's nascent political party, the National Revolutionary Party (PNR). The PNR brought together competing political factions, military leaders, and political bosses under the umbrella of one party. Designed to foster political stability at such a turbulent time, it gave local party branches a wide amount of latitude to run their own affairs, while national affairs were dominated by Calles. Under this system, the president was reduced to merely being an administrator; political insiders and even foreign observers understood that Calles dominated the political affairs of the country and that regional and local officials often governed without federal government intervention. Local strongmen in turn were crucial in lending their support to the anti-Chinese campaigns.[75] The party, which in 1946 would be renamed the Institutional Revolutionary Party (PRI), governed Mexico from 1929 to 2000, and made Calles an extraordinary force in national politics, even without holding political office, from 1929 until his exile from the country in 1936.[76]

The precursor of the PNR, northwest Mexico's Partido Revolucionario Sonorense, had made an early calculation to ally itself with anti-Chinese associations. When Adolfo de la Huerta campaigned for governor of the state of Sonora in 1919, he endorsed many of the hateful demands of the anti-Chinese associations, including the abrogation of Mexico's Treaty of Amity and Commerce with China, "and the expulsion of Chinese nationals and their descendants from Sonoran territory." After de la Huerta's victory, the anti-Chinese associations were incorporated into the Partido Revolucionario Sonorense, and the Sonoran government provided financial support for their activities. Moreover, de la Huerta lent his support to passing the 1919 Labor Law, including an 80 percent labor provision targeting Chinese business owners.[77] Once in power nationally, the PNR understood the political uses of anti-Chinese activity. Luis L. León, one of the party's founders, argued that anti-Chinese and other xenophobic activity "will . . . give us strong sympathy in all of the republic."[78] In the years after the formation of the National Revolutionary Party, Chinese diplomats saw anti-Chinese activists as an important part of the party's membership; the party even provided them with office space.[79] This incorporation into the official state party caused them to radicalize further and spread throughout the country.

With a political leader and a national party committed to *antichinismo,* it was no accident that the anti-Chinese campaigns were most intense during the Maximato, particularly during the presidency of Pascual Ortiz Rubio (1930–32), who was politically weak and worked with a congress that was largely loyal to Calles and the PNR instead of the president.[80] Chinese diplomats and residents were in agreement. Not only did federal officials disapprove of anti-Chinese activities, but the president was also deeply concerned about how the anti-Chinese campaigns would hurt Mexico's reputation abroad. But ultimately they saw Ortiz Rubio as such a weak political figure that negotiating with him was useless.[81] Ma Jixiu, a Chinese who had lived in the country for twenty years before being deported, noted that since "Calles dominated the congress, orders from the president [to protect Chinese] would not work."[82]

Sonora had some of the fiercest anti-Chinese associations in the country, but it also had some of Calles's strongest political allies. Two of his relatives served as governor during the anti-Chinese campaigns: his uncle, Francisco S. Elías; and his son, Rodolfo Elías Calles.[83] As anti-Chinese activists intensified their activities in the summer of 1931, both Francisco Elías and Rodolfo Elías Calles (who took office on September 1, 1931) pledged their support. Francisco Elías gave his reasons for supporting the anti-Chinese campaigns in a telegram to the Mexican Subsecretary of Foreign Relations. The governor made mention of the Tong Wars to help justify the campaign: "the existing rivalries between their mafias has been a constant threat in our cities . . . on various occasions there have been true gunfights in the [streets] harming peaceful citizens." But the expulsion of the Chinese, argued Elías, also presented opportunities for Mexican workers to obtain employment. "If you keep in mind that in this entity [state] there exist around nine hundred Chinese businesses and if you calculate an average of three employees each, you will see that there would be two thousand seven hundred Mexican employees who would be consumers and breadwinners."[84] Rodolfo Elías Calles in turn was reported to have said several times "that he would not tolerate the existence of a single Chinese in the whole state."[85] The open support of government officials helped anti-Chinese activists obtain what they had worked for since 1916: the expulsion of Chinese migrants from Sonora.

THE ANTI-CHINESE EXPULSION IN SONORA AND SINALOA

Chinese minister to Mexico Samuel Sung Young (Xiong Chongzhi) and consul in Sonora Yao-Hsiang Peng (Peng Yaoxiang) were well aware that the advent of the Great Depression in 1929 provided anti-Chinese activists with a crucial pretext to intensify their anti-Chinese activities, to argue for preventing future Chinese immigration, and to expel those who were already in the country. In Mexico the impact of the Great Depression fell primarily on the working class. Moreover, it provoked a crisis for the government, as revenues fell by 34 percent.[86] Mexican economic woes were further compounded when U.S. officials deported or encouraged the exodus of hundreds of thousands of Mexicans and Mexican Americans from the southwestern United States to Mexico.[87] Once they arrived, they joined the swelling ranks of the unemployed in Mexico. Indeed, anti-Chinese activists often mentioned "the Great Repatriation," both to compare the status of repatriated Mexican migrants with that of Chinese merchants and to give their petitions a sense of urgency. "Day by day deported [Mexicans] arrive in our Mexico," read a petition from one anti-Chinese association, "and this makes our situation even more difficult."[88] Chinese immigrants, especially those who naturalized as Mexicans, represented an unwanted competition for Mexican unemployed workers, especially those who were pouring south of the U.S.–Mexico border. Thus, allowing the Chinese to remain "discards the element which is truly national."[89]

With the advent of the depression, anti-Chinese activists moved from more overtly racist measures against the Chinese, such as banning intermarriage with Mexicans and proposing special ghettos for Asian residents, to primarily enacting economic restrictions, in particular the 80 percent labor provision. The provision specified that 80 percent of the workforce of foreign-owned businesses was to be supplied by Mexican labor. In practice, this meant that, for every Chinese worker a Chinese business employed, it would have to hire at least four Mexican workers to be in compliance. Just like other restrictions against the Chinese, it specifically included naturalized Chinese Mexicans.[90] The 80 percent labor provision provided a way for anti-Chinese activists and the Mexican government to curry favor with unemployed Mexicans by promising them future employment. Although initially passed by the Sonoran legislature in 1919, it was largely unenforced until 1931, when a strengthened 80 percent provision was enacted. The provision was also incorporated into the Federal Labor Law the same year.[91] From 1931 to 1933, this provision, along with increased taxes on Chinese businesses and a new registry of foreigners in the state, was used for future repression against the Chinese, and in particular as the justification for the expulsion of Chinese from the state of Sonora.[92]

Anti-Chinese associations made use of legislation like the 80 percent labor provision to encourage Mexicans to declare boycotts of Chinese businesses that were not in compliance. Just one month after the passage of the new state law, anti-Chinese activists began to give speeches, spread leaflets, and discourage Mexicans from patronizing Chinese businesses. Eventually, they would surround Chinese businesses to prevent Mexican customers from entering them. Their boycotts were extralegal actions. Anti-Chinese associations were not empowered under Sonoran labor legislation to determine whether Chinese businesses were in compliance with the law, nor were they allowed sanction them for noncompliance. None of these actions were officially condoned by local authorities, who preferred the deniability of having anti-Chinese campaigns organized by nongovernmental organizations. Anti-Chinese associations carried out boycotts anyway, carrying weapons to enforce their mandates. As local and federal government officials refused to intervene, anti-Chinese associations began to act with impunity. In Sonora, where anti-Chinese associations used these tactics most frequently, Chinese residents and diplomats were stymied in their attempts to intervene and rescue the livelihoods of Chinese residents.

In practice, anti-Chinese associations cared little about the 80 percent labor provision. Many Chinese business owners did try to comply with Sonoran labor legislation, even though it had disastrous effects for Chinese workers. Because the law stipulated that Chinese hire four Mexicans for each Chinese worker, those who complied were forced to fire almost their entire Chinese staff. Ching Chong y Compañía, a large business in Navojoa valued at over 500,000 pesos, complained that it complied with the demands of anti-Chinese activists to implement the 80 percent labor provision by firing its Chinese employees and hiring Mexican workers, only to face increased taxes and a new boycott from anti-Chinese activists three months later. Ultimately the owners saw themselves compelled to sign a contract stipulating that they would sell their goods and leave the region.[93] As this tactic became rapidly replicated, then, it led to the unemployment of thousands of Chinese workers. A letter from a Chinese group in Mazatlán, Sinaloa, illustrates what happened to them. After they were fired, Chinese workers were unable to sleep or eat at their former businesses and were forced to find a living elsewhere. As anti-Chinese campaigns became more numerous, "newly and previously unemployed overseas Chinese are everywhere." Chinese associations tried to support them temporarily, but once their resources ran out after one or two months, the only alternative would be for the workers to try to migrate to a tertiary country or return to China.[94] Despite this displacement of Chinese workers for Mexican labor— the stated goal of anti-Chinese associations—activists nevertheless continued to boycott Chinese businesses. Although occasionally Chinese migrants would negotiate a peaceful end to the boycott, far too often the stated goals of anti-Chinese associations were simply a pretext to close Chinese businesses.

Not simply relying on the Chinese diplomatic corps to protect them, Chinese migrants in Sonora and other states tried to organize themselves for their own protection. When Chinese migrants were detained, they attempted to meet with local officials to secure their freedom, and sent representatives to Mexican jails to ensure that Chinese prisoners were well taken care of. Migrants also often sought protection from the Mexican court system.[95] In addition to appealing extensively before Mexican officials, they also met extensively with Minister Sung Young and Consul Peng. The Mexican branch of the Guomindang sent appeals to the central party leadership in mainland China, while other organizations wrote to the Ministry of Foreign Affairs or the Executive Yuan. Migrant appeals before both Mexican and Chinese officials suggest the use of strategic nationalism, appealing to officials on both sides of the Pacific Ocean in an attempt to remain in Mexico.[96]

Chinese organizations also stressed unity to face the threat against them. The central committee of the Guomindang in Nogales, Sonora, sent a message addressed not only to all its party branches but to the Chinese Mexican world in general. It called specifically for Chinese to put the division forged during the Tong Wars behind them: "No matter what faction of overseas Chinese, [all] must do away with all dividing lines [and] unite as one in order to seek realistic protection, in order to be the rearguard of the diplomatic corps" or risk a disastrous future. It ended with a sober warning: "[We] wish our compatriots in Mexico will quickly wake up to the truth."[97] Unfortunately, the two factions did not heed the advice of the national GMD headquarters.

As the summer of 1931 wore on, what was initially called a boycott of Chinese businesses became more and more brazen. A visit by legation secretary Zhang Tianyuan and consul Peng Yaoxiang illustrated the dire conditions of Chinese merchants in the state. In the state capital of Hermosillo, the anti-Chinese association marched on the evening of July 5. Two days later, the association "dispatched people to stand in front of the doors of businesses it believed were not following the law, prohibited other people from entering to buy." Mexicans who tried to enter Chinese businesses anyway "were prevented through force of arms." One Chinese business operated solely by the proprietor, and thus exempt from the 80 percent provision, was nonetheless boycotted by the anti-

Chinese association, who argued that the business needed to employ Mexicans before it could reopen.

The result was the rapid closure of Chinese businesses across Sonora. In Navojoa, only two Chinese businesses continued to operate by early July, both of which employed Mexican workers. Nevertheless, on July 10 anti-Chinese activists surrounded one of these shops and, using megaphones, tried to persuade Mexicans not to purchase from the Chinese. In Ciudad Obregón, seven large-scale Chinese businesses had not only complied with the law but even obtained a certificate from local authorities as proof of their compliance. Anti-Chinese activists, however, refused to recognize the document and, declaring the businesses in violation of the labor law, demanded that each pay a fine of 30 pesos before it be allowed to reopen. All seven closed by July 1. The same situation was repeated in Nogales as well as the smaller towns of Huatabampo, Cócorit, and Esperanza. The Chinese legation alleged that Calles had telegrammed civil officials around the state and encouraged them to support the campaigns.[98] Emboldened, anti-Chinese associations began fining Chinese businesses that had already gone out of business several hundred to over a thousand pesos, and confiscating merchandise from those who were unable to pay. Eventually, anti-Chinese activists began stealing Chinese property without even the pretense of a fine.[99]

At the same time, anti-Chinese activists were also aggressively forcing Chinese farmers off of the state's farmlands. In Santa Bárbara, for example, anti-Chinese activists robbed Chinese farmers, damaged their homes, and pillaged their farmlands.[100] Soon after, the landowner canceled the Chinese farmers' lease and evicted them from their lands. In Ciudad Obregón and Bacanuchi, hacendados also forced Chinese off their farmlands, suggesting that it was due to pressure from authorities.[101]

In early August, anti-Chinese associations declared a deadline for Chinese businesses to settle their affairs and leave the state. This deadline is notable, as nowhere in the labor law or anywhere in the Mexican constitution were foreigners subject to deportation for failing to comply with labor legislation. Yet as the state and federal government turned a blind eye, anti-Chinese associations felt empowered to do just that. Were Chinese to ignore the order to abandon Sonora, anti-Chinese associations warned, they "would not be responsible for protecting them."[102] Zhang Tianyuan and Peng Yaoxiang met with state civil and military officials, who promised the Chinese diplomatic officials that they would work to protect local Chinese businesses but in practice did nothing.[103] President Ortiz Rubio, while meeting with the Chinese minister, asserted that Chinese businesses should ignore the unconstitutional order, but the legation feared that since "the president has no real power," he would be unable to protect the Chinese.[104]

The deadline for Chinese to leave was pushed back several times. On August 30 and 31, despite the fact that the deadline had been postponed, the towns of Huatabampo and Arizpe began detaining and deporting Chinese migrants on their own. In Huatabampo, anti-Chinese activists robbed and beat Chinese before forcing them to take the train out of town or even to flee on foot. Some hid in their rooms for days, helped by their neighbors, who provided them with loaves of bread so that they would survive. In Arizpe, Chinese farmers were stripped of their farming tools and other property and pushed off of the lands they were planting. Chinese from those two towns fled to Cananea and as far as Los Mochis, Sinaloa.[105]

The pressures on Chinese migrants in the state only intensified. Under pressure from the governor and the state's Secretary of Gobernación, Mexican landowners were abruptly canceling their leases with Chinese business owners and farmers, meaning that "Chinese businessmen have no place to rent, Chinese farmers have no land to plant."[106] In October, following a new decree allowing for the detention of Chinese who still ran their businesses in the state, Chinese in Nogales and Navojoa were thrown in prison without explanation.[107] The following month consular officials reported soberly that the Chinese "have no hope of reopening their businesses."[108] By then, Chinese diplomats, instead of protesting, pleaded with state officials to at least allow Chinese businessmen time to sell their goods and farmers to harvest their produce before deporting them, but Rodolfo Elías Calles refused to meet with Chinese officials or even return their telegrams. Consul Peng feared "that there will be no more trace left of the Chinese in this state."[109]

The success of the anti-Chinese campaigns in Sonora encouraged anti-Chinese organizations in the neighboring state of Sinaloa to conduct aggressive actions against the Chinese. The inauguration of an anti-Chinese governor convinced anti-Chinese associations in Sinaloa that they would not be punished. Following the example of government officials in Sonora, officials in Sinaloa increased business taxes on the Chinese several times over in 1932, hoping to force them to close their businesses and leave the state.[110] On February 10, 1933, local authorities in Los Mochis, Sinaloa, rounded up approximately one hundred Chinese residents and loaded them onto trucks for removal to the state of Nayarit. Anti-Chinese associations conducted similar detentions in Sinaloa's other major cities, including Mazatlán and Culiacán. The Chinese loaded onto trucks were not allowed to take any possessions with them, and shortly after they were taken away, anti-Chinese associations sacked their homes and businesses. On their journey south to Nayarit, the migrants were given neither food nor water nor any protection from the cold. "Criminals and prisoners of war are treated with more consideration and humanity," protested Minister Sung Young.[111] Other Chinese immigrants in the state of Sinaloa were also expelled northward, toward the U.S.–Mexico border, where they would be detained by INS agents and deported to China.[112] The governor of Sinaloa agreed to suspend the extrajudicial detentions of Chinese only if the Chinese community agreed to leave the state within a specified period of time.

Chinese diplomats watched helplessly as extrajudicial detentions of Chinese migrants only intensified. In February 1932, Rodolfo Elías Calles gave an order to local authorities "for the arrest and subsequent deportation from Sonora of all Chinese residents."[113] Chinese in Cumpas reported being detained and given fifteen days to leave the state. As they were taken into custody their personal possessions were taken away, and while they languished in jail their homes were sacked. Chinese residents in the small towns around Agua Prieta, Sonora, reported that authorities were detaining them and forcing them to cross the U.S.–Mexico border into the United States. Local authorities in Nogales reportedly took twenty-seven detained Chinese to the border and, when the Chinese hesitated crossing the border, beat them with clubs and threatened to shoot them until they crossed.[114] Officials in Sonora, in spite of incontrovertible proof that anti-Chinese associations and local officials were forcing the Chinese out, continued to dispute the accusations levied against them, and Rodolfo Elías Calles continued to assert that Chinese were fleeing the state "of their own free will."[115]

Just as pressing as cataloging and protesting the abuses against Chinese migrants was dealing with the increasing refugee crisis. Chinese were pouring out of the state, many toward the United States. Long-standing residents, even those who were Mexican citizens, left Sonora and Sinaloa; some had to abandon businesses valued at close to a million dollars. "Those who have assets either return to China or move to other states," noted Minister Sung Young, while "poor overseas Chinese . . . sneak into the United States and . . . have the U.S. government spend the money to send them back to China." An estimated nine hundred had already been deported in this fashion—a number that would swell to over four thousand by the end of the anti-Chinese campaigns. Those who remained in Sonora either sought desperately to sell their real estate or, being "utterly destitute, have no way of moving [and] sit and wait to be rescued."[116]

The expulsion of Chinese from the state of Sonora made headlines around the world and led to protests in China against the Mexican government. Articles on the Chinese expulsion in Sonora were printed in the United States, China, and Japan.[117] After arriving in Shanghai, expelled Chinese reported on the extralegal detentions and deportations committed against them between 1931 and 1933.[118] The honorary consul in Shanghai, Mauricio Fresco, following the growing condemnation in the Chinese media of the Mexican actions, denied that the anti-Chinese campaigns were even taking place. "Some Chinese left Mexico," admitted Fresco, "[but] they are the ones who would not submit to the laws of our country, but the majority of Chinese are well in Mexico and are under the protection of the authorities."[119] Fresco noted that Chinese media outlets were not convinced. According to the French-language *Journal de Shanghai,* Chinese newspapers condemned the expulsion as barbaric and rejected the idea that Chinese migrants were emigrating of their own free will.[120] Even journalists in the United States, a country that carried out a similar repatriation of hundreds of thousands of Mexican migrants, similarly condemned the Mexican expulsion of Chinese. The *St. Louis Daily Globe Democrat* tried to distance the two repatriations in an editorial on March 8, 1933, entitled "There Is a Difference," that condemned the "heartless treatment" and compared it "with our sympathetic and helpful repatriation of our excess Mexicans."[121]

The two governors of Sonora during the anti-Chinese campaigns, Francisco S. Elías and Rodolfo Elías Calles, kept former president Calles informed about developments regarding the Chinese question. Francisco Elías, for example, boasted prematurely that by the end of his term "there would not be a single Chinese business in this [state]."[122] Plutarco Elías Calles was aware of the crisis caused by the mass deportations of Chinese but believed them to be a necessary solution to what he considered "the Chinese problem." The former president, writing to his son Rodolfo, encouraged him not to "become alarmed at the situation," especially at the flight of capital from the state, since soon Mexican capital would fill the void.[123]

Not content with expelling the Chinese, xenophobic organizations in Mexico turned their attention to other economic competitors, especially Jewish and Arab merchants. A xenophobic organization in San Luis Potosí pledged to organize for a law "that will restrain the immigration of Turkish, Syrian-Lebanese, Czechoslovakians, Poles, and Jews, or of any nationalities of the many that are invading the markets with serious injury to the National commerce."[124] The Workers Union Chamber of Ciudad Juárez, Chihuahua, petitioned that Jews, Arabs, and Japanese be prohibited from "selling fruit and other articles" because it would create "unfair competition for Mexican merchants."[125] Unlike the Chinese, other immigrants were not expelled from the country. However, nationalist groups continued to hound foreign merchants during the late 1920s and 1930s. These protests had an impact on Mexico's 1934 immigration law, which prohibited not only workers from entering the country, but also businessmen wishing to work in commerce.[126]

The anti-Chinese campaign began to wane only during the presidency of Abelardo Rodríguez (1932–34), a period when the influence and prestige of Plutarco Elías Calles began to dim. Although Rodríguez never publicly broke with Calles, he "increasingly found space to oppose the influence of the *jefe máximo*."[127] In regard to the anti-Chinese campaigns, whereas Ortiz Rubio was much more hesitant to push back in light of Calles's endorsement, Rodríguez expressed his displeasure more freely. On May 15, 1933, the Mexican Secretary of Foreign Relations, José Manuel Puig Casauranc, wrote the governors of Sonora and Sinaloa at the behest of the president. The notes to the two governors appear to have been prompted by an earlier conversation between the secretary and the governor of Sinaloa, Manuel Páez. Pressed for an explanation of the anti-Chinese campaigns in Sinaloa, Páez reassured the central government that the state had reached an agreement with the Chinese consul to effect the departure of all remaining Chinese. The explanation was a lie, and in the interim anti-Chinese associations continued to carry out extrajudicial detentions of Chinese residents.

Rodríguez, who had been governor of Baja California, was no friend of the Chinese; in 1933, the Secretaría of Gobernación under his administration issued another secret circular banning the Chinese, along with other undesirable races, from immigrating to Mexico.[128] But as governor, asserted Puig Casauranc, Rodríguez had "attacked the problem in a very different way." Robbing the Chinese of their possessions, placing them on trucks, and carrying them out of the state, he asserted, had done grave harm to Mexico's international standing. Because the federal government understood that another deadline had come for the Chinese to evacuate Sinaloa, the president wished for the governor to put an end to the anti-Chinese campaign before the federal government took the blame for actions "in which it does not take the most remote participation and does not authorize."[129]

Given the fact that the governor of Sonora, Rodolfo Calles, was the son of the *jefe máximo,* Puig Casauranc's letter to him was more cordial but equally forceful. Puig Casauranc argued that although expelling the Chinese might be in the best interest of the wider Mexican nation, how it was effected created grave problems for the federal government. At the time Puig Casauranc wrote Calles, the U.S. government had incontrovertible proof that Chinese who entered the United States in the month of March had been forced to do so by Sonoran authorities. Although the embarrassed Mexican government considered paying for the cost of deporting those migrants to China, it worried about opening itself up to the responsibility of paying for the deportation costs of all Chinese Mexicans detained by the United States. Moreover, the risk of angering the United States by deporting the Chinese was too great to run. "The President and I, I insist, well understand the special difficulties [of] such a serious problem [the Chinese question]," wrote Puig Casauranc, "but having been resolved in a general sense, we hope that the naked presentation of the dangers that come from these questions could improve things and avoid similar incidents in the future."[130]

Chinese diplomats in Mexico saw Calles's downfall—the former president would board a plane for exile in the United States in 1936—as the definitive end to the anti-Chinese campaigns. Yet the note of displeasure indicates that as early as May 1933 the administration of Abelardo Rodríguez was committed to ending the abuses that drove Chinese migrants from the country. Activists in Sonora and Sinaloa had gone too far, by deporting Chinese migrants without justification and deporting them from the state. The federal government made clear that it would no longer be able to hide behind the misrepresentations of the anti-Chinese campaigns made by anti-Chinese organizations and instead would take direct responsibility over the actions committed by local associations and authorities. It needed to take greater control because anti-Chinese associations, in expelling the Chinese, had caused problems not only with the Chinese government but, more important, with the United States. After May 1933, the federal government discouraged use of the methods utilized by anti-Chinese associations. Although anti-Chinese associations in other states tried similarly to expel the Chinese, they found that the federal government was more committed to protecting, and better able to protect, the Chinese still in the country.

CONCLUSION

Sonora was the center of Chinese organizational activity in Mexico, was the center of a national network of anti-Chinese activists, and was the home state of the national politicians who would support the anti-Chinese campaigns from 1931 to 1933. Chinese associations, poorly understood by local observers, helped new migrants arrive and settle in Mexico, served as interlocutors between Chinese communities, Mexican neighbors, and Mexican authorities, and increased ties between Chinese Mexicans and their sending communities in southern China. The organizations Chinese migrants founded around the country demonstrated that their interests went much further than illicit activities or even mutual aid. The divisions among Chinese associations in the country, which regrettably crystalized into the Tong Wars of the mid-1920s, demonstrated that Chinese immigrants had different visions of a consolidated Chinese government. These divisions would last for the rest of the twentieth century. Although violence never recurred between the Guomindang and the Chee Kung Tong, they never again trusted each other and found it difficult to cooperate on matters relating to Chinese politics.

Violence between the two organizations provided ammunition to anti-Chinese associations, which wanted nothing more than to rid themselves of the Chinese. Having already argued against the Chinese presence as a threat to Mexican commerce and mestizo nationalism, they pointed to the Tong Wars as evidence that the Chinese presence was dangerous to everyday Mexicans. The Great Depression provided another justification. As local Mexican workers suffered from unemployment and as Mexican repatriates arrived from the United States, anti-Chinese activists argued that Chinese jobs should belong to Mexican workers.

As Mexico began to embark on a project of political stability and consolidation after the Mexican Revolution, prominent government officials supported the anti-Chinese campaigns and incorporated anti-Chinese associations into the structure of Mexico's new ruling party. Plutarco Elías Calles's support was crucial to the success of anti-Chinese campaigns. Also crucial was the support of Calles's local and state political allies, particularly in Sonora and Sinaloa. Once anti-Chinese activists had unofficial government backing, they radicalized to the point that they implemented crippling boycotts against Chinese businesses and the expulsion of Chinese migrants from the state of Sonora. Although Chinese migrants tried to resist the anti-Chinese campaigns, appealing to both Mexican and Chinese officials to safeguard their lives and businesses, the political strength of the anti-Chinese associations and the emerging Mexican state prevented them from finding relief. The result was the exodus of Chinese migrants from the state, and the destruction of Chinese organizations throughout much of northwestern Mexico.

All around the country, anti-Chinese activists tried to replicate the success of the Sonora expulsion, but outside of Sonora and Sinaloa, they would find greater resistance. Chapter 2 turns to the effort to expel Chinese from the states of Tamaulipas, Baja California, and Chiapas. In these areas, anti-Chinese associations lacked both the popular and government support that made the Sonoran anti-Chinese campaign so successful.

CHAPTER 2

Those Who Remained and Those Who Returned

Resistance, Migration, and Diplomacy during the Anti-Chinese Campaigns

Thousands of Chinese immigrants fled the northern Mexican state of Sonora in 1931, chased out by anti-Chinese associations that decreed a six-month limit for migrants to close their shops, settle their affairs as best they could, leave the area, and never return. The wealthiest Chinese were able to purchase a steamship ticket to China, but those less fortunate fled to neighboring states or crossed illegally into Central America or the United States—often carrying only the clothes on their backs and begging for food along the way. Whatever they had accomplished was washed away in just a few years.

Not content with the expulsion in Sonora, anti-Chinese activists during the late 1920s extended their campaigns across the entire country. Even before Sonora expelled its Chinese, far-flung towns suddenly opened anti-Chinese associations; their newspapers published anti-Chinese cartoons and opinion pieces; their streets witnessed anti-Chinese marches; and anti-Chinese activists surrounded *paisano* businesses. Many such towns specified a time limit, anywhere from a few months to a few days, for all Chinese in the vicinity to settle their affairs and leave the country.

But despite their drive to replicate the Sonora expulsion, anti-Chinese groups found that, outside of Sonora, *paisanos* could resist their tactics. In the state of Nayarit, for example, the state government sided with Chinese migrants after self-declared "Green Guards" staged a boycott of local Chinese commerce and surrounded the entrances of Chinese businesses. The state quickly grew tired of the Green Guards, who "not only attack Chinese merchants, but even our nationals who have the right to buy from [the Chinese]." The Secretaría de Gobernación repeatedly gave guarantees to the Chinese in the state, and those guarantees apparently persuaded the local governor to protect them.[1] The outcome of the campaign in Nayarit challenges the conclusions frequently drawn about anti-Chinese violence in postrevolutionary Mexico. First, it demonstrates that Mexicans had continued to shop at Chinese businesses even after the Green Guards declared a boycott. Furthermore, state authorities could ignore nationalist arguments about Mexican economic interests and instead move to protect the Chinese.

Far removed from the state of Sonora, anti-Chinese campaigns varied considerably in their causes and outcomes. In Tamaulipas, along the Gulf Coast, land was taken away from wealthy Chinese farmers, but a full-scale expulsion did not take place. On the northwestern peninsula of Baja California, an anti-Chinese boycott closed Chinese businesses, but it collapsed after the federal government intervened to protect the Chinese. And in the southern state of Chiapas, anti-Chinese activists repeatedly tried to expel the Chinese but never, it appears, found popular support. At the conclusion of the anti-Chinese campaigns, these three areas would hold the largest Chinese populations in the country. Indeed, Chinese in Sonora would flock to these areas as potential places of refuge and resettlement.

In much of the country, Chinese migrants did not simply accept their fate and pack up their belongings. They made use of local, national, and transnational connections to help convince local officials to safeguard their presence. New associations were established and old ones strengthened, all of which did their best to protect Chinese lives and properties by harnessing connections on both sides of the Pacific. Certainly, Chinese reached out to their diplomatic officials in Mexico; countrymen in San Francisco and mainland China also wrote on their behalf, scandalized by the news of their plight. But, too keen to pretend that China's diplomats alone could save them, Chinese associations were increasingly active in Mexican circles. They sought protection in Mexican courts, harnessed connections with local and federal officials, and encouraged friendly Mexican organizations to intercede on their behalf. The resistance shown by Chinese Mexicans during the anti-Chinese campaigns demonstrates the ways in which both local and transnational ties could facilitate their remaining in Mexico. Chinese associations contributed funds not only to China but also to local Mexican communities, demonstrating early claims to belonging to their areas of settlement. Once the anti-Chinese campaigns began, migrants appealed to both local and Chinese officials. Finally, the campaigns produced a counterintuitive cooperation: Chinese migrants and diplomats worked together to ensure that migrants retained the freedom to remain in Mexico. Ultimately, Chinese migrants persuaded authorities in several states to break up anti-Chinese marches, shut down meeting halls, and confiscate propaganda. Admittedly, by any measure the anti-Chinese campaigns across Mexico were devastating. In just three years, three-quarters of Mexico's Chinese population fled the country; total losses were estimated at over 10 million Chinese yuan.[2] But many communities were able to survive the anti-Chinese campaigns and remain in Mexico through much of the twentieth century.

Those *paisanos* who were able to remain in the country by resisting the anti-Chinese campaigns achieved what they undoubtedly saw as major victories in the face of daunting odds. This chapter examines their resilience. The anti-Chinese campaigns led to the strengthening of Chinese associations around the country, which defended communities like those of Tamaulipas, Chiapas, and Baja California from xenophobic attacks. After the anti-Chinese campaigns came to a close, the climate improved so much that even Chinese who had been expelled from the country sought to return to Mexico to rejoin their families and resume their business activities.

THE ANTI-CHINESE CAMPAIGNS ACROSS MEXICO

Studies on the anti-Chinese campaigns primarily focus on the northwestern Mexican states of Sonora and Sinaloa. One historian referred to these campaigns as "a peculiarly *norteño* phenomenon."[3] But they were conducted in all corners of the country: "where there are Chinese, there are anti-Chinese organizations," noted one diplomatic source.[4] In cities and towns across central and southern Mexico (see map 2), nativists were inspired by the hateful message of activists like José Ángel Espinoza, one of the main intellectual proponents of the anti-Chinese campaigns, to form their own anti-Chinese organizations in hopes of ousting the Chinese. Once formed, these groups used propaganda and marches to help spread their message to Mexicans in the surrounding area.

The rapid spread of anti-Chinese associations was likely due to redoubled efforts of a small number of anti-Chinese activists. José Ángel Espinoza believed that the "organization of anti-Chinese leagues in the

MAP 2. Cities and towns across Mexico with a significant Chinese population.

spacious territory of the Republic" was the only way the movement could succeed.[5] To this end, it had to be easy for new associations to spring up around the country. (See figure 1.) If the movement were to expand nationally, not only would it garner increased support; it would also be more difficult for federal officials to arrest their activities. Espinoza's *El problema chino en México* contains a sample charter for anti-Chinese associations to use, meaning that even uneducated racists could "immediately and in any part of the country organize as many anti-Chinese leagues as necessary."[6] The charters were broad enough, Espinoza noted proudly, that they could be used in the future against other undesirable foreigners: "Turks, Syrians, Poles, etc."[7] More than vitriol, then, Espinoza offered a plan that would ultimately successfully expel most Chinese immigrants from the country.

Despite the rhetoric of anti-Chinese activists, their associations were quite small. In 1932, anti-Chinese activists alleged that they had created 215 anti-Chinese associations with a total membership of two million people, suggesting an average membership of nine hundred people per

Mexicano: El color amarillo que ves en la carta geográfica de tu patria, es la demostración del dominio mongol. Ves a Sonora limpio de la mancha asiática, pues sigue el ejemplo de este pueblo batallador y pronto harás de tu patria chica una entidad que podrás llamar tuya y de los tuyos.

FIGURE 1. José Ángel Espinoza encourages Mexicans around the country to follow Sonora's example and expel the Chinese, after which, says Espinoza, "you will make your hometown a place that you can call yours." From Espinoza, *El ejemplo de Sonora*.

association.[8] But even in Mexico's largest cities, rare was the anti-Chinese petition that garnered more than a few dozen signatures. Rather than deriving their strength from their alleged large membership, anti-Chinese organizations engaged in actions that overcompensated for their small membership and spread their influence beyond the place of their founding. Different anti-Chinese associations replicated the same tactics, which then overwhelmed Chinese diplomats and residents seeking to respond. The anti-Chinese organization in Torreón, Coahuila, for example, was one of the most active, petitioning at least ten states around the country to pass anti-Chinese legislation.[9] Even cities without anti-Chinese associations, then, could come under the influence of the racist rhetoric coming from neighboring states. Legislators in the state of Yucatán received several petitions from local and state government officials in northern and central Mexico banning Chinese immigrants, even though that state was opposed to such legislation.[10]

The extant literature on the anti-Chinese campaigns underestimates the ability of Chinese Mexicans to survive them, particularly because of the failure of the Sonora Chinese to stay in the country. But the Chinese themselves were never dismissive of their own ability to persevere. Chinese diplomats played an important supporting role by encouraging Chinese Mexicans to organize, as well as by negotiating on their behalf before the Mexican government and the League of Nations. The consulates and associations are a large factor in explaining the permanence of a fragment of Mexico's Chinese population after 1934.

During the 1930s, the utility of Chinese native-place, clan, and mutual-aid associations to combat anti-Chinese pressure encouraged locations without any Chinese associations to establish their own. *Paisanos* established these associations when anti-Chinese activities had spread to their cities or to neighboring locations. For example, the Chinese of Ciudad Madero, Tamaulipas, organized a Chinese association in 1935, when anti-Chinese activists proposed discriminatory labor legislation; they were organized in part by the *paisanos* in neighboring Tampico.[11] In Mexico City, which never witnessed a serious anti-Chinese campaign, early acts of anti-Chinese violence in northern Mexico prompted the Chinese community there to form the Organization for Overseas Chinese across Mexico (Quanmoguo Huaqiao Zongjiguan). The group organized *paisanos* in the capital as well as provided aid for Chinese victims of violence in various parts of Mexico. It dissolved in 1932, when Chinese in the city believed the environment had improved.[12] In Ensenada, *paisanos* formed a Chinese association in 1931 in response to the campaigns in Sonora and Sinaloa, even though an anti-Chinese campaign did not begin in Ensenada until 1934.[13]

Both *paisanos* and anti-Chinese activists saw different attacks around the country as part of the same protracted struggle. In each affected area, Chinese migrants made the argument that they had contributed to the development of the local area and that the campaigns lacked popular support. Letters from Chinese associations around the country made mention of anti-Chinese campaigns not only in Sonora but also in Tamaulipas, Chihuahua, Baja California, and Coahuila, among others. Even if they were not personally affected, Chinese leaders urged Chinese diplomats to do their utmost to protect Chinese lives and properties. Even though the frequent protests of the Chinese legation failed in Sonora and Sinaloa, in other locations the efforts of Chinese diplomats and associations were successful. Having few remaining options, *paisanos* inevitably turned to each other and to the diplomatic corps as their last bastion of defense in the country.

VILLA JUÁREZ, TAMAULIPAS

When Mexican authorities detained and expelled eighty-two Chinese residents of Villa Juárez, Tamaulipas, on false charges that they lacked lawful documentation to reside in the country, Chinese diplomats and area residents leaped to their defense. They vigorously protested the extrajudicial detentions and demanded that those arrested be released and allowed to return to their homes. Although there is some evidence of local resentment against the success of Chinese migrants, the detention of the Chinese was spurred not by xenophobia or economic nationalism but by local and national politicians who coveted productive Chinese-owned farmlands. Because of overbearing pressure from former president Calles, Chinese protests largely fell on deaf ears, and the expelled migrants were unable to return to their homes. But the Villa Juárez Chinese ultimately avoided being deported from the country. Moreover, the campaign pushed Chinese in the area as well as around the country to organize for their own self-defense. Unlike Sonora, Tamaulipas did not expel its Chinese residents. Some of the Villa Juárez Chinese would resettle in the state's major port city of Tampico, which maintained the largest Chinese community in the country after the anti-Chinese campaigns.

Villa Juárez (now El Mante), just outside of Tampico, Tamaulipas, has been largely understudied by scholars of the Chinese diaspora in Mexico. Chinese immigrants had been arriving in the region since the late nineteenth century, many working on the railway line between San Luis Potosí and Tampico. Many others entered the country through the Gulf Coast ports of Progreso, Tampico, and Veracruz.[14] Another wave of Chinese migrants arrived during the Mexican Revolution, as an oil boom took place along the Gulf Coast. They worked primarily in support industries for oil workers—as food vendors, launderers, cooks, tailors, and cobblers.[15] By 1930, most of the migrants there dedicated themselves to operating Mexican grocery stores.

In addition, a sizable minority excelled in agriculture, incensing Mexican farmers without access to land. This was the case with an early influential Chinese businessman, Wong Foon Chuck (Huang Kuanzhuo). Born in Taishan County, Guangdong Province, Wong immigrated to the United States at thirteen but eventually would resettle in Mexico. In 1896, Wong would establish a five-thousand-hectare hacienda in Villa Juárez known as Hacienda Cantón (Guangdong Yuan), developing the area well before Mexicans were interested in the land.[16] Hacienda Cantón and another hacienda, Nuevo Cantón, continued to be "highly productive" until 1930, producing sugar, rice, and sesame seed.[17] Indeed, as noted by the U.S. consul, "The Chinese are really responsible for the prosperity of El Mante."[18]

Early but sporadic hostility against *paisanos* encouraged them to form associations. In 1918, Chinese Tampicans established a general Chinese association, the Zhonghua Huiguan, because they had been harassed and did not yet have a Chinese consulate. The association contributed to the development of the city, donating funds to purchase ambulances and stoplights. In 1924, after an anti-Chinese organization began to agitate against them, Chinese organized a second association incorporating Chinese in the neighboring state of Veracruz and made contacts with local authorities and the local military chief to protect their presence.[19]

By 1929, however, there was still a general climate of animosity toward the Chinese. Local government officials had begun to harass Chinese business owners, increasing taxes and dispatching health inspectors to perform audits. The area was developing the agrarian sector of its economy, and the Chinese consul noted the presence of *agraristas* (supporters of agrarian reform) who wanted to make sure that the fruits of Mexican economic development remained in Mexican hands.[20] Chinese-owned farms, including Hacienda Cantón, drew their ire. The local Chinese consul reported that the governor of Tamaulipas told a large gathering of local residents: "The area of El Mante [including Villa Juárez], Tamaulipas, is a new agricultural area of Tamaulipas; the state government is determined not to allow it to be infected with foreigners." Shortly thereafter, allegations emerged that a Chinese farmer at Hacienda Cantón shot a Mexican thief on the property, incensing the local population, which pressed for local authorities to act on the Chinese problem. Local officials, in turn, having no legal way to expel Chinese from the territory, asked the Secretaría de Gobernación, in particular the Department of Migration, for help ridding the state of unwanted Chinese.[21]

The raids on Chinese migrants in Villa Juárez and the nearby farms of El Limón and Hacienda Cantón took place in September 1930. According to initial reports, migration officials went to each Chinese business in the town, first searching for contraband, then demanding to see immigration paperwork. All workers were detained except the main owners, who were left behind to watch over their businesses. The rest, eighty-two migrants, were loaded onto two boxcars, in which they initially stood during the eight-hour journey to Tampico. Later, with the intention that they arrive in a decent manner, "as any other passenger," they were transferred to second-class passenger cars.[22] Upon their arrival, the Chinese were taken into custody and placed in the local prison. While they languished in jail, their businesses and residences were plundered; local Chinese estimated the total losses at 500,000 Mexican pesos.[23] Reports emerged that the governor had issued an order that Chinese businesses should suspend all activities within four days and that their owners should leave the country. That evening, local newspapers warned that immigration authorities would continue to conduct similar raids in Tampico.[24]

Although the Department of Migration characterized the detention of the Villa Juárez Chinese as an immigration issue, subsequent reports reveal that the Secretaría de Gobernación lied to Chinese diplomats about the legal status of the detained migrants. Despite the fact that all of the detained migrants possessed legal documentation to reside in the country, government agents never bothered to check.[25] This oversight occurred because the detention was carried out not by the Department of Migration, as the government initially maintained, but by Braulio Junco and Guillermo Davis, special agents of the Secretaría de Gobernación personally dispatched by Rodolfo Elías Calles, son of the former president. The agents' sole objective, according to the confidential document, was to "ensure that [the Chinese] do not return to Villa Juárez."[26] According to the agents, Rodolfo Elías Calles had personally paid for the transportation of the Chinese to Tampico; a close business associate accompanied the Chinese to ensure that they left Villa Juárez for good. Knowing the sensitivity of the expulsion, Rodolfo Elías Calles asked "that on this matter his name not be mentioned."[27]

The documents make clear that only the Chinese had acted in accordance with the law, while the agents of the Secretaría de Gobernación acted with impunity. The detained *paisanos* had broken no laws and were in fact in possession of legal documentation to remain in the country. Mexican authorities took advantage of the fact that Chinese had registered themselves and their businesses, giving the legal addresses of their homes and workplaces. It was thus extremely easy for Mexican authorities to round them up. Their trust in legal procedures explains why, after the raid on Villa Juárez, Chinese in the area "all . . . felt in danger."[28] At the same time, Mexican officials failed to follow the law in extending the protections that the Chinese were entitled to. When journalists and the Chinese consul boarded the train, the two agents lied about their own names and refused to release the names of the detainees, hampering the effort to free the Chinese.[29] While Mexican federal officials limited themselves to promising a full investigation, local and state officials ignored urgent telegrams from the Chinese consulate, which sought to negotiate for their freedom. Appeals that Chinese deportees had legal proof of residency fell on deaf ears.

Chinese residents and the local consul would eventually concur on the nature of the problem: not the legal status of Chinese migrants, nor agents of the local Department of Migration, but former president Plutarco Elías Calles.[30] The consul in Tampico saw the detention of the Villa Juárez Chinese as part of an attempt "to take away Mexican national [Wong Foon Chuck's] land."[31] Although former president Plutarco Elías Calles did not directly order the raid, the confidential report from the Secretaría de Gobernación suggested that he was pleased, while the Anti-Chinese Committee in Tampico, writing directly to the former president, applauded the raids and asked that they be extended to Tampico.[32] It is revealing that special envoy Samuel Sung Young (Xiong Chongzhi) intended to negotiate not only with Mexican federal officials, but also with Calles.[33] Chinese diplomatic officials believed that Calles wished to entice popular support by suggesting that Chinese-owned lands might be nationalized and divided among landless Mexicans as part of the country's agrarian reform, but really wished to keep these lands for himself.[34] After Calles and a close associate, Aarón Sáenz Garza, opened a nearby sugar estate, Chinese diplomats reported that migrants found it more difficult to obtain business licenses, and those who did saw their taxes increase.[35] The fact that the Chinese diplomatic corps saw Calles as the chief instigator complicated efforts at negotiation. Out of office, Calles was unaccountable to the Mexican government, but continued to be respected by local officials around the country.[36]

Chinese migrants and diplomats immediately protested the extralegal immigrant detentions. Chinese associations convened a meeting of all local Chinese residents, and planned to dispatch representatives to meet with the governor. Meanwhile, local paisanos pooled resources to hire a lawyer to argue their case, and a court ruling initially ordered the release of the Chinese. Allies in the Mexico City Chinese association also launched a protest against the treatment of the Villa Juárez Chinese.

Samuel Sung Young, the Chinese minister to Mexico during most of the anti-Chinese campaigns, immediately went to the affected area, interceding before the governor of Tamaulipas and the Secretaría of

Foreign Relations. He delivered an official document of protest and asked that the eighty-two Chinese who were detained be released and that the Mexican president order that Chinese throughout the country be safeguarded. Chinese migrants later had nothing but praise for Sung Young, writing that he "negotiated the entire day, did not waste a minute, worrying beyond belief at the state of the Chinese and going through all kinds of hardships and difficulties."[37]

The detained Chinese were set free only after repeated negotiations.[38] They hesitated, however, to return to Villa Juárez, where there was no guarantee that they would be protected from similar actions in the future.[39] Gradually, approximately thirty *paisanos* gambled on returning to the village and resuming their businesses. But on December 5, they were once again detained, allegedly under orders from Rodolfo Elías Calles. They then were forced to sign a pledge to leave the area within ten days. Two weeks later, the chief of police of Villa Juárez led raids on Chinese haciendas, detaining approximately three dozen Chinese. Like the eighty-two detained the previous year, they were apprehended without being allowed to collect their possessions, held without food or drink, and subsequently escorted on foot into Tampico.[40] After the second raid, the federal government ultimately proved reluctant to intervene. Some returned to China, while others resettled in Tampico to start up new businesses. It was evident to the consulate that crucial to the resolution of this case "was the support of the powerful and prestigious former president"; both local and federal officials ultimately proved reluctant to contradict former president Calles and intervene in favor of the Chinese residents.[41] Despite the displacement of the Villa Juárez Chinese, however, and despite the calls of anti-Chinese associations to remove other Chinese communities from the area, Chinese in other parts of the Gulf Coast were not expelled from the country.

The case of the Villa Juárez Chinese is not simply a case of nationalization of foreign-owned lands, or of agrarian reform in postrevolutionary Mexico. Even as local landless Mexicans hungered for the Chinese-owned land, what became the El Mante complex "benefitted not *ejidatarios,* but private landowners, many of them friends and relatives of former president Plutarco Elías Calles." After Calles's exile, he and his associates would lose the very land they seized from the Chinese. After the land was nationalized, a sugar mill was constructed in El Mante, and cooperatives were formed to plant sugar on the site of the former Chinese hacienda, in what became "a shining example of a successful project under the agrarian law."[42]

ENSENADA, BAJA CALIFORNIA

The campaign in Ensenada, Baja California, occurred when anti-Chinese activists argued that *paisanos* failed to comply with Mexican labor legislation and as a result should be expelled from the country. Just as in Sonora and Sinaloa, members of the league declared a boycott of Chinese businesses and surrounded the shops in order to force compliance among the Mexican population. Although the anti-Chinese organization was nearly successful in expelling *paisanos* from the city of Ensenada, the local Chinese association was able to use its connections to other Chinese communities on the peninsula as well as Mexican government officials and Chinese diplomats to break the boycott and reopen their businesses. More important, the campaign in Ensenada did not spread to the larger cities of Tijuana and Mexicali.

Although some Chinese arrived from California in the late nineteenth century, most arrived after the turn of the twentieth century. The majority of *paisanos* there worked the cotton fields of the Mexicali Valley, a move facilitated by the Colorado River Land Company and then governor Esteban Cantú (1915–20). The Mexicali Valley had such a high percentage of Chinese migrants that in the early twentieth century these migrants called Mexicali "little Guangzhou."[43] Large groups of Chinese also lived in Tijuana and Ensenada, arriving from the United States and from other parts of Mexico after the anti-Chinese campaigns in those areas. The Chinese population surged to the point where it had become the largest ethnic group in the territory. While Abelardo Rodríguez served as governor of Baja California (1923–30), he counted seven thousand Chinese nationals and six thousand Mexican citizens.[44] The decline in the price of cotton encouraged many to leave the cotton fields for Baja California's major cities—Mexicali, Tijuana, and Ensenada—and open general stores that served Chinese and Mexicans alike.[45] There were so many Chinese-owned general stores that, in the local language, to go to the store was to visit "*el chino* on the corner." These stores were popular with Mexicans because they were conveniently located and kept long hours.[46] Their success in Ensenada made them targets for nativists.

Two of the businesses anti-Chinese activists targeted were Yun Kui y Compañía and Rafael Chan y Compañía. Yun Kui had been an Ensenada institution for about as long as Ensenada existed. Liang Changmao and his two brothers Rumao and Jingmao, who moved to Ensenada in the 1880s and 1890s, founded Yun Kui in 1898. The store sold both Chinese and Mexican goods and obtained the business of both Mexican and Chinese Ensenadans.[47] Advertisements for the store appear in one of the first newspapers to be published in the city, *El Progresista,* in 1903.[48] Mexican residents of Ensenada had high opinions of Yun Kui, Rafael Chan, and other Chinese businesses in the city; one wholesaler describes their owners as "men who could be trusted, who would obtain goods on credit and repay us, even without a bill of sale, simply at our word."[49] The two companies contributed a portion of their profits to the construction of schools and nurseries in Ensenada and the repair of local roads.[50] Both firms grew from humble beginnings into large enterprises, eventually supplying necessities such as clothing, perfume, tools, and riding equipment. In addition, they provided wholesale goods for twenty-five other Chinese-owned general stores in Ensenada, which in effect meant that the two companies controlled a large share of the retail commerce in the Baja California city.

Just as in other areas of northwestern Mexico, their success generated intense resentment, which eventually led to the creation of anti-Chinese associations. The Nationalist League of Ensenada attacked longstanding Chinese businesses like Yun Kui and Rafael Chan, denouncing their owners as trespassers who built their fortunes on the backs of everyday Mexicans.[51] Even before the Ensenada campaign, advertisements in one local newspaper repeatedly exhorted readers to buy from Mexicans and avoid buying from foreigners. One gas-station advertisement implored readers, "Protect your countrymen, buy from 'El Indio.'" Another declared, "To buy from Mexican businessmen is to perform a patriotic act." A Jewish-Lithuanian immigrant in Ensenada who understood the business environment renamed his business "El Azteca."[52] However, nativists targeted the Chinese in particular because of their success and visibility.[53]

Labor unions and nationalist groups, seizing on fears that Mexico might lose Baja California to U.S. annexation, described the large waves of U.S. and Chinese citizens to the region as nothing short of an invasion. "Baja California . . . finds itself invaded by a thick wave of Chinese," wrote the president of the Comité Pro-Raza Rodolfo Elías Calles of Mexicali to President Pascual Ortiz Rubio (1930–32). The fact that the Chinese population exceeded the Mexican population in certain areas of the territory underlined fears of a foreign takeover. The Comité Pro-Raza advocated curbing Chinese migration to northwestern Mexico and encouraging Mexican settlement in the territory to stave off a U.S. or Japanese invasion.[54] Their rationale directly connected territorial defense to Chinese exclusion, and linked their race-based movement to working for the benefit of the territory and the nation.

Both the tactics and the stated aims of the Nationalist League of Ensenada strongly recalled other anti-Chinese campaigns across the country. As a result, when the Ensenada campaign began, Chinese across Baja California instantly recognized the magnitude of the threat. Chinese communities in Baja California's major cities, formed during the Sonora expulsion, convened an emergency meeting to respond to the campaign. Wealthy Chinese Ensenadans took refuge in nearby Tijuana and Mexicali.[55] The three communities also hired a lawyer to help defend themselves in Mexican courts. Finally, they alerted the Chinese diplomatic corps in Mexico. The Mexicali Chinese Association, the Zhonghua Huiguan, asked the local Chinese vice-consul, Hu Yianjie (Hu Yanji), to travel to Ensenada and investigate the campaign. Vice-Consul Hu took photographs of the campaign and then met with the governor to present his concerns.[56]

Hu and the Chinese minister, W. S. Wong (Huang Yunsu), then presented a formal protest before the office of the governor in Mexicali and the Secretary of Foreign Relations in Mexico City. From the Mexican capital, Secretary of Gobernación Eduardo Vasconcelos and Secretary of Foreign Relations José Manuel Puig Casauranc tried to understand conflicting reports from the northwestern territory. While the territorial governor, Agustín Olachea, shielded the actions of the Nationalist League and dismissed the reports as a local conflict blown out of proportion, the Chinese community in Ensenada accused the governor and his staff in the city of complicity in trying to close Chinese-owned businesses. In addition to the fear of displacing the Chinese, this conflict presented a special complication: fear that the Chinese might cross into the United States, adding to perceptions of Mexican barbarity toward Chinese migrants and worsening U.S.–Mexican relations. All of the above governmental agencies and associations had to move quickly to respond to the growing crisis caused by the Nationalist League.

At the same time, anti-Chinese activists in Ensenada and their supporters tried to construct the campaign as a popular movement in order to establish its inevitability. Governor Olachea told Vice-Consul Hu that the campaign was an expression of the popular will and should end in no other way but with the exodus of Chinese from the territory.[57] Two weeks after the start of the campaign, Olachea sent pictures of an anti-Chinese march in Ensenada to Secretary Vasconcelos in an attempt to make a similar point. These pictures of the march, which likely included many curious locals, were meant to show that the nationalists had won over the majority of the population.[58]

Vice-Consul Hu's interviews with members of the Chinese community in Ensenada, Tijuana, and Mexicali, however, suggest that the campaign was not a popular phenomenon caused by long-simmering tensions between the Chinese and Mexicans in Ensenada. During meetings with Hu, Chinese merchants denied that there had ever been any major problems between Chinese and Mexicans. All of them employed Mexican workers, thus negating the 80 percent labor clause as the reason behind anti-Chinese protests in Mexico. According to the Chinese community in Ensenada, the campaign was started by "a few ignorant people," and Chinese leaders in the city "believe[d] that the city's anti-Chinese [league] takes advantage of this opportunity to push the Chinese out, simply to gain economically."[59] The fact that many of the members of the Nationalist Committee in Ensenada were also members of the Ensenada Chamber of Commerce helps support their view.[60]

Just as in other campaigns, news of the Baja California campaign spread quickly and caused protests and diplomatic incidents around the world. After one protest at the Mexican embassy in Washington, the ambassador sent a telegram to the Secretaría of Foreign Relations to ask what exactly was happening in Ensenada.[61] The Chinese consul in Los Angeles criticized the campaign as a "deplorable act" in interviews with the *Los Angeles Times*.[62] Articles on the campaign published in the official newspaper of the Chinese Nationalist Party, the Nanjing daily *Zhongyang Ribao* ("Central Daily News"), incensed Chinese on the mainland.[63] Mauricio Fresco, Mexican minister to China, sent reports on the Chinese reaction to the campaign from Shanghai.[64]

As the federal government had not yet stepped in, the league and Governor Olachea continued to carry out their campaign against Chinese migrants. On February 18, ten days into the campaign, Olachea sent a message to the Secretary of Gobernación announcing that every restaurant and commercial establishment owned by Chinese in Ensenada had now closed. As the activists had acted within the limits of the law, wrote Olachea, he would not intervene to stop their actions.[65] Five days later, Olachea announced that the Mexican Nationalist League and Chinese merchants had reached a final resolution. "One month was given to some, three months to others to completely liquidate their businesses," wrote Olachea, after which they would leave the territory permanently.[66] The agreement bound all Chinese in Ensenada regardless of citizenship—Chinese or Mexican. The three signatories later alleged that the Mexican Nationalist League had appointed the three of them "leaders" of the community who could agree to leave the country on behalf of all other Chinese in the city, and that they had signed the agreement only after being threatened with pistols.[67] This tactic directly paralleled the situation in Sonora and other states, in which Chinese business owners were given a time limit to liquidate their businesses and leave the state. After the Mexican Nationalist League made the agreement public, the territorial government declined once again to intervene, now because the matter appeared settled and because it could not interfere in a private agreement.

The agreement between business owners and the Mexican Nationalist League alarmed the Chinese legation. If the federal government upheld the agreement as valid and binding, anti-Chinese groups in other regions of Mexico could likewise designate their own leaders of the Chinese community to expel them throughout the country.[68] On March 8, Chinese Minister Wong wrote a strongly worded note to the Secretary of Foreign Relations protesting recent anti-Chinese agitation, local and federal government inaction, and, in particular, the idea that Chinese business owners and Mexican nationalists had found a solution to their conflict. Wong was offended by the idea that physically blocking the entrances to Chinese businesses could constitute some form of lawful and passive resistance. Addressing Olachea's pretext for inaction, Wong wrote, "Mr. Secretary, I don't see [how] the activities executed by the anti-Chinese leagues could fit within the law." To prevent the crimes being committed, authorities in Baja California "have the precise obligation to prevent the use of force from restricting the liberty of Chinese businessmen to sell as well as that of Mexicans outside the anti-Chinese leagues to buy."[69]

It was at this point that the secretaries of Gobernación and Foreign Relations finally agreed on the need for direct intervention in the Ensenada campaign.[70] As Olachea and Wong presented opposite views of the legality and justice of the anti-Chinese campaign, the central government seemed more worried about the result: "as the Territory of Baja California depends directly on the Executive of the Federation, [the Federal Government] could not avoid responsibility" if the Chinese were driven from Baja California.[71] The Secretary of Gobernación ordered Governor Olachea to impede the actions of the Nationalist League, no matter how legal he believed them to be.[72] The order drew a quick reaction from nationalist groups. On receiving the news that their license to march in Ensenada was now denied, these groups along with the territorial National Revolutionary Party (PNR) sent three telegrams to the Secretary of Gobernación asking him to reconsider. While two of the messages were cordial, the president of the regional PNR was much more direct, asserting that "[t]he Mexican Nationalist League considers it the evil work of anti-Mexican elements."[73]

Nevertheless, the ban on anti-Chinese activity appears to have endured, for in the month after these three telegrams there is no record of any marches, or of nationalist groups physically blocking the entrances to Chinese businesses. When Olachea and territorial agents for public health dragged their feet in giving the Chinese the necessary permits to reopen their businesses, the federal government intervened again to expedite the process.[74] In late March and early April, Chinese businesses began to reopen in Ensenada—a fact that frustrated anti-Chinese activists. After a long and arduous campaign, complained one, "[we] managed to close all [the businesses] but two of the most powerful Chinese are reopening [them] and I believe that soon the rest will open and our work will remain on the ground."[75]

Although the Ensenada campaign was not the last anti-Chinese campaign in Baja California, subsequent campaigns were dispersed more quickly. When nationalists began to congregate before a planned 1935 march in Mexicali, the military forcibly disbanded them and arrested the leaders of the movement. The lawyer for the Chinese community in the city dismissed the movement as one of "hungry mobs that tried to take control of foreign commerce."[76] In 1937, another campaign, this time under the Regional Confederation of Mexican Workers (CROM), sought the expulsion of foreigners under the slogan "Mexico for the Mexicans." Though theoretically directed at foreigners of any nationality, the organization declared that anyone caught owning a business for or otherwise helping foreigners would be declared a "Chinese Mexican." In imparting guarantees to the Chinese residents of the territory, an official from the Secretaría of Foreign Relations justified protecting foreigners in the peninsula by reminding the Secretary of Gobernación about the difficulties generated during February and March of 1934 in Ensenada.[77]

SOCONUSCO REGION, CHIAPAS

The weakest support for anti-Chinese campaigns was likely in the Soconusco, an area in the Pacific Coast region of Chiapas along the border with Guatemala. Even as anti-Chinese associations were continuously formed in the Soconusco, they never obtained the support of the local population or of state officials. As opposed to the campaigns in Sonora and Baja California, anti-Chinese associations were never even able to stage an anti-Chinese boycott, suggesting that they did not have the popular appeal that they did in other regions of Mexico.

By the emergence of the anti-Chinese campaigns, Chinese migrants had lived and worked in Chiapas for about fifty years. According to the local community, the first migrants to arrive in the late nineteenth century were Chinese who left Panama after working on the canal.[78] More Chinese arrived to work on local railways, hired by the Compañía Mexicana de Navegación del Pacífico in 1895.[79] By 1914, the Soconusco already had five hundred Chinese; the mayor of Tapachula estimated that the Chinese formed 80 percent of local commerce. More than simply profiting from local commerce, the Chinese had contributed to the development of the region, constructing public works like "city halls, schools, [and] parks."[80] By the time of the anti-Chinese campaign there were nearly seven hundred Chinese in the state, not only running small businesses but also farming.[81]

Compared with northern Mexico, residents of Chiapas had few reasons to engage in anti-Chinese attacks. The Mexican Revolution had come relatively late to Chiapas; "[w]hen the revolution finally came to the state, it triggered very little of the popular mobilization experienced elsewhere in Mexico."[82] Moreover, the tumult that did occur did not specifically target foreigners. Revolutionary factions did harass and loot Chinese businesses, as occurred periodically in the railway nexus of Arriaga from 1914 onward, but Chinese were not singled out in these attacks.[83] Initial labor reforms after the outbreak of the revolution did not appear to be concerned with foreign ownership of Mexican business, as in northwestern Mexico. While the northwestern states of Sonora and Sinaloa expelled their Chinese residents as a byproduct of postrevolutionary consolidation, "Chiapas was a state still characterized more by Porfirian continuity than by revolutionary change."[84] Thus, the Chinese community still dominated local commerce along the Pacific coast of Chiapas into the 1930s.

The anti-Chinese campaigns were initially triggered by a small group of business owners who wanted to rid themselves of economic competition. In 1930, the Secretary of Gobernación received a petition from twenty-two small business owners complaining about the Chinese and asking the government to remove them so that the Tapachula market would be "truly national, which is to say all Mexican businesses."[85]

Chinese business owners had already warned the diplomatic corps that Mexican business owners would push the Chinese out in an attempt to "divide up" their property.[86]

In Tapachula—the Soconusco's largest city—the anti-Chinese league liberally borrowed both ideology and tactics from anti-Chinese associations in northern Mexico. In June 1929, for example, the weekly newspaper *El Heraldo,* in Huixtla, Chiapas, published a piece three straight weeks entitled "Out with the Chinese from Our Communities!!" alleging that the Chinese presence would only degenerate the Mexican race and proposing a ban on interracial marriages and the creation of special ghettos for the Chinese.[87] The newspaper obtained these articles from *El Istmo* in Puerto México, Veracruz (now Coatzacoalcos), which in turn reproduced an article edited by the Nationalist Pro-Race League in Tampico, Tamaulipas.[88] The following year, fifty "Mexicans by birth" declared the formation of the first "Mexican Anti-Chinese League" in the state of Chiapas, a group that was "inspired by the patriotic work of the anti-Chinese Leagues and Committees established in different states." It ended its message to the central government by promising, "[U]nited . . . we will desinify [*deschinatizaremos*] Mexico."[89] Its charter, sent to the Secretary of Gobernación the same day, bears a remarkable similarity to José Ángel Espinoza's sample charter. The stated goals were similar as well: like its northern counterparts, it wished to limit Chinese immigration (especially to the Soconusco region of Chiapas), end naturalized citizenship, and create special ghettos for Chinese.[90] The league then began to spread leaflets around the city calling for a boycott of Chinese businesses and asking for the "expulsion of the Chinese who have invaded this State and primarily the Department of the Soconusco."[91] Rather than producing leaflets and other propaganda on its own, the league obtained much of its material from the "Directive Center of the Nationalist Campaign" in Mexico City, the same material the center distributed "to the 250 similar groups which exist in the Republic."[92]

Even a month into the campaign, Chinese Mexicans reported that the Mexican Anti-Chinese League still had not achieved any of its goals. Although local officials were hesitant to shut down the league, it continued to lack the support of local residents, officials, and the local media: after *El Heraldo,* local newspapers did not publish defamatory articles about Chinese.[93] Frustrated by its lack of success, the association tried to organize surrounding towns and villages. In Mapastepec, one single league member visiting from Tapachula went door to door inviting residents to an open anti-Chinese gathering. In Huixtla, league members began to conduct anti-Chinese marches, and local authorities declined to suppress their activities. Individuals distributed leaflets in small hamlets, such as Tonalá and Arraiga.[94] Anti-Chinese activists also resorted to violence. In Pueblo Nuevo, local officials conspired to ambush and kill one Chinese merchant, making it clear to Chinese throughout the area that their lives and businesses were now in danger.[95]

In response, the Chinese organized an association of their own to respond to the hateful actions of the Mexican Anti-Chinese League. That same month, major Chinese associations in the state—such as the Chinese Business Association, the Guomindang, the Chee Kung Tong, and the Lian Sheng Tang—formed a united association, the Chinese Chamber of Commerce and Agriculture, to negotiate with Mexican authorities for their protection. The Chinese Chamber argued that local Sinophobes simply lacked popular support. Writing to the central government, its president, Samuel Juan, argued that local authorities could "attest to our hard work and trustworthiness" and asked for guarantees that they would remain unmolested.[96] In a subsequent letter, the Chinese Chamber noted that the acts of the anti-Chinese league were "propagated by a small group of Mexicans [while] the immense majority of citizens . . . respect the law."[97]

Chinese also sought the alliance of friendly Mexican groups. On November 28, 1930, the Secretary of Gobernación received a petition from the "Fraternidad" Masonic lodge in Tonalá, Chiapas, alleging that "less scrupulous individuals, under the pretext of a nationalism poorly understood, are carrying out anti-Chinese propaganda" against the Chinese who "work honestly and among which there are some brothers." Although the Chee Kung Tong was not exactly a Masonic order like its Mexican counterparts, it did ally itself with Mexican Masonic orders, and turned to them to support the Chinese community in times of trouble.[98]

Chinese resistance encouraged local officials to begin shutting down anti-Chinese aggression. Police began to break up anti-Chinese meetings.[99] Local officials were not on board with the anti-Chinese campaigns, either. The local migration chief declined to deport Chinese, which led to the league accusing him of being biased toward the Chinese. In Tapachula, the mayor warned the league that its actions were against the law and demanded that it take down its anti-Chinese propaganda or see its offices closed.[100] The governor, noting that most foreigners in the state had nationalized as Mexicans, also asserted that they overwhelmingly complied with Mexican labor legislation.[101] Ultimately, local military officials would tear down anti-Chinese billboards throughout the city. Admitting that their cause had little support from local Mexican residents or politicians, the anti-Chinese league lamented the "painful disgrace" and declared it "a great shame that, in so many bad Mexicans who are ostensibly helping them, the Chinese have so many assistants to plot their intrigues."[102]

The Chinese Chamber wrote once again in February 1932 after the Mexican Anti-Chinese League planned yet again to distribute flyers and conduct marches against the Chinese community of Tapachula. The Chinese minister to Mexico worried that Chinese lives were once again threatened.[103] Exasperated, the city council of Tapachula wrote the Mexican Anti-Chinese League, accusing them of being "on the margins of our current laws, of morality and of good manners." Any future propaganda against the Chinese or any other nationality, as well as any future meetings that denigrated a foreign group, would lead to the prosecution of the leaders of the league. Nationalism, it admonished the league, wasn't carried out by insulting foreigners, or by inciting Mexicans to violence.[104]

As an anti-Chinese association in San Luis Potosí remarked, the Tapachula case was not the first time that Chinese wrote Mexican officials "with the end of prohibiting the persecution" of Chinese migrants.[105] Nor was it the last time that the tactic worked. Although there would be subsequent anti-Chinese campaigns in Chiapas, they appear to have been about as successful as the campaigns described above. Aside from isolated incidents of homicides of Chinese nationals, anti-Chinese activists appear never to have gained traction among Mexican nationals in Chiapas, nor did they obtain the cooperation of Chiapas government officials; they were unsuccessful in expelling Chinese from the Soconusco or any other part of the state.[106]

POPULATION DISPLACEMENTS CAUSED BY THE ANTI-CHINESE CAMPAIGNS

Any successes that Chinese associations and the Chinese legation may have had in protecting the rights of Chinese in Mexico did not ultimately stop the exodus of Chinese from the country in the early 1930s. In all, an estimated three-quarters of the Chinese population present in

Mexico in 1930 fled the country by 1940. Many were naturalized Mexican nationals or natural-born Chinese Mexican children. To the Chinese community in Mexico, expulsion was a trauma that was never forgotten; it challenged their integration into Mexican society and their sense of belonging to Mexico.[107] The number of Chinese who obtained Mexican nationality suffered a steep decline after the anti-Chinese campaigns, and for reasons discussed below, many more Chinese lost than gained Mexican nationality during the 1930s.[108]

After 1934, however, the anti-Chinese campaigns were no longer a threat to foreign merchants. The Chinese legation, which had blamed Calles for much of the movement, looked favorably on the conditions of Chinese merchants during the Cárdenas administration (1934–40).[109] Moreover, even years after the conclusion of the campaigns, the Chinese legation maintained that they had never been a popular phenomenon; not only did "the average person [have] no ill will towards overseas Chinese [in Mexico]," but the success of the movement was due only to the fact that it had unofficial government backing. As a result, when the movement lost its powerful patron, it crumbled.[110]

The anti-Chinese campaigns scattered migrants who were expelled from the states of Sonora and Sinaloa. Some were able to join friends or family members in other territories where the campaigns were not so ferocious. Others were left to the mercy of strangers. One report from the legation, for example, tracked a few hundred Chinese from Sonora and Sinaloa who found refuge in Nayarit, and eventually Guadalajara, Jalisco. Only about a tenth of the refugees either had enough funds to be self-sufficient or could stay with family or friends. The majority had no money. Their clothing was unkempt. Initially these migrants landed in Acaponeta, Nayarit, where locals gave them food to eat and allowed them to stay for four days. Chinese in large cities such as Mexico City, as well as the small towns of Acaponeta and Santiago Ixcuintla, Nayarit, and Barranca, Jalisco, donated funds for refugees. In some areas, they were even helped by Mexican business associations (*xiren shanghui*). One train conductor on the Tren del Pacífico ("Pacific Railway") took pity on the penniless Chinese and took them in groups of twenty to Guadalajara for free.[111] One consul tracked Chinese in Sonora heading to neighboring states of Chihuahua and Sinaloa, but also much farther, to Nayarit and Chiapas.[112] Others would flee as far as Guatemala.[113] The areas that took them in did not necessarily welcome them: newspapers in states such as Nayarit disdained these migrants and suggested the state act as Sonora and Sinaloa had and expel them.

As a result of these displacements, the anti-Chinese campaigns led to three major demographic changes for the Chinese community. First, whereas Chinese residents concentrated in Mexico's northwest during the early twentieth century, after the anti-Chinese campaigns those who remained were much more evenly spread around the country. A large share resided in four regions: Baja California, Tamaulipas, Chihuahua, and Mexico City. Although Chinese settled in Mexico City during the early 1910s, the capital did not support a large settlement of Chinese until after the anti-Chinese campaigns. Many of those who opted to remain in the country during the anti-Chinese campaigns nonetheless considered Mexico City a safer location. Several sources suggest that other Chinese attempted to return to the places where they had previously settled in Mexico, especially after the anti-Chinese campaigns ended. As small numbers of Chinese began to return to Sonora in June 1934 following the calming of anti-Chinese agitation, activists began to call for new anti-Chinese campaigns.[114]

Second, those who remained were overwhelmingly middle-class Chinese businessmen. Before the campaigns, there were sizable numbers of Chinese traders (*huashang*) and workers (*huagong*), including small shop owners around the country as well as the large population of cotton pickers in the Mexicali Valley. But anti-Chinese activists overwhelmingly targeted vulnerable Chinese Mexican workers, who were largely unable to resist expulsion from the country. After Mexican labor groups began to agitate against Chinese workers, and the 1931 Labor Law limited the ability of Chinese business owners to hire their countrymen, the proportion of Chinese workers among the Chinese Mexican population declined significantly. Moreover, new legislation made it difficult for workers to return to Mexico. The 1936 Law of Population, passed after the anti-Chinese campaigns, imposed a new quota system that limited new entrants from countries outside of the Americas and Spain to just one hundred per country per year. It also required new arrivals to invest at least 10,000 pesos in Mexican businesses. Although this legislation was likely not passed with the Chinese in mind, it did prevent the Chinese Mexican population from growing as it had before the anti-Chinese campaigns, and meant that new arrivals were almost certainly businessmen with means to invest or members of their families.

For those in China, returning to Mexico was much more difficult. The majority of those who were chased out of cities across Mexico left the country without the necessary documentation to return. Obtaining that documentation provided additional challenges. With the closure of the Mexican consulate in Hong Kong in 1930, Chinese who wanted to return to Mexico were obliged to disembark in Yokohama, Japan—the country that had invaded Manchuria in 1931 and would invade much of rest of China in 1937—to obtain the necessary documentation.[115] In addition to the distance involved, the unfamiliar territory, and the language barrier, the limits on freely going ashore made the process of routing through Japan difficult for Chinese. The costs of the trip, including passage across the Pacific Ocean and the sojourn in Yokohama, were prohibitive for those who in Mexico had been workers and business owners of modest means. The difficulties were compounded when transpacific travel became nearly impossible after the outbreak of the Second World War.

After longtime residents (*jiuke*) returned to China, many petitioned to return to Mexico. Some found themselves in dire economic conditions after their return, while others were confident that the anti-Chinese campaigns had ended once and for all. Although *paisanos* did not claim a strategic sense of nationalism as Chinese Mexican women and children would, they did assert their rights as Mexican citizens to return to the country.[116] A few Chinese petitioned the Secretaría de Gobernación directly, explaining that they had been forced out by the anti-Chinese campaigns and asking for special permission to return.[117] In some cases, these requests were successful. In 1936, Augusto Chan Tac wrote the Secretaría from Guangzhou seeking permission to return to the country. A naturalized citizen since 1924, Chan Tac explained that due to an anti-Chinese campaign he had left the country in a hurry, without obtaining the necessary documentation to reenter. The Secretaría approved his request to return to Mexico.[118] Miguel Sam Lee, another Mexican citizen, obtained permission to reenter Mexico after taking his family to the Portuguese colony of Macau.[119]

Many more Chinese Mexicans would lose their Mexican citizenship during the 1930s, however, and with it their right to return to Mexico. According to the Immigration and Naturalization Law of 1886—a law that preceded the anti-Chinese campaigns by half a century—any naturalized citizen who had spent more than two continuous years in the country of his or her birth would lose Mexican citizenship. The provision applied to Chinese migrants no matter how long they had lived in Mexico, even those who had established Mexican businesses or started Mexican families. The difficulty of obtaining the necessary documentation and making the return trip to Mexico meant that many were not able to return within the two-year limit. Losing their citizenship made it virtually impossible for longtime residents to return to Mexico.[120]

The cases in which naturalized Mexicans lost their nationality after returning to China were numerous. Esteban Lee became ill near the end of the two-year deadline and was thus unable to return to the country in time. The Secretaría later denied a request to return, as he had "become a foreigner once again [*ha vuelto a ser extranjero*]."[121] Esteban Cinco "lost his Mexicanness [*perdió la calidad de mexicano*] for being outside of the country for more than two years."[122] Alfonso Chee was labeled a "Chinese citizen" and denied reentry into Mexico.[123] In all of these cases, descriptions of the individuals in question always refer to them as "foreigners" or "Chinese citizens," never as Mexicans. Because the law predated the anti-Chinese campaigns, it did not include any mechanism to help those forcefully displaced from the country.

In light of the extraordinary circumstances, other Chinese tried to obtain the help of the Chinese government to return to Mexico. Huang Hanrong had lived in Mexico for over twenty years and owned a thriving business, but was driven out by the anti-Chinese campaigns. Three years later, Huang lived in Nanjing but still experienced great social and economic difficulties. With the help of the Ministry of Foreign Affairs he hoped to obtain the necessary documentation to return to Mexico.[124] After they heard that the Mexican government had changed and that the anti-Chinese campaigns had ceased, eighty-two Chinese in Zhongshan County, Guangdong Province—a region that traditionally sent Chinese to Mexico—wrote the Chinese Ministry of Foreign Affairs seeking help returning to the country. According to the letter, these Chinese Mexicans were now unfamiliar with China, and uncertain about their prospects for the future. The eighty-two migrants were part of a much larger group who initially may not have wanted to return to Mexico, but for whom Mexico became more appealing after their return to China.[125] All had proof of long-term residency in Mexico—either a 1924 passport or their registration in the 1932 National Registry of Foreigners—and wanted the Ministry of Foreign Affairs to negotiate their return to Mexico so they could reopen their old businesses.[126] The Chinese legation recognized that many old sojourners had lost their nationality and permanent residence because of forces outside of their control, but was reluctant to pressure the Mexican government regarding its own requirements for residency and citizenship.

The Mexican government proved amenable to making exceptions for Chinese migrants of means, including land and business owners, but did not allow Chinese workers to reenter the country. Those married to Mexican women would also be able to return to Mexico, though they would have to find the funds on their own.[127] Although there are no statistics as to how many men returned to Mexico after the anti-Chinese campaigns, they likely included only those with the resources to once again make the transpacific voyage and start their businesses anew.

How many Chinese remained in Mexico at the conclusion of the anti-Chinese campaigns? Chinese diplomatic sources make clear that more Chinese remained in Mexico than previously acknowledged. In the absence of better data, scholars have relied on Mexican census data and the National Registry of Foreigners to arrive at the following conclusion: of eighteen thousand Chinese present in Mexico in 1930, fewer than five thousand remained in 1940.[128] But the anti-Chinese campaigns encouraged migrants to avoid Mexican officials, leading to large doubts about the accuracy and completeness of both sets of data.[129] For example, fully a quarter of Chinese in the Tampico consular district failed to register for the National Registry of Foreigners.[130] Although the embassy never had an accurate count of Chinese migrants in the country, its regular contact with Chinese associations gave it a much better idea of how many Chinese lived and worked in the country, as well as their social and economic conditions.[131]

In 1943, ten years after the anti-Chinese campaigns, the Chinese diplomatic corps estimated that there were 12,400 Chinese in the country. This number is more than double the estimate of Chinese in the country in the census of 1940, and nearly as high as the estimate in the census of 1930. Seven cities across the country had Chinese populations of at least three hundred people: Mexicali, Baja California; Chihuahua, Chihuahua; Tampico, Tamaulipas; Torreón, Coahuila; Mexico City; Tapachula, Chiapas; and Mérida, Yucatán. Significantly, the diplomatic corps' estimate counts only Chinese men, not women or Mexican-born children. For example, the estimate from the consular district of Tampico counted native-born children only if they were over twenty years of age and had taken the initiative to register with the legation—a grand total of eight young men and women in 1940.[132] Because of immigration restrictions and the difficulty of returning to China during the Sino-Japanese war, the Chinese Civil War, and the Communist control of mainland China, the community remained rather static during the twentieth century, shrinking largely through the death of its members.

CONCLUSION

The methods used by anti-Chinese groups, begun in Sonora and later spread across the country, add a new dimension to current scholarly understandings of the anti-Chinese campaigns. Outside of Sonora, the anti-Chinese campaigns across Mexico were coordinated efforts. Anti-Chinese activists shared propaganda and approaches to expel the Chinese, and middle-class businessmen and politicians around the country made use of these mechanisms to appropriate Chinese-owned property.

During the anti-Chinese campaigns, Chinese migrants depended on each other to weather the personal crises caused by displacement. Chinese associations around the country appealed to Mexican and Chinese government officials to help shield them from the harm caused by anti-Chinese associations. Where they were successful, Chinese migrants remained through much of the twentieth century. Where they were not, Chinese associations donated funds to provide aid to displaced refugees and petitioned both governments to allow them to return to Mexico.

The Chinese associations that grew and strengthened during the anti-Chinese campaigns continued to act on behalf of the Chinese community well after 1934, when the Mexican government began to safeguard the rights of foreign nationals on Mexican soil. Although the anti-Chinese campaigns were a lasting trauma for the community, during future challenges the memory also reminded them of the power of joining together. As the next chapter will show, the anti-Chinese campaigns also made them painfully aware of China's weakness on the international stage. Although Chinese immigrants who remained in Mexico were largely unable to return to China during the Second World War and the Cold War, the experience of the anti-Chinese campaigns encouraged them to maintain a great deal of interaction with their homeland's politics. The Chinese associations that were formed during this period would help support the government of the Republic of China during the Second World War and the Cold War. At the same time, the peace they found after the conclusion of the anti-Chinese campaigns allowed these associations to participate more actively in Mexican society.

CHAPTER 3

We Won't Be Bullied Anymore

The Chinese Community in Mexico
during the Second World War

The full-scale Japanese invasion of southern China in 1937, including the traditional sending communities in Guangdong Province, shook the Chinese Mexican community to its core. Shocked by the devastation that the Japanese onslaught wrought upon Guangdong Province, and aware of the need for a stronger China internationally, many Chinese Mexicans spared no expense to support China in the Second Sino-Japanese War—a conflict that would become a part of the Pacific Theater of the Second World War. Between 1937 and 1945, Chinese associations across the country would work together to make a substantial financial contribution to the war effort by selling war bonds and collecting donations for the government of the Republic of China as well as for China relief agencies.

The motivations of *paisanos* to take part in the war effort, as captured in Chinese Mexican memoirs, newspaper accounts, and government records, center on a desire to end racist hostility against them and a yearning to overcome the trauma caused by the anti-Chinese campaigns. New Chinese associations called War of Resistance organizations represented the first instance in which Chinese Mexicans conducted public diplomacy activities outside of their community. Their message sought to change not only Mexican public opinion regarding the Japanese invasion of China but also the opinions of Chinese Mexicans themselves. Because they saw international politics and domestic racism as tightly interconnected, Chinese Mexican leaders participated in the war effort in part to seek greater acceptance into Mexican society. In this regard the community was largely successful. At the end of the war, increased friendliness between *paisanos* and Mexicans signaled a shift in the perception of Chinese Mexicans from harmful and menacing during the anti-Chinese campaigns to esteemed foreigners at the end of the war. This change generated tangible benefits, including the legalized status of Chinese undocumented migrants in the country.

Chinese migrants were not the only residents of the Americas to engage in transnational political activity in support of the governments of their ancestral country. During the early twentieth century, diasporic communities across the Americas mobilized in support of both allied and Axis governments. Like the Chinese, other diasporic communities were motivated by local concerns, including domestic racism as well as barriers to political participation.[1] The volatile course of the war helped determine the fate of several diasporic groups in the Americas. After the Americas entered the war, some Latin American countries would cooperate with the United States in interning their German and Japanese residents, and many of those who were not interned were nonetheless affected by relocation orders and property seizures. In contrast, the status of Chinese communities throughout the Americas tended to improve, with a relaxation of immigration restrictions and a decrease in anti-Chinese rhetoric.

CHINESE MEXICANS AFTER THE ANTI-CHINESE CAMPAIGNS

Once the anti-Chinese campaigns ended, Chinese migrants passed the rest of their lives largely undisturbed by further xenophobic violence. National-level anti-Chinese groups did not disappear, continuing their agitation until at least 1937, when a presidential resolution, in the name of protecting small-scale merchants, ordered the government to inspect the migratory status and commercial activities of foreign businessmen.[2] Nevertheless, unlike the close relationship that these groups enjoyed with the PNR during the Maximato, during the Lázaro Cárdenas administration (1934–40) they found themselves out of the government's favor. Moreover, the government was turning away from revolutionary nationalism and instead toward industrial development as a way to neutralize class struggle and harmonize the divisions between the left and right. This especially meant a closer relationship with the United States, but also with other countries as a way of highlighting Mexican openness and modernity.[3] To this end, xenophobic activity was counterproductive. Thus when the presidential resolution was issued, it nonetheless asked xenophobic associations "not to cause useless agitation among foreign elements."[4] Xenophobic activities like those described in chapters 1 and 2 continued, though more sporadically and less successfully. Despite the fact that racism against the Chinese never completely disappeared, Chinese diplomats noted a much more hospitable environment for Chinese migrants. During an inspection tour of Chinese communities, the legation reported that none of the ten cities visited showed any signs of tensions between Mexicans and Chinese. In Ciudad Juárez, Mexicans had "friendly feelings" toward Chinese residents. In Torreón, where a 1911 massacre ended in the deaths of over three hundred Chinese, the legation reported vastly different conditions and asserted that Chinese maintained a "good relationship with Mexicans."[5]

Although many businesses failed to grow to the extent that they had during the beginning of the twentieth century, after the early thirties they began to expand once again and were lucrative enough for the community to subsist. Most Chinese continued to operate small-scale retail shops, including grocery stores, perfume shops, cafés (especially the *cafés de chinos* in Mexico City), and laundries. Certain Chinese businesses were particularly successful. Take the case of Huang Xiangfu, the founder of Chocolate Wong in Mexico City, which at its height shipped across the Mexican Republic. The firm occupied a ten-story building in the *centro histórico* of Mexico City, in which Huang also rented out space for a store and a cinema. Other successful enterprises included that of Yun Kui in Ensenada and a large general store operated by Peng Da in Torreón.[6] After the boycotts of the anti-Chinese campaigns came to an end, Mexican customers once again began to patronize Chinese shops and cafés. A rise in the wages of everyday Mexican workers meant that they had more to spend on Chinese businesses, whose owners saw their earnings rise.[7]

Although *paisanos* once again found peace after the conclusion of the anti-Chinese campaigns, they continued to worry about demographic challenges facing the community. By the late 1930s, the Chinese community in Mexico was aging fast—a result of the anti-Chinese campaigns as well as migratory legislation that made it difficult for new Chinese immigrants to settle in the country. Because many Chinese had arrived in Mexico in the first two decades of the twentieth century, by the 1940s many Chinese were either in middle age or close to retirement age. In the consular district of Tampico, for example, only about 2 percent of the district's Chinese were under the age of thirty, whereas nearly 80 percent were between the ages of forty and sixty-five.[8] This unnerved Chinese leaders around the country, who worried about the fate of their businesses after their deaths and feared that the Chinese population of Mexico might die out. As a result, many business owners requested that the Chinese legation negotiate immigration provisions with the Mexican government that would facilitate the entry of younger relatives.

Apprehensions that Chinese immigrants might stop arriving in Mexico in large numbers also fed concerns about the cultural attachments of second-generation Chinese Mexicans. These children were generally born of Chinese fathers and Mexican mothers. In Monterrey, for example, only two of fifty-five male Chinese residents had female Chinese partners, while more than half had Mexican partners. In all, these men had 210 Chinese Mexican children.[9] In part because their mothers were community outsiders, these children were perceived not to have a deep familiarity with Chinese language and culture. According to an assessment from the legation, fathers were too busy earning a living to teach their children about China, and schools were difficult to maintain since amenities were difficult to find and teachers were paid little. During the war, schools were founded in Mexico City, Tampico, Chihuahua, and Mexicali, serving up to one hundred Chinese Mexican students each, but most of them closed before the end of the decade, usually due to lack of instructors or funding.[10] As a result, reported the Chinese legation, children were "Mexicanized"—"other than knowing that their fathers are Chinese, they don't recognize their identity [and] don't see themselves as Chinese."[11] Although the assessment is too categorical, it did document concerns that subsequent generations of Chinese Mexicans would lose touch with their Chinese ancestry. In Guadalajara, Mazatlán, and Tampico, organizations for second-generation Chinese Mexicans attempted to foster community among these children and encourage them to identify with their Chinese roots.[12]

DIVIDED AT THE HEART

Although the Chinese Mexican population experienced drastic changes during the 1930s and early 1940s, one constant was continuing divisions among Chinese migrants, both between middle- and working-class Chinese and between members of the Guomindang and members of the Chee Kung Tong. By the late 1930s, differences between the GMD and the CKT that had been tabled during the anti-Chinese campaigns came back to the surface during China's moment of crisis. Resolving these differences fell to Minister Cheng Tien-ku (Cheng Tiangu). Dispatched to Mexico in May 1940, Minister Cheng would seek throughout his three years in Mexico to bring the two sides together to facilitate the war effort.

Even fifteen years after the Tong Wars and after the anti-Chinese campaigns called attention to the perils of a divided community, Chinese ministers to Mexico continued to find that the CKT and the GMD remained very much estranged. Three factors complicated the division between the two groups. On the surface, the competition for profits from casinos and opium intensified the conflict. Although the Mexican government prohibited gambling, many *paisanos* continued to frequent both CKT- and GMD-owned casinos, and their owners quietly paid bribes to keep them open.[13] Although just a small fraction of the members of both factions participated in illicit activities, it complicated the efforts of diplomats to mediate their differences. Moreover, members who might have been opposed to the illicit trade preferred not to intervene. The Chinese legation, however, disapproved of these activities: Minister Cheng called casino owners "corrupt individuals" and "unworthy members," while his predecessor, Minister Tan Shaohua, criticized them for "using the name of the association to pursue selfish objectives" and blamed them for the enduring rivalry between the two factions.[14] Other members of the GMD resented the CKT's numerical advantage and thus proved unwilling to negotiate with them.[15]

A further complicating factor was that the two groups continued to maintain rather different opinions on transpacific politics. A report from a prominent Chinese Mexican, Deng Chuanshan, made no mention of the competition over opium and smuggling and suggested that political differences were the most significant factor in their feud. Deng asserted that the CKT disapproved of the way that the GMD governed mainland China and as a result the two groups "were as incompatible as fire and water."[16] Into the 1930s, the CKT continued to deny that the GMD was the legitimate government of China. During the Second World War, most chapters of the CKT in Mexico did not fly the Chinese Nationalist flag but instead flew either the dragon flag or five-colored Chinese flag—banners that had been used in China before the Guomindang consolidated its political control over much of mainland China.[17] Although the distinction might have been lost on Mexican residents, the open display of contempt scandalized GMD officials in Mexico. "Those who do not respect our flag do not respect our country," concluded a report from the Chinese legation.[18] The Mexican GMD tried negotiating directly with the CKT on the issue of the flag, and when that failed, the Chinese legation, using the rationale that the subversive flag threatened the relationship between the two countries, tried to persuade Mexican authorities to forcefully take it down.[19] The controversy over the national flag suggests that political differences were an important part of their rivalry, complicated further by local conflicts.

Another major conflict involved a labor dispute among Chinese café workers in Mexico City. Mexico City had over three hundred Chinese-owned cafés, and their workers and owners were an overwhelming proportion of the city's twelve hundred Chinese. Chinese workers who remained in Mexico after the anti-Chinese campaigns were able to make a living but faced difficult conditions in the country. Although many were motivated by the desire to earn enough money to raise the socioeconomic status of their families in Guangdong Province, because wages were relatively low in Mexico, after years of toil many Chinese laborers had not saved enough to afford a return trip to their home villages. Additionally, since many had both Mexican and Chinese families, these workers saw their wages stretched thin as they supported wives and children on both sides of the Pacific.[20]

The large disparity in conditions between Chinese workers and businessmen pushed café workers to seek better working conditions. In the summer of 1941, Li Youfu attempted to organize these workers into the Mexican Overseas Chinese Labor Union. The union initially had few members, but in December 1941 it issued an edict calling upon Chinese café workers to enter the union, and at the same time sought to join a Mexican federation of labor unions, the Confederación General de Trabajadores (CGT), affiliated with Mexico's ruling party. On January 7, the union issued a threat to Chinese café owners across the city: if they did not allow their workers to join, it would ask the Mexican Secretary of Labor to dispatch inspectors to each recalcitrant Chinese café. Café owners were repulsed by the attempt of the union to incorporate their employees. But they were also afraid that if they were compelled to pay their employees higher wages, they would be forced out of business. As a result, they declared that they would fire any employee who joined the Mexican Overseas Chinese Labor Union. The dispute quickly escalated. The union filed a lawsuit and solicited the intervention of a government labor arbitration board, the Mexican Junta Local de Conciliación y Arbitraje. Café owners, for their part, allegedly fired and threatened union members. By February 1942, even the CGT felt obliged to ask the

Chinese legation to mediate the acrimony between the owners and their employees.[21]

The Chinese legation was deeply concerned about the labor dispute because it presented Chinese migrants as well as the working conditions of the cafés in a negative light. Café owners, by admitting that acceptance of the terms of the labor unions would force them out of business, recognized that they paid their workers below the living wage. If Mexican authorities had cracked down on the cafés it would have led to many of them closing, with the loss of livelihood for both owners and employees. The legation also feared that it might even spark a resurgence in anti-Chinese activities. For this reason, the proposed solution from the legation, which was signed by both the union and the café owners, returned the labor situation to the status quo ante, requiring café owners to rehire fired workers and compensate them for lost wages, while obliging the labor union to withdraw its lawsuit and its case before the Junta de Conciliación y Arbitraje. Most important, the first clause stated that "if a dispute happen[ed] with other countrymen, [Chinese] should not utilize the strength of foreigners to pressure [each other]."[22] A solution would have prevented Chinese labor leaders from airing their dirty laundry in public, but both sides appear to have violated the settlement.

Although the conflict exposed tensions between Chinese Mexican workers and owners, the community and the legation did not appear to be concerned yet with Communist infiltration and agitation. One minister to Mexico, Cheng Tien-ku, believed that the CGT "contained no shades of Communist thought" and would eventually collaborate with the labor union confederation on public diplomacy activities.[23] But the conflict nonetheless underscores why Communism would largely be unappealing to Chinese Mexican merchants after the Second World War: any attempt to redistribute wealth would be regarded as a threat to their businesses and livelihoods.

CHINESE MEXICANS AND THE WAR EFFORT

Chinese Mexican activities in support of China in the Second Sino-Japanese War lasted eight years, from 1937 to 1945, though hostilities between the Chinese and Japanese had run high long before then. As part of the settlement after the First Sino-Japanese War (1894–95), the Qing dynasty ceded the island of Taiwan to the Japanese. After the First World War, the Treaty of Versailles transferred the German concession of Shandong to Japan, leading to widespread protests on the mainland.

In 1931, following the Mukden Incident of September 18, Japan invaded Manchuria in northeastern China and created the puppet state of Manchukuo under the last Qing emperor, Puyi. In spite of the outbreak of hostilities in 1931, only the Chinese community in the state of Chiapas appeared to have organized in opposition, launching an anti-Japanese boycott.[24] The invasion of Manchuria coincided with the beginning of the anti-Chinese campaigns, and so the Chinese communities in affected areas had more immediate concerns. (As noted in chapter 2, the Chinese community in Chiapas was largely spared.) Additionally, the Guomindang until 1937 had a policy of nonresistance against Japan, preferring to fight Chinese Communists first before the Japanese.[25] This may have led Guomindang chapters in Mexico to follow suit.

The Guomindang policy of nonresistance changed abruptly just after July 7, 1937, when Japan took advantage of minor hostilities between Chinese and Japanese soldiers at the Marco Polo Bridge to invade the major cities along China's east coast. The director-general of the Guomindang, Chiang Kai-shek, announced China's policy of resistance against Japan three days later.[26] The Japanese invasion of southern China—the provincial capital of Guangzhou would fall in October 1938, but Hong Kong and nearby villages would not fall until 1941—cut off all communication between Chinese Mexicans and their home villages and placed tremendous hardship on their relatives in China. After the fall of Hong Kong, Chinese Mexicans had no reliable way to send remittances to their relatives, and after "the Japanese seized the region's crops to feed their own troops, many locals simply starved to death." Others were forced to sell "first their jewelry and furniture, then their homes, and finally themselves" in order to feed themselves and their children. In Taishan County, to which a plurality of Chinese Mexicans traced their origins, one in four would die by the end of the conflict.[27]

All around the world, Chinese migrants responded by boycotting Japanese goods, donating to the war effort, and attempting to convince Western nations to support the Nanjing government. In Mexico the impulse was no different. Many members of the Chinese community in Mexico felt the need to come to China's assistance, well aware of China's weakness on the international stage. One Chinese described this nationalist impulse as "to have a country and then to have a home," arguing that "when [China] was strong, overseas Chinese would finally be protected."[28]

The "home" that he mentioned referred both to the ancestral communities in Guangdong Province and to the community's settlements around Mexico. Because Chinese Mexicans maintained transpacific ties to their communities of origin in Guangdong Province, they were dismayed and outraged by the Japanese invasion. In addition to being worried about the well-being of their relatives, many were concerned that a long-term Japanese occupation of China would sever them from their roots. "The enemy does not allow us to belong to the Republic of China," noted an editorial in *Qiaosheng Yuekan / El Vocero de la Colonia China* ["Voice of the Chinese Colony monthly"], a newspaper published by the Chinese community during the war, and were China successfully conquered, Chinese Mexicans would lose a critical part of their own identity and rootedness.[29] At the same time, "home" referred to the Chinese Mexican community's new places of settlement across the Pacific. "Mexico is our second home, but has all along discriminated against us," noted one editorial; the anti-Chinese campaigns and other atrocities committed against Chinese Mexicans "linger in our minds."[30]

Paisano editorials stressed the interconnectedness of both senses of home. Hu Erqin, a prominent Chinese who lived through the Sonora anti-Chinese campaign before moving to Mexico City, suggested that a strong Chinese government was crucial to the stability of Chinese Mexican residents.[31] Beginning with the Torreón Massacre in 1911, asserted Hu, Chinese Mexicans faced a difficult past that involved incredible loss, devastation, and hardship. Moreover, since anti-Chinese activity in Mexico coincided with a tumultuous period in Chinese history, Chinese Mexicans had to face this history alone. This lack of help from China only emboldened anti-Chinese activists. Since "nobody interfered," Mexicans' "prejudice grew deeper, [and] they began to reject Chinese even more without fear."[32] Unlike the Chinese of the United States, Chinese Mexicans do not appear to have been motivated by a desire to demonstrate themselves as worthy citizens of their host country.[33] Yet to them the desire for peace and tranquillity on Mexican soil was undoubtedly a motivating factor. One group, like its counterparts in the United States, referred to its mission as "to save China, to save ourselves."[34]

One of the leaders of the Chinese Mexican community during the Second World War was an unlikely figure, coming from outside of the Cantonese-speaking community. Yu Shouzhi was born in Yibin, Sichuan Province, in 1911, the year of the Xinhai Revolution. After attending Sichuan University and studying education, Yu was dispatched to Mexico City in March 1937 to head the new Chinese school in the capital.[35] The start of the Second Sino-Japanese War, just a few months after his arrival, changed the nature of his appointment. Yu's leadership during the war was exceptional for two reasons. First, at twenty-six years of age Yu was much younger than the majority of the Chinese community in Mexico and the only one born outside of Guangdong Province. Although some Chinese in Mexico may have spoken Mandarin, Yu likely faced language difficulties when communicating with some of the Cantonese-speaking Chinese Mexicans. Second, Yu's training and passion were not concerned with political or party affairs but rather with Chinese education.[36] Because Chinese Mexican parents longed for education opportunities for their children, Yu's vocation would allow him to connect with Chinese residents at a time when the community was so fractured.

Yu's activities on behalf of the Chinese Mexican community—including the publications, Cantonese operas, and public celebrations he helped produce during the war—took place as the GMD and the CKT tried to work together to provide aid to the Chinese government. On July 31, the Zhonghua Shanghui in Mexico City convened a representative assembly of all nineteen Chinese organizations in the city, not only the GMD and CKT but native-place organizations like the Haiyan Gongsuo and the Sanyi Huiguan, and clan organizations like the Lishi Gongsuo. The organizations unanimously elected to create a new organization, the Mexico City National Salvation Organization to Support the Anti-Japanese War of Resistance (Mojing Kangri Jiuguo Houyuanhui). Yu Aihe, a member of the Guomindang, was elected chairman of the organization, while Yu Shouzhi was elected secretary. This committee called a representative meeting of Mexico City's Chinese organizations once a year, during which time it elected new leadership.[37] After the formation of the War of Resistance organization in Mexico City, Chinese in big cities and small towns across Mexico formed their own War of Resistance organizations, with the largest located in the cities of Mexicali, Tampico, and Tapachula. Although the committees were open to members of all Chinese organizations, in practice most organizations were headed by members of the GMD.[38]

To help coordinate activities between War of Resistance committees across the country, two newspapers were founded, thus filling a large vacuum in Chinese Mexican society. "Even in peace times Mexico should have a newspaper, a vehicle to transmit information and enlighten the people," argued Minister to Mexico Tan Shaohua in an introductory message to one of the two major newspapers, *Qiaosheng Yuekan*. "[The fact that] Mexico has ten thousand overseas Chinese but still lacks a Chinese-language newspaper is certainly a huge pity."[39] For years, Chinese in Mexico had tried and failed to sustain a Chinese-language newspaper that served the entire community.[40] The CKT published its own newspaper, *Moguo Gongbao,* a monthly that counted nine hundred subscribers, but according to Yu it was mainly concerned with its own activities.[41]

The dearth of Chinese newspapers before the Second Sino-Japanese War encouraged Chinese Mexicans to look elsewhere in search of information on their home communities. At the time of the outbreak of the war, most of Mexico's Chinese subscribed to newspapers in the United States: members of the GMD would subscribe to San Francisco's *Guomin Ribao* or Chicago's *Sanmin Chenbao,* whereas CKT members subscribed to San Francisco's *Shijie Ribao* or New York's *Niuyue Gongbao.* Some Chinese without any party affiliation subscribed to San Francisco's *Zhongxi Ribao.* The editorials in each newspaper affected the way that Chinese migrants understood long-distance politics. Newspapers from the United States took on average a week to arrive in Mexico, meaning that Chinese migrants in the country received only dated pieces of information.[42] The immediate predecessor of *Qiaosheng Yuekan* was a short bulletin named *Kangri Xinwen* (Resistance against the Japanese News), a daily bulletin edited by Yu Shouzhi that translated news about the war in Mexico City dailies from Spanish into Chinese. The newspaper eventually obtained three hundred subscribers, who paid two pesos per issue. In contrast to *Kangri Xinwen, Qiaosheng Yuekan* was more focused on the Chinese Mexican community and on its efforts to assist the Republic of China. The magazine, which published more than eighty issues during the eight years of the war, was distributed for free and supported entirely through donations and advertising.[43]

Qiaosheng Yuekan, which sold eight hundred copies, and *Moguo Gongbao,* which had nine hundred subscriptions, appear to have small circulation numbers, but the papers were nonetheless influential among GMD and CKT members as well as the wider Chinese public. Both newspapers were distributed to regional party branches and independent associations across Mexico, thus ensuring that they reached a wide audience. Moreover, the circulation figures are comparable to those in the United States—which had more Chinese but also more Chinese newspapers, and where Chinese newspapers rarely published more than one thousand copies.[44]

Undoubtedly, the major goal of *Qiaosheng Yuekan* was to increase contributions and support for the war. The first issue declared that "this magazine's greatest mission is to spread consciousness of the popular War of Resistance among the overseas Chinese masses [*qiaozhong*]."[45]

At the same time, *Qiaosheng Yuekan* fulfilled an important secondary goal: "[i]n addition to providing information on the war [it was] an avenue for people to express their opinions, exchange ideas—a common organ to benefit the entire overseas Chinese community."[46] The monthly was also a vehicle for the announcement of celebrations, commemorations, performances, contribution drives, war-bond sales, and the establishment and closing of Chinese associations around the country. Even though the magazine was run largely by members of the GMD, any Chinese Mexican from any organization in the country could submit a piece for publication, although in order to avoid polemics, the leader of the author's organization had to approve and seal the submission.[47] Thus, any Chinese Mexican, regardless of class or political differences, could participate in the propaganda arm of the War of Resistance organizations.

War of Resistance organizations were primarily dedicated to financial and propagandistic activities. They collected donations in each city and remitted them to the central authorities of the Chinese government, as well as sold war bonds. Donations could be included among remittances from U.S. Chinese, or they could be sent directly to Chinese banks in New York, San Francisco, or Hong Kong.[48] In some locations, residents swore to "national salvation pacts" in which they pledged to contribute 10 to 15 percent of their monthly salary to the Chinese government. Finally, the donations were not solely monetary. The Chinese communities of Manzanillo, Colima, and Torreón, Coahuila, for example, sponsored a clothing drive for Chinese officers and soldiers.[49] For the sake of transparency, after each pledge drive, War of Resistance organizations would publish information about the drive in *Qiaosheng Yuekan*, including how much was collected and how it was remitted back to China.

Moreover, "national salvation through aviation" organizations raised money to buy airplanes for the war effort, thus helping relieve the wartime capital at Chongqing of constant air raids.[50] The disparity between the Chinese air force and its Japanese counterpart was tremendous: "[a]t one point Nationalist China possessed fewer than ninety planes in safe working condition, compared to more than two thousand in the Japanese military."[51] Mexico's aviation associations may have been influenced by similar organizations in the United States. According to Japanese intelligence, Chinese Americans arrived in Mexico seeking the help of Chinese Mexicans to buy over twenty airplanes originally destined for Republican Spain during its civil war.[52] Mexico had three known aviation associations. One was located in Tampico, Tamaulipas, and collected over US$16,000 from Chinese along the Gulf Coast.[53] There was also an aviation association in Torreón, established a few years before its Mexico City counterpart, that boasted over two hundred members.[54] The Mexico City aviation association was led by Liang Meizu, exceptional because he was one of the few Mexican-born Chinese who was active in the War of Resistance organizations, but also because he had pledged to donate all of the profits from his store—the Golden Dragon perfume shop in Mexico City—to the war effort. At one meeting of the aviation association on January 31, 1941, Chairman Liang personally donated the equivalent of 200,000 Chinese yuan to buy one airplane, after which he was personally telegrammed by Chiang Kai-shek as a gesture of appreciation.[55]

In addition to soliciting donations and selling war bonds, the War of Resistance organizations held fund-raising events that brought different sectors of Chinese Mexican society together. These gatherings included performances of both Chinese and Mexican songs and dances, illustrating the community's cultural ties to both sides of the Pacific Ocean. A night of entertainment on August 21, 1938, for example, was organized by the War of Resistance committee in Mexico City, and hosted by Yu Shouzhi. The Chinese school chorus sang patriotic songs, and female students performed butterfly dances. The night also featured performances of Chinese boxing and lion dances, as well as a performance by both Cantonese opera troupes in the city. Proceeds from the tickets— more than 10,000 Mexican pesos—were remitted via New York's Bank of China to the Guangdong provincial government.[56] On October 10, 1938, a National Day celebration in Mexico City featured butterfly dances and patriotic songs, but also Spanish-language musical numbers and even traditional dances from the state of Chiapas.[57] These events demonstrate the creativity with which the War of Resistance organizations approached their activities, seeking contributions not through coercion but through an attempt to foster patriotism and create community among Chinese Mexicans.

Yu also wrote and directed a series of plays, proceeds of which went to the war effort. According to Yu, the two Cantonese opera troupes in Mexico City began to cooperate at the beginning of the war, staging Cantonese operas every month and on Chinese holidays. (See figures 2 and 3.) During these plays, the troupes sought donations for the Chinese army. Eventually, however, the audience grew tired of "still the same people, the old scripts, the old songs."[58] After Yu wrote his first play, he cast actors among the Chinese youth, who rehearsed every

FIGURE 2. A Cantonese opera troupe performs in Mexico City's El Teatro del Pueblo. Photo courtesy Fototeca Nacional INAH.

FIGURE 3. An audience enjoys the opera performance. Photo courtesy Fototeca Nacional INAH.

evening at the Chinese school, and later performed the play at the capital's Teatro del Pueblo. The script sought to increase financial contributions to Mexican aviation associations. In the play, the home of the protagonist was bombed by Japanese airplanes, causing the main characters to lament the fact that they hadn't given the government money to buy airplanes for national defense. According to Yu, the youths' first performance "caused a sensation." The performance collected 3,000 pesos in ticket sales and 4,000 pesos in donations. Future plays— presented, like the Cantonese operas that preceded them, approximately once a month and on national holidays—had a regular cast of actors, stressed Cantonese themes, and included Cantonese and patriotic songs. The stories Yu crafted, "in addition to depicting the cruel violence of the Japanese army, the pain of refugees and the national volunteer army, inserted a few familial and love stories, so that it could obtain [the audience's] approval and touch them emotionally." In total, Yu estimated that he wrote and directed over twenty plays for the Chinese community in Mexico City.[59]

Chinese communities around the country made substantial financial contributions to the Chinese government. The War of Resistance organization of Mexicali purchased war bonds totaling over US$80,000 and 40,000 Mexican pesos. The Chinese residents of Ciudad Juárez donated 40,000 pesos and sold war bonds several dozen times during the war. The much larger Chinese community in Mérida collected more than 200,000 pesos during the war. The Chinese of Chiapas donated approximately 800,000 pesos to the war effort. And the community of Tampico collected over 1 million pesos in bonds and donations, the largest contribution of the entire country.[60]

The above activities were most successful among the Chinese population in Mexico, but Chinese propaganda activities in Mexico were in theory designed for the entire country—that is, for Chinese and Mexicans alike. Minister Cheng, for example, believed that people's diplomacy should be the centerpiece of War of Resistance activities, and encouraged Chinese Mexicans to engage in popular diplomacy whenever possible.[61] Although most events were conducted in Chinese, meaning that they would have not been accessible to Mexicans or even native-born Chinese Mexicans, some events in Mexico City were designed to include Mexican residents. For example, the Zhonghua Shanghui held a social event to which representatives from Mexican civic associations were invited. Speeches made in Chinese and Spanish explained the significance of the Second Sino-Japanese War, after which there were *vivas* for Mexico and the Republic of China. The same month, the Guomindang participated in a world peace conference organized by the Confederation of Mexican Workers (CTM).[62] Two events at Mexico's Palace of Fine Arts celebrated the "brave Chinese fighters" and were attended by Mexicans from different sectors of society.[63] More than simply social events, these events represent the beginnings of Chinese political activity in Mexico, during which Chinese were able to improve their own image and call attention to China's war against Japan.

Such events had only a limited impact on Mexican public opinion. A major challenge was Mexican apathy toward the war effort and wariness of sending troops to war.[64] The consul in Tampico, for example, noted that "the local population [did] not have a deep interest in the situation in the Far East."[65] Because it believed that Chinese organizations in the area lacked the talent to come up with propaganda for the Spanish-speaking world, the consulate suggested that it could write editorials for Spanish-language newspapers as well as provide news content sympathetic to the Chinese side.[66] Other editorials suggested more drastic action. One opinion piece in *Qiaosheng Yuekan*, for example, suggested that the War of Resistance organizations join left-leaning Mexican organizations in pursuing their goals. For example, since Mexico sold oil to Germany and Japan, the author suggested joining Mexican anti-Fascist organizations and protesting, even picketing at ports where Mexican oil was to be shipped. Additionally, Chinese Mexicans could coordinate a boycott of Japanese products.[67] The fact that Mexico had not yet declared war on Japan and that the suggestions were so overtly political—under Article 33 of the Mexican Constitution foreigners could be deported for interfering in Mexican politics—probably explains why Chinese did not go to such lengths.

Despite the successes that Chinese Mexicans experienced in the war effort, continuous divisions between community factions represented a continuing challenge. In contrast to the United States, where the outbreak of the Second Sino-Japanese War encouraged "all feuding parties [within the Chinese community] to shelve their differences to concentrate on national salvation activities," Chinese Mexicans found that putting aside their differences was much more difficult.[68] Differences over transnational politics constituted the most significant challenge to War of Resistance activities. The CKT remained suspicious not only of the GMD in Mexico, but also of the GMD on the mainland and its handling of the war. The CKT's suspicions were evident on October 21, 1938, when the Japanese military took Guangzhou, provincial capital of the sending communities of Chinese Mexicans. After 1938, most of China's east coast and all of its major cities were in the hands of the Japanese military or collaborationists. Skepticism of the GMD strategy in the Sino-Japanese War came to a head. After 1938, the strategy of the Chinese military was to "trade space for time," retreating to the interior in hopes of exhausting Japanese supply lines and eventually obtaining economic and military aid.[69] The strategy likely disheartened many Chinese Mexicans, since it would delay the liberation of Guangzhou for some time. After the fall of the city, the CKT withdrew from the Mexico City War of Resistance organization, contending that Chiang Kai-shek had not fulfilled his obligation to defend Chinese territory and "had allowed their hometown to fall into enemy hands."[70] Minister Tan tried to mediate between the GMD and the CKT without success.[71]

Although the CKT did make donations on its own to the war effort, its withdrawal from the War of Resistance organization was a blow that crippled the donation effort from Chinese across the city.[72] In Mexico City, Tijuana, and Mexicali, the CKT made donations on its own and did not cooperate with the War of Resistance organizations in those cities. Baja California War of Resistance committees in turn petitioned the Chinese legation to find a way to punish the Baja California CKT, but the legation thought it best not to get involved.[73] In some regions outside the capital, especially in Tampico and Chiapas, there was no open hostility between the CKT and the GMD, and as a result the War of Resistance organizations in these cities made greater contributions.[74]

An early priority for Minster Cheng Tien-ku, who arrived in Mexico in May 1941, was to find a way for the two groups to cooperate. Soon after taking his post, for example, he tried to persuade members of the CKT to hoist the national flag. Minister Cheng visited Torreón, a city that despite his pleas continued to show open conflicts between GMD and CKT members. Furthermore, the Torreón chapter of the CKT continued to fly the five-colored flag, even after the Chinese legation requested that they remove it. Upon hearing of the minister's arrival, the CKT prepared a special welcome at its headquarters and a large banquet at a prominent local hotel, and invited prominent local civil and military officials to attend. After arriving, however, Cheng threatened to boycott both events, since he was "the representative of the Republic of China" and would not be treated "as a government official of the Manchus." Cheng made clear that the CKT's disdain for the GMD in Mexico had the effect of embarrassing the diplomatic representative of the Chinese government. The CKT acquiesced, borrowing a flag from the

GMD for the minister's visit. After that, suggested Cheng in his memoirs, one by one CKT branches across Mexico began to fly the national flag.[75] The CKT headquarters in Mexico City finally began to fly the national flag on National Day (October 10), 1941.[76]

The low point in the conflict between the two groups occurred in May 1943, when Mexican authorities raided Chinese opium dens—cases that received widespread attention in Mexico City dailies. In response, Minister Cheng called for a meeting of all Chinese groups in Mexico City's Teatro del Pueblo. Making the argument that their legal troubles represented a setback for China's public-diplomacy activities in the country, Cheng reprimanded local Chinese for "last week's grotesque trouble which was published in every newspaper in the capital and lost national prestige." Thus, he admonished them that if they "sincerely love[d] [their] country, love[d] [their] home no less than [their] countrymen in China," they would unite rather than squabbling with one another and "causing trouble and complaints." Not doing so would have "the effect of ruining the prospects of the War of Resistance."[77] Following this meeting, after promised changes in the War of Resistance organization in Mexico City (changes that would decrease the GMD's dominance over them), the CKT rejoined.[78] In 1943, when China and Mexico negotiated a new treaty, the CKT sent a telegram to the Mexican Secretaría of Foreign Relations expressing its congratulations and approval.[79]

Despite the enmity between the GMD and the CKT, and despite the continued mediation that was required to enable Chinese Mexican community organizations to work together, the story of the War of Resistance movement in Mexico is not one of missed opportunities but of challenges overcome, of the necessary resolution of its internal problems and of its own definition against a backdrop of war. In spite of considerable challenges, the community made a substantial contribution in support of the Nationalist government. In total, Chinese Mexicans donated about US$2 million to the war effort.[80] A large part of the estimated four thousand Chinese Mexicans who contributed to the war effort donated a considerable portion of their disposable income to the government of the Republic of China.[81]

CHINA AS WARTIME ALLY

After the bombing of Pearl Harbor, much of the Western Hemisphere would belatedly and hesitantly join the Second World War. After the December 1941 attack, reports began to emerge regarding Mexico's small

Japanese community, many of whom resided on the strategically critical peninsula of Baja California. Intelligence and even some journalistic reports cast doubt on the loyalty of Mexico's Japanese and even asserted that the Japanese migrants wished to use Mexico as a staging ground for an attack on the United States.[82] Japanese were ordered to relocate from the coasts into the interior of the country, and Japanese assets in the country were frozen.[83] Mexico suspended diplomatic relations with the Axis powers, but it did not officially declare war until May 22, 1942, after a German submarine sank the Mexican oil tanker *Potrero del Llano*.[84]

Chinese nationals, while not affected by orders for relocation, were troubled by Mexican military preparations for the war. On November 25, 1942, the *Diario Oficial* published a decree requiring the citizens of allied countries to register for the Mexican military, to receive military training, and to participate in the war if it came to Mexico.[85] The military eventually projected that Mexican youth and co-belligerent nationals would serve in the military in one-year tours of duty. The order affected Chinese nationals between the ages of fifteen and forty-five—about 30 percent of foreign-born Chinese Mexicans; native-born Chinese Mexicans, as Mexican citizens, were already required to register for the military.

The vast majority of the Chinese population in Mexico appears to have been opposed to this decree and unwilling to comply. For some, their difficulty with the Spanish language made them uneasy about submitting to military training from Mexican officials. Others thought their businesses would be affected if they or their employees were called to serve in the military. While some believed that their participation in the war would make Mexicans think better of the Chinese population in the country, for others the idea of taking up arms with Mexicans, who not even a decade prior had expelled the vast majority of their countrymen, must have made them uncomfortable. Moreover, Chinese recruits had no control over where they would be sent after Mexico mobilized for war, and they may not have felt any connection to conflicts unrelated to the Second Sino-Japanese War.

Responses to the order for military registration ranged from support to passive resistance to outright hostility. The Chinese community in Mexico City petitioned the Chinese legation to negotiate with the Mexican government in its implementation of the decree. Since the Chinese in Mexico City were primarily concerned with language differences with Mexican citizens and the effect that military service would have on their businesses—military training was proposed for Sunday mornings, when Chinese cafés were normally open—the legation proposed that

FIGURE 4. During the Second World War, Chinese Mexicans in Tijuana formed a self-defense group under Ma Wenye and underwent military training. From Chen Kwong Min, *Meizhou huaqiao tongjian*.

Chinese in the city form a military squad that would train separately from Mexicans, at a more convenient time for café owners and workers. The legation would arrange for a translator to interpret military commands for the Chinese recruits. Additionally, the legation proposed that Chinese organizations in Mexico City be responsible for the logistics of military registration and training, which, despite constituting an interference by the consulate in Mexican domestic affairs, presumably would raise the rate of compliance. Still, Mexico City Chinese appear not to have registered for or participated in military training.[86]

In two cities, the Chinese community responded with the formation of its own military squads. In the city of Tijuana, Baja California, local Chinese decided to form a military squad. Composed of a few dozen men, it was led by a local Chinese, Ma Wenye, but under the command of the local military, and received military training each week.[87] (See figure 4.) In Mérida, the response to the military decree was enthusiastic: a few dozen Chinese formed a military squad and participated in military training, earning the praise of local Mexicans. They also participated in a military parade that was widely reported in Spanish-language newspapers.[88] (See figure 5.) Although it is unclear why the Chinese communities of these two cities were the only ones to organize

FIGURE 5. The War of Resistance Committee in Mérida, Yucatán, marches during a celebration of the Day of the Revolution (November 20, 1942). From Chen Kwong Min, *Meizhou huaqiao tongjian.*

Chinese squads, it is significant that neither city had experienced an anti-Chinese campaign or had ever had a nativist association.

In Ciudad Juárez, Chihuahua, the decree led to a dispute between the CKT and the GMD. When local authorities began preparations for military training, the CKT believed that Chinese should join the military and "thus receive a favorable opinion among the populace." In contrast, the GMD was much more hesitant to receive military training, and the fact that the local general Chinese association, the Zhonghua Gongsuo, was dominated by members of the GMD meant that the organization did not motivate local Chinese to register and receive military training. In order to press the issue, the CKT, which had extensive ties to the Mexican community of Ciudad Juárez, had an editorial released in the local daily *El Orbe* accusing the Chinese of shirking their military responsibilities. The editorial accused a "nationalist" group (the Guomindang, or the Chinese Nationalist Party) of engaging in suspicious and potentially traitorous activities. Because many residents of Ciudad Juárez were unaware of the political differences between the

CKT and the GMD, the editorial could have been damaging to the entire community, raising suspicions of Chinese nationals during wartime. Nevertheless, it appears to have had its desired effect: the Chinese legation encouraged the local branch of the GMD to sign up for military service, especially if the CKT planned to do so.[89]

Eventually, the Chinese community in Mexico realized that this requirement would not greatly affect them. Mexican budgetary appropriations did not keep up with the military's zeal for preparing for war. After the declaration of war, military spending in Mexico did not increase appreciably; barracks and other military installations had not yet been built. According to the Chinese legation, there was no "atmosphere of war preparation."[90] Moreover, it appears Mexicans did not want to participate in military training either. According to the consul in Tampico, only a third of military-age men received military training, and less than half of eighteen-year-olds registered for service. Among those who did attend, the drills were creating "more resentment than enthusiasm."[91] After the president made clear that these activities were considered voluntary, attendance at military training in Tampico dropped by 94 percent.[92] The requirement eventually was not enforced to such an extent that, the legation suggested, it "disappeared."[93]

But attitudes about military service are notable because they reveal the mind-set that Chinese had about serving with their Mexican neighbors, as well as demonstrating the continued effect that the anti-Chinese campaigns had on the Chinese community in Mexico. Chiang Kai-shek had encouraged Chinese abroad to serve in what he called "their second homeland": "They should participate in all kinds of wartime activities, enlist when they are called for military service and fight to protect the country in which they live as religiously and as valiantly as their brothers and sisters are fighting to protect their fatherland."[94] But, save for the Chinese military squads of Mérida and Tijuana, most Chinese were reluctant to serve, and even those who were willing appear to have been opposed to serving alongside Mexicans. While Soong May-Ling (popularly known as Madame Chiang Kai-shek), during her trip to the United States in 1943, expressed her wish that "wherever her compatriots go, into whatever land they are adopted, they become loyal citizens of that country," the Chinese in Mexico knew that their Mexican citizenship was much more tenuous.[95] Unfortunately, not much is known about native-born Chinese Mexicans who received military training, but a small number of them did renounce their Mexican citizenship in order to avoid serving in the military—an indication of how much they feared such service.[96]

The entry of Western powers into the war had profound consequences not only for the Republic of China but also for Chinese settlements across the Americas. The wartime alliance between Mexico and
China encouraged the Mexican government to regularize the migratory
status of Chinese undocumented immigrants, even as it did not allow
large numbers of new Chinese migrants to settle in the country. For
Chinese Mexicans without legal documentation, the 1943 legalization
was a crucial step toward their stabilization in the country.

After the Second Sino-Japanese War became integrated into the Pacific
Theater of the Second World War, China's relationship with its allies
improved dramatically. China's status in the United States began to rise,
and its War of Resistance was increasingly viewed as heroic.[97] Just after
the U.S. entry into the war, President Franklin Delano Roosevelt praised
the Chinese as "those millions who for four and a half years have with-
stood bombs and starvation and have whipped the invaders time and
again in spite of superior Japanese equipment and arms."[98] As allies
praised China, they began to pay attention to their own past aggressions,
including the unequal treaties imposed on China after the Opium Wars
of the mid–nineteenth century, as well as Chinese exclusion. In 1943, on
a visit to the United States, Soong May-Ling reminded members of Congress that the "repeal of the Exclusion Acts would boost Chinese morale
and thus contribute to the war effort."[99] The effects of repeal were not
immediate: a quota was set of only 105 Chinese immigrants per year.[100]
However, the repeal, along with the 1945 War Brides Act, "changed the
composition of Chinese America," allowing families to reunite and the
Chinese community in the United States to grow.[101]

It was in this context that Chinese-Mexican relations also improved
during the Second World War.[102] After Mexico joined the war in May
1942, the Republic of China likewise became a wartime ally. Like U.S.
government officials, Mexican officials had kind words for the Chinese
in their effort against Japan. In his third annual *informe de gobierno*—
similar to a State of the Union address in the United States—President
Manuel Ávila Camacho praised "the great Chinese people, heroic warriors in a long war that anticipated the current conflict."[103] In 1943,
Mexico and China elevated their respective legations to embassies, and
Mexico dispatched its first ambassador to China, José Gómez Esparza,
to the wartime capital of Chongqing. (Unfortunately, however, travel
conditions prevented Gómez Esparza from making the trip.)[104] The Chinese government, for its part, nominated Chen Chieh (Chen Jie) as the
first Chinese ambassador to Mexico.[105] The elevation of legations to

embassies also provided these countries with an opportunity to renegotiate a bilateral treaty, since the previous treaty had lapsed in 1926.

The new treaty heightened expectations for increased Chinese immigration to the country; for Chinese Mexicans, the international situation and the migratory situation were linked. After the Chinese Mexican population shrank after the anti-Chinese campaigns, the 1936 Ley de Población, limiting Chinese migration to just one hundred per year, seemed to make it almost impossible for the community to grow again. What Chinese community leaders sought from the treaty—free movement between China and Mexico—was important not only because it would allow young Chinese to once again settle on Mexican soil and afford family members in war-torn Guangdong Province a new place of settlement, but also because it would allow Chinese Mexicans to travel more freely to China to look after their relatives.[106]

The most difficult negotiations between the two governments were on the issue of Chinese immigration. Despite broad agreement on most of the proposed bilateral treaty, the Chinese and Mexican governments spent months exchanging notes on the two articles that would affect Chinese migration to Mexico: Article V, which governed the entry of nationals of one country into the territory of the other, and Article VI, which governed foreign residency. The Chinese government wanted its nationals to enjoy "[the] liberty to enter or leave the territory of the other under the same conditions as the nationals of other countries."[107] Under this clause, objected the Mexican Secretaría de Gobernación, China could ask for an unlimited migratory quota, similar to those of nationals of Spain and the Americas. The Chinese objected to the Mexican counterproposal—that foreign nationals could enter the other country "in accordance with the stipulations of their respective legislations"—due to the fact that it could allow for de jure discrimination against Chinese nationals.[108] Ultimately, in April 1944 China accepted the final revisions to the Chinese-Mexican treaty, which contained no special concessions from the Mexican government on migration—a result that deeply disappointed Chinese Mexicans. The result was a steady decline of the Chinese population in Mexico as longtime residents (*jiuke*) grew old and died in their adopted country.[109]

Disappointment over immigration provisions, however, masks the improved status that the Chinese community in Mexico enjoyed as a result of the Second World War. From a position of vulnerability, the Chinese community in Mexico experienced a period of stability and tranquillity they had not seen since before the Mexican Revolution.

While Axis nationals were affected by blacklists or forced removals, the Chinese population quietly regularized its migratory status. Shortly after declaring war the Mexican government, fearful of the actions of fifth columnists and Axis sympathizers, carried out a registration of all foreign nationals in the country. Moreover, it announced its intention to deport any foreigner lacking legal documentation to remain in the country. Around three thousand people, notably Chinese residents along the western edge of the U.S.–Mexico border, had no legal status in Mexico, and were thus alarmed by the registration order.[110] After several rounds of negotiations, the Chinese embassy successfully negotiated with the Mexican government to provide identification for these migrants and accord them permanent resident status.[111] The reason behind the successful negotiation, asserted Cheng, was the fact that the status of the Chinese Mexican community had improved: it was due "to the heroes inside of [Mexico] who fought the War of Resistance, [it] caused foreigners to respect and admire, [and] the status [of Chinese] was raised."[112] Moreover, migrants along the border obtained special permission to cross the U.S.–Mexico border to conduct business. With a new treaty governing Sino-Mexican relations and with China's elevated status internationally, the Chinese community in Mexico no longer feared for its own safety on Mexican soil.

VIVAS FOR CHIANG KAI-SHEK

The Second Sino-Japanese War came to an end with the unconditional surrender of Japanese forces on August 15, 1945. Although the Republic of China emerged from the conflict considerably weakened, for the moment it had consolidated its hold across much of mainland China, and reclaimed the island of Taiwan. With China as one of the five victorious powers after the war, the status of the Chinese community in Mexico also seemed to rise. Yu notes that Mexicans on the streets gave Chinese the thumbs-up and screamed, "¡Viva Chiang Kai-shih!"[113] Just ten years after the anti-Chinese campaigns, Chinese in Mexico were acutely aware of how China's victory in the war changed their status in Mexico. According to Yu, after the war "overseas Chinese are very important and admired in Mexican public opinion, poles apart from the anti-Chinese campaigns."[114]

Rather than celebrate alone, Chinese communities around the country celebrated alongside Mexicans. In cities and towns across the country, prominent civil and military officials dined and toasted with Chinese associations, and celebrations—some of which were broadcast over Mexican radio—included the general Mexican public and featured speeches in both Chinese and Spanish. Chinese associations that during the anti-Chinese campaigns might have appeared insular and secretive now opened themselves to outsiders.

The most prominent celebration occurred in the capital, where Ambassador Chen Chieh held a lavish banquet whose invitees included cabinet secretaries, military officers, members of congress, labor and business leaders, chiefs of mission of foreign embassies in Mexico City, and leaders of foreign associations in Mexico. These leaders lined up to congratulate Ambassador Chen on China's victory, after which they mingled freely with invited guests from the various Chinese associations in Mexico City.[115]

In other areas of the country, Chinese communities opened their celebrations to the larger public. After representatives of the Japanese government signed the instrument of surrender, Chinese in Baja California and Chiapas closed their stores for three days in celebration of the end of the war. In Mexicali, the Chinese community staged a large parade and a barbecue that fed three thousand people, while a banquet in Tijuana fed an additional eight hundred guests.[116] The celebration in Tapachula, Chiapas, featured an open bar serving beer and "oriental beverages." Local newspaper *El Apagón* passed along an invitation to the public "to take advantage of the magnanimity of the *chinitos*."[117] Many other towns invited local Mexican and Chinese guests to dances. From the city of Torreón, which invited a thousand guests to the lavish Casino de la Laguna and broadcast the celebration on radio station XETB, to the small town of Cacahoatán, Chiapas, where the Chinese association entertained its guests with traditional marimba music, guests danced into the early morning hours to celebrate the end of the war.[118] Many of these social engagements, such as the ones in Torreón and Manzanillo, marked the first time that Chinese and Mexican guests had celebrated together.[119]

The celebrations allowed migrants to demonstrate their sense of belonging to both Mexico and China, even in towns that had recently tried to expel them from the country. Typical was the commemoration of the war in El Mante, Tamaulipas. Chinese residents of the city raised both the Chinese and Mexican flags and played both national anthems. After the guests bowed three times before pictures of Manuel Ávila Camacho and Chiang Kai-shek to show their respect, they enjoyed performances of Chinese and Mexican music. Whereas fifteen years earlier civil officials had tried to evict the majority of Chinese residents, in 1945 the mayor asserted that relations between Chinese and Mexicans were warm and friendly.[120] In Cacahoatán, Chiapas, a full-page advertisement in the local newspaper extended greetings to President Ávila Camacho and the governor of Chiapas and expressed its desire that the "amity which has always tied the Chinese and Mexican peoples will, now in [time of] peace, grow even stronger."[121]

These celebrations were instances of public diplomacy between China and Mexico as well as between Mexican and Chinese residents. They attempted to capitalize on the Chinese victory in the war to improve the social standing of the Chinese community in the country. Moreover, they demonstrated that Chinese associations were no longer insular, and for the moment were not divided. In Torreón, for example, the Guomindang held part of its celebration at the headquarters of the Chee Kung Tong, whose members had momentarily dropped their objections to the government of Chiang Kai-shek.[122]

But the following year provided an even larger indication of just how much the community's status had changed. In 1946, a Chinese Navy fleet touring the Americas accepted an invitation from President Manuel Ávila Camacho to visit Mexico. The fleet consisted of eight ships—two destroyer escorts, two 180-foot-long patrol escorts, and four 180-foot light minesweepers, with 72 officers and 980 sailors. The U.S. Navy provided an escort for the fleet, which had visited Guantánamo, Cuba, and crossed the Panama Canal before arriving in Mexico.[123]

Even before the fleet docked in Mexican waters, the Chinese embassy in Mexico notified the Chinese community in Mexico City about the upcoming festivities. It in turn spread word of the visit to other communities across the country and formed a committee to prepare for the fleet's arrival. When Chinese Mexicans raised funds to prepare for the naval visit, they were not just showing their loyalty to China; rather, they believed that the arrival of the fleet showcased their social progression in Mexico and the increased respect that Mexicans held for the Chinese community as a result of the war effort.

For Hu Erqin, the visit of the Chinese Navy demonstrated the benefits that *paisanos* reaped as a result of War of Resistance efforts. Chinese Mexicans "rose up for [their] defenseless country to defeat the enemy" and launched an eight-year struggle to support the Republic of China. Beyond simply helping China, the war effort also had positive effects for the Chinese community. Mexicans saw the community's efforts and as a result changed their attitude toward them: "all began to treat our overseas Chinese with increased respect."[124] At the same time, Mexico had joined the war, sending an air force squadron to the Philippines, and improving its diplomatic relationship by exchanging full ambassadors. The naval visit was a manifestation of both improvements: not only did it show increased amity between China and Mexico; it also underscored the fact that Chinese government officials could finally visit Chinese Mexicans and extend their greetings, something *paisanos* "all along had thirsted for and had not received."[125]

The victory celebration was notable, then, in that it combined a public celebration of the newly invigorated diplomatic relationship with a celebration of the Chinese communities and associations around the country. The navy could not visit every community—the Chinese Association in Mazatlán wrote Chiang Kai-shek several times to ask that the navy spend a week in Sinaloa, but the request was turned down—but the selection of cities helped ensure that Chinese across the country could visit the celebrations. Chinese young and old traveled from the periphery of the country to Acapulco, Mexico City, and Puebla to see the Chinese Navy. In each city, *paisanos* were made a central part of all victory celebrations—a powerful reminder that Chinese authorities recognized their contributions in the War of Resistance movement and that the victory celebration was theirs as well.

The arrival of the fleet on May 1 paid tribute to Acapulco, an important and symbolic city for the Chinese–Mexican relationship. In the colonial period, the Manila galleon (*nao de china*) connected the cities of Manila and Acapulco, sending Mexican silver to Asia, bringing fine Chinese artwork and crafts to the Americas, and connecting the peoples on both sides of the Pacific.[126] Making reference to the *nao*, captain Lin Tsun declared, "[W]e don't bring cloth or ivory, only a sincere greeting from my country."[127] Despite the fact that Acapulco did not have a sizable Chinese community, the landing of the fleet there—and the continued visits of Chinese officials to the Mexican city since then—points to the long-lasting relationship between the two countries. Wrote Eduardo Tellez, reporter for the Mexico City daily *Excélsior,* "[T]he warships brought a brotherly hug from a bloodied China to its darling sister: Mexico."[128] Chinese Mexicans waited at the dock, holding the flags of both countries, and greeted the navy at the port of Acapulco with flowers. (See figure 6.) That evening, the Chinese community welcomed both the Chinese Navy and Mexican officials at a banquet at Acapulco's Hotel Casa Blanca.[129]

The sailors were then honored with several days of activities in Mexico City, where they were enthusiastically received by the capital's

FIGURE 6. A Chinese Mexican welcoming committee celebrates the arrival of the Chinese Navy to the Mexican port of Acapulco. From Chen Kwong Min, *Meizhou huaqiao tongjian.*

Chinese community. On May 3, the Chinese Navy marched from Chapultepec Park to the Angel of Independence victory column, where they offered flowers.[130] From there, they marched down the Paseo de la Reforma and Juárez and Madero avenues to the Zócalo, concluding their triumphal march at the National Palace. Behind them, *paisanos* vigorously waved Chinese and Mexican flags as they marched along the parade route. The throng was accompanied by a contingent of the Mexican Navy as well as its marching band, which played both Chinese and Mexican songs.[131] Along the route, "the *pueblo* applauded the bravery of the sailors from the friendly country."[132] The commander of the Chinese fleet met with the Mexican Secretary of National Defense, the Secretary of the Navy, the Secretary of Foreign Relations, and the governor of the Federal District, while the commanders of each of the eight ships met with President Manuel Ávila Camacho. Afterward, the fleet had lunch with the Chinese community in the capital and then toured the Chinese organizations in the city. In the evening, the troops were treated to Cantonese theater, of the kind that had helped raise funds for the war effort. *Paisanos* who traveled to the capital were impressed by the dignified manner of the soldiers and the cordial reception of the Mexican people.

In addition to the march in the Zócalo in Mexico City, the invitation to march at the head of the May 5 parade in Puebla was indeed a special honor, since Cinco de Mayo commemorates the iconic 1862 battle in which overmatched Mexican forces successfully repelled a foreign aggressor. The symbolic connection with China's recent victory was impossible to overlook. On May 5, 1946, the Chinese community of Puebla provided breakfast for the troops, after which the Chinese sailors marched in the Cinco de Mayo parade. Observed Yu Shouzhi: "People turned out en masse, fighting to see the elegant demeanor of China's warriors; [it] added luster to [our] country, and elevated our overseas Chinese."[133] When the Chinese fleet set sail on May 6, the Chinese community saw them off.

For both the embassy and the Chinese community in Mexico, the parade was an unqualified success. In a country with a large suspicion of foreigners and a wariness of foreign armies, the Mexican government had honored the Chinese Navy with several days of celebrations in three of Mexico's major cities, recognizing China as an important partner and as a new postwar power. *Paisanos* were given a chance to thank the Chinese armed forces for their tenacity during eight difficult years of resisting the Japanese invasion, and the Chinese Navy in turn was able to thank the community for its contribution during the Second Sino-Japanese War. At the same time, the parade allowed for a moment of catharsis about the anti-Chinese campaigns while assuring Chinese in Mexico that, with China's new strength, another anti-Chinese campaign would not be repeated. Yu noted that sixty- and seventy-year-old *paisanos* wept along the parade route in Puebla, and though Yu had not lived in Mexico during the anti-Chinese campaigns, his own reaction testifies to the War of Resistance and the anti-Chinese campaigns as milestones in the community's history. According to Yu, despite years of effort, the Chinese community received "no medals or merits." Still, the rewards were far greater: "What is important is we triumphed, the Chinese people rose up, overseas Chinese will not be bullied by the anti-Chinese [movement] any more, our lives and property are guaranteed."[134]

CONCLUSION

Major factions of the Chinese Mexican community cooperated on the activities benefiting the War of Resistance against Japan. The support for China was not a reflexive support of their home country and the Nationalist government in power. Instead, it responded to two desires, one international, one local. The first was a desire to counteract the invasion that had hurt their home communities in Guangdong Province, and the belief that the best mechanism for ending the invasion was through support of the Nationalist government. The second was that if China's status could rise internationally, their own status in Mexico would move from persecuted minority to that of respected foreign nationals. If unity required mediation between the GMD and the CKT, in the end both factions were in agreement on the desires that motivated their support for the War of Resistance.

At the same time, the Second World War did not eliminate political differences between the GMD and the CKT. The CKT began the war as the largest Chinese organization in Mexico. During the war, and particularly as the Nationalist government began to win, the GMD appeared to have won the trust of much of the Chinese community, and membership in the party surged throughout the country. But there appeared to have been no corresponding decline in CKT membership, and it ended the war as still the largest Chinese organization in Mexico. Nevertheless, outright antagonism between the two groups declined. And as the CKT government sent a congratulatory note to the Mexican Secretaría of Foreign Relations and began to fly the Nationalist flag, it recognized the Nationalist government as the legitimate government of China.

During the Second World War, unlike the Japanese, Italians, and Germans, the Chinese were not under any suspicion from the Mexican government. If the Mexican government was aware of the activities of the GMD, it was not alarmed by the actions of a foreign party on Mexican soil. Moreover, anti-Chinese actions were not revived, despite a nationalist conjuncture that could have led to a wider movement against foreign shop owners and businessmen. The resulting environment—in which Chinese were not encouraged to obtain Mexican citizenship and assimilate, as in the twenties, or in which they were rejected as foreigners, as in the thirties—provided the Chinese community with the space to sort out its attitudes toward the war and toward long-distance political questions. It helped that the community was composed of a large proportion of small businessmen—people with the resources and the time to devote themselves to long-distance politics.

Perhaps the greatest satisfaction after the conclusion of the war was that Chinese Mexicans could once again see family and friends across the Pacific and take up long-delayed plans that had been shelved during wartime. This was the case with Yu Shouzhi, now in his early thirties, who returned to Chongqing and got married. Rather than continue their life in China, however, the couple move to Mexicali, encouraged by the business environment in Mexico. Although Yu left behind his work as school headmaster, he remained committed to fostering the education of second-generation Chinese Mexicans and sponsored scholarships for second-generation students to return to China.[135] Moreover, in Mexicali he remained engaged with Chinese politics, helping the communities in Baja California navigate the difficulties that lay ahead.

CHAPTER 4

The Golden Age
of Chinese Mexicans

Anti-Communist Activism under
Ambassador Feng-Shan Ho, 1958–1964

The pride Chinese Mexicans felt in connection with the Chinese government's defeat of invading Japanese forces would not last. Soon after the victory over Japan, the civil war between Nationalists and Communists resumed once again with equal ferocity.[1] Upon the resumption of the Chinese Civil War, wrote Yu Shouzhi, "overseas Chinese once again fell into despair."[2] The sense of despair deepened when Nationalist (ROC) forces were routed by the Communists. On October 1, 1949, Communists proclaimed the People's Republic of China (PRC), with a capital in Beijing, while the Republic of China government retreated to the island of Taiwan, setting its new capital in Taipei. (See map 3.) Once again, Chinese Mexicans found themselves largely separated from their relatives in mainland China, this time for the duration of the Cold War.[3]

After the conclusion of the civil war, armed conflict gave way to other forms of competition. Chief among them was the scramble for diplomatic recognition abroad. From 1949 into the twenty-first century, both governments argued that they were the true and only legitimate government of China. Although the People's Republic of China controlled the mainland, at the conclusion of the civil war most countries continued to recognize the Republic of China as the legitimate Chinese government. This jockeying for recognition would soon spread to much of the Third World, involving trade overtures, technical and agricultural assistance, and cultural diplomacy. Through the 1950s, the PRC began to gain ground, establishing diplomatic relations with

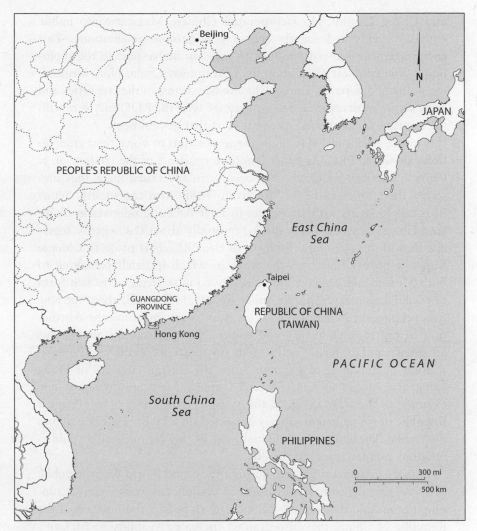

MAP 3. The People's Republic of China and the Republic of China (Taiwan) after 1949.

several developing countries in Asia, Africa, and the Middle East. These diplomatic setbacks alarmed the ROC and made it fearful of becoming increasingly isolated from global politics.

ROC ambassadors like Feng-Shan Ho acutely understood the need to influence public opinion throughout the Third World on the question of the two Chinas. Once selected as ambassador to Mexico, he turned to *paisanos* to convince Mexicans to be wary about embracing Communist China. Continuing the policies of his predecessors Tan Shaohua and Cheng Tien-ku, Ho incorporated Chinese Mexicans into public embassy events and eagerly encouraged *paisano* celebrations. This encouragement allowed *paisanos* to take an active part in the diplomatic discussion on recognition for Communist China. Notwithstanding political differences among Chinese Mexicans, in the late fifties and early sixties most continued to sympathize with the ROC and were willing to argue for continued recognition of that government.

Chinese Mexicans were in a unique position to voice their reservations about the PRC. As either longtime residents of the country or as Chinese Mexican youth who had been born and raised there, they presented their criticisms of the PRC from within Mexican society. Yet as Mexican residents with strong ties to East Asia and relatives in mainland China, they could also speak personally about the negative repercussions of the 1949 establishment of the PRC. This phase in Chinese Mexican history illustrates the ways in which heartfelt belonging to both Mexico and China could be deployed in strategic ways as a form of public diplomacy. *Paisanos* spoke openly, in Spanish, about the horrors propagated in mainland China after 1949, including the destruction of the region's history and culture, the persecution of religious adherents, and the misery and tragedy on agrarian collectives. The repatriation of hundreds of *paisanos* from the foreign enclaves of Hong Kong and Macau in 1960, argued Chinese Mexicans, was just one example of the ways in which the 1949 establishment of the People's Republic of China had negatively impacted their family members across the Pacific. The embassy would make use of this argument in its public-relations campaign against the PRC.

Like the activities organized during the Second World War, the public activities that the embassy organized in conjunction with Chinese communities around the country did more than bolster the position of the Republic of China; they also granted increased visibility to Mexico's *paisanos*. Ambassador Ho's cooperation with local Chinese, particularly with old community associations formed during the early twentieth century and new ones established to face the Cold War, helped bring the community together and give it a new raison d'être. The public demonstrations and letter-writing campaigns conducted by *paisanos* and their children refuted common stereotypes about the Chinese in the country. Two activities in particular presented a rather different image of Chinese Mexicans: the annual pilgrimage of the Chinese of Mexico City to the Basílica de Nuestra Señora de Guadalupe, one of Mexico's holiest sites; and the Chinese Mexican protest of the 1963 Economic and Commercial Exposition of the People's Republic of China. Because the cooperation between *paisanos* and the embassy led to tangible benefits for both the Republic of China and the Chinese Mexican community, the ambassador referred to his tenure in the country as "the golden age of Chinese Mexicans."[4]

The jostling between the PRC and the ROC in Mexico, which led to the fervent political activity of the Chinese Mexican community, illustrates Mexico's special position during the Cold War.[5] In contrast to other countries in the Americas, Mexico maintained relations with several Communist countries, including the USSR, countries in the Eastern Bloc, and Cuba.[6] This relative independence explains why the People's Republic of China sought Mexican diplomatic recognition during the administration of Adolfo López Mateos (1958–64), a courtship that the United States largely tolerated. Mexico's relatively independent foreign policy afforded its government the appearance of greater legitimacy and autonomy and allowed the government to mediate tensions between the left and right wings of the Institutional Revolutionary Party (PRI).[7] The People's Republic of China sought to appeal to Mexico's ruling party, not by exporting its revolution to Latin America, but rather by offering to open its large market to Mexican businessmen and thus prolong Mexico's midcentury economic boom. As a result, from 1949 to 1971 important segments of the ruling party argued for recognizing the PRC.

The Cold War challenged the political allegiances and identities of Chinese communities around the world. Many Chinese communities remained loyal to the Nationalists, while others were fractured along political lines.[8] Several grew disillusioned both with the radical reforms of the People's Republic of China and with the heavy-handed tactics of the Republic of China. Additionally, since Chinese communities in several countries were largely separated from mainland China for at least a full generation—their members unable to return to China and they themselves unable to receive new Chinese immigrants—many began to identify more strongly with the country of settlement.[9] In this challenging environment, the Republic of China worked furiously to maintain the allegiance of Chinese communities around the world and encourage identification with the ROC government even as it was no longer on mainland China.[10] Additionally, it sought to use Chinese migrants in public diplomacy campaigns against the PRC.[11]

The diplomatic efforts of Ambassador Ho thus serve as an example of the Republic of China's concerted effort during the late 1950s and early 1960s to strengthen its relationship with much of the Third World, thus preventing it from losing its seat in the United Nations, and main-taining its international legitimacy. Certainly, the diplomatic backing of the United States helped the Republic of China maintain diplomatic relations with countries in Asia, Africa, and Latin America. In Latin America, moreover, the promotion of conservative, anti-Communist governments had the side effect of preserving the status of the Republic of China in the region.[12] But the tireless effort of the ROC's diplomatic corps, especially in countries that may have otherwise recognized the People's Republic of China, helped the government retain its seat in the United Nations in a "substantial, if not overwhelming victory for Nationalist diplomacy."[13]

THE WITHDRAWAL OF THE ROC FROM MEXICO

After the retreat of the ROC government to Taiwan, the government's foreign relations were in disarray. Few nations established diplomatic missions at the new ROC capital in Taipei. Major non-Communist powers instead recognized the People's Republic of China, including Great Britain, India, and Israel. With fewer resources at its disposal, the ROC was forced to shrink its diplomatic corps. Early in 1949 the Republic of China maintained 135 missions abroad, but after the Com-munist victory the number shrank to 55; the work force of its Ministry of Foreign Affairs was cut in half.[14] In Mexico, the ROC closed its con-sulates in Tampico, Mazatlán, Tapachula, and Mexicali, leaving only a small staff at its embassy in Mexico City. Their closure distressed Chi-nese Mexicans, who worried about losing the protection of the diplo-matic corps from further violence. Although the embassy assured *paisa-nos* that the closures were merely temporary, the consulates in Tampico, Tapachula, and Mazatlán never reopened.[15]

While the ROC retrocession forced its government to reduce its con-tact with the outside world, the PRC took only a passive interest in Latin America. As a practical matter, the PRC could not afford to encourage Latin America along its socialist road. Embroiled in the Korean War in the early 1950s, the PRC certainly lacked the resources to challenge the United States in its self-proclaimed "backyard." Instead, the PRC's first priority was to increase Mexican support for diplomatic relations, in part by winning over influential Mexican leaders. This effort included incipient trade overtures and cultural missions. For example, in August 1959 Beijing held a "Mexican film week" featuring director Alejandro Galindo and his famous cautionary tale on migration to the United

States, *Espaldas mojadas.*[16] The PRC also invited prominent Mexican intellectuals to mainland China at great expense. Once there, "Chinese leaders appear[ed] always to have time to receive Mexican visitors." The PRC's open door to prominent Mexicans was an attempt to showcase the successes of the Chinese Revolution, not an attempt to train Communists or foment revolution in the region. Indeed, noted the U.S. Department of State, during the late 1950s the People's Republic of China, even more than the Soviet Union, excelled at "winning friends and influencing people in Mexico."[17] Even as China experienced radical changes domestically, its foreign policy in this period was "absolutely [. . .] non-revolutionary."[18]

The increasing attractiveness of the PRC led to a vociferous argument over diplomatic recognition for "New China" (the People's Republic of China). The question of Chinese recognition was undoubtedly the most important issue in Mexico's policy toward East Asia, dividing the left and right wings of Mexico's ruling Partido Revolucionario Institucional. Among those most in favor of recognition for the People's Republic of China were prominent Mexican leftists, who quickly became enthralled with New China. Vicente Lombardo Toledano, prominent labor leader and founder of the Partido Popular Socialista, visited China shortly after the 1949 revolution. Upon his return to Mexico, he gave public lectures on the PRC and published books and articles praising its successes.[19] Former presidents Emilio Portes Gil (1928–30) and Lázaro Cárdenas (1934–40) both traveled to Beijing, each meeting with Chairman Mao. The latter affirmed that he found the new government's successes, particularly in the area of agrarian reform, "startling."[20] Several other Mexican intellectuals, bureaucrats, and generals who slowly began to visit China also returned with positive impressions of the country. As President Adolfo López Mateos (1958–64) later told Milton Eisenhower, "those Mexican leftists who visit the Soviet Union and China, when they come back to Mexico, many of them are disillusioned about the Soviet Union but very enthusiastic about Communist China."[21] The government of the PRC hoped that such enthusiasm would pressure the Mexican government to extend diplomatic recognition and support PRC membership in the United Nations.

In contrast, the right wanted Mexico to stand with anti-Communist nation-states and stand firm its support of the Republic of China. Wary of dangers of Communism for domestic Mexican politics, conservatives argued that the Mexican government should maintain its recognition of the Republic of China as a government in exile. Although the Mexican government, in keeping with one of the central pillars of its foreign policy, usually maintained relations with any government holding effective control, an important precedent had been set when it continued relations with the Spanish Republic in exile in 1939.[22] Mexican conservatives argued that it was too soon to determine whether the PRC had effective control over mainland China, and that the Mexican government should join the United States and other Western democracies in providing support to the government of Chiang Kai-shek in Taiwan.

For their part, the administrations of Adolfo Ruiz Cortines and Miguel Alemán wavered between the Communist and Nationalist governments. On December 1, 1949, the Mexican representative to the United Nations argued that China should be free to choose its own political system, but then announced that Mexico would not support a Soviet motion to admit the People's Republic of China into the United Nations.[23] One year later, the Mexican government appeared ready to recognize the PRC, sending messages through the Polish embassy in Mexico "announcing the desire of President Alemán to establish diplomatic relations with New China and making clear that for the government of Mexico the Guomindang diplomats were foreign citizens who did not represent the legitimate government of the Chinese people."[24] The Polish government transmitted the message directly to PRC Premier Zhou Enlai. As the Polish government facilitated initial moves toward diplomatic recognition, however, the PRC intervention in the Korean War forced the Mexican government to reconsider.[25] U.S. pressure on Latin American governments vis-à-vis the People's Republic of China was a decisive factor. When the government of the United States decided to postpone its recognition of the PRC indefinitely, it sent word through its embassies in Latin America that it hoped "the American Republics would confer with each other before recognizing that regime or changing its relationship to the Nationalist government of China."[26]

One of the major factors explaining the Mexican government's ambivalence on the "two Chinas" question was that, until the mid-1950s, the debate remained largely ideological. Mexico derived few tangible benefits from its relationship with either country and thus saw little incentive to change its recognition policy. Since Mexico and China produced similar goods, there was little prospect of even a symbolic trade relationship; Mexico was not even one of the PRC's five major trading partners in Latin America.[27] For the moment, the Mexican government limited itself to impersonal, off-the-record relationships with government officials in the PRC.[28] At the same time, it was also not enthusiastic about its relationship to the ROC after 1949: "the island was not very attractive, was full of problems, and was the cradle of an extremely authoritarian government, even by Mexican standards; as if that were not enough, trade never grew, the topic of migration hung about like a ghost, and the constant clashes between nationalists and communists only had small echoes in Mexico."[29] Mexico never established a diplomatic presence in Taipei, and its dealings with ROC officials were limited to communiqués and matters of protocol.[30]

Paisanos greeted the start of the Cold War just as ambivalently. In a worrisome sign for the relationship between the ROC and the Chinese community, whereas the community's response to the Second World War had been enthusiastic, its initial reaction to the Cold War was tepid. Just as during the Second World War, one of the ways that the ROC reacted to the Cold War was through the formation of a national salvation association—in this case, the Overseas Chinese Anti-Communist National Salvation Association (Huaqiao Fangong Jiuguohui), in 1953. The association was tasked with preventing Communist infiltration and supporting the ROC in its struggle to retake the mainland. It also made donations to the central government, ostensibly to care for refugees who escaped the mainland and resettle them in Taiwan.[31] The organization, however, appears to have been small, especially in comparison to its counterpart during the Second World War. There are few records of its donations to central authorities, of its activities, or of exactly how ROC officials wanted Chinese Mexicans to accomplish the organization's goals.

Although the two rival Chinese governments appeared deadlocked, international developments pushed the ROC to reconsider its strategy toward Mexico. During the early 1950s, the PRC's involvement in the Korean War deterred foreign governments from establishing diplomatic relations with the Communists. According to Donald Klein, "no nation recognized [Beijing] from the spring of 1950 (Indonesia) until mid-1955 (Nepal)."[32] In 1955, however, sixteen new countries joined the United Nations, and in 1956 twelve of the sixteen voted to support the PRC's seat at the United Nations. That same year, Egypt, Yemen, and Syria recognized the Communist government. Suddenly the ROC's position in the United Nations, and its international legitimacy, had come into serious doubt. Were Latin American countries to recognize and support the PRC, the ROC might lose its seat at the United Nations.[33]

As a result, in the late 1950s the ROC placed renewed emphasis on its foreign relations, and in particular its relations with Latin America and the Middle East. A central focus was Mexico, whose lackluster support for the ROC had become obvious by 1957. That year, the ROC's vice-minister of foreign affairs, C.H. Shen, embarked on a tour of several Latin American countries, during which he would inspect overseas Chinese affairs and meet with high-level Latin American officials. However, Mexican officials suggested that Shen's visit to their country came at an inconvenient time and requested he postpone his trip.[34] At first, the office of the president assured Ambassador Liu Qin-wu that the delay was "not at all caused by bad intentions."[35] Yet, despite the fact that Vice-Minister Shen deferred his trip until October, Ruiz Cortines's administration let the entire summer go by without considering a date to give the ROC embassy in Mexico, nor did it provide a satisfactory explanation for the delay. In June, the Secretaría of Foreign Relations communicated to the embassy that "the President, busy with party affairs, could not consider—yes, even consider—matters of protocol until after Parliament or Congress opened on September 1." The ROC ambassador to Mexico was exasperated by his inability to obtain a date for the vice-minister's visit, and the Taipei government thought the delay unusual and suspicious.[36] The following year, the ROC would name a new ambassador to Mexico, Feng-Shan Ho, who had more experience in dealing with countries ambivalent about their relations with the two Chinas.

THE COLD WARRIOR

"Mexico is very important," said ROC President Chiang Kai-shek to his newly appointed ambassador to Mexico, Feng-Shan Ho, when they met on April 24, 1958. "The Chinese Communists are very strong. They will surely try to subvert us in that country."[37] As the Republic of China began to prioritize its diplomatic relationship with Mexico, it pushed for a change in its embassy in the country. Ho's long history with the Ministry of Foreign Affairs explains his appointment. Throughout his career, as Consul General in Vienna during the Second World War, and as ambassador to Egypt (1947–56), Ho promoted the interests of the Republic of China at difficult moments for the ministry by engaging in popular diplomacy in conjunction with the local Chinese population. In 1949, even as some members of the diplomatic staff defected to the PRC in the wake of the Communist victory, he remained faithful to the Nationalist government. The ambassador's main priority in Egypt was to preserve the diplomatic relationship between the ROC and Middle Eastern countries, visiting government officials in Saudi Arabia,

Ethiopia, Lebanon, Iraq, Iran, Sudan, Syria, Jordan, and Yemen. The ambassador also worked with his Middle Eastern counterparts in the United Nations, hoping to secure their support on resolutions concerning the two Chinas.[38]

Ho understood that the PRC made use of trade to pursue incrementally expanded relations with countries in the Third World—what he called the "silver bullet policy." In 1956, a PRC trade delegation bought surplus Egyptian cotton, and established a commercial office in Cairo. A few weeks later, the People's Republic of China held a commercial exposition in Egypt. Even as the Egyptian foreign minister denied any political significance to the PRC's overtures, Ambassador Ho began to see the warning signs of Egyptian recognition of the PRC. When Egyptian President Gamal Abdel Nasser abruptly announced the establishment of relations with Beijing, Ambassador Ho was left with no choice but to return to Taipei.[39]

Even as Ho had failed to maintain a diplomatic relationship with Egypt, his understanding of the PRC offensive in that country and its importance for ROC foreign policy in the Middle East made him an exceptional candidate for the post of ambassador to Mexico. When he met with Chiang Kai-shek just before leaving for Mexico City, Ambassador Ho remarked, "The importance of Mexico in Latin America is very similar to that of Egypt among the Arab nations. When the Chinese Communists wanted to establish relations with the Arab nations, they first tried to succeed in Egypt. Now that they want to establish relations with nations in Latin America, they will first concentrate on Mexico. I believe there will be a fierce struggle between the Communists and us."[40] Maintaining friendly relations with Mexico and the rest of Latin America would be his first priority during his tenure.

Once Ambassador Ho arrived in Mexico City in May 1958, his approach involved increased contact with local officials as well as members of the local Chinese community. The ambassador quickly became friends with Subsecretary of Foreign Relations José Gorostiza, and soon developed a working relationship with Secretary of Foreign Relations Luis Padilla Nervo. The ambassador also "made contact with the immigration authorities, the customs bureau, and various news media to be aware of the latest intelligence regarding the activities of Communist China in Latin America."[41]

Ambassador Ho used his contacts with members of the Secretaría of Foreign Relations to try to block visits from the PRC to Mexico, all of which he understood to be "communist infiltration." The ambassador was less concerned that these citizens of the PRC would foment revolution than that they would promote a positive image of the People's Republic of China. For example, the ambassador tried to block the entry of Chinese intellectual Kuo Mo-jo into Mexico, dismissing the Chinese Academy of Sciences as "nothing more than an official communist organization"; he accused Kuo of "subversion and infiltration [. . .] under the pretext of culture and science."[42] Similarly, in persuading the Mexican government to block the entry of a Chinese opera troupe from the mainland, Ho wrote that the group would attempt to enter Mexico "under the disguise of a goodwill mission" when their true intention was to foment discord among Chinese communities around the world, establish cultural relations, pave the way for future "infiltration," and, ultimately, obtain PRC recognition.[43] Although Ambassador Ho did not succeed in blocking the entry of every Communist group to Mexico, Mexican officials denied or canceled several PRC entrance visas after the ambassador's protests. His constant objections thus served as a strong barrier to Mexican government officials establishing a cultural relationship with the PRC.

The ambassador also prodded Chinese Mexicans to participate more actively in Cold War politics. He first met with Huang Xiangfu, founder of Chocolate Wong and one of the wealthiest Chinese in the capital. Although Huang initially had few contacts with the rest of the Chinese Mexican community, Ambassador Ho convinced him to begin participating in the community's activities. The ambassador met with and encouraged prominent Chinese Mexican businessman Pablo Fong (Feng Bao) to participate in Chinese events and help the community improve, but Fong seemed less receptive.[44] On September 27, Ho called a meeting of members of the Chinese community in Mexico City. At a difficult time for the Republic of China, Ho and *paisano* leaders agreed to raise money for troops on the Taiwanese islands of Jinmen and Matsu, as well as for refugees moving into Hong Kong.[45]

After Ho took up his post, then, Chinese Mexicans began to figure more prominently in embassy-sponsored cultural celebrations. On the morning of October 10, 1958, the National Day of the Republic of China, Ambassador Ho and a group of Chinese Mexicans presented flowers before the Monument to the Niños Héroes in Chapultepec Park. Although visiting a Mexican historical monument on an ROC holiday might seem incongruous, such an action would not only generate good press but also showcase the dual loyalties of *paisanos*. In December, the embassy invited the diplomatic staff of thirty missions in the capital as well as the city's Chinese community to a special reception to celebrate the inauguration of President Adolfo López Mateos (1958–64).[46] These festivities increased the profile of the embassy as well as the Chinese community it represented.

THE CHINESE MEXICAN REPATRIATION OF 1960

The repatriation of nearly three hundred Chinese Mexican refugees from the European enclaves of Hong Kong and Macau added symbolic weight to the embassy's public-relations campaign against the PRC. Portrayals of the refugees as a group of Mexicans who had suffered under Chinese Communism signaled a greater acceptance of the Chinese community as part of the Mexican nation and suggested that the country's Chinese residents would not sympathize with the PRC. While the ROC embassy in Mexico appears to have taken no part in the repatriation or resettlement of refugees, their arrival served as added evidence of the missteps and dangers of the People's Republic of China under Mao Zedong. After 1960, groups of repatriates participated in the embassy's public activities, and *paisanos* made reference to the repatriation in order to bolster their argument.

The repatriates who arrived in 1960 at the airports of Mazatlán, Sinaloa, and Guadalajara, Jalisco, had departed Mexico three decades prior—the casualties of the anti-Chinese campaigns and the Chinese expulsions in Sonora and Sinaloa. As demonstrated in chapter 1, these refugees had arrived in China carrying little aside from the clothes they had on their backs. Frequently, the Chinese men who were expelled from Mexico returned to China with their Mexican wives and Chinese Mexican children. Many of the Mexican women and children who arrived in East Asia spoke little or no Chinese, making it difficult for them to integrate to their new surroundings, support themselves, or find appropriate aid.

Beginning in the late 1930s, many of these refugees began to consider returning to Mexico. As noted in chapter 2, in addition to their troubles in China, many believed that the anti-Chinese movement had died down and that the Chinese community in Mexico was now safe. Initially, however, Mexican government officials ignored the hardships of the refugees and were slow to appropriate funds to aid the return of destitute women and children. Additionally, they stubbornly refused to allocate funds to repatriate Chinese-born men. In 1937–38, a small repatriation under President Lázaro Cárdenas returned some Chinese families to the country, while others obtained permission to reenter Mexico through family-reunification provisions of Mexican immigration law, paying for their own return to the country.

The limited repatriation of the 1930s meant that, at midcentury, many members of the community remained trapped in southern China. Some were unable to prove their Mexican citizenship, making their repatriation difficult. Even for those who could, travel to Mexico was made difficult by the outbreak of the Second World War and later the Cold War. The Japanese invasion of southern China, the Communist victory in 1949, and the radical changes that mainland China experienced under Mao Zedong placed enormous strain on and displaced many of the refugees from Mexico to the British enclave of Hong Kong and the Portuguese enclave of Macau. Many of those who remained relied on help from the Catholic Church, in particular the Asociación Hispano-Americana de Nuestra Señora de Guadalupe. Participation in religious celebrations allowed the repatriates to build a sense of community. Every December 12, for example, the community on Macau celebrated the feast day of the Virgin of Guadalupe.[47]

One example of the ways in which displacement to China brought deep challenges is the life story of Jorge Cinco. Born in Sinaloa in 1930, Cinco, together with his family, was forced to flee Mexico during the anti-Chinese campaigns. His family lost its Sinaloa business, which they had entrusted to a caretaker. During the Second World War, he lost his father in the Japanese bombardment of Manila. His mother remained in China, speaking no Chinese and with only one other Latin American friend. The family was dealt a final blow during the Communist takeover of Guangzhou, when the family lost everything. Escaping to Hong Kong, Cinco became a spy for the ROC government and later was one of the repatriates to Mexico in 1960. Even after he was repatriated, he had to struggle to obtain the proper documentation and the funds to repatriate his mother and sister. After arriving in Mexico, Cinco would speak openly of the tribulations his family experienced after the Communist takeover of mainland China.[48]

In the late 1950s, a new push began to repatriate the remaining Chinese Mexicans in East Asia. In her pioneering study, Julia Maria Schiavone Camacho argues that they deployed a strategic and heartfelt nationalism that persuaded government officials to help them return to Mexico. Because simple claims to citizenship were insufficient to receive help from the Mexican government, Chinese Mexican refugees began to press their cultural claims to belonging in Mexican society in order to spur the Mexican government into action. In doing so, "Chinese Mexicans pushed the boundaries of what it meant to be Mexican."[49] Antonio Lay Mazo helped lead the effort. A Chinese Mexican born in Sinaloa and raised in Taishan County, Guangdong Province, Lay Mazo began to write letters to President Adolfo López Mateos in 1959. His letters emphasized two main points. First, they stressed the Mexicanness of the community. He asserted, for example, that those who remained still did not speak Chinese and had little knowledge of Chinese customs. His second point, however, was that Chinese Mexicans were suffering as a result of New China and the policies of Mao Zedong.[50] According to Schiavone Camacho, "Cold War politics framed the intense nationalistic rhetoric and ideology they elaborated."[51] Lay Mazo "drew on the stories he heard from countrymen to appeal to the Mexican government to 'liberate' Mexicans from communist China, describing the hardships and persecution some had faced under the new regime."[52] This point appealed to López Mateos's internationalist impulse and his determination to use Mexico's independent foreign policy to make an impact on the Cold War. Thus, pressure from inside and outside Mexico led to the 1960 repatriation of the remaining Chinese Mexicans in China, Hong Kong, and Macau.[53]

Once in Mexico, the repatriates could speak to "the hardships that followed from the captivity they suffered in China" and help mobilize their community against the PRC. A booklet on the refugees, entitled *Chinos-Mexicanos cautivos del comunismo*, described itself as "a series of *testimonios* on the truth about Communism." For example, after his arrival in Mexico, Francisco Chong López harshly criticized the authorities of the PRC who he claimed "had enslaved [his] countrymen," and asserted that forced labor had contributed to his contraction of tuberculosis. Lay Mazo affirmed that those who remained in China were living in a "total hell," suffering under the rule of Mao Zedong, who had "experiment[ed] with millions of people, taking away their personality and dignity and snatching away their private property." Lay Mazo also attacked PRC agrarian collectivization, which he asserted had led to death from hunger and exhaustion. He described the small rations of food that were given to Chinese farmers, even to women and children. One of the repatriates stressed that, no matter the difficulty of the transition in Mexico, what mattered was that "we no longer suffer the nightmare of Communism that tormented us day and night. In Mexico there is freedom, and it's foolish to think that there are Mexicans who dream of being happy [if] Communism takes over our country. I want to talk to each and every one of them and tell them of the dangers of this harmful and oppressive doctrine." In a sharp reversal of Mexico's image during the anti-Chinese campaigns, Mexico now became the land of freedom and opportunity for Chinese Mexicans—a framing that required the whitewashing of the history of the anti-Chinese campaigns' restrictions and misfortune. Even though the repatriates also left Mexico under miserable conditions, none of the *testimonios* emphasized the anti-Chinese movement. Forgetting the past, they focused on the present, including Communism and the danger of association with the People's Republic of China.[54]

For Chinese Mexicans who were not displaced from the country during the 1930s, the repatriation allowed families to reunite and the community to grow. For those who welcomed their family members back to the country, however, the rationale for repatriation was as important as the repatriation itself. If Chinese Mexicans became Mexican in China, as Schiavone Camacho argues, their nationalism and repatriation also helped *paisanos* in Mexico achieve the acceptance they had been denied for much of their history in the country.[55] Far from a community of potential Chinese Communist subversives, *paisanos* portrayed themselves after repatriation as the group who had suffered the most under the excesses of the Communists and those who would work hardest to prevent Mexican recognition of the People's Republic of China.

THE CHINESE MEXICAN PILGRIMAGE TO THE BASÍLICA DE NUESTRA SEÑORA DE GUADALUPE

Like the repatriates, *paisanos* in Mexico also deployed Mexican religious and cultural imagery in their political messages. A major example is a cultural tradition, begun in 1958, that continues into the present: the annual Chinese Mexican pilgrimage to the Basílica de Nuestra Señora de Guadalupe. While on the surface a simple Catholic ceremony, the pilgrimage echoed themes presented by the repatriates concerning the Catholic devotion of the Chinese community in the country and of the dangers of Chinese Communism. Like the repatriation, it demonstrates how heartfelt expressions of Catholic identity and Mexican belonging could be used for strategic ends. Initially planned to challenge perceptions of the People's Republic of China, the tradition was embraced by Chinese Mexicans as a way to challenge stereotypes and present a respectable image of the community.

On the surface, the Chinese procession was similar to countless other pilgrimages carried out at the basilica. Its point of departure was, like

FIGURE 7. Chinese Mexicans march in Mexico City during the second annual pilgrimage to the Basílica de Nuestra Señora de Guadalupe. Photo courtesy Pilar Chen Chi.

other pilgrimages, the Glorieta de Peralvillo, just outside the center of Mexico City. Its destination was the Cerro de Tepeyac, three and a half kilometers away—the exact spot where, over four hundred years prior, an indigenous peasant by the name of Juan Diego had been graced with the holy presence of the Virgin. In total, the faithful numbered approximately seven hundred.[56] Walking along the Calzada de Guadalupe, they carried Mexican flags as well as banners displaying her image. (See figure 7.) Many of the banners carried a prayer in her honor: "Ave Maria Our Lady of Guadalupe, Queen of Mexico and Empress of the Americas, the Chinese community of Mexico City comes to kneel before Your Miraculous Image to express our gratitude and veneration for all the favors received, both in terms of health and well-being in this blessed land. May you always be worshipped for Your Grace and Blessing." Other worshippers carried signs in Chinese that expressed the message more concisely: "Mexico City Chinese Worship the Virgin María."[57]

While in many ways similar to other processions, the pilgrimage was strikingly different visually. Many of the women wore traditional *qipao* dresses. The Mexico City newspaper *El Universal* referred to the "beautiful and exotic costumes" and the "exotic sounds of the Chinese orchestra" during the 1960 pilgrimage. Some of the men carried a Chinese lion costume while others played traditional Chinese instruments on the way to the basilica. An account of the 1961 pilgrimage mentioned the "signs with symbolic inscriptions" carried by the pilgrims, referring to Chinese characters. But most notable was the annual presence of the staff of the embassy of the Republic of China, led by Ambassador Feng-Shan Ho and his wife, Shao-yun Hwang. Some newspaper reports on the pilgrimage identified him as the representative of the Chinese community in Mexico City. In addition to Mexican flags, moreover, some Chinese Mexicans carried ROC flags as well. Unsurprisingly, these visual differences meant that many more Mexicans paid attention. Ambassador Ho's estimate that "fifty thousand spectators" witnessed a lion dance performance just outside of the basilica is likely an exaggeration, but it underscores the fact that, on a Sunday at the basilica, the dances would have drawn the attention of hundreds if not thousands of Mexicans. After their performance, the ambassador led the pilgrims into the basilica, where they were seated in a special section. Twelve Chinese Mexican girls stood surrounding the altar.

The pilgrimage was a cooperative effort between the ROC embassy and the Chinese Mexican community. According to the ambassador's memoirs, shortly after arriving in the country, the ambassador realized that "Mexicans, including the Mexican-Chinese, are ardent Catholics," and he admitted he helped organize the pilgrimage "to strengthen cultural propaganda."[58] He believed that the faith of the Chinese community could be used to "deliver a sharp blow to Communist infiltration" in Mexico, particularly by emphasizing the persecution of fellow Catholics in mainland China after the advent of the PRC, as well as the government's nationalization of the Catholic Church.[59] While the church was being repressed in mainland China, it was becoming much more vocal in Mexico, speaking out against the evils of Communism, particularly after the success of the Cuban Revolution.[60] The conflict between the Vatican and the Chinese government likely explains why Mexican Catholic clergy so eagerly cooperated with Ambassador Ho and the pilgrims.

Rather than separating politics from religion during Mass, the pilgrimage served as an avenue to present the political views of the Chinese community and the Republic of China. The sermon argued for freedom of religion and freedom from religious persecution and incorporated anti-Communist slogans. Part of the service was given in Chinese.[61] The ambassador, who took the podium, "pleaded for the unity of the Catholics in China and Mexico, the promotion of the spirit of Christ, and the defeat of the common enemy," referring to

Communism. Countering the image the PRC wanted to promote as a friend of the peoples of the Third World, the pilgrimages to the basilica and the sermons delivered inside sought to paint a picture of New China as an aggressor—an enemy of free religious practice and a threat to global peace. Ambassador Ho even described the PRC as the "public enemy of humanity."[62]

At the same time, the pilgrimages sought to portray the Republic of China as a greater friend to the Mexican people. A central component of that friendship was its shared faith. Chiang Kai-shek and Soong May-ling (Madame Chiang Kai-shek) were both Methodists, and the number of Catholics on the island of Taiwan was quickly expanding—numbering about two hundred thousand by 1960. The ROC had a Catholic archbishop, Yu Bin, who was ardently anti-Communist and who moved his diocese to the island of Taiwan after the Communist takeover of the mainland.[63] During the 1963 pilgrimage, Ambassador Ho presented a flag of the Republic of China, which he asserted represented "the hearts of the Chinese people." He then thanked the Lord for "protecting the peace and happiness of Chinese Mexicans." With the Lord's help, asserted the ambassador, mainland China would emerge from its "sea of suffering."[64]

The Chinese community's annual pilgrimage to the basilica was powerful in part because of its status on the margins of both Chinese and Mexican society. Chinese Mexicans turned to one of the few institutions that Mexicans without wealth or power could reliably turn to: the Catholic Church. In this way, they demonstrated their powerlessness and humility as a way to win the hearts and minds of the Mexican people. Moreover, showcasing the Catholicism of the Chinese community was a way to dispel the notion of the Chinese as a potential fifth column and show that it was eager to join the global alliance against Communism. Through their religious devotion, the Chinese demonstrated their integration into Mexican society. Moreover, because the Virgin was considered Empress of the Americas, in showing their devotion they made the implicit argument that after decades on Mexican soil they were also people of the Americas—that the Mexicans' *virgencita* was their *virgencita* as well. (See figure 8.) Newspaper articles celebrated the faith of the Chinese community in Mexico and never questioned their devotion.

At the same time, other aspects of the pilgrimage displayed the pride that the Chinese community felt for the culture of their native country and made the argument that Chinese Mexicans had not completely

FIGURE 8. Chinese Mexicans clutch the flags of the Republic of China and Mexico as well as the banner of the Virgin of Guadalupe inside of the Basílica de Nuestra Señora de Guadalupe. Photo courtesy Pilar Chen Chi.

severed their ties to China. Presumably, the attire of the pilgrims—and the conscious decision to make the pilgrimage so visually different from most pilgrimages to the basilica—not only attracted the attention of city residents along the pilgrimage route and on Tepeyac Hill, but was a visual connection between the Chinese community in the city and those who the embassy argued were suffering on the mainland.[65] This visual connection put the faithful in a unique position to talk about the "two Chinas" problem, to pray for an end to the division of China and by extension for world peace.

The pilgrimages were also some of the first events to begin to build unity among different sectors of Chinese society, including first-generation *paisanos,* second-generation children, and returned refugees from Hong Kong and Macau in 1960. Women, the daughters of Chinese migrants, also made an appearance in the community ritual, challenging images of Chinese Mexican society as overwhelmingly male. Because of the participation of wider sectors of the community, the group grew year after year as other Chinese associations, some of them new ones, began to join the pilgrims, including the Chinese Catholic Association and the Mexico City Chinese Chamber of Commerce (Mojing Huaqiao

Shanghui).[66] Chinese Mexican youth also began to form lion-dancing troupes, which allowed them to preserve ancestral traditions.

As a result, the pilgrimages provided an annual activity in which Chinese Mexicans could speak for themselves and challenge established stereotypes of the Chinese as opium smokers and gamblers who self-segregated and resorted to violence over illicit activities. The pilgrimage presented an image of the community on the righteous path, of a community that had established deep roots in the country and had strong emotional bonds to Mexico and its people. Even as it may have begun as a response to international politics across the Pacific Ocean, it became an avenue for Chinese Mexicans to celebrate their Catholicism and their Mexicanness. It was also a striking example of using "television diplomacy" to reach audiences outside of Mexico City.[67] Each year, in addition to the thousands of Mexicans who lined the parade route to see the spectacle, the pilgrimage made headlines in Mexico City newspapers and was broadcast on television and in newsreels, thus ensuring a wide distribution and good press for the Chinese community. Images of the pilgrimage even circulated across the Pacific Ocean. A commemorative book that the Guomindang politician and ROC leader Chiang Ching-kuo sent to U.S. President John F. Kennedy included a photograph of "the Chinese Catholics in Mexico."[68] Thus, in addition to the importance that the pilgrimage had for international politics, the religious procession had a much deeper significance for the community.

THE ECONOMIC AND COMMERCIAL EXPOSITION OF THE PEOPLE'S REPUBLIC OF CHINA

The criticism of the PRC was much more pointed during the Economic and Commercial Exposition of the People's Republic of China, staged in Mexico City in December 1963. Despite the fact that Mexico and the PRC had few goods to trade, the ROC embassy was deeply worried about the exposition, for it believed it might lead to diplomatic relations. Indeed, the PRC had an ambitious agenda for the trade fair, one that went far beyond trade. Telling was the fact that it advertised the fair as far away as Santiago de Chile, some four thousand miles distant. A November 1963 ad in the Santiago daily El Mercurio displayed a solitary building with a Chinese architectural design and carrying the national emblem of the People's Republic of China. Flying both the PRC and Mexican flags, the building clearly evoked a future embassy for the PRC in Mexico, and by extension the establishment of diplomatic relations between Latin America and the PRC in the near future. The caption, in Chinese and Spanish, announced that the Economic and Commercial Exposition of the People's Republic of China was to open the following month in the Mexican capital.[69]

The advertisement in *El Mercurio* suggests that the 1963 trade fair not only was significant for the trade relationship between mainland China and Mexico, but also had wide political implications for the United States, the Republic of China, and Latin America. The PRC invested a large amount of personnel, time, and money in the exposition. It was the first exposition organized by the PRC in Latin America outside of Cuba and much larger than any the PRC had ever held in Havana. The display and sale of cultural products and artifacts were designed to win the support of everyday residents of the capital and to deemphasize the mainland's struggles since the establishment of New China. Ultimately, the trade fair was a part of the PRC's "silver bullet policy," designed to win quick recognition of the People's Republic of China. "The first phase was to buy goods, to entice with profit," Ambassador Ho wrote in his memoirs. "The second was to apply for opening a trade fair, in order to exchange delegations and establish a permanent trade relationship. The third phase was to shift from commerce to politics, the final purpose being to request diplomatic recognition."[70] Central leaders in the PRC were so confident about the initiative that they hoped to stage the trade fair in Chile and Brazil the following year.

The decision to hold the trade fair split the cabinet of president Adolfo López Mateos (1958–64). Secretary of Foreign Relations Manuel Tello and of Gobernación Gustavo Díaz Ordaz opposed the exposition.[71] Secretary of Industry and Commerce Raúl Salinas Lozano was enticed to support the exposition by a Chinese offer to purchase $6 million in surplus Mexican cotton as well as coffee and petroleum. He believed that, particularly after the Sino-Soviet split, Mexico could enter the large Chinese market.[72] Salinas Lozano was joined by influential ex-President Lázaro Cárdenas (1934–40) and labor leader Vicente Lombardo Toledano, who enthusiastically supported the trade fair for ideological reasons.

Ultimately President López Mateos was motivated by his own desire to see Mexico assume a leadership position in global affairs and reduce its economic dependency on the United States. While he did not want to jeopardize Mexico's relationship with the Republic of China or with the United States, the trade fair afforded Mexico the opportunity to display its self-proclaimed independence in international affairs, which depended upon "the friendship and respect of numerous countries" around the globe. For example, the president cooperated extensively with countries inside and outside Latin America on nuclear disarmament and nonproliferation. During the previous year, the president had visited four countries in Asia and five in Europe, seeking to strengthen Mexico's political and economic ties.[73] Even as he didn't mention the PRC by name, the trade exposition was López Mateos's opportunity to continue to diversify Mexico's economic and political relationships, to show that it was not beholden to U.S. policy in East Asia, and, by placing Mexico's desire for international peace above all others, to elevate himself to a leadership position capable of defusing Cold War tensions.[74]

At the same time, however, the López Mateos government feared the repercussions of openly embracing the People's Republic of China. Wary of embracing the PRC outright, it stipulated that only a private company could hold the fair. Official organizers Guillermo Nasser Quiñones, Carlos Villanueva, José Luis Ceceña, and their Committee for the Development of Sino-Mexican Economic Relations lent their name to the trade fair.[75] In reality, however, the fair was organized by workers from the PRC, who began arriving in June 1963.[76] The Mexican government also tried to limit its political exposure by denying the PRC an appropriate venue. Most foreign expositions were held at the large and prestigious Auditorio Nacional, but the administration prohibited the Auditorio and other large exposition venues from working with the committee. By forcing the committee to scramble for an exposition site, it likely wanted to force the exposition into a much smaller venue that would limit its exposure and the political fallout. The administration appeared to obtain its wish when initial reports surfaced about the committee selecting an abandoned tobacco factory in the San Juan de Letrán market, outside the historic center and the posh districts of the city, as the exposition site.[77]

The PRC group worked furiously to turn that factory—twenty-four hundred square meters—into a showcase of China's development in the fourteen years since the establishment of New China, into an example that Latin Americans nations would want to emulate. The PRC group employed approximately one hundred Mexican workers to remodel the exhibition site over the course of six months, spending approximately US$400,000 in the process. The facade of the building was made to look like Beijing's Imperial Palace in the Forbidden City.[78]

Despite the fact that Mexico wished to shed any political implications for the trade fair, PRC organizers primarily had political goals for the exposition. The PRC's goals, significantly, made little mention of trade between the two countries, but included "an appropriate display of Chinese socialism, especially its building the national economy; displaying the foreign policy orientation of China; allowing both peoples to increase their understanding of each other; . . . and encouraging Mexicans to increase their anti-imperialist consciousness."[79] It would display Chinese products in agriculture, heavy and light industry, textiles, handicrafts, and cultural products, though the embassy of the United Kingdom noted that the products were of inferior quality and generally not for sale. More important were large photographs along the walls depicting Chinese advancements after 1949. Many of the cultural items to be prominently displayed—modern literature, scientific advances, and films—also were not for sale and had little to do with trade. The PRC intended to complement these articles with several tons of propaganda and political treatises, including writings by Chairman Mao Zedong.[80] The exposition's program expressed the desire that it would "bring about the development of commercial and economic relations between China and Mexico, and similarly a growth in the friendship between the Chinese and Mexican peoples."[81]

This message was tailored specifically to the Mexican audience. Since Mexico and China both had long histories, it wished to bring ancient artifacts and handicrafts to show China's success at preserving its ancient history and culture. Identifying Mexico as a country whose economy was exploited by the United States, the PRC also sought to portray itself as a government whose trade policy encouraged equanimity and mutual benefit. Moreover, because Mexico had experienced its own problems with agrarian reform, the PRC wished to show the successes of Chinese agricultural collectivization. Specifically, "because corn is Mexico's most important grain, both in its history and in everyday life, and the one that Mexicans are most interested in, we plan to show our production process for corn and compare the production process at each stage with the Mexican corn production process."[82]

Advertisements for the exposition attempted to make a similar point in enticing Mexicans to attend the trade fair. In one large poster advertising the exposition, a large flag of the People's Republic of China flew in front of two large gears, symbolizing the country's industrial progress and prowess. The gears are complemented in the lowest register by stalks of maize, making reference to the PRC agrarian reform, collectivization, and its increasing ability to feed its own people. In the center of the poster, the Imperial Palace symbolized the current Communist regime and the government that had achieved advances in industrialization and farming. No matter who legally sponsored or organized the exposition, the poster made it clear that the exposition was driven solely by the People's Republic of China.[83]

Ambassador Ho understood the political aims of the PRC exposition and did his best to convince Mexican government officials and journalists of the political dangers of the trade fair. Ambassador Ho organized a press conference to make a simple argument: because the PRC had low levels of industrial production—its drive to ramp up industrialization during the Great Leap Forward had been a failure—it had few products to display and fewer products to trade with Mexico. As a result, the ambassador argued, the exposition "could only be a ruse of a political and ideological [nature] to succeed in the Communist infiltration of the Latin American continent."[84] His warnings before the Secretary of Foreign Relations grew darker, asserting that the PRC would use Mexico as a base for Communist infiltration and violent governmental overthrow of the rest of Latin America and implying that Mexican government officials would be responsible.[85]

By October 1, the National Day of the People's Republic of China, Ambassador Ho must have realized that he would be unable to put an end to the trade fair. That day, one of the trade delegates who had secured Secretary of Industry and Commerce Salinas Lozano's assent to the trade fair had returned to Mexico City and celebrated National Day with the Sociedad Mexicana de Amistad con China Popular and other prominent leftist organizations in the Mexican capital.[86] A few days later, the English ship *West Breeze* arrived at the Mexican port of Veracruz with 186 tons of materials for the exposition, including 10 tons of propaganda materials destined not only for Mexico but for much of Latin America.[87] The following month, the PRC announced purchases of Mexican cotton and wheat and announced that it would dispatch another delegation to Mexico to discuss trade.[88] Ambassador Ho explained to his superiors that the PRC's actions in Mexico, a repeat of the "silver-bullet policy" it enacted in Egypt in 1956, could lead to the establishment of trade and diplomatic relations with Mexico in the near future.[89]

Once it realized it could not stop the exposition, the ROC embassy began to mobilize the Chinese Mexican community, hoping to counter positive impressions of the exposition and to argue against diplomatic recognition of the PRC.[90] Near the ROC's National Day, it encouraged Chinese communities around the country to send a message to President Adolfo López Mateos expressing their opposition to the PRC trade fair.[91] This gesture marked the first time that Chinese immigrants on their own would write to the Spanish-language press, and the first time they would speak for themselves rather than relying on the embassy. Newspapers around the country published the letters on October 10. Most of the letters began by praising the Mexican president and people. The Unión Fraternal Asociación China in Ciudad Juárez, Chihuahua, in a letter signed by Horacio Chew and Luis Wong Keang, "recognize[d] [the president's] meritorious work and effort for peace." Under his command, wrote Arturo Lamshing, representing the Chinese community in Tapachula, Chiapas, the country "reach[ed] its patriotic greatness and the true democratic triumph of the Mexican Revolution." *Paisanos,* then, omitted the anti-Chinese campaigns and echoed the sentiment that, like the repatriates, they were much better off in Mexico than in China. The Chinese community in Tampico, Tamaulipas, represented by Filiberto Chew, expressed its appreciation to the president and the Mexican people "for the welcome that we have received during our time in Mexico, a country that we hold dear." The community in Mexico City expressed its appreciation "for living in and enjoying the hospitality of this great country where prosperity, tranquillity, and peace prevail."[92]

The second part of the letter compared their good fortune in Mexico with the trials their relatives were undergoing in mainland China. Like the Catholic pilgrims, these letter writers echoed the repatriates in presenting a rather negative image of mainland China under Mao Zedong. Mainland Chinese were, according to the Chinese association in Tampico, "governed by a regime that disavows high human values." On the mainland, affirmed the community in Mexico City, "our brothers . . . are suffering from slavery, hunger, and misery under the Communist regime." "[They are] suffering the misery and vexations of Communism," affirmed the community in Ciudad Juárez. To underscore their point, the community in Mexico City made mention of "the 282 Chinese-Mexican refugees which Your Excellency had the kindness to repatriate from Hong Kong and Macau, [who] are live witnesses to what we express."[93]

The last part of the letter denounced the trade exposition. The letter from Ciudad Juárez referred to it as "Communist infiltration disguised as a trade move." The association in Tampico described the PRC agents who organized the exposition as "countrymen who betray Mexican hospitality." The community in Tapachula asserted that the exposition, if allowed to proceed, would be a black mark on the president's otherwise brilliant record.[94] Even if the trade fair were allowed to continue, they hoped to influence Mexican public opinion enough that the Mexican government would refrain from moving closer to the PRC. Their announced intention to protest the exhibition likely had the same motivation.[95]

Ultimately, the letters from the Chinese community did not prevent the fair from opening as scheduled on December 7, 1963. Even more disheartening for the ROC, relations between the PRC and Mexico had grown startlingly close. When Ambassador Ho complained to Mexican officials about the convention's name and its use of PRC flags in the exhibition hall—the embassy argued that they would make the exhibition look like an official exposition of the PRC—exposition organizers simply ignored him. Even more disheartening for the Republic of China, high-level Mexican government officials participated in the opening of the exposition. The embassy had been assured just days before that the Mexican government would not participate.[96] Yet the day before the official inauguration, Mexican President Adolfo López Mateos toured the exposition site, declaring, "There is no doubt that these people have progressed. This exposition demonstrates it."[97] (See figure 9.) The following day, after a band played the national anthems of the People's Republic of China and Mexico, Secretary of Industry and Commerce Salinas Lozano cut the ribbon on the exposition, announcing that "Mexico proposes to increase trade with all countries independently of the ideologies they profess."[98] Before reporters, PRC organizers argued that the mainland's eight hundred million people represented "a big market" for Mexican surplus goods, and Mexican editorials asserted that "all of Mexico's economic problems are now solvable." The PRC's success at the exposition, warned Ambassador Ho, would put the Republic of China in a precarious position in Mexico.[99]

From the opening of the trade fair, the Mexican government's denials that the trade exhibition had political connotations were belied by the statements and actions of prominent political figures. On December 9, prominent leftist and former president Lázaro Cárdenas visited the exposition. The leader of the PRC delegation, Chang Kuang-tau, accompanied the former president in visiting every display. Cárdenas expressed his admiration for the objects displayed at the exhibition, and upon leaving he wrote in the guest book, "The Economic and Trade Exposition of the People's Republic of China is very significant and was organized very well, it objectively suggests the huge development in all areas of the People's Republic of China. . . . We admire the Chinese People's surprising effort to develop their country."[100] President López Mateos

La vieja China casi no tuvo industria pesada.
La Nueva China, despues de su fundacion,
aplicando una política de apoyo principalmente
en sus propias fuerzas, y despues de mas de
10 años de esfuerzos, ha creado una industria
pesada con una base apreciablemente poderosa
y con muchas ramas completas.

FIGURE 9. Mexican President Adolfo López Mateos (*center right*) tours the 1963 Economic and Commercial Exposition of the People's Republic of China. The text on the wall behind him contrasts "Old China" [the Republic of China], which had very little industrial development, with "New China" [the People's Republic of China], which through ten years of hard work developed heavy industry. Photo courtesy Fototeca Nacional INAH.

also wooed the delegation when he hosted them the following month, receiving a fine Chinese carpet and other luxurious gifts.[101] In contrast, Mexico's right wing continued to show discomfort with the trade exposition. The Secretary of Gobernación and future president, Gustavo Díaz Ordaz, left town for the opening ceremony and did not meet with Chang Kuang-tau.[102]

In response to the opening of the trade fair, the ambassador, in conjunction with local Chinese residents, conducted a public-relations campaign against the PRC. On December 7, during the opening ceremony of the exposition, the ambassador stood outside the exhibition hall and distributed articles and pictures documenting PRC atrocities on the mainland. The ambassador also shared the information with *La Extra del Domingo* and *Ovaciones*. On the same day, the Mexico City Overseas Chinese Anti-Communist National Salvation Association (Mojing Huaqiao Fangong Jiuguohui) published an open letter in the Mexico City daily *Excélsior* sharply criticizing the decision to continue with the exhibition. "Beware of the Bloody Hands of the Chinese Communists," warned the title. It dismissed the trade fair as merely a "pretext" for closer economic relations between Mexico and the PRC. The editorial went on to describe the PRC as a rogue state, as an aggressor to world peace and a nuclear threat. PRC policies, argued the letter, resulted in the death of approximately sixty-four million men and women, and twenty million alone from famine in 1961. Mexican visitors to the PRC trade exhibition, then, needed to remember the bloody history of mainland China: "[T]he products that are being exhibited [at the exhibition] . . . are nothing more than a personification of the tears, the blood and the flesh of the enslaved Chinese population. With this the Communists try to deceive the Mexican people, making [them] believe that the Chinese continent has happiness and prosperity" to encourage the improvement of relations between the two countries. Finally, the letter calls on "our Mexican friends" to be wary of the "venomous intrigue from the Chinese Communists." The editorial was surrounded with images of misery and death in mainland China, furnished by the ROC embassy. In addition to the editorial, the Anti-Communist National Salvation Association later sent private letters to various trade organizations and labor unions in the city.[103]

Meanwhile, Chinese Mexican youth stood in front of the entrance to the exposition and around the exposition site in San Juan de Letrán market to distribute the open letter to passersby. Their goal, on the day when the PRC sought to earn the friendship and trust of the Mexican people, was to "increase popular antipathy toward [the People's Republic of China.]"[104] Other youth sneaked into the exhibition site, writing graffiti on the guest book signed by President Cárdenas and other prominent leftists. "Overthrow the traitor Mao Zedong!" they scribbled. "Long live President Chiang [Kai-shek]! Long live freedom!" To help combat the pro-PRC propaganda that was freely distributed inside the exhibition hall, a group of Chinese Mexican youth sneaked inside the exposition and placed their own propaganda materials on small tables near the entrances and exits. By the time the organizers discovered the propaganda, wrote Ambassador Ho, visitors to the exhibition had already taken most of the pro-ROC flyers.[105] These actions certainly caught the attention of the exposition organizers. The PRC's own assessment of the exposition described the youth as "reactionary forces" who "continue[d] to cause trouble" and wanted to "prevent the influence of the exhibition."[106]

In addition, Chinese Mexicans granted interviews to local journalists in which they presented their views on the conditions in mainland China. Businessman Antonio Yon Chiem, for example, presented a rather negative image of "enslaved China" after 1949, including the persecution of Catholics and Catholic missionaries, the death of twenty million from famine, and the flight of refugees toward Hong Kong and Macau. He didn't have to mention the trade fair, since the article was published just one day after its inauguration.[107] Fernando Chi Kim and Luis Chan, interviewed at the Mexico City Chinese Chamber of Commerce (Mojing Huaqiao Shanghui), argued that trade between China and Mexico was unlikely and would serve only as a pretext for Communist infiltration into the country.[108]

Despite these interruptions, PRC organizers believed the 1963 Economic and Commercial Exposition of the People's Republic of China was largely successful. When the first few days of the exposition saw a low turnout, organizers agreed to extend it by an extra two weeks, increase publicity, and allow Mexicans to enter the exposition for free after Christmas.[109] In total, organizers estimated that the exposition drew an attendance of 230,000 over the course of the thirty-one days it was open. This included many Mexican leftists who, unable to visit the mainland, eagerly consumed evidence of economic progress in the People's Republic of China and extensively praised the Communist government in the guest book. Organizers estimated that 45,000 guests attended one of 362 film screenings, contributing to its deep political impact. Although the Mexican government denied the PRC permission for a trade office with diplomatic protection, exposition organizers believed they had laid the foundation for a future strengthening of relations between Mexico and the PRC.[110] The perceived success of the exposition led the PRC to attempt to stage it in other Latin American countries, including Chile, Brazil, and Peru.[111]

For the Mexican government, the exposition also achieved important objectives. The most immediate benefit was the PRC's purchase of excess Mexican goods totaling millions of U.S. dollars, and the potential to continue to sell to the expanding Chinese market.[112] At the same time, the exposition satisfied Mexican leftists as well as influential former president Lázaro Cárdenas. Finally, the Mexican government's restraint from throwing its full weight behind the exposition, as well as its refusal to establish a trade office or official commercial relations, or to allow any sign of strengthened relations with the PRC, appears to have satisfied the U.S. government. Ambassador Ho did speak with U.S. officials about the trade exposition, including U.S. Ambassador to Mexico Thomas Mann, but the latter simply suggested that President Johnson would address the matter in his next meeting with President López Mateos.[113] Johnson may not even have done that, since the Department of State's memorandum for the presidential visit suggests that it believed López Mateos never seriously considered recognizing the PRC. The State Department understood that the López Mateos administration granted the exposition to help mollify the left, especially Vicente Lombardo Toledano and Lázaro Cárdenas.[114] The memorandum asked President Johnson not to raise the issue during the meeting. If it was raised, Johnson "should let [López Mateos] know we are aware of his assurances."[115]

Rumors circulated for months after the exposition that Mexico would recognize the PRC. The López Mateos administration, however, put those rumors to rest. When Charles de Gaulle visited the Mexican capital the following year, just after France recognized the Communist government, Mexican President López Mateos announced that "during his administration Mexico would maintain relations solely with the Chinese Nationalists."[116] Expectations for Mexico to establish relations with the PRC would be further diminished during the administration of López Mateos's successor, the conservative Gustavo Díaz Ordaz (1964–70).[117]

While the PRC tried to capitalize on the success of its 1963 exposition in Mexico City, its efforts to strengthen its relationship with the rest of Latin America faced obstacles. For example, its hopes to replicate its trade exposition in Brazil would be dashed by Brazilian internal politics. The leftist administration of João Goulart granted the PRC permission to hold its trade fair in Brazil.[118] However, the April 1 coup that overthrew Goulart interrupted those plans. Shortly after the coup, Brazilian authorities arrested nine Chinese, including PRC workers in charge of planning the exposition and journalists from the New China News Agency (NCNA; Xinhuashe).[119] The Chinese were tried on charges of subversion and handed ten-year prison sentences, but expelled from the country the following year.[120]

On April 20, 1965, Feng-Shan Ho was notified that he would soon be recalled as ambassador to Mexico. The reasons for his recall are unclear; just a few months earlier Ho had been praised in the ROC press as "an outstanding ambassador to Mexico." In addition to negotiating a new trade agreement, signed September 25, 1964, the ambassador convinced new president Díaz Ordaz to nominate an ambassador to the Republic of China in 1965. According to Ho's memoirs, when he was recalled the ambassador was negotiating with Mexican authorities for the entry of Chinese immigrants, but his departure interrupted those plans.[121]

On June 20, the Guomindang in Mexico City organized a farewell reception for Ambassador Ho. The speeches from leaders of the Mexico City Chinese community were full of praise. "He has maintained the honor of our country, he has contributed to the welfare of the community, he has promoted Chinese culture, he has organized the youth of our community, and he has confronted the Communists in a bitter struggle," asserted a Chinese Mexican leader. The ambassador, referencing his struggles in Egypt and Mexico, believed that his efforts had made the Republic of China stronger. "The objective of the Communists to establish diplomatic relations has failed," he asserted. "This is a great victory in diplomacy."[122]

CONCLUSION

Ambassador Feng-Shan Ho helped bolster the position of the Republic of China in Mexico by preventing Communist infiltration in the country and arresting the improving relationship between the People's Republic of China and Mexico. Having already witnessed the establishment of relations between the PRC and Egypt in 1956, the ambassador worked with officials from the Mexican Secretaría of Foreign Relations to block the entry of "Communist infiltrators" who could serve as emissaries for the PRC, ranging from scientific groups to cultural performers. Moreover, through the pilgrimages to the Basilica of Guadalupe as well as the repatriation of Chinese Mexicans, the ambassador was able to present a different image of the PRC—one of a despotic regime that persecuted mainland Chinese.

Unable on his own to prevent an improvement in relations between Mexico and the PRC, Ambassador Ho relied on the Chinese community to campaign actively on behalf of the ROC. Even if the ambassador could prevent representatives of the PRC from entering the country, the PRC continued to receive favorable media coverage in Mexico, and pro-PRC groups persisted in promoting the image of the Communist government. Although there were few Chinese left in the country, their long history in Mexico and their position between Mexican and Chinese society made them ideal interlocutors for the anti-Communist message of the Republic of China. Ambassador Ho made effective use of the

Mexican media to amplify their message, spreading awareness of their declarations and marches to everyday Mexicans. When combined, their efforts were effective at delaying Mexican recognition of the PRC.

The Chinese community in Mexico, however, was not simply a tool that the embassy could use for political purposes. The embassy's activities, in addition to serving as public diplomacy, also improved the image of Chinese Mexicans. They brought disparate sectors of Chinese Mexican society together and for the first time allowed them to present a positive image of themselves. Whereas newspaper reports had previously described them as opium-addicted illegal immigrants who supported the Chinese Communists, their public activities portrayed them as pious and upstanding Catholic Mexicans. During the pilgrimages, they prayed for the mainland Chinese masses they said were suffering under the excesses of Chairman Mao, especially after the repatriation of Chinese Mexicans in 1960. Chinese Mexicans marshaled this negative image of the PRC as they protested the 1963 Economic and Commercial Exposition of the People's Republic of China, arguing that a diplomatic recognition of the PRC would negatively impact their community.

The activities planned by Ambassador Ho also afforded the community the opportunity to proudly display elements of its Chinese heritage while at the same time demonstrating adaptation to local society and laying claim to a sense of belonging to local communities. The situation of the Chinese community in Mexico, then, presents a sharp contrast with that of the Chinese community in the United States. Chinese Mexicans did not seek political participation in Mexican politics, both because the Mexican political system was relatively closed and because their numbers were too small to represent a significant political force, even in local elections. In contrast, these events of public diplomacy allowed Chinese Mexicans to make an impact far beyond their numbers, and to make claims to Mexicanness that were respected. When the Chinese community made its annual pilgrimage to the Basílica de Nuestra Señora de Guadalupe, newspaper accounts did not attack the Chinese for being too foreign, nor did they mock the Mexicanness of the longtime residents of the country. Furthermore, as Chinese Mexicans protested the 1963 Economic and Commercial Exposition, journalists did not attack them as foreigners meddling in Mexican affairs. This treatment of the Chinese community suggests that, in the course of the thirty years since the anti-Chinese movement, public hatred and suspicion of the Chinese Mexicans had virtually disappeared, and Mexican society was more willing to accept them as part of the Mexican nation.

Not all Chinese Mexicans were willing to collaborate with the ROC embassy, however. As chapter 5 will demonstrate, as the Cold War dragged on, a growing minority of Chinese Mexicans vocally questioned their ties to the Republic of China. Because having the support of Chinese Mexicans was so important to the ROC's diplomatic mission during the Cold War, the ROC embassy sought to punish and silence anyone who diverged from the embassy's official propaganda.

CHAPTER 5

The Cold War Comes to Chinatown

Chinese Mexicans Caught between
Beijing and Taipei, 1955–1971

After 1949, two governments claimed not only the exclusive right to rule mainland China but also the allegiance of Chinese diasporic communities around the world. Throughout the Cold War, the Republic of China (ROC) and the People's Republic of China (PRC) openly competed for the loyalty of Chinese communities, often dividing them between those who supported the Beijing and Taipei governments. The rivalry between the two governments had a profound impact on Chinese communities, since it had the "power to define and shape who they [were] as Chinese subjects . . . . [I]t involve[d] debates about ideology, Chinese history, modernity, cultural authenticity, and identity."[1] Try as they might, Chinese could not avoid these kinds of divisive conflicts, since they were caught in the politics of the East Asian Cold War regardless of citizenship or cultural attachment. As "their Chinese ethnicity link[ed] them to China culturally, historically, and sometimes even politically," so, too, were they associated with Chinese Communism after 1949.[2]

In this context, Mexico's small but influential Chinese community came under substantial scrutiny during the Cold War, particularly after the People's Republic of China began to seek closer ties to Mexico and Mexican diplomatic recognition. In the aftermath of the December 1963 Economic and Commercial Exposition of the People's Republic of China, hosted by the PRC in Mexico City, the attitudes of Chinese Mexicans toward Chinese Communism attracted international attention. Government reports and newspaper articles in the United States began to present Latin America, and in particular Mexico, as a likely point of Communist subversion and a weak link in the Cold War. In particular, the existence of a Chinese community of dubious loyalty at the doorstep of the United States became a matter of grave concern not only to both Chinese governments but also to those of the United States and Mexico. This concern materialized even though by the mid-1960s there were perhaps only five thousand *paisanos* left in the country, most of whom were quickly dying off from old age.

During the Cold War, the relationship between Chinese Mexicans and the ROC, the PRC, and Mexico were in flux, and questions of political loyalty and allegiance intersected with questions of belonging and citizenship. The relationship between the Republic of China and Chinese Mexicans was forged during the 1910s, as it began to consolidate its hold over much of mainland China, including Guangdong Province. But the retrocession of the same government to the island of Taiwan—away from the province most Chinese Mexicans still considered "home"—forced the community to confront new geopolitical realities.[3] This process of redefinition continued throughout the Cold War as the Republic of China failed to complete its promised invasion of mainland China and "its very legitimacy in the eyes of both the overseas Chinese and the outside world was called into question."[4]

A clear example of the ROC's predicament may be found in an article from the Mexico City English-language daily *The News*, which asked four individuals if the People's Republic of China should be admitted into the United Nations. Luis Fong, identified in the article as a "Chinese-born Mexican," affirmed the difficulties that Chinese Mexicans had in envisioning the government on Taiwan as their government. "To us Canton [Guangdong] is the heart of China," he answered. "I would like to see China in the United Nations, but not the China we have now. The China that was a republic under Sun Yat Sen. To us Formosa [Taiwan] is not China. It is just an island." Although Fong does not express Communist sympathies, he notes how difficult it was for Chinese Mexicans to support a government that governed "just an island" and no longer had any connection with the migrants' home communities. His response demonstrates that the longer that the government of the ROC spent in Taiwan, the more difficult it was for some Chinese Mexicans to envision the Nationalists as the legitimate government of China. Yet not everyone agreed with his views; the article drew quick and sharp condemnation from four Chinese associations in the capital, dismissing Fong as an ignorant waiter at Restaurant Luau, "known neither in the field of Chinese studies nor in anything related to China," who could thus not represent "[any] of the sections of either the Mexican community or the Chinese community in Mexico."[5] The denunciation of Fong's views demonstrates that, to some Chinese residents and diplomats, not all transnational attachments to China were viewed in a positive light. In fact, during the Cold War some attachments to mainland China were increasingly seen as liabilities, and the ROC thus sought to discourage such ties as much as possible. Once the People's Republic of China exercised control over mainland China, the ROC discouraged any contact with the Communist government or travel to ancestral lands. This took place just as the PRC began to make contact with Chinese communities around the world in hopes of securing their political allegiance.

These questions grew more pressing as *paisanos* grew older and as their separation from mainland China lengthened. Their attitudes toward the Republic of China and the People's Republic of China changed. A large share held firm in their support of the Republic of China and, under the encouragement of the ROC government, continued to donate to the Nationalist government and the Guomindang, and visited "China" on Taiwan; as they heard reports of the Nationalists' progress in Taiwan, and of the Communists' struggles on the mainland, they kept hope alive that the ROC would one day retake mainland China. Others longed for their home villages and decided to visit their relatives in Guangdong Province while they still could, violating the ROC prohibition on travel to the mainland. During the Cold War, they used Mexican passports to travel to Hong Kong, from where they surreptitiously entered Guangdong Province. Still others praised the People's Republic of China, angering the ROC embassy. When attacked, some *paisanos* made reference to their Mexicanness to argue that they were far from being Communist sympathizers, and many began to feel a sense of belonging both to their home villages and to their local communities of settlement. In the face of social and political forces in both East Asia and North America that placed them under scrutiny, Chinese Mexicans increasingly asserted their willingness to define themselves.

Yet Chinese Mexican attempts at self-definition unleashed the fury of the embassy of the Republic of China in Mexico, undercutting the efforts of Chinese Mexicans to maintain dual loyalties to both Mexico and China and exposing the perils of sustained ties with the ROC. Regardless of their actual ideological orientation, during the 1960s the embassy labeled any Chinese Mexican brave enough to speak out against the Nationalist government a "Communist sympathizer," and shared intelligence on any such individuals with a Mexican national security agency, the Dirección Federal de Seguridad (DFS), with the Federal Bureau of Investigation (FBI), and with journalists on both sides of the U.S.–Mexico border. Moreover, it requested the authority to deny Chinese Mexicans the travel documents necessary to return to mainland China, even if they were Mexican citizens. In a reversal of its position during the anti-Chinese campaigns, it was even pleased when the Mexican government implicitly threatened pro-PRC Chinese Mexicans with deportation if they continued to engage in political activities. Altogether, these initiatives demonstrated the embassy's willingness during the late 1950s and 1960s to intervene in the daily lives of Chinese Mexicans, be they of Mexican or Chinese citizenship. Moreover, even as the ROC continued to claim that one of its most important roles was to protect the Chinese residents in the country, its pressure on Chinese Mexicans to follow the ideological line espoused by the Nationalist government put the community under great strain.

This pressure stemmed from the fact that the Republic of China depended on the ability of Chinese Mexicans to influence Mexican public opinion, particularly since the ROC feared losing its United Nations seat. But the ranks of those opposed to the ROC was growing. While a few were suspected of collaborating with Communist front organizations in Mexico, many others were what the embassy considered "fence sitters"—wary of the Communists, but exasperated with the Nationalists and tired of being separated from family members in their home villages. This latter group increasingly questioned the ideology put forth by the ROC embassy, and as a result became less willing to participate in ROC diplomatic activities. The embassy believed that dissenting voices among the community dulled the influence of pro-ROC Chinese Mexicans, prompting its response.

Thousands of miles from East Asia, the Cold War demonstrated the potential to disrupt the daily lives of ordinary Chinese Mexicans—what Greg Grandin referred to as the "politicization and internationalization of everyday life and familiar encounters."[6] In Canada and the United States, the Guomindang and the Chinese diplomatic corps monitored and intimidated Chinese who they believed were growing too friendly toward the PRC.[7] In Mexico a similar dynamic took hold. For expressing their opinion on international politics or for traveling to mainland China, a small group of *paisanos* and their children were condemned as Communists and saw their reputations tarnished inside and outside of Mexico. Although the first reports on pro-PRC Chinese emerged in

1955, the ROC embassy was not concerned about them until 1963, when it believed that the Mexican government might extend recognition to the People's Republic of China. Once it feared that the Chinese Communists sought "to cause the trust of Chinese Mexicans toward our government to waver," it sought to silence dissenting voices, as well as regain the community's trust and support.[8]

CHINESE MEXICAN COMMUNITIES DURING THE EARLY COLD WAR

During the 1950s, the ROC, Mexican, and U.S. governments largely ignored initial contacts between Chinese Mexicans and the People's Republic of China. The lack of concern had three causes. First, the People's Republic of China was slow to establish contact with *paisanos* and their children, and demonstrated a misunderstanding of Chinese Mexican history and community needs. Second, those who sympathized with the People's Republic of China were a small minority, and during the 1950s were largely ignored by pro-ROC Chinese. Third, and most important, between 1949 and 1963 the embassy of the Republic of China believed that Mexico would not recognize the People's Republic of China, no matter what the PRC or Chinese Mexicans did. Largely ignored by the ROC diplomatic corps in this period, Chinese Mexicans had more freedom to explore alternative forms of belonging. Some Chinese Mexicans began to claim belonging to their Mexican communities, even if they remained loyal to the ROC. Some demonstrated early support for the PRC, participating in Mexican Communist organizations and celebrating the National Day of the PRC, but no action was taken against them.[9] Nor did the ROC try to prevent small numbers of Chinese from traveling to mainland China in this period. Although ROC ambassadors to Mexico before 1963 recognized the potential threat, they were not yet alarmed by the left-leaning politics of some Chinese Mexicans.

During the Cold War, contact between the government of the Republic of China and Chinese Mexican communities, especially those in the countryside, suffered a marked decline. As noted in chapter 4, once the Communists took over mainland China, the ROC permanently closed its consulates in the Mexican cities of Tapachula, Mazatlán, and Tampico. One measure of the ROC embassy's lack of knowledge of the outside communities was the fact that it no longer had a reliable estimate of the number of Chinese in the country. In 1942, the Ministry of Foreign Affairs estimated 12,500 Chinese Mexicans, based upon its constant contact with Chinese communities in that period. Yet because Mexican immigration law made it difficult for new Chinese migrants to enter the country, as Chinese Mexicans passed away of old age and illness the population gradually declined. During his tenure, Ambassador Feng-Shan Ho estimated "eight or nine thousand" Chinese—in their majority, men.[10] Toward the end of his tenure, however, the embassy confessed that it had no "actual reliable number" of Chinese in the country, and chose instead to rely on the 1960 Mexican census as the most accurate estimate. That census counted 4,492 Chinese men and 593 Chinese women, nearly half of whom lived in either Baja California, Tamaulipas, or the Federal District of Mexico City.[11] The census results give an idea of how much the community's population had declined during the 1950s and 1960s. Although the Mexican census results do not account for Mexican citizens of Chinese descent, including Chinese migrants who adopted Mexican citizenship and Chinese Mexican children, the ROC embassy continued to consider the latter groups as Chinese, and thus under its informal jurisdiction.

Around the world, the competition for hearts and minds among Chinese communities called attention to the marginality and vulnerability of these communities within their places of settlement. At the outset of the Cold War, "every Chinese was suspected of being a communist, or at least a sympathizer, whose loyalty could never be trusted."[12] To outside observers, "the diaspora's cultural, linguistic, and familial ties to China [. . .] raised alarm about the loyalties of the overseas Chinese in the 1950s."[13] In the United States, fear that the rise of Communist China might lead to the internment of Chinese Americans led sociologists like Rose Hum Lee and Francis L. K. Hsu to call for abandoning Chinese citizenship and assimilating to American culture.[14] In Thailand, the Cold War similarly "created an overarching atmosphere of suspicion" of local Chinese.[15] In Panama, concerns about the rise of China led to a "reevaluation of Chinese belonging in the nation."[16]

In Mexico, these fears presented themselves early on: in September 1951, when the Chinese community in Mexicali sent a panicked telegram to central authorities of the Guomindang in Taipei. Members of the community had heard a rumor that Chinese business owners along the U.S.–Mexico border would be resettled in concentration camps. Although Mexicali Chinese professed loyalty to President Chiang and to anti-Communism, "Communist sympathizers are also Chinese and [we] deeply fear that foreigners will not be able to distinguish good [Chinese] from bad."[17] Although they did not mention it in their telegram, Mexicali

Chinese likely feared a reprisal of the concentration of Japanese nationals in Baja California during the Second World War, which destroyed Japanese lives and businesses along the U.S.–Mexico border. Central authorities briefly considered issuing identification cards to party members, which they thought would distinguish them from Communists and thus spare loyal Chinese from harm.[18] The ROC embassy later claimed it was a simple "misunderstanding" that Chinese Mexicans were taken for Communist sympathizers, and insisted that after the embassy intervened, internment of Chinese Mexicans never again surfaced as an issue.[19]

Even after the threat of internment subsided, Chinese Mexicans must have been aware that during early Cold War, Mexico was hostile to foreign ideas and wary of foreign-born people, particularly those connected to the Communist world. The government used the Law of Social Dissolution "to imprison anyone convicted of endorsing 'foreign ideas' that led to 'rebellion, sedition, riot, or insurrection.'"[20] Moreover, it routinely blamed unrest against the ruling party—notably during the 1956, 1958, and 1968 student movements—on *manos extrañas,* or foreign agents.[21] *Paisanos* and their children surely understood that political action, particularly in favor of the People's Republic of China, risked being seen as foreign subversion, particularly since many members of the community were foreign born.

After the withdrawal of the consulates in the late forties, many Chinese Mexicans began to reevaluate their relationship to Mexico and China. Documents written by Chinese Mexicans in the forties, written in Chinese, stressed the community's loyalty to the government of Chiang Kai-shek. Yet the first book published by the community in Spanish, entitled *La honorable colonia china en la república mexicana,* instead highlighted the community's local ties. It presented the Chinese community as exemplary neighbors and loyal citizens who had contributed to the development of Mexico by starting Mexican businesses and families. In contrast to earlier depictions of Chinese migrants that disparaged them as gamblers and opium smokers, *La honorable colonia china* presented *paisanos* as hardworking businessmen and farmers. Salvador Wong Kam, for example, managed shoe and candy factories in Hermosillo, Sonora, before moving to Mexicali, Baja California, and establishing a general store. Juan G. Wong, of Torreón, Coahuila, was a farmer before establishing the "La Bonanza" general store.[22] Clearly written for other Mexicans, the introduction expresses hope "that in a not so distant future we Mexicans will . . . grant them the place they deserve . . . in the conglomeration of our great nation."[23]

The book was a short history of *paisanos* around the country and their associations, giving brief life histories and providing an account of their political and charitable activities. A result of the cooperation of *paisanos* in sixteen states and Mexico City, it included both Guomindang members, who would have been most supportive of the ROC, and Min Zhi Dang[24] members, who would have been more skeptical. It distanced the Chinese Mexican community from associations with Chinese Communism and mentions few Chinese government officials or diplomats. It provided the names of individual migrants in Spanish, not in Chinese. Moreover, despite being published just after the ROC's National Day in 1957, it was dedicated to Mexican President Adolfo Ruiz Cortines, "for his outstanding and fruitful work benefiting the great Mexican nation."[25]

The Chinese presented in this directory had not abandoned their ties to China and Chinese associations, but, more than in Chinese-language directories, also expressed pride in having set down roots in Mexican cities and towns. Migrants described their activities with the Guomindang and Min Zhi Dang, and the directory published photos of Chinese associations celebrating the National Day of the Republic of China. But rather than emphasize these activities, as Chinese Mexicans had done in Chinese-language directories, descriptions in this directory focused on what the Chinese associations had done for the benefit of Mexican communities, making the argument that they were good residents and neighbors. The Chinese Association in Mexicali, Baja California, for example, donated 12,000 pesos for the construction of public housing. Chinese in Huixtla, Chiapas, helped provide funds for the construction of the local city hall and hospital. In Casas Grandes, Chihuahua, Chinese residents each gave several thousand pesos for the construction of local roads. Chinese across the state of Yucatán contributed to the O'Horán hospital in Mérida.[26] Moreover, individual Chinese around the country participated in local civic organizations including local chambers of commerce, the Rotary Club, the Lions Club, and especially the Red Cross.

Claims to Mexicanness are nuanced. In the book, there is no use of the term "Chinese Mexicans," though it notes that the document concerns "persons of Chinese descent." But the Chinese Chamber of Commerce in Mexico City (Mojing Huaqiao Shanghui) expressed its willingness to cooperate with local civil and military authorities "to achieve a better Mexico." The Chinese association in Manzanillo, Colima, noted that each year it celebrated the National Day of the ROC but also was swept up in the "widespread joy" during Mexican Independence Day celebrations, while the Chinese association in Mexicali described itself as loyal and patriotic.[27] Others gave witness to the long time they had spent in the country and their efforts to help develop their communities. Luis L. Siam, for example, had been a resident of Mexicali for nearly twenty-nine years, had been president of the city's Chinese association for fourteen, and described himself as an ally of local civil and military authorities. Jim Woo Bunping had lived in Mexicali for over forty years. Before his death in 1952, he had helped build a school in the city.[28]

Others claimed rootedness in the country by talking about the families they had created in Mexico. Like many other documents from Chinese Mexicans in this period, *La honorable colonia china en la república mexicana* contains biographical information only on men.[29] Many profiles, however, proudly listed the names of the men's Mexican wives and children, and some include family photographs. Their presence is notable, since women and children normally went unmentioned in Chinese-language directories. Juan Ham Lai of Mexico City, shown with his wife, Paula Chande de Ham, was proud of the fact that the oldest of his four children attended university. José Ham of Campeche was similarly photographed with his wife, Rosalia Gunam de Ham, and their six children, emphasizing that he wished to "make of [his children] useful beings to the Community in which they live."[30] Through their community and family connections, *paisanos* were actively involved in the prosperity of their local communities, and by extension of the country at large. They may not have claimed Mexicanness outright, but they were clearly invested in Mexico as a place where they spent their lives and raised their families.

Despite initial apprehensions on the part of Chinese Mexicans that the Cold War would quickly and negatively impact them, they were largely left alone for nearly a decade after the foundation of the People's Republic of China. While the ROC downsized its presence in the country, the PRC took several years to come into contact with Chinese communities in Latin America, and the latter's interactions were characterized by missteps and misunderstandings.[31] For example, unlike the ROC, which developed an intimate relationship with Chinese Mexican communities during the anti-Chinese campaigns, the PRC seemed unaware of past anti-Chinese violence. In 1952, Zhong Renjin, a former resident of Ahome, Sinaloa, wrote the PRC's Ministry of Foreign Affairs concerning the 1930s anti-Chinese campaigns. He complained that the embassy of the ROC in Mexico had done nothing to seek redress for past abuses, and asked the PRC to be an effective representative for Chinese in the country. The letter was transmitted to the PRC's Overseas Chinese Affairs Committee but did not inspire any further action.[32] Even as late as 1960, when Mexican government representatives hoped to obtain permission to enter Guangdong Province to repatriate Chinese Mexican refugees there, the PRC Ministry of Foreign Affairs confessed it still had no knowledge of the anti-Chinese campaigns, and was not aware "of the number of Mexicans in China or whether there were Mexicans in China or their political situation." The ministry recommended asking returned Chinese (*guiqiao*) from Mexico about the community's history, but for the moment denied the representatives' request to enter mainland China.[33] Moreover, like the ROC, it initially produced audiovisual material in Mandarin and as a result was unable to reach the Cantonese- and Spanish-speaking Chinese Mexican population.[34]

A small number of Chinese Mexicans demonstrated early support for the People's Republic of China, but these Chinese were initially not considered threatening or subversive. The first indications of pro-PRC Chinese emerged in 1955, when a Spanish-language newspaper published a report on conflicts between pro-PRC and pro-ROC Chinese in Mexico. The article paid particular attention to Francisco Ham Cheem Jr. (Tan Xuanpan).[35] After visiting the People's Republic of China, Ham Cheem Jr. began to spread propaganda for the PRC, and celebrated the PRC's National Day with the Mexican Sociedad Mexicana de Amistad con China Popular (SMACP). As the SMACP pressured the Mexican government to establish relations with the People's Republic of China, it naturally would welcome the presence of Ham Cheem Jr. and other left-leaning Chinese Mexicans. According to reports, Ham Cheem Jr. even attempted to organize a Mexican chapter of the Chinese Communist Party.[36]

Soon reports began to emerge on other dissident Chinese Mexicans. Fernando Chi Wi Ling (Zhu Huaniao) was taken into custody in December of the same year and charged with embezzling 30,000 pesos. An exposé on Chi published in *Últimas Noticias de Excélsior* shortly after his arrest accused him of heading a secret Chinese Communist organization. The report alleged that Chi headed a group of "addicts of opium, gambling, and Mao Tse Tung," a "commune" pervading the entire Chinese Mexican community, obligating them, after they had allegedly entered the country illegally, to contribute to the Communist cause.[37] The article was troubling because its description of the Chinese community in Mexico was a reprise of anti-Chinese propaganda disseminated during the 1930s, with anti-Communist rhetoric included almost as an afterthought. The objective of the sensationalist article was to increase suspicion of the Chinese community and cast them as "pernicious foreigners" capable of corrupting Mexican society during the Cold War. According to the embassy, after Chi's arrest Mexico City newspapers published many similar articles on the Communist threat posed by the Chinese community in the country.[38]

Although the journalist reporting on Chi's arrest likely took some liberties in his report, later investigation showed that it was based in part on factual evidence. An ROC embassy report confirmed Chi as the leader of the "Chinese Communist Party" in Mexico. Chi helped distribute Communist propaganda and screened pro-PRC films at his café to help celebrate the country's National Day. Moreover, "[Chi] and others receive[d] the support of Mexican Communists as well as commands from high levels [of the Communist Party of Mexico]."[39] Some reports maintained that Chi was bailed out by prominent Mexican leftist Vicente Lombardo Toledano.[40] The embassy was further distressed by reports that the arrests of Ham Cheem Jr. and Chi Wi Ling, both former members of the Min Zhi Dang, had been instigated by the Guomindang. In other words, the Cold War allowed for *paisanos* to find new meaning in old rivalries. Although the Guomindang denied the report, the embassy considered the rumor serious enough to bring both leaders in to the embassy and encourage them to find a way to coexist.[41]

Extant sources do not permit a general profile of Chinese Mexicans sympathetic to the People's Republic of China. They appear, for example, not to have left any written documents or testimonials. From what is written about them, it appears that ideologically committed Communists were few. In contrast to Spanish-language articles, most embassy and Chinese Mexican reports before 1963 make clear that individuals like Ham Cheem Jr. and Chi Wi Ling were exceptions, and that the Chinese community was overwhelmingly loyal to the government of the ROC. One observer, *paisano* Huang Yibin, dismissed those who celebrated the PRC's National Day as "old ignorant Chinese beggars" who had been bribed to come to the celebrations and take pictures.[42] Despite such a characterization, those Chinese had reasons to distance themselves from the ROC. Over the course of the twentieth century, some had become disgusted with the corruption of the Republic of China and saw the People's Republic of China as an alternative. Others marveled at the political and economic advances that China was undergoing under the rule of Mao Zedong, which would have benefited their family members in Guangdong Province. Although most Chinese Mexicans remained committed to the Republic of China, opting to preserve the bond they had formed during the anti-Chinese campaigns, there were ample reasons to rethink this alliance during the Cold War.

While the embassy could have sought out and punished Chinese Mexicans who associated with Communist organizations, it doubted the potential for individual Chinese to engage in subversion. It initially believed that Spanish-language newspapers were merely offering sensational articles to red-scared Mexicans: "Spanish newspapers have exaggerated the other side's strength," wrote the embassy, which asserted that most Chinese Mexicans simply ignored Ham Cheem Jr. and his Communist Party. Moreover, the embassy assured the Ministry of Foreign Affairs that despite Ham Cheem Jr.'s efforts, his attempt to change Mexican foreign policy was "currently impossible."[43] The embassy's relationship to Chinese Mexicans was thus predicated on the international situation. In other words, because it believed that Mexico was unlikely to recognize the People's Republic of China, it did not see a reason to persecute individuals like Ham Cheem Jr. and Chi Wi Ling, who the embassy believed were at any rate going to fail.

Instead of prosecuting dissident Chinese Mexicans, then, the embassy sought to use voices from loyal Chinese Mexicans to drown them out. It asked Chinese Mexicans to write editorials in favor of continued recognition of the ROC (see chapter 4). Moreover, because some Chinese attended a 1955 celebration of the PRC's National Day, it encouraged the Chinese community to throw an even larger celebration for the ROC's National Day. "To encourage the full expression of overseas Chinese loyal patriotism," the embassy "specially mobilized every overseas Chinese organization to prepare for an expanded celebration on the afternoon of [October] tenth." Nearly a thousand Chinese, claimed the embassy, attended the event. The audience received Chinese- and Spanish-language materials that editorialized against the Communist incursion into Mexico. At an evening reception for Chinese Mexican leaders, Ambassador Feng warned the community to guard more strictly against propaganda from the People's Republic of China.[44]

During the 1950s and early 1960s, the ROC embassy dismissed articles on Chinese Mexican Communists, and even pushed for their retraction. A series of articles published during Ambassador Ho's tenure in *Últimas Noticias de Excélsior* made damaging allegations against Chinese Mexican individuals, and slandered the entire community. First, alleged the series, secretive Chinese organizations known as "tongs" were fighting over profits from illegal casinos, the smuggling of Chinese immigrants into the country, and the trade in narcotics. In violence reminiscent of the Tong Wars (see chapter 1), the article alleged, a dead Chinese was found on Calle Dolores, in Mexico City's Chinese neighborhood. Second, the articles alleged that Chinese made use of the immigration papers of deceased Chinese to allow new Chinese immigrants to enter the country—a tactic referred to as "transmigration." The articles implied that it was not possible to know how many dangerous, drug-smuggling, potentially violent Chinese lived in the country. After the intervention from the embassy, however, *Últimas Noticias de Excélsior* published a full retraction in which it admitted that the allegations were "completely inconsistent with the truth." The retraction further asserted that no "tong" existed in Mexico, and that "transmigration" was absurd and would be impossible to carry out in practice. Finally, it extolled the virtues of Chinese Mexicans, who loved Mexico as much as their countrymen, and declared that criminal Chinese in no way reflected on the larger group as a whole. Ambassador He noted that Chinese Mexicans "rejoiced" when they read the retraction, believing that it restored their sullied reputations.[45]

The fact that only a few years later the embassy would become so preoccupied with suspected Communist sympathizers is thus surprising. Only four years after the embassy asked for a retraction of the *Últimas Noticias de Excélsior* articles, the ROC embassy built a close relationship with members of the U.S. and Mexican news media and would make use of sensationalist articles to tarnish the reputations of Chinese Mexicans who were perceived to be disloyal. This reversal indicates the extent to which the embassy feared losing Mexican diplomatic recognition, as well as its fear of the impact the words and actions of any one Chinese Mexican could have on its relationship with the country.

A "PEIPING SPY RING"

In the aftermath of the 1963 Economic and Commercial Exposition of the People's Republic of China (see chapter 4), journalists and government agencies in the United States began for the first time to report on Chinese Communist activities south of the U.S.–Mexico border. Most immediately, they speculated as to whether the exposition implied that the Mexican government would soon establish diplomatic relations with the PRC. Other reports went further, focusing on the Mexico City branch of the New China News Agency (NCNA; *Xinhuashe*). Established during the planning stages of the Economic and Commercial Exposition, it was the only agency the PRC left behind after the conclusion of the exposition. Journalists and government agencies questioned the agency's motives. FBI reports alleged that the agents spoke little Spanish and were not there for news-gathering activities.[46] U.S. journalists went further, speculating that the NCNA was a cover for Chinese undercover operations, and that its agents might plan activities that could reach the United States through the porous border between the two countries.

Reports about the exposition, Chinese-Mexican relations, and the NCNA agents included Chinese Mexicans as obvious potential collaborators in PRC activities. Reporter Hal Hendrix, for example, asserted that the NCNA was actually Beijing's "spy base in Mexico." The five members of the bureau's staff were "all known to be welltrained [sic] Intelligence [sic] agents, not foreign correspondents," who met with "operatives" traveling from Cuba and collaborated with the Sociedad Mexicana de Amistad con China Popular. One of the potential dangers of the agents was that they could convince Chinese Mexicans to surreptitiously cross the U.S.–Mexico border and conduct subversive activities in the United States. According to Hendrix, the eighty-five hundred Chinese in the country, and especially the two thousand Chinese in Baja California, were "a matter of concern to U.S. authorities" because of their proximity to the U.S.–Mexico border. Even those who were loyal to the Republic of China were nevertheless suspect because "many of the pro-Western Chinese still have relatives in Red China [the PRC] and are subject to pressures from Peking agents." Hendrix thus suggested that all Chinese Mexicans were worthy of suspicion, since their familial ties to Guangdong Province would pressure even the most loyal Chinese Mexicans to engage in pro-Communist activity. Hendrix's article implied that any Chinese south of the U.S.–Mexico border with transnational ties constituted a potential threat to the national security of the United States.[47]

By 1964, the embassy no longer dismissed articles like Hendrix's as speculation and sensationalism, as it had done during the previous decade. By the time the report emerged, the embassy was quietly conducting its own investigation of suspected Chinese Communist activities in Mexico. The embassy scrutinized Chinese who met with the PRC trade delegation and NCNA agents, as well as those who spoke out on the two Chinas and traveled to mainland China. The stories of three *paisanos*—Pepe Chong, Francisco Ham Cheem Jr., and Pablo Fong— help us understand how Chinese Mexicans who visited the People's

Republic of China came under increased scrutiny, even if they had been perceived earlier as steadfastly loyal.

Pepe Chong (Zhang Baisi) came under scrutiny for visiting mainland China along with his family and talking about his trip after he returned. A coffee and cotton planter in the southern Mexican city of Tapachula, Chiapas, and a Mexican citizen, Chong had participated in the local chapter of the Guomindang and was well respected not only in Tapachula but "by every compatriot in the southern [Mexican states]."[48] As a Guomindang member, he would have been expected to maintain hostile attitudes toward the PRC. But as he began to approach seventy years of age, Chong decided to visit his older brother and younger sisters, whom he had not seen in over fifty years, and took his wife and children along with him. According to early reports, Chong's second son, Rafael, a student at the National Autonomous University of Mexico, had turned Communist and persuaded his father to visit mainland China via Hong Kong. Even though three separate Chinese Mexicans visited Chong in Tapachula and attempted to dissuade him from his trip, he was firm in his resolve.[49] When he returned to Tapachula three months later, his impressions of mainland China were included in a Tapachula newspaper article reporting widespread literacy, the rectification of gender inequality, and the establishment of order. They were dangerous precisely because they could disrupt the narrative of chaos and destruction advanced by the ROC. To central authorities, Chong's comments were proof of his defection: from his comments, "one could see that the Chinese leadership in southern Mexico, in only four months, ha[d] absorbed the poison of the People's Republic of China."[50] From Tapachula, the newspaper clipping including Chong's comments was sent to the Mexican Dirección Federal de Seguridad (DFS).

The story of his trip that Pepe Chong told members of the Guomindang in Tapachula was markedly different from that which he told the Spanish-language press. Chong's story before the GMD emphasized manipulation and government control, presenting a negative image of the PRC. From Tapachula, Chong had arranged to travel to his ancestral village of Taishan, outside of the provincial capital of Guangzhou. After arriving in Hong Kong, however, he was told that, because of the "current political situation . . . it would be inconvenient to obtain permission" for Chong and his family to visit Taishan. Instead, Chong and his family would have to wait for his family members to make the trip to Guangzhou. During his ten days in the city, Chong alleged that he was surrounded with government officials from different agencies and not allowed to speak to his family in private. Shortly before they were to leave, Chong was notified that the government of Taishan County had arranged a special car to take the Chong family to his ancestral village, but by then his wife was fed up with the city, and his family members from Taishan seemed reluctant to allow Chong to return with them. Chong left Guangzhou unsure if what he saw was a picture of actual conditions in Guangdong Province or a fabrication created by the government.[51] Although it is unclear why Chong gave two rather different accounts of his trip, the latter account appears to have mollified ROC and Mexican authorities. A DFS agent paid a visit to Chong while on a trip to the city and concluded that he was not a Communist sympathizer.[52] Moreover, a subsequent embassy report on potential Communist sympathizers does not mention Chong.

Francisco Ham Cheem Jr., an ROC national, drew scrutiny for his business links with the People's Republic of China, which the ROC embassy took to constitute Communist subversion. Ham Cheem Jr. was tracked on a September 1964 trip to mainland China, Hong Kong, and Macau. The embassy shared information on him with Mexican DFS and U.S. FBI agents, both of which began to produce surveillance reports on him.[53] DFS reports present Ham Cheem Jr. as dangerous and allege that he was in direct contact with NCNA officials in the country and that his business activities were really a cover for his pro-Communist activities.[54] FBI reports, in contrast, suggest that Ham Cheem Jr. was less of a threat. Although he may have had connections to the drug trade in Mexicali, he was also a medicinal-herb importer. Ham Cheem Jr. may have been a Communist, but his business interests more likely explained his contact with Chinese Communist commercial agents as well as his trips to the mainland. Moreover, the FBI asserted that Ham Cheem Jr. was deeply disappointed with his 1964 trip, including the difficulties of traveling to the mainland and making contacts in East Asia.[55] Like Pepe Chong, this suggests that Ham Cheem Jr. would have been unwilling to cooperate with the Chinese Communists. It is unclear how the FBI arrived at a more optimistic assessment, though the information contained in the DFS reports likely came directly from the ROC embassy.

The person whom ROC, Mexican, and U.S. reports most concerned themselves about was Pablo Fong (Feng Bao). Born in Jiujiang, Nanhai, Guangdong Province, Fong had spent the vast majority of his sixty years in Mexico. That he was accused at all is rather surprising, because before 1964 he had stellar anti-Communist credentials. He had operated his Mexico City business—Perfumería La Moda—for over forty years and also invested in real estate. He was married to a Mexican woman and had five Mexican-born children. Fong had served the Guomindang as a member of its financial affairs committee. Moreover, during the Korean War he was a leader of the anti-Communist National Salvation Society (Fangong Jiuguohui).[56] As late as 1959, he was considered by the embassy as one of the six *paisanos* who had done the most to spread anti-PRC propaganda.[57] In 1963, the same year as the PRC exposition, Fong hosted a farewell gathering for Mexican ex-president Miguel Alemán Valdés, who was to visit the island of Taiwan. At the party, Fong praised ROC Ambassador Feng-Shan Ho "for his leadership that has enhanced the prestige of the [Chinese] community."[58] But while some of his compatriots protested the 1963 Economic and Commercial Exposition of the People's Republic of China, Fong attended the exposition and marveled at what he found inside. During the exposition, Fong declared, "China's shame of a hundred years has been washed away. Mexico will not have another anti-Chinese campaign." Exposition organizers cited Fong's statement to demonstrate its impact on Chinese Mexicans.[59]

What happened after Fong attended the PRC exposition is a matter of dispute. Around the time of the trade fair, his attitude toward the Republic of China changed; the ROC embassy accused him of becoming "opportunistic." According to this account, written by the ROC embassy in Mexico, Fong wrote Chairman Mao, thereby "establish[ing] relations with the Communists." In September 1964, Fong traveled to the People's Republic of China, staying for three months. After he returned, reports alleged that Fong attended a meeting of the Min Zhi Dang (MZD) on conditions in New China. Later, he would collaborate with them in spreading leaflets among the Chinese population of Mexico City attacking the Nationalist government of Chiang Kai-shek, "under the instigation of New China News Agency cadres in Mexico." Fong's actions were dangerous because they intended "to damage our country's prestige, to sway the patriotism of our compatriots."[60]

In order to shame and embarrass Chinese Mexicans who sympathized and cooperated with the PRC, Ambassador Feng-Shan Ho collaborated with U.S. journalist Jack Anderson. Anderson and Ho met during the swearing-in ceremony of President Gustavo Díaz Ordaz (1964–70), and Anderson immediately took an interest in the political sympathies of Chinese Mexicans. "The Red Chinese," asserted Anderson, "have sought for years to infiltrate Mexico."[61] During one meeting between them, Anderson told Ho that the only way to fight the PRC diplomatic offensive in Mexico was to shock the United States, and especially the Democratic

Party, into action. The implication was that, after information on suspected Communist infiltration came to light, the U.S. government would place pressure on its Mexican counterpart to be more wary of its relationship with the People's Republic of China. Perhaps because they shared a vision, Anderson and Ho became good friends in Mexico City. The two were together during much of Anderson's weeklong stay in the capital; the ambassador even took him to visit the pyramids at Teotihuacán.[62] During this time, Ho shared the embassy's intelligence on suspected Chinese Mexican Communists with the columnist.

The resulting article, published in February 1965 in *Parade* magazine—a weekly insert into newspapers nationwide—raised concerns about the Chinese under investigation by the ROC embassy, as well as the larger community as a whole. Like Hendrix's article, it alleged collaboration between Chinese Mexicans and the NCNA to engage not only in Communist subversion, but in drug trafficking, gambling, and smuggling. According to Anderson, Wu Chu, chief of the Mexico City NCNA bureau, had "quietly buil[t] up a formidable underground that [was] smuggling dope into the U.S. and defense secrets out." Rather than focus on the NCNA headquarters in the upscale Polanco neighborhood of the capital, however, Anderson centered his exposé on the "Chinese spy ring" in a "sleazy [Mexicali] gambling joint that may prove to be one of the most sinister spy traps in the Americas." According to Anderson, the owner of the casino, Chinese Mexican Ham Cheem Jr., used the location as "a recruiting post for American traitors and misfits" and used gambling debts to force others to perform favors for Communist organizations in the country. Thus the article framed his ties to both Mexico and China as dangerous; Ham Cheem Jr. was much more dangerous than the recent arrivals of the NCNA precisely because he had integrated into Mexican society. Unlike them, he had lived in Mexico for over twenty years, and according to Anderson had acquired a "Latin flamboyance" and "could pass for a Mexican but is actually Chinese."[63] His knowledge of the people and customs thus made him an ideal tool for the Chinese Communists. After traveling to mainland China in 1957, allegedly to undergo training "as a spy and agitator," Ham Cheem Jr. returned to Mexicali to open the gambling den, also dealing in drugs and "the other excitements Mexicali has to offer." The article also alleged that, during a sojourn in Mexico City, Ham Cheem Jr. convinced Pablo Fong to travel to mainland China. The fact that he had visited the mainland was evidence that "Mr. Fong" had become "entangled in the Red web," converted to Communism by Ham Cheem Jr. and the staff of the NCNA.[64] Anderson presented Chinese

Mexicans as dangerous not only because they had integrated, but also because they were mobile—capable of traveling across the Pacific and even of penetrating the U.S.–Mexico border—and able to convince one another to support the People's Republic of China.[65]

Anderson's article had a broad impact on both sides of the Pacific Ocean. As noted above, the article was printed across the United States; the Chinese embassy seemed pleased that the article would "attract serious attention from all corners [*gefang*] in the United States and Mexico."[66] After the publication of the article, rumors were accepted as fact and further embellished when they were retold. Picked up in the United States, it was sent to the Mexican Secretary of Foreign Relations, who then informed Mexican President Díaz Ordaz.[67] Elements of Anderson's article were broadcast on Mexico City television news stations the following day.[68] In July of the same year, an article in the Mexican daily *El Universal* named Fong as a link in a Mexican network of Chinese Communist spies; it described Fong as a "well-known drug [trafficker]" dealing in Mexico and the United States.[69] Two ROC newspapers, the English-language *China Post* and the Chinese-language *Central Daily News,* synthesized Anderson's article on the "Peiping Spy Ring" carrying out subversive activities in Mexico.[70]

The ROC embassy continued to follow Pablo Fong for months after the emergence of the report, hoping to intimidate not only him but also other Chinese Mexicans who considered supporting the People's Republic of China. In July 1965 an ROC report tracked him on a trip to San Francisco, affirming that he sent postcards to a few "Mexico City Chinese Communist sympathizers" but not specifying his other activities.[71] Seven months later, Ambassador Chen Chih-ping, meeting with the Mexican Secretary of Foreign Relations, "earnestly and sincerely declared that the Communist bandits [i.e., the PRC] were infiltrating overseas Chinese society."[72] The report the embassy shared with the Mexican government named Fong as one of those who "ha[d] been affiliated in the past two years with the Chinese Communists and . . . is being used by them as a tool."[73] Privately, the embassy made clear that it wished to make an example of Fong to keep other *paisanos* in line. It noted that it "looked forward to the Mexican government placing special attention on the traitor [Fong]. If the Mexican government can impose restrictions on [Pablo Fong's] activities, then other overseas Chinese sympathizers will afterward be vigilant."[74]

Fong attempted to clear his name and set the record straight on his trip to mainland China. In two open letters sent to the U.S. embassy as well as to former presidents Emilio Portes Gil and Miguel Alemán Valdés, Fong angrily denounced the accusations against him. Rather than seeing his visit to mainland China as evidence that he had defected to the Communists, Fong presented it as one characterized by filial piety. In February 1964, wrote Fong, he became very ill and spent some time in the hospital. While in his hospital bed, he began to reflect on how "he had been to most of the world, except to the place where [he] was born." After he was released from the hospital, he decided to travel to Guangdong Province before it was too late, and in September of that year, in the company of his Mexican-born son, he arrived in his home village "without incident," visited his sisters, and arranged his parents' tomb. The trip was Fong's first trip to East Asia in over forty years. When Fong returned to Mexico City, his friends and countrymen—none of whom had had the opportunity to visit mainland China since the Communist takeover in 1949—asked Fong about conditions in mainland China. "As was natural," wrote Fong, "I spoke to them about the progress in education and cleanliness that China has had recently; in particular my village had not been able to recuperate from the destruction that it suffered during the war against the Japanese in 1939, until now."[75] Fong's letter suggests that he was not spreading propaganda for the Communists as much as remarking on the political and social advances of Guangdong Province. Fong likely would have been invested in the province's development, regardless of which government was in power, because many of his relatives still lived there.

His trip to mainland China, and the comments he made about progress on the mainland, were the beginning of his troubles with the embassy of the Republic of China. His friends in the embassy staff "turned into [his] enemies," saying he was a "propagandist for the People's Republic of China." When Anderson's *Parade* magazine article was published in newspapers around the United States, many of his friends in that country read the allegation that he was a secret Communist operative. For a businessman with international contacts, the allegations must have been a profound embarrassment.

Like those in *La honorable colonia china,* Fong presented himself as neither Communist nor Nationalist, but rather as a Mexican patriot. Asserting that he was "completely separate from international politics," Fong used his experiences in Mexico to help deflect charges that he was a Communist. In 1952 Fong became a Mexican citizen, and had since become a member of the Institutional Revolutionary Party. In the letter he declared that he was a Catholic and loved "our tricolor flag." In addition, Fong participated in a number of Mexican civic groups, including the YMCA, the Red Cross, the Lions' Club, and other anti-Communist civic organizations. At a previous international conference of the Lions' Club, Fong joined the Mexico City delegation wearing the "traditional regional costumes" of his second home. His open letter argued that his participation in these organizations, and not the articles published about him in the United States, Mexico, and Taiwan, were the true testament to his character. In addition, his five Mexican-born children, all Catholic, grew up admiring the United States; many studied at the American School in Mexico City.[76] By explaining his activities and asserting his status as a proud Mexican, Pablo Fong suggested that attacks considering him a Chinese Communist sympathizer were absurd.

Fong argued that these attacks stemmed from the embassy's desire to control the Chinese Mexican community, even those who were no longer Chinese nationals. In his open letters, Fong used his denunciation of the embassy's tactics to also condemn the politics of Chiang Kai-shek and the Chinese Nationalists. Even though very few Chinese Mexicans liked Chiang, most were afraid to speak out publicly for fear of having their reputations tarnished like Fong's. "The Chinese embassy," Fong concluded bitterly, "has relied on false elements to attack and threaten the Chinese [community], since at the moment that an absolutely impartial Chinese decides to visit his family in China, he's considered a 'Communist.'" Those who went to PRC cultural events, even out of curiosity, were also labeled Communists. Those who said one disparaging comment about Chiang, those who "comment[ed] about any news about the Chinese continent," and those who left the Guomindang were all labeled communists. Fong suggested that the ROC sought control over Chinese Mexicans similar to its control over the island of Taiwan, where Chiang himself had clamped down on all dissent, turning himself into an "emperor."[77]

Both the embassy's report on Fong's activities and Fong's defense appeared to agree on the fact that Fong's comments about the ROC and his visit to mainland China were his true transgressions. The embassy of the ROC did not present evidence to corroborate their allegations—either the pamphlets he was said to have distributed or any intelligence reports placing him with staff of the NCNA. But his prominence within the community, his attendance at the 1963 exposition, and his visit to mainland China all made him a potential threat to the ROC embassy in

Mexico. From the accusations against Fong, it's clear that the ROC wanted to discourage transnational ties with mainland China. It expected only positive comments about the Nationalists and President Chiang, denunciations of the Communists, and visits to Taiwan, not mainland China, even as their relatives in Guangdong Province were growing very old. Their impressions of mainland China could challenge the image of death, disease, and starvation that the ROC wished to project on the Mexican people. Any deviation from this enforced nationalism was tantamount to aiding the enemy. This was the patriotism that the ROC embassy had come to expect of the Chinese community in Mexico.

Intelligence sharing with U.S. and Mexican officials, tracing the movements of suspected subversives, and reporting on the activities of pro-PRC Chinese Mexicans succeeded, if only briefly, in silencing them. A few weeks after the *Parade* article, the ROC embassy in Mexico reported that the Mexican DFS was investigating eighteen Chinese Mexicans for alleged ties to Chinese Communists—nine Mexican citizens and nine ROC citizens. The eighteen were interrogated by DFS agents, "sternly warned," and then set free. The embassy noted that the detention seemed to have had an impact on Chinese like Pablo Fong. Though Fong initially sang the praises of Communist China, reported the embassy, after his detention he expressed "extreme anti-Communism." Fong himself was interrogated for two or three hours, during which he protested that Mexico had no anti-Communist legislation and asked for the legal rationale for his detention. The stern warning from the DFS was short but powerful. "Although you people are Mexican citizens," Fong was reportedly told, "you were not born here and are still Chinese. Foreigners at least are not allowed to take part in political activities."[78]

When the DFS shared details of their detention with Ambassador Ho, Ho took this statement to mean that the federal government would imprison Chinese Mexicans if they went too far. But the detained Chinese probably understood the larger implication. The DFS referred not to Article 145 of the penal code, a vague statute punishing Mexicans who brought in foreign ideas to disrupt the social order, but rather to Article 33 of the Mexican Constitution of 1917, which specifically targeted foreigners. Article 33 forbids foreigners from participating in Mexican politics but also allows the president to deport anyone whose presence is deemed inconvenient. By calling them "still Chinese," the DFS suggested that Fong and others were not shielded from deportation were they to go too far in supporting the People's Republic of China.[79] The statement may have been an empty threat (although deportations under Article 33 were difficult to challenge), but as noted by the ROC ambassador, the detained took the statement very seriously. This is why Pablo Fong declared his anti-Communism; this is why the chairman of the Min Zhi Dang "suddenly expressed cooperation on everything"; and why the Chinese Mexican political world went from great concern to "peace and quiet."[80] The treatment of Pablo Fong and others suggests that Chinese Mexicans were limited in their desire to find their own way between a Chinese and a Mexican political identity. While Fong's letter loudly proclaimed his Mexican citizenship and identity, the actions of the DFS and the Chinese embassy, in contrast, reduced his identity to that of an overseas Chinese, who was to obey the dictates of the embassy (at least on the question of the People's Republic of China) or suffer the consequences.

The above reports on suspected Communist subversives suggests that the embassy's definition of a suspected Communist was rather broad and actually reflected its own fears about losing Mexican diplomatic recognition. Those accused of surreptitiously visiting mainland China to receive indoctrination from Communist operatives had likely merely tried to conduct business trips, or visited their elderly family members and tended to their parents' tombs. Those accused of spreading Communist propaganda had only expressed satisfaction at developments in mainland China or voiced dissatisfaction with the Republic of China. But because the embassy's version of events carried greater weight, these suspected Communist sympathizers became surveillance targets for ROC, Mexican, and U.S. intelligence agencies.

PREVENTING COLLABORATION BETWEEN CHINESE COMMUNISTS AND CHINESE MEXICANS

The stories of Ham Cheem Jr., Fong, Chong, and others who came under the scrutiny of the ROC embassy and by extension the DFS and the FBI reveal that by the mid-sixties the embassy openly worried about increasing contact between Chinese Mexicans and the People's Republic of China. The agency saw three solutions to this complicated problem. First, it wished for greater control over Chinese Mexicans, especially the ability to prevent them from legally traveling to East Asia. Second, it sought once and for all to mediate conflicts between the Guomindang and the Min Zhi Dang, in hopes that the latter would end its flirtation with supporting the People's Republic of China. Finally, it wanted to end contact between Chinese Communist proxies and Chinese Mexicans, especially by removing the New China News Agency from the country. Whereas the first effort largely failed, the latter two efforts were more successful.

Travel to mainland China was a sensitive issue for many Chinese Mexicans, especially as over the decades they continued to be separated from their relatives in Guangdong Province. To be sure, many Chinese Mexicans continued to support ROC policy, boycotting products from the People's Republic of China and forming groups to "visit China" (*fanghua*) on Taiwan.[81] Lü Shifeng, for example, led a delegation every year to celebrate National Day in Taipei—but an account of one of the trips suggests that only GMD members participated.[82] But those who visited mainland China grew more numerous over the course of the decade, and in the case of Mexican citizens, there was little the embassy could do in response. Fong and Chong, holding Mexican passports, did not need travel documents from the ROC embassy to travel outside of the country. By 1966, the embassy was aware of a tour group composed of at least five Mexico City Chinese and ten Mexicali compatriots who hoped to enter mainland China via Hong Kong.

In response, the embassy of the ROC hoped that the Mexican government would place a special travel restriction on Chinese residents of Mexico: "for the benefit of both countries . . . any Chinese resident in Mexico that seeks a visa or identity or travel document should be asked for his passport from the Republic of China, and in case he sustains that [he is] not a national of the Republic of China, they would have to prove this, obtaining a certificate from the Embassy of the Republic of China. This, we believe, will at least help the embassy and the Mexican authorities to know exactly who are nationals of the Republic of China and who are Chinese who have no nationality and are loyal to other countries [the People's Republic of China]."[83] The ROC embassy once again asked for authority over Mexicans of Chinese descent that it normally would not enjoy, including the power to authenticate the citizenship of Mexican nationals and maintain veto power over their travel. The fact that the embassy asked for this restriction multiple times indicates that it was likely not implemented.

Moreover, infighting between the Guomindang and the Min Zhi Dang not only could swell the ranks of the Communist sympathizers but could threaten the entire community, even loyal Chinese Mexicans, with being labeled as Communist sympathizers. Even though most Chinese in Mexico still supported the government of the ROC, community leader Tan Xinmin warned that the strength of Communist sympathizers was "increasing daily."[84] Although the Guomindang was favored by the government, the Min Zhi Dang was still larger and "often expresse[d] dissatisfaction with the government." As a result, the Min Zhi Dang was the primary target of those who wanted to infiltrate the Chinese communities in Mexico. Although Fong and Chong were not members of the MZD, several other suspected Communists, including those suspected during the late fifties, were current or former members. According to an ROC Ministry of Foreign Affairs report, there were so many suspected Communist sympathizers in the MZD that the organization had attracted the attention of the U.S. Federal Bureau of Investigation.[85]

A core group of MZD members early on welcomed the PRC diplomatic offensive in Mexico—a position that put them at odds with the embassy. Since 1958, members of the Guomindang had been complaining that the MZD's periodical, the *Gongbao,* had contained articles and editorials unfavorable to the Nationalist government. For example, two articles written by a Guadalajara Chinese writing under the pen name Yun Hang "energetically propagandized for the Chinese Communists."[86] When the PRC acrobat and opera troupes sought to perform in Mexico, the ROC embassy tried desperately to block their entry into the country, while the MZD planned welcoming festivities for the performers at two Chinese casinos: Club Central and Club Cantón.[87] Members of the MZD were also alleged on multiple occasions to have celebrated the National Day of the People's Republic of China, sometimes alongside Mexicans.[88] Even more damning, the MZD was alleged to have provided favorable coverage of the 1963 exposition of the PRC.[89] In 1965, when ROC government officials considered Guillermo Leetonway (Li Dongwei) for the position of delegate to the National Assembly, the Mexico City Chinese Chamber of Commerce wrote a letter opposing him, arguing that Leetonway, a former chairman of the MZD, was a "Communist sympathizer" whose *Gongbao* spread Communist propaganda and editorials criticizing President Chiang.[90] Even more damning, they accused Leetonway of holding a PRC passport, indicating where his true sympathies lay.[91] The number of MZD members who took positions at odds with that of the government deeply concerned the embassy in Mexico.

The embassy concentrated its attention on a core group within the MZD, the Group of United Workers and Businessmen (Gongshang Lianweituan). This core group, established in 1951 exclusively from the membership of the MZD, had a separate meeting place from the rest of the group. The core group was headed by Eligio Ley, who the embassy believed had hated the Guomindang for years, had collaborated with the Communists, and had expanded his control of the MZD. By the early sixties, when the core group was composed of nearly forty members, the NCNA developed ties to Ley and later other members of the group, including Anastasio Tea (Xie Chun), helping turn it into what the embassy considered a "Communist sympathizer group" (*fugong qiaotuan*). This put the core group at odds with the larger membership of the MZD. In September 1965, the core group tried to persuade the larger MZD to change the date of its celebration of China's National Day from October 10 to October 1—indicating its support for the government of the People's Republic of China—but the larger group was reluctant, and the measure failed. That year, while most of the MZD met on October 10, inviting embassy staff and members of the Mexico City branch of the GMD to the celebration, the core group allegedly met separately on October 1 with NCNA staff and the SMACP. In January 1966, at a celebration of the fifteenth anniversary since the core group's founding, the group carried out a banquet and invited members of the NCNA, as well as members of the Mexican Communist Party. At a celebration of the larger MZD that same month, some members sought to screen four films on the People's Republic of China, but some of the membership objected and the films were not shown. It was clear to the embassy that, even as most of the members of the MZD were still loyal to the government, the members of the core group were Communist sympathizers and sought to turn the larger MZD into a welcoming space for the People's Republic of China and its supporters. Even as "members of the [MZD] do not agree with the actions of [Eligio Ley] and other Communist sympathizers, . . . up to now no one has dared to take the initiative" to oppose their actions.

By the mid-sixties, the embassy faced a complicated task. It could afford to punish individual Chinese like Pablo Fong, but it could not afford to alienate the MZD, or else risk "the Chinese Communists controlling all of the MZD." The effort to win over the MZD, beyond the scope of the embassy, required the "active support" and "understanding" of a Guomindang that didn't like the MZD and preferred to consider its members as Communists.[92] Continued enmity between the two organizations, the perception that the embassy favored the GMD, or the perception that the embassy was punishing members who in their majority were members of the MZD could turn more members of the MZD away from the Nationalist government and make them supporters of the PRC. Because of the "large amount of influence" the MZD still had in Chinese Mexican society more generally—MZD members outnumbered GMD members in Ensenada, Baja California; Chihuahua, Chihuahua;

Ciudad Juarez, Chihuahua; and Tampico, Tamaulipas—losing the MZD could lead to losing the support of Chinese Mexicans in vital sectors of the country.[93] This delicate balancing act explains why the ROC embassy energetically persecuted individuals sympathetic to the PRC, but was hesitant to act too forcefully in attacking the MZD.

This attitude toward the MZD marked the difference between the two ROC ambassadors to Mexico during the Cold War, Ambassadors Ho (1958–65) and Chen (1965–71). Ambassador Ho, like ambassadors to Mexico before him, was pessimistic about the prospects of winning over the MZD. According to Ambassador Ho, the MZD was poorly organized, and its members were too uneducated; additionally, the organization seemed uninterested in participating in activities that involved other Chinese organizations. Although he noted the existence of "unworthy members of that party" who seemed to sympathize with the Communists, he did not take the MZD's potential for subversion seriously, and noted that the MZD was not in contact with its counterparts in the Philippines and the United States.[94] Ambassador Chen, in contrast, believed the MZD could harm the embassy's diplomatic objectives, and actively sought out members of the MZD who were not Communists.[95] Shortly after arriving in Mexico, Ambassador Chen made links with both the GMD and the MZD. At a banquet that included the leadership of both organizations, Ambassador Chen exhorted both sides to unite. "If there's no country [then] there are no individuals," admonished the ambassador. "If there's no unity, [then there's no existence]."[96] The following year he invited to the ambassador's residence in Mexico City high-level officials of the MZD—a group that included those members of the MZD "deceived and lured by the Communists, Eligio Ley and Anastasio Tea." While they were at the ambassador's residence, Chen exhorted the MZD members in attendance "not to hold a fence-sitting attitude," but to remain loyal to the government.[97] Ambassador Chen also sent telegrams to party chapters across the country asking for their support in establishing links with MZD members who were "non-Communist, anti-Communist and supporters of our government."[98]

Although problems with the MZD had no easy solutions, the problem that the embassy could solve quickly was that of reporters from the New China News Agency. Its internal reports on Chinese Communist subversion focused on Chinese Mexicans. Yet its report to the Mexican Dirección Federal de Seguridad, "Summary of the Activities of the Chinese Communists in the Chinese Community in Mexico," privileged the

NCNA, blaming its reporters for encouraging subversion in the Chinese Mexican community. Hardly mentioning the activities of Mexican leftists, including the SMACP, the report instead focused on activities involving NCNA reporters and Chinese Mexicans, including Ley, Tea, and Fong. "We have concrete evidence to believe that they were working very hard to . . . infiltrate the [MZD]," asserted the report.[99] In providing the report, the goal of the embassy was not only to make Mexican authorities increase their surveillance of NCNA staff and Chinese Mexican Communist sympathizers, but additionally to "gradually provide the Mexican side [with] all the material needed to expel the [PRC] reporters."[100]

Already, the activities of the NCNA news bureau in Mexico City had raised considerable suspicion. Jack Anderson's *Parade* article asserted that NCNA bureau chief Wu Chu directed all subversive operations around the country, including those executed by Chinese Mexicans. In response, Wu Chu was transferred from Mexico, while the U.S. Department of State ordered its ambassador to Mexico, Fulton Freeman, to investigate the NCNA's activities, which only increased pressure on the Mexican DFS to investigate the bureau.[101] In November 1966, the journalists suddenly returned to mainland China. They left so quickly and mysteriously that different explanations were advanced as to their departure. One report asserted that the NCNA grew frustrated because "its efforts in [that] country have not been effective."[102] Chen Chih-ping told the U.S. embassy that the journalists returned to China due to the emergence of the Cultural Revolution: they would be indoctrinated in "Red Guard tactics," which they would then use among Mexico's restive student population and among Chinese Mexicans.[103] Privately, the ROC embassy believed that the NCNA journalists may have fled because they received reports of being investigated by the DFS.[104]

When the journalists applied to return to Mexico the following year, Ambassador Chen alerted the U.S. Department of State, and affirmed that the journalists, now indoctrinated during the Cultural Revolution, "would use [their tactics] to incite rebellion among university students and among the Chinese-Mexican community."[105] As proof, it cited the case of Roberto Ching, a native-born Chinese Mexican, who "was involved in a plot to start an organization of 'red guards'" in the country.[106] The embassy readily admitted that the report on Ching's activities might not be credible, but it still asserted that the Mexican government should take the threat seriously. The tactic appears to have worked: the U.S. embassy, because of the "long common border" between the two countries, expressed a desire to prevent the NCNA journalists from returning.[107]

In July 1967, with the NCNA journalists still outside of the country, Mexican DFS officials arrested thirteen Mexican distributors of PRC literature affiliated with the NCNA. That day, newspapers across the capital blared headlines alleging that the distributors, financed by the NCNA, "intended to turn Mexico into a socialist state."[108] They were also accused of forming guerrilla organizations throughout the country. The bulk of the government's proof consisted of the twelve tons of pro-PRC propaganda they discovered, including writings by Marx, Lenin, and Mao as well as Chinese-language textbooks. While Secretary of Foreign Relations Antonio Carrillo Flores characterized the plot as a foreign intervention propagated by the People's Republic of China, no Chinese or Chinese Mexicans were arrested, and Carrillo Flores maintained that Mexico had no plans to submit the case to an international tribunal.[109] The U.S. embassy noted with pleasure that the allegations that the NCNA financed the plot "should rule out its bid for a return to Mexico."[110]

As with the ROC embassy's accusations against Chinese Mexicans, it is difficult to understand whether its accusations against the NCNA were the result of legitimate intelligence or were rather an attempt to silence an organization capable of fomenting dissent against the Nationalist government. The distributors and their allies reacted angrily to the accusations, asking for an end to the repression of Mexican leftists.[111] One of the reporters of the Mexico City bureau of the NCNA, Pien Chen, sent a letter to several members of the Chinese Mexican community protesting the fact that the NCNA's operations were shut down. The charges, he maintained, were simply false and had been fabricated by the Mexican government to respond to international and domestic politics. Despite the fact that Chen's letter contained no calls to action, in the embassy's reading of the letter, Pien Chen "incite[d] . . . the Chinese residents in Mexico to dedicate themselves to subversive activities."[112]

With the NCNA gone, reports of Communist activity among the Chinese Mexican community also diminished. If the original reports from the embassy are to be believed, the decline in Communist activity was due to the fact that Chinese Mexicans no longer had NCNA agents to fund and organize their activities, or due to the fact that these Chinese Mexicans opted to move more cautiously. If not, the embassy may have been less concerned about PRC sympathizers after the administration of President Díaz Ordaz so clearly broke with agents from the People's Republic of China. In any case, after the departure of the NCNA, Ambassador Chen Chih-ping would try once again to increase contact between the ROC embassy and Chinese communities around the country, mediate old problems, and encourage the community to unify to face down propaganda from the People's Republic of China.

CONCLUSION

While the embassy encouraged Chinese Mexicans to speak for themselves, it was not prepared for the possibility that they would use that voice to speak against the Republic of China. Although some Chinese Mexicans resisted the embassy's efforts to silence them, the embassy appeared to have the upper hand, using surveillance and coercion as well as cooperation with the U.S. and Mexican governments to force *paisanos* and their children to remain quiet and avoid becoming too close to the People's Republic of China.

The experience of the Chinese Mexican community during the Cold War offers sharp contrasts to that of Chinese in the United States. As in the United States, the Cold War was a moment of tension for the Chinese community in Mexico, particularly between steadfast supporters of the Nationalist government of Chiang Kai-shek and those who began to see the Chinese Communist government as better representing their interests.[113] Just as in the United States, the association with Communism made the Chinese community suspect, and some worried about being placed in internment camps.[114]

One major difference separates the cases of the United States and Mexico—the migrant status of the Chinese community. Despite the fact that a limited number of family reunifications took place in Mexico during the Cold War, new entrants were not "paper sons" as some were in the United States. As explained in chapter 3, Mexican concerns with Chinese immigrant status ended during the Second World War, when immigration authorities allowed for the regularization of the migrant status of the entire community. This appears to have permanently laid to rest the issue of migratory status among Chinese Mexicans. Even as newspaper articles shed negative light on the Chinese Mexican community during the Cold War, there was no official scrutiny of the migratory status of Chinese Mexicans.[115] Nor did Mexican authorities seem concerned with deporting or even arresting those who were suspected of Communist activity. During the crackdown on the New China News Agency, when Mexican authorities were best able to arrest and deport Chinese Mexican Communists, they took no action against the community.

The fact that Chinese Mexicans did not suffer greater harassment or deportation in this period has two main causes. First, the Mexican government, even during conservative administrations, appeared less concerned about Chinese-influenced Communist movements and more concerned with native-born leftist activity. As demonstrated during the crackdown on NCNA propaganda in 1967, the Mexican government's concern with "*manos extrañas*," or foreign agents, was less an actual fear of foreign subversion than an excuse to crack down on Mexican leftists. While ROC diplomats, particularly Ambassador He, saw the two as connected, Mexican authorities did not. Second, Mexico's ambivalent role in the Cold War did not put it at odds with the PRC. In the United States, the outbreak of the Korean War placed the Chinese American community under suspicion much before that of their Mexican counterparts. In contrast, after the Sino-Soviet split many Mexican leftist groups, including the Mexican Communist Party (PCM), were less supportive of the PRC.

On balance, Chinese Mexican political organizations also appeared to be less progressive than their U.S. counterparts. Unfortunately, records that shed light on how the Mexican Dirección Federal de Seguridad considered the political leanings of Chinese organizations remain classified. But despite the accusations from the embassy of the ROC, no Chinese Mexican organization was as progressive as the Chinese Hand Laundry Alliance of New York or other left-leaning Chinese associations in the United States.[116] Even as the core organization of the Min Zhi Dang sympathized with the People's Republic of China, it made only minor efforts to convince other Mexicans or Chinese Mexicans on the question of the PRC. The fact that so few Chinese Mexicans openly supported the PRC was in part due to the political environment in the community, but also due to the fact that many were businessmen wary of the PRC's redistributive measures.

By the end of the sixties, Ambassadors He and Chen had done as much as they could to prevent Mexican recognition of the PRC. But the fact that some Chinese Mexicans began to question their ties to the ROC foreshadowed how they would feel after the ROC's ultimate departure. When the ROC left the country, some would continue to miss them, while others quickly moved on to support the People's Republic of China.

CHAPTER 6

A New China,
a New Community

The year 1971 not only witnessed a sharp break in the relationship
between Mexico and the Republic of China; it also saw a severed relationship between the ROC and Chinese Mexicans. *Paisanos,* who by
this point had already reached advanced age, immediately closed all
Chinese associations with ties to the Republic of China, including the
Guomindang, Chinese chambers of commerce (*shanghui*), and cultural
associations. In so doing, they removed an important pillar of community life as well as a vehicle for Chinese community engagement. Native-
born Chinese Mexicans largely turned away from the community associations founded by their parents and sought out different ways to form
community and identify with their roots. While some put their effort
into cultural associations, such as dragon-dancing groups, others
removed themselves entirely from Chinese community activities. Finally,
Mexico's new relationship with the People's Republic of China allowed
a large new wave of Chinese migrants to settle in the country. These
recent migrants founded their own immigrant associations serving their
economic and political interests.[1] The rapid changes experienced by the
Chinese community in Mexico after 1972, both diplomatic and demographic, have made it difficult for the community to recover memories
of Chinese political activity during the mid–twentieth century. These
changes have also challenged the community to rethink its relationship
to both Chinese governments, particularly as the PRC has come to
embrace both native-born Chinese Mexicans and new immigrants. As a

result, the Chinese community, in the present, "is composed of groups with diverse ways of expressing their Chineseness, defining their identities, constructing mechanisms of belonging to different collectivities, and establishing networks tying them to the primary locus of the cultural origin of the diaspora: China."[2]

THE END OF ROC–MEXICAN RELATIONS

Up until 1971, the embassy of the Republic of China in Mexico continued to engage in the same kinds of activities designed by Ambassadors Feng-Shan Ho and Chen Chih-ping, targeting Mexican public opinion and cooperating with the Chinese community in Mexico for the sake of public diplomacy. Activities that purported to merely celebrate Chinese culture were imbued with political significance. For example, in response to mainland China's Cultural Revolution of the late 1960s and early 1970s, during which several ancient Chinese archaeological and cultural sites were destroyed, the ROC carried out several public diplomacy activities. In holding an exposition of Chinese art in the city of Mazatlán, Sinaloa, in 1969, the Republic of China tried to position itself as the guardian of Chinese culture. During his opening remarks, Ambassador Chen praised ancient Mexican and Chinese culture and railed against the Chinese Communist government for encouraging the destruction of Chinese history. "Since their usurpation of [power on] the Chinese continent in 1949," argued Ambassador Chen, "the Communist regime began immediately to persecute intellectuals in the aim of destroying our traditional culture; the brutality of which has never been seen in Chinese history." Prominent Sinaloa Chinese showed their support, including José Wong, president of the Chinese association.

Remarkably, even decades after the Communist takeover of the mainland, the ROC continued to argue that the collapse of the PRC was imminent. The Cultural Revolution had made the government fragile, it argued. "[I]gnorant youth" serving as Red Guards sowed terror through the mainland. Were the political situation to deteriorate, the ROC promised it would capitalize on the ensuing chaos in order to restore the ROC government on the mainland. In the event of any revolt against the leadership of Mao Zedong, asserted the ambassador, "within six hours our navy [and] air force will immediately rush to the rescue." Ambassador Chen's statement was meant to reassure Chinese Mexicans that, even as the Nationalist government had not recovered mainland China in seventeen years, *paisanos* still should not give up hope, instead uniting with the government to "counterattack the mainland [and] construct a new, free, democratic China."[3] Thus, the Republic of China reaffirmed its promise to Chinese Mexicans that it would "achieve the sacred mission of recovering the Chinese mainland, under the great direction of our President Chiang Kai-shek, not only for the salvation of our people but for the consolidation of world peace."[4]

By the late 1960s, however, not only was the Republic of China's mission to recover mainland China increasingly unlikely; it also was quickly losing international support. In 1969, the Canadian government "communicated with Washington its intention to establish relations with Beijing, without finding any objections."[5] Latin American governments no doubt took notice of the tepid U.S. response. A more significant development took place in July 1971, when U.S. president Richard Nixon announced his intention to visit the People's Republic of China the following year, indicating a thaw in relations between the PRC and the United States. That same day, President Nixon called his Mexican counterpart to request Mexican support for a compromise proposal in the United Nations that would allow both Chinese governments a seat at the international body.[6]

News of Nixon's upcoming visit reverberated globally and soon reached Chinese Mexicans. Understanding the importance of the announcement from Washington, both pro- and anti-Communist Chinese Mexicans reacted quickly. On July 24, the ROC embassy in Mexico City received a telegram signed by Manuel Kong Chong, claiming to be "President of the United Chinese [Community] of the Mexican Republic." Wrote Kong Chong, "[T]he Chinese [Community] of the Mexican Republic and the whole world is celebrating" the news of Nixon's visit; Chinese on the mainland "had wished . . . for 25 years to have only one . . . legitimate China and not a puppet China like Taiwan."[7] Just like its investigation of other Chinese Mexicans (see chapter 5), the embassy investigated Kong Chong, and came to the conclusion that he likely did not exist: the address Kong Chong provided on the telegram was either falsified or incorrect, and the street "only had one Chinese café." The telegram could have been sent by a leftist organization that understood the importance of the Chinese community to Mexican–ROC relations or by a member of the Chinese community in Mexico who was afraid of the repercussions of taking such an openly political stand. In contrast to the telegram from Kong Chong, four major Chinese groups in the state of Baja California—the Chinese associations in Mexicali, Tijuana, and Ensenada as well as the Mexican Overseas Chinese

Anti-Communist National Salvation Organization—sent a telegram to President Chiang Kai-shek and Vice-President Chiang Ching-kuo expressing their support. Denouncing Nixon's visit as a "presumptuous and ignorant action," the telegrams declared that the Chinese community in Mexico was deeply opposed to Nixon's visit, and pledged their support and faith in Chiang's leadership.[8]

The administration of Luis Echeverría (1970–76) saw in the possible recognition of the People's Republic of China an opportunity to obtain domestic and international political benefits. The economy had slowed as the country reached the end of the long economic boom known as the Mexican Miracle, and sorely needed new potential markets and trade opportunities. The political left was deeply dissatisfied, particularly after the Mexican government massacred student protestors at Tlatelolco in October 1968—a repression in which Echeverría had a prominent role. During Echeverría's presidency, moreover, the Mexican military pursued guerrillas in the center-west state of Guerrero.[9] Scholars have suggested that Echeverría saw increased international engagement and advocacy on behalf of the Third World—including greater participation in international organizations, welcoming exiles from South American dictatorships, and strengthening ties to Communist countries such as Cuba and China—as an opportunity to make peace with Mexico's left. Finally, since the United States had not yet established diplomatic relations with the People's Republic of China, it was an opportunity for Mexico to demonstrate its independence from the United States.[10]

Sensing the importance of the historical moment, Echeverría went personally to New York in October 1971 to address the United Nations General Assembly on the question of Chinese representation. In his remarks, the Mexican head of state went further than Nixon had requested, announcing that Mexico would support expelling the Republic of China from the United Nations and admitting the People's Republic of China. Responding to the proposed two-state solution, Echeverría declared that "sovereignty and territorial integrity are legally indivisible," implying that only the People's Republic of China should have representation in the United Nations.[11] The final vote—seventy-six for, thirty-five against, with seventeen abstentions—for the first time gave the People's Republic of China a seat in the international body. Sensing the inevitable, diplomats from the Republic of China withdrew from the United Nations a week before the vote.[12]

The end of Mexican relations with the Republic of China came soon after the 1971 vote in the United Nations. Despite Mexico's role in the political setback, the ROC embassy did not believe that the Echeverría administration would so quickly break with the Republic of China. The two countries had enjoyed diplomatic relations for sixty years; Chen Chih-ping, as the longest-serving ambassador in Mexico City, was dean of the diplomatic corps. Assuming that the Republic of China would at least be provided with time to arrange its affairs before departing, ROC Ambassador to Mexico Chen announced that relations with Mexico "[would] continue to be normal and cordial."[13] On November 9, however, Mexican Secretary of Foreign Relations Emilio O. Rabasa informed Chen that, in accordance with Echeverría's statement at the United Nations on territorial integrity, Mexico would announce its break in diplomatic relations with the Republic of China one week later, after which custom dictated that the ambassador leave the country as soon as possible. Chen, taken aback, replied that he would not be prepared to depart from the country in a week, and asked for forty-five days to arrange for the closure of the embassy. Rabasa "countered that he would ask President Echeverría if an announcement could be made in two weeks instead of one."[14] Ambassador Chen left the country on November 15, two days before the Mexican government made the announcement.[15]

The U.S. embassy in Mexico was highly displeased by the move, not because the Mexican government had defied the Cold War imperatives of the United States but because of the lack of respect with which the Mexican government had treated Chen and the ROC. "[W]e had assumed Mexico would move toward [Beijing] in good time and in any event independently of us," noted U.S. Ambassador to Mexico Robert McBride, but described Rabasa's treatment of Chen as "in poor taste," "regrettably typical," and "inelegant and unnecessary."[16] Although Rabasa later expressed regret over what McBride referred to as an "unhappy episode," he did not adequately explain why Mexico felt such pressure to hasten Chen's departure. The most plausible explanation is that President Echeverría wanted to establish diplomatic relations with the People's Republic of China as soon as possible and saw the expulsion of the Republic of China as a necessary step to that end. Rabasa explained to McBride that the Mexican government took a principled position with regard to the question of Chinese representation, but this is belied by the fact that Echeverría days before had inquired about the possibility of maintaining two Chinese embassies in the Mexican capital. Nevertheless, the Mexican government's justification of indivisible sovereignty seemed to satisfy much of the domestic political sphere. Though the ruling Institutional Revolutionary Party and the right-wing National Action Party expressed support for Echeverría's action, the left-wing Party of the Democratic Revolution pointed out that this principled position made no sense, "using two Germanys, two Koreas, and two Viet Nams" as examples.[17]

The rapid break in relations between Mexico and the Republic of China meant the immediate closure of the ROC embassy and the consulates in Mexicali and Guadalajara.[18] The consul general in Mexicali, Liu Tung-Wei (Liu Dongwei), bade the residents in his consular district farewell with a message in Chinese, "to his beloved brothers and sisters," thanking local Chinese for their close cooperation with the consulate over the years. The Chinese of his consular district, affirmed the consul, had not only made a tremendous contribution to Baja California's development, but had also won over the esteem of their neighbors by following the law and being good residents. Moving forward, only by staying united would they avoid being intimidated or threatened by others, and they should continue to cooperate with Mexicans and the local government for the development of the state and for their common prosperity. Even as the consular staff now had to withdraw from the state, admonished the consul, all Chinese Mexicans in the area were now ambassadors for the Republic of China.[19]

A few Chinese migrants gathered solemnly to witness the closure of the embassy and consulate. The closure of the Mexicali consulate drew nearly fifty Chinese from around the state. The national anthem of the Republic of China played as the ROC flag was lowered one last time, and Chinese Baja Californians, with tears in their eyes, lined up to kiss it.[20] Photographs of weeping Chinese were prominent on the front pages of Baja California newspapers the following day. A similar lowering ceremony in Mexico City drew a dozen Chinese.[21] Despite the outpouring of emotion, however, Chinese migrants or associations would make no public comment about Mexico's break with the ROC.

The ROC continued its relationship with Mexico even after the closure of the embassy and consulate, although that relationship would be much more restrained and lack diplomatic standing. In keeping with its policy of maintaining "whatever relations are feasible with any nonhostile country," the ROC obtained approval from the Mexican Secretaría de Gobernación for the establishment of a commercial office.[22] In addition, the ROC reopened its former consulate in Mexicali just across the U.S.–Mexico border, in Calexico, California, still headed by Consul Liu Tung-wei. Consul Liu declared that the new consulate would have jurisdiction over the Imperial and Mexicali Valleys and thus "guarantee the protection of approximately 2,000 Chinese Nationalists living in Baja California."[23] ROC diplomatic officials also continued to meet with Chinese residents in Baja California, issuing ROC passports to any Chinese willing to accept them. The fact that holding an ROC passport made it easier to obtain a U.S. visa meant that many migrants in this period held both ROC and PRC passports.[24] Nevertheless, after 1971, ROC staff in Mexico and Southern California were limited in their ties to Chinese Mexicans. No longer would they be able to meet with Mexican officials on behalf of Chinese residents, since they had no official standing in the country. This meant that Chinese Mexicans could no longer turn to them in times of trouble.[25]

Mexico and the ROC maintain a relationship into the present, driven primarily by economic concerns. A strengthened ROC economy and strong Taiwanese investment in Mexico have led Mexican businessmen to argue for sustained and deepened contact between the two governments. Mexican government officials have carried out unofficial visits to Taipei, despite the discomfort it causes Mexico in its relationship with mainland China. Nevertheless, the relationship has not expanded into other areas, and it is unlikely that the Republic of China will ever regain any form of official recognition from the Mexican government.[26]

IN TEN YEARS, THERE WILL BE NOTHING LEFT OF US

Mexico's break with the Republic of China occurred at a time when the Chinese Mexican population was in free fall and members of the community were remarkably pessimistic about the future. As one anthropologist who studied the Chinese community in Tampico just two years after Mexico established relations with the People's Republic of China noted, one *paisano,* Juan San-Chi, remarked bitterly, "Unfortunately you come to study us when we are almost dead, in ten years there will be nothing left of us, not even the memories of our good [times], around the thirties."[27] The population of *paisanos* was on the decline, as were the organizations they founded. The demise of Chinese associations was hastened by the closure of the ROC consulate and the rapid closure of Guomindang branches throughout the country. The closure of these associations and the passing away of the migrants who founded them erased any memory of the associations' activities or their complicated political legacy and are the most important reasons behind the lack of narratives on the community between 1934 and the early 1970s.[28]

By the late 1960s, the low numbers of surviving *paisanos* already threatened to close the Chinese associations in the country. The Republic of China had never obtained any concessions from the Mexican government on Chinese migration, and thus never saw the Chinese population of the country grow. Whereas the 1960 Mexican census counted 5,085 Chinese men and women in the entire country, the 1970 census counted less than half that number—1,847.[29] Estimates from the ROC government were only slightly higher: in 1972, it estimated forty-eight hundred *paisanos* and twelve thousand native-born Chinese Mexicans.[30] Both figures suggest that *paisanos* had nearly vanished from the country. The signs of population decline as well as physical and mental fatigue were evident. In 1970, the normally robust New Year's celebration hosted by the Asociación China (Zhonghua Huiguan) in Mexicali drew just three hundred attendees, while a similar celebration of the Tijuana Asociación China (Zhonghua Xiehui) drew just one hundred guests, including local Mexicans.

Finally heeding demographic trends, in the late 1960s Chinese Mexicans belatedly created more associations for second-generation Chinese Mexicans and those of subsequent generations. "Because most compatriots in Mexico married Mexican women," read a report from the ROC embassy, "the place of *huayi* youth [of Chinese descent] in overseas Chinese society is important."[31] During its time in the country, however, the embassy had not done enough to reach out to them. Ambassador Chen Chih-ping personally tried to introduce eight native-born Chinese Mexican youth into the Tampico chapter of the Guomindang, hoping that other local chapters would follow suit and introduce "new blood" into the aging Chinese organizations. Additionally, the ambassador suggested placing Mexican-born youth in leadership positions, which would allow them to take over as older generations retired from party politics.[32] Finally, in order to attract the participation of Chinese Mexican youth, the ambassador and other Chinese leaders thought it best to plan activities specifically designed for them, including film screenings and dances.[33] Whereas few organizations had historically existed that explicitly involved second-generation Chinese Mexicans, by 1971 Mexicali's Asociación China had sponsored three, including a Chinese-language school, a youth group, and a music group.[34] Similarly, in Tapachula, Chiapas, there was a Club de Mestizos that catered to children of unions between Chinese and Mexicans.[35]

Although Chinese associations were threatened by demographic changes, no one thought that they would close as quickly as they did. On the night of the November 15, 1971—the night of Ambassador Chen's departure—the committee of the Mexico City Guomindang met secretly at the embassy and resolved to transition to "underground activities."[36] In practice, this meant that they would no longer conduct any activities in public, or meet with Mexican officials. It also meant that Guomindang offices around the country would be closed. In Mexicali, members quickly sold the party chapter for fear that the new embassy of the PRC would want to claim it.[37] In Chiapas, the party chapter would remain in the hands of Chinese residents, but fall further and further into disrepair. Any organizations affiliated with the Guomindang also closed. A recently founded organization, known as the Mexico All-Chinese General Association (Quanmo Huaqiao Zonghui), which was meant to bridge all Chinese associations in the country and finally integrate members of the Guomindang and the Min Zhi Dang, saw its savings liquidated, the proceeds of which allowed some of its members to move to the United States.[38] Second-generation Chinese Mexican clubs, including those in Chiapas and Mexico City, also ended their activities.[39] Jorge Prieto Laurens, a staunch anti-Communist and a friend of the embassy, tried to organize Chinese communities in Mexico City, Monterrey, Guadalajara, and Mérida to form a group known as the "Friends of Taiwan," but his effort appears not to have been successful.[40]

Although neither the migrants nor the diplomats realized it at the time, contacts between the Republic of China and Chinese Mexicans would never again reach the intensity they had during the 1960s. After 1978, internal political changes led the Republic of China to increased democratization and more native Taiwanese in positions of power. Taiwan's major opposition party, the Democratic Progressive Party (DPP), pushed for Taiwanese autonomy and a government focused more on Taiwan and less on the recovery of mainland China. Under the DPP, which ended the Guomindang's exclusive hold on power in 2000, the government office in charge of overseas Chinese affairs, now without a Cold War mandate to organize Chinese around the world, survived calls for its closure, but shifted its focus to overseas Taiwanese rather than overseas mainland Chinese. In 2001, a majority of commissioners were Taiwanese—an indication of the loss of status of earlier waves of Cantonese-speaking migrants.[41] The Republic of China has effectively ceded much of its contact with Chinese overseas to the People's Republic of China—an important change for a government that saw overseas Chinese as the mother of the revolution and an important part of its foreign policy after 1911.

With time and with the passing away of its members, other mutual-aid associations not affiliated with the Guomindang also closed. In Mexicali, for example, native-place and clan associations such as the Haiyan Gongsuo and the Huang Jiang Xia Tang held on to their meeting halls into the twenty-first century but effectively stopped carrying out activities due to lack of members.[42] The Min Zhi Dang is also effectively extinct. Just as with the Guomindang, this suggests that native-place and clan associations in Mexico were slow to incorporate members of the second generation, or that second-generation Chinese were less willing to carry on those traditions.

The rupture with the Republic of China forever affected Chinese Mexican political activities as well as the memory of those activities. Older migrants, who no longer openly celebrated Chinese Nationalist holidays or identified themselves with the Guomindang, preferred to recall them as social organizations. "The Kuo Min Tan [Guomindang] for instance organized the best parties and dances for the paisanos," recalled one immigrant. "The dance of October the 10th was very famous and many locals joined in. Also when they held Chinese banquets, the food was the best."[43] Because October 10 was less easily celebrated as the National Day of the Republic of China, it was remembered instead as a social celebration. Others recalled the organization's mutual-aid activities, including its provision of aid to those who were destitute or of advanced age.[44]

While older generations downplayed the political work of organizations such as the Guomindang, later generations had fewer memories about the political activities of the Chinese community. Alicia Woong Castañeda, for example, who spent some of her childhood in China before settling in Guadalajara, noted that all the paisanos chinos got together to "speak their language and talk about political affairs," while the children played table tennis or ate snacks. She also better remembered the social events sponsored by the Guomindang, such as dances for youth and festivals (kermesse) incorporating the major foreign communities of the city, both of which ended when, "with time, the [Guomindang] ended."[45]

Juan San-Chi's fear, then, that there would be nothing left of his generation shortly after 1972 was largely correct in two crucial respects. First, paisanos largely vanished from the country, having begun their steep demographic decline during the 1960s. Second, without the embassy of the Republic of China or mutual-aid associations to serve as an institutional memory, much of the record of their activities faded away.

MEXICO AND THE PEOPLE'S REPUBLIC OF CHINA

After severing its relationship with the ROC, Mexico proceeded quickly to strengthen its relationship with mainland China. Mexico and the PRC established diplomatic relations on February 14, 1972, the seventy-third anniversary of Mexico's establishment of diplomatic relations with the Qing government. Both Echeverría and Rabasa argued that the moment was significant for Mexico, with Rabasa calling it "historic" and Echeverría arguing that it would contribute to world peace.[46] Within months, the PRC would dispatch its first ambassador to the country as well as a consul in the northwest city of Tijuana.[47] While elements of the U.S. diplomatic corps in Mexico were concerned that the PRC embassy would become a source of Communist subversion, the embassy appears to have primarily concentrated on soft power activities, of the kind that the PRC government had carried out in Mexico before 1972.[48]

Some Chinese Mexicans took advantage of the recognition of the PRC to travel to China, ending their long separation, which had continued almost without interruption since the Second Sino-Japanese War. In this sense they joined Chinese in other parts of the world, who also took advantage of recognition of the PRC to reacquaint themselves with the mainland.[49] One migrant visited China in 1977 and remained for six months, returning in 1981 and 1983. Other Chinese brought along their Chinese Mexican children so that the family could reconnect with their roots.[50] Still others visited for political reasons. On October 1, 1972, Pablo Fong, MZD chairman Eligio Ley, and their families traveled to Beijing to celebrate the country's National Day, now without fear of retribution from ROC authorities.[51] Fifteen members of the Asociación China of Mexicali traveled to mainland China in 1984 to celebrate the thirty-fifth anniversary of the foundation of the PRC.[52]

Despite the groups of Chinese Mexicans traveling to mainland China, the larger Chinese Mexican community appears to have given the embassy of the PRC a much more ambivalent reception. In the month after the arrival of PRC Ambassador Xiong to Mexico City, the embassy conducted several activities geared toward winning the support of the local Chinese population, but largely was unable to convince many Chinese Mexicans to take part. A celebration for Chinese Mexicans in front of the presidential palace, for example, drew only a few attendees. Additionally, PRC employees had difficulty encouraging Chinese Mexicans to register at the new embassy, even after they worked with members of the Min Zhi Dang to build support. Unless they registered, PRC embassy staff warned, the embassy would not be able to protect them. Nevertheless, the Taiwan Office for the Promotion of Commerce reported that few people were convinced to comply.[53]

In Baja California, the establishment of relations with the PRC led to an open conflict among local Chinese. When a volleyball team from mainland China visited Tijuana, the ROC consulate in Calexico attempted to organize a boycott, while pro-PRC Chinese tried to organize a welcoming committee. Chair Ma Wenye of the Tijuana Asociación China (Huaqiao Xiehui) convened a meeting to propose welcoming the volleyball team, as well as celebrating China's National Day on October 1 (the National Day of the PRC). Some members of the community also announced their intention to hang the red and gold flag of the People's Republic of China. In response, another member of the community declared his opposition to the volleyball team's visit, arguing that the team was not from his ancestral country and would not be welcomed in his name. Moreover, he declared his opposition to celebrating the PRC's National Day. According to reports, during the meeting of the Asociación China, members fought animatedly about the two proposals. The fight caught the attention of nearby Mexicans, who drew closer to the meeting hall to witness the spectacle. The attendees parted on bad terms, without coming to an agreement—something that the ROC consulate in Calexico, given the circumstances, considered a victory. Nevertheless, when the volleyball team arrived, Ma Wenye and other Chinese arrived at the airport to welcome them in a personal capacity.[54] In Mexicali, the reception of the PRC similarly divided the community. The Asociación China there would not hang the PRC flag until November 1975, after the PRC ambassador personally visited the city and encouraged them to do so; even then, the vote was seventeen in favor to ten opposed.[55]

At least on a symbolic level, Mexico has prized its relationship with the People's Republic of China after the establishment of diplomatic relations. Luis Echeverría visited Beijing in 1973, the first Latin American head of state to do so after Cuban president Osvaldo Dorticós Torrado—and met with Mao Zedong, Zhou Enlai, and Deng Xiaoping.[56] After Echeverría's visit, every Mexican president since has visited the Chinese mainland. Moreover, since the 1980s, several PRC heads of state have visited Mexico.[57]

Mexican leaders who predicted during the 1960s and 1970s that recognizing the People's Republic of China would bring increased trade were correct, but that trade has presented Mexico with several challenges. Instead of Mexico obtaining access to the large Chinese market, as Mexican leaders had envisioned during the 1960s, Chinese products have largely flooded the Mexican market. Mexico's trade deficit with the People's Republic of China reached $60 billion in 2014, while Chinese products compete with Mexican ones for the U.S. market.[58] As a result, calls for increased tariffs and investigations of alleged Chinese dumping practices have grown louder.[59] At the same time, Chinese direct investment in Mexico is low, representing one-tenth of 1 percent of all foreign investment in the country from 1999 to 2013.[60] Rather than seeing the People's Republic of China as an opportunity, then, many Mexicans now "perceive the Chinese presence as more of a threat."[61] This perception presents a substantial challenge to the relationship between Mexico and China as well as to the Chinese community in Mexico moving forward.

SECOND-GENERATION CHINESE MEXICANS AND THE NEW CULTURAL ASSOCIATIONS

The descendants of the first wave of Chinese Mexicans are currently second-, third-, or fourth-generation Chinese. Most have both Chinese and Mexican ancestry. After a lapse of several years, new associations for these native-born Chinese Mexicans began to slowly replace the associations that closed during the ROC departure. No longer created in an environment of anti-Chinese hostility, however, they had a purpose markedly different from that of earlier associations. Political activities were largely deemphasized. Instead, cultural organizations predominated, which, instead of protecting second-generation Chinese Mexicans from discrimination, served to demonstrate their pride in their roots and recover memories from the time of their ancestors. Together these organizations represent a multiplicity of forms of demonstrating belonging to the Chinese diaspora.[62]

In Mexico City, for example, the association Comunidad China de México was founded in 1981 to replace the Chinese Cultural Association, which closed in the early seventies.[63] The organization's lion-dancing troupes continue to perform during Chinese New Year and Mid-Autumn Festival at Calle Dolores, the traditional Chinatown (barrio chino) of Mexico City. The Chinese pilgrimage to the Basílica de Nuestra Señora de Guadalupe, analyzed in chapter 4, may also have been suspended for a time, but in the present the tradition of the annual pilgrimage to Mexico's holiest religious site continues.[64] In the Soconusco region of Chiapas, the Chinese community formed a new Chinese association known as the Asociación China del Soconusco. Founded in 1983, it was open to anyone of Chinese descent or who had a Chinese relative. This latter organization, however, has had difficulty retaining members. One interview subject claimed that the organization was effectively closed for nine years at the end of the twentieth century.[65] As a result, it has expanded to include not only descendants of Chinese Mexicans, but anyone interested in Chinese culture. In both Tapachula and Huixtla, organizers maintained that descendants were less interested in Chinese culture, and that as a result the majority of dancers had no familial links to China. A Chinese dance group for women, also established in Mazatán in 1984, similarly chose to incorporate Mexicans with no Chinese ancestry, although the director confessed to incorporating lighter-skinned dancers to avoid people "saying that they weren't Chinese."[66]

Chinese Mexicans have sought out different forms of building community and recovering memories from their parents' generation. The online group Inmigraciones Chinas a México, founded in 2012 and composed of nearly nine hundred descendants of Chinese Mexicans of different generations currently residing around Mexico and in other countries such as China and the United States, shares photographs and memories of the community at midcentury to recover Chinese Mexican history, both of those who remained in the country after the anti-Chinese campaigns and of the repatriates who arrived in Mexico in 1960. In addition, the group has organized the first commemoration of the 1960 repatriation and an academic conference on Chinese Mexican history.[67]

THE NEW IMMIGRANTS

Another major change affecting the Chinese community in Mexico is the global resurgence in Chinese migration across the Americas. Countries as diverse as Canada and Peru began to welcome new Chinese migrants, at first distant family members of earlier waves of migrants and then migrants with different regional, language, and class backgrounds.[68] Reversing the Republic of China's decades-long inability to obtain relaxed immigration provisions, the People's Republic of China did secure new avenues for Chinese migrants to arrive once again in Mexico. During the 1990s, the Mexican government allowed new categories of Chinese immigrants to enter the country, including those who had a child, a spouse, or another close relative already present in the country, while those who wanted to visit friends or conduct business could more easily obtain visas. Some of those in the latter category overstayed their visas, becoming undocumented migrants in the country.[69] The smuggling of Chinese migrants to Mexico has also increased, although just as in the early twentieth century, many migrants see the United States as a final destination.[70] The result has been a substantial increase in the Chinese population in the country in the past twenty years. In Mexico, as in the rest of the Americas, this new immigration produced immediate tensions with earlier waves of Chinese migrants.

Much of this new Chinese migration has been to Baja California. The state experienced considerable economic and demographic growth beginning with the 1965 Border Industrialization Program and continuing in the wake of the 1994 North American Free Trade Agreement—phenomena that drew more Chinese to the region. From 1995 to 2006, after the North American Free Trade Agreement went into effect, the number of workers in the city's low-wage assembly factories known as *maquiladoras* doubled. These workers in turn spurred an increased demand for low-cost fast food, leading to a sharp rise in Chinese restaurants and Chinese migrants in the region. From an estimated 60 Chinese restaurants in Mexicali in 1990, there were over 300 such restaurants in the city in 2006. In Tijuana, in addition to the sharp rise in Chinese restaurants—there were an estimated 120 Chinese restaurants in 2001—there has also been an increase in the number of Chinese who work in manufacturing, such as in the factories near Plaza 5 y 10. These workers are seen as more willing to work long hours and as more vulnerable to mistreatment than their Mexican counterparts.[71]

More work opportunities have increased Chinese migration to the region. Early in the twenty-first century, Chinese migrants paid $10,000 to $15,000 to migrate to Mexico, with many of them going into debt for several years to make the journey. Though many would like to travel onward to the United States, few ultimately travel north of the border, likely due to tougher immigration controls along with the higher fees for transporting Asian migrants.[72] The rise in immigrant smuggling has meant that, once again, estimates of the Chinese population of the country are difficult to verify. According to the National Institute of Migration, only 10,247 Chinese resided in Mexico in 2009.[73] Chinese association leaders, in contrast, estimated thirty thousand Chinese—twenty thousand in Baja California and ten thousand in Mexico City.[74] Mexican scholars place the estimate even higher, at seventy thousand.[75] Whatever the number of Chinese immigrants in the country, it represents a large demographic shift for the Chinese community: it is the largest Chinese population in the country since the anti-Chinese campaigns, and may be the largest Chinese population in Mexican history. The passing away of earlier generations of Chinese migrants, and the new wave of immigration of Chinese to the country, have shifted the center of population once again to Mexico's northwest, especially the state of Baja California.[76]

Dubbed the "new immigrants" (*xin yimin*), the new arrivals from mainland China may have family ties to established Chinese Mexicans but have substantial cultural differences. Native-born descendants of the first wave of Chinese migrants speak Cantonese or Spanish, and their elders for the most part were anti-Communist. New arrivals grew up after the establishment of New China, primarily speak Mandarin, and may have trouble communicating in Spanish. Most come from outside of Guangdong Province, and some arrived from another country in Western Europe or the Americas. The diversity of the Chinese Mexican community means that there are large numbers of Chinese Mexicans who speak Spanish, English, Cantonese, Mandarin, or a combination of these languages.[77] In part due to the language barrier, Chinese Mexican associations serving the second generation and beyond communicate infrequently with associations of recent arrivals, and receive little attention or support from the PRC government.[78] Intracommunity differences continue to manifest themselves even as, among Mexicans, all Chinese Mexicans may all be lumped together as *chinos*.

The boom in the population of both native-born Chinese Mexicans and recent Chinese arrivals has transformed those Chinese associations in Mexico that still remain open. For example, the Asociación China in Mexicali offers services to both recent and older Chinese migrants. It helps process passport applications, for example, to ensure that migrants maintain a regular migratory status, and mediates conflicts with local Mexicans. Finally, it runs Chinese schools and plans local celebrations, including the celebration for Chinese New Year. Other clan and nativeplace associations house recent migrants, accepting very little for lodging, to ensure that migrants are able to get a good start.[79]

In addition, new immigrants have formed their own economic associations to look after their business interests. In 2001, with the encouragement of the embassy of the People's Republic of China in Mexico, and having invited Luis Echeverría as a guest of honor, PRC businessmen formed the Cámara de Empresarios Chinos en México (Moxige Zhongguo Huaren Shanghui); like the Mexico City Chinese Chamber of Commerce (Mojing Huaqiao Shanghui), formed eighty years prior, it is a "nongovernmental organization with the full support of the Chinese embassy in Mexico." In addition to concentrating the efforts of the businessmen it represents, the organization sees itself as having a major role in promoting economic relations between China and Mexico.[80] Although the community still lacks a nationwide newspaper, websites such as Mo Hua Tang, OneMex (Moxige Huaren Zixunwang), and ChinoMX (Zhongmo Luntan) update migrants on major news stories and provide information on how to navigate immigration procedures and access basic services, and even how to understand basic aspects of Mexican culture.[81]

The past decade has also witnessed the growth of some associations, composed of old and new migrants, that have embraced politics and called for a peaceful reunification between the People's Republic of China and the Republic of China on Taiwan.[82] Chinese in Baja California and Sonora have formed the Northwest Mexico Pro-Peaceful Unification of China Association (Moxige Xibei Diqu Zhongguo Heping Tongyi Cujinhui); a periodical published by the organization, *Moguo Qiaoxun*, runs articles favoring the reunification of China, including messages from high-level PRC officials such as Hu Jintao. Their frequent trips to mainland China give the leaders a status not given to other Chinese migrants. For Eduardo Auyón Gerardo (Ouyang Min), who was a repatriate from Hong Kong and Macau in 1960 and is now one of the leaders of the organization, the change in attitude toward the People's Republic of China is remarkable. It is unclear to what extent their views and organization have the support of the rest of the community, but their message nonetheless has spread quickly throughout the country.[83]

OUR CHINESE HEARTS

Among the songs Chinese from Tijuana and San Diego came together to sing during a 2002 Chinese New Year celebration was Hong Kong singer Zhang Mingmin's "Wo De Zhongguoxin" ("My Chinese Heart").[84] The song, performed in Mandarin at the 1984 CCTV Spring Festival Gala, has been tremendously popular in mainland China and in the diaspora ever since. The song takes the perspective of an overseas Chinese who has not visited mainland China for several years, has acculturated to Western ways and wears Western clothing, but has nonetheless preserved his "Chinese heart"—something that living abroad "cannot possibly change." While scholars have seen this and other nationalist songs as evidence of the Chinese state's attempt to promote "a great, united and indestructible Beijing-centric Chinese identity," its continued popularity thirty years after its release suggests that the message has found some resonance within the Chinese diaspora.[85]

That a Chinese Mexican along the U.S.–Mexico border can feel comfortable singing such a nationalist and pro-PRC song during a prominent Chinese cultural celebration indicates how much has changed within the community at the close of the twentieth century. It suggests that, as the status of China has risen in recent decades, Chinese Mexicans, particularly descendants of the first wave of migrants as well as newer immigrants, have come forward to express their allegiance and affinity to mainland China. These expressions—just like expressions of loyalty to the Republic of China that allowed *paisanos* to renegotiate their position in Mexican society—have eagerly been welcomed in mainland China, which displays them as expressions of loyal Chinese overseas and their descendants. Just like the song "My Chinese Heart," reports on Chinese Mexicans from mainland China frequently use metaphors of heart and blood to suggest their continued belonging despite their integration into Mexican society. Just as Live Yu-Sion has found for the island of Réunion, this sense of belonging holds even among Chinese Mexicans who "no longer speak their ancestral language . . . and have lost the essential cultural elements of their parents or grandparents."[86]

While the Republic of China was disengaging from Chinese communities abroad, the People's Republic of China was increasing its contact with overseas communities. This change was also due to dramatic internal political changes, including the end of the Cultural Revolution and China's Reform and Opening-Up policy. In 1978, the PRC reopened its State Council for Overseas Chinese Affairs, and subsequently organized committees on overseas Chinese affairs in other government bodies. These new government bodies implied "that the Chinese governments, from the central to the local level, now paid attention to the overseas Chinese, which had never been the case before."[87] Additionally, from its contact with Chinese Mexicans and other parts of the diaspora, it's clear that the PRC is following the example of the ROC's contact with Chinese diasporic groups during the twentieth century.

Although the PRC does not claim Chinese abroad as its own citizens, as the ROC did, it does assert a cultural link between these migrants and mainland China.[88] Evoking the same Zhang Mingmin song, a 2001 news article on the work Chinese Mexican artist and community historian Eduardo Auyón Gerardo (Ouyang Min) was titled "Bainian bubian zhongguo xin" ("One Hundred Years of Unchanging Chinese Hearts"), referring to the community's hundred-year presence in the country as well as asserting its enduring Chineseness. Glossing over the significant cleavages in the Chinese Mexican community, including differences in language, culture, politics and religion, the article suggested an essentialized Chinese identity loyal to the People's Republic of China. "Loving their country, loving their birthplace is their tradition," asserted the article. Although the community supported the Republic of China in the past, the article argued that in the present it was firmly in support of the People's Republic of China.[89]

While the article asserted unequivocal patriotism on the part of Chinese Mexicans, the reality is much more nuanced. During the past forty years, increasing ties between the PRC and Mexico have allowed Chinese Mexicans to express pride in their Chinese heritage even while also asserting their Mexicanness. This positioning vis-à-vis the ancestral country of Chinese Mexicans began early in the relationship between the PRC and Mexico. Vicente Mack, a native-born Chinese Mexican, early on established a relationship with PRC representatives and visited the People's Republic of China shortly after relations were established. When the director of the Bank of China visited the country, Mack welcomed him "in the name of the Chinese colony of Mexico." Moving beyond the traumatic history of the Chinese community during the anti-Chinese movement, Mack instead argued that "Chinese immigrants in this hospitable land have found opportunities to work to live better and progress. Here all men are equal." While presenting Chinese Mexicans as substantively Mexican, Mack also expressed affinity with mainland China. "We, the new generation born in the country, are Mexicans by right and primarily by desire, by conviction," he declared, but then asked to send a greeting "from the Chinese colony in Mexico to the land (*pueblo*) of its ancestors and to President Mao." The director, in response, asserted that Chinese Mexicans were "the base of our [diplomatic] relations. Our best tie is [that of] blood." The bank director accepted Mack as being Chinese because he had Chinese blood, even as he was Mexican by desire, and Mack had no problem celebrating his Chinese roots even if he defined the community primarily as Mexican.[90]

The president of Mexico City's Comunidad China de Mexico (Mohua Shetuan), Alfonso Chiu Hu (Zhao Chongxi), expressed a similar sentiment in 1990, when Chinese president Yang Shangkun met with over one hundred Chinese Mexicans during a visit to the city. Despite the fact that the visit was the first-ever meeting between Chinese Mexicans and a sitting Chinese president, Chiu Hu emphasized the community's affinity for its Chinese heritage but also for its Mexican present: "We are all proud of our blood ties and names. Although our feet are firmly planted in Mexico, we are kindred spirits with the country of our ancestors, because the same blood flows in our veins." Yang's speech to the Chinese Mexican representatives contained admonishments similar to those of the Republic of China during the mid–twentieth century: to unite as one to help develop mainland China, to preserve Chinese traditions, to get along with Mexicans, to work for Mexico's development, and to promote friendly Chinese–Mexican relations.[91] It's clear from the words of Mack and Chiu, as well as from the uncritical reception their words garnered in periodicals such as the *People's Daily/Renmin Ribao*, that expressing belonging to both Mexico and China were not in opposition, but rather could be complementary. As during earlier meetings between Chinese officials and the Chinese Mexican community, the meeting served to benefit both Chinese Mexicans and the Chinese government. Chinese Mexicans could engage in public diplomacy activities and serve as interlocutors in the Chinese–Mexican relationship, at the same time obtaining prestige from a rising China. Thus, not only did senior Chinese officials continue to meet with them during their visits to Mexico; their meetings were also covered favorably in the Chinese-language press.

Coverage of Chinese Mexicans visiting mainland China had a similar effect: it suggested the continued loyalty of a community that saw itself as firmly integrated into Mexican society, even after several decades of being unable to visit the mainland. The most salient example is of the Ley family, one of the wealthiest Chinese families in Mexico. That family has a long history in the country, arriving in 1905 and moving around northwestern Mexico in the first half of the twentieth century. In 1954, Juan Ley Fong (Li Zhaokai) arrived in the city of Culiacán, Sinaloa, and opened a market, Casa Ley. When Ley Fong passed away in 1969, his son, Juan Manuel Ley (Li Huawen), converted Casa Ley into a supermarket, slowly expanding into a supermarket chain. After securing a large investment from Safeway supermarkets, the supermarket chain began to expand rapidly throughout northwestern Mexico. During the early twenty-first century, there were over 150 Ley supermarkets in twelve states in northern, western, and central Mexico.[92] Aside from his supermarkets, Juan Manuel Ley was president of a Mexican baseball team, the Culiacán Tomateros. Yet in the twenty-first century Ley became interested in visiting the land of his ancestors, arriving in Guangdong Province in 2003 and returning several times thereafter. In 2009, at seventy-six years of age, Ley returned to attend the premiere of the Central and South American edition of a documentary entitled *The People of Zhongshan Abroad* and declared, "We always believed ourselves to be overseas Chinese."[93] While affirming his difference, then, Ley also took considerable pride in his roots. Chinese media reported on the visits of the entire Ley family to their ancestral village, including his two younger sisters and his younger brother, Sergio Ley (Li Ziwen), who served as Mexico's ambassador to China from 2001 to 2006. Consistent with second-generation language-retention rates analyzed above, of the entire family, only Juan Manuel Ley's son, studying at Peking University, was able to speak Chinese, but the newspaper coverage nonetheless asserted that their inability to communicate did not hamper their personal connection to their ancestral village, as "their hearts were interlinked."[94]

Finally, cultural celebrations such as Chinese New Year and Mid-Autumn Festival have been used to bring together different parts of the Chinese Mexican community and serve as moments of cultural diplomacy within Mexico. Ximena Alba has noted that, in Mexicali, Chinese New Year is the only time when second-generation Chinese Mexicans celebrate alongside more recent migrants.[95] Reports of Chinese cultural celebrations depict native-born Chinese Mexicans as proud of their heritage. In 1991, for example, amid dragon and lion dances, a Chinese Mexican youth identified only as "Patty" noted that "traditional culture and customs make us think to our own roots, yearn even more for distant China. We always are proud of our Chinese blood [*xueyuan*]."[96] In addition, such celebrations serve as moments of contact between Chinese Mexicans, Chinese diplomats, and Mexican attendees.

Renmin Ribao, for example, covered Chinese New Year celebrations in Baja California and in Mexico City in 1997. An evening Chinese New Year celebration in the city of Tijuana, for example, drew seven hundred Chinese migrants and Chinese Mexicans. Like previous cultural celebrations, it drew not only the Chinese ambassador to Mexico and the Chinese consul in Tijuana, but also representatives of the mayor of the city and the governor of Baja California. In his remarks, the president of Tijuana's Asociación China thanked the Chinese government for "caring for overseas compatriots" and expressed his desire for the reunification of China and Taiwan. Consular staff also attended the New Year celebrations in the nearby city of Mexicali and in distant Mexico City.[97]

Although business and political organizations are reemerging, PRC contact with new immigrants and native-born Chinese Mexicans has been to emphasize family and cultural links with mainland China and to increase friendly feelings toward the new Chinese government. In comparison with the ROC era, friendly contact between the PRC and Chinese Mexicans seems less overtly political, but it nonetheless allows mainland China to make claims as to the affinity and loyalty of these diasporic groups.

CONCLUSION

The changes of the past forty years—a reduced role for the ROC, a greater openness on the part of the PRC, and a globalized Mexico now much more exposed to world markets—have allowed the Chinese community of the country to grow once again, but have also changed the composition of that community and challenged it to rethink its identity toward both sides of the Pacific Ocean. Among the questions left to be resolved are whether the different elements of the Chinese community in the country will unite or organize separately; whether they will actively support the People's Republic of China or remain more apolitical; and whether the children of recent Chinese migrants will retain their ties to the People's Republic of China or articulate a different sense of belonging.

What seems evident is that, even as there is some tension between Mexico and the People's Republic of China, there is also a greater acceptance of the Chinese presence in the country and of the community's history during the twentieth century. There is also a greater acknowledgment of Mexico's past aggression against Chinese migrants. Incorporating interviews of Chinese migrants and their descendants, television programs and newspaper reports commemorate the anti-Chinese campaigns and the 1960 repatriation of Chinese Mexicans, while also giving testament to Mexico's incredible if little-noticed ethnic diversity.[98] Over time, Chinese Mexicans themselves have been increasingly willing to take part in this project. As noted by Jorge Cinco, who as a child left the country during the anti-Chinese movement and returned during the 1960 repatriation, "It is no longer as it was before in the time of President Calles. Now many people like for me to talk to them about China, and I like to do so. It is no longer like the time when my father lived here. Now we Chinese are treated well and are accepted as both Chinese and Mexican."[99]

The reevaluation of twentieth-century mestizo nationalism and the increased openness to pluricultural notions of Mexican nationhood open a window for Chinese Mexicans to argue for their place in the

Mexican nation and offer the possibility that migrants and their children will increasingly be willing to identify as Mexican.[100] In addition to singing "My Chinese Heart," then, migrants might also be willing to sing songs like "El Cachanilla," which one Chinese Baja Californian did during a Spring Festival celebration in 2008, "with all his heart and with an excellent *ranchera* intonation."[101] Singing the song, whose title denotes a native of Mexicali, allowed him to perform his sense of belonging to the region of his birth. Beginning with the cotton fields, which Chinese migrants helped develop, and then moving through Tijuana, Mexicali, and Ensenada, all of which had Chinese communities, the song was as much about his history as it was about the history of any other resident of the state. Soon, it could belong to the children of recent Chinese migrants as well. "I am pure *cachanilla,* I say it unpretentiously," they might sing. "I am from Baja California, a northerner at heart [*norteño de corazón*]."

Conclusion

Near the historic center of the Mexican capital, just outside the old Secretaría of Foreign Relations building, the Chinese Clock Tower, commonly known as El Reloj Chino, has stood witness to the tumultuous history of the Chinese Mexican community during the twentieth century. The tower was originally presented as a gift from the Chinese community, then known as the *colonia china,* to the Mexican people on the hundredth anniversary of the cry for independence, and meant to be a symbol of the lasting friendship between the Mexican and Chinese peoples. On its surface, the clock tower harks back to an age when *colonias,* or foreign enclaves, saw themselves as fundamentally separate from the social sphere in which immigrants to Mexico lived and worked.[1] Other foreign enclaves made similar gifts, including a statue of George Washington from the American community; one of Giuseppe Garibaldi from Italian residents; and an Ottoman clock from the Syrian-Lebanese community.[2] Yet since its initial dedication, the clock tower has slowly evolved, mirroring changes in the Chinese community during its long presence in the country.

Just one year after its dedication, both the Qing government and Porfirio Díaz would fall from power, but Chinese immigrants continued to arrive, and the clock remained standing. But it would last only a short time in its original form. During the "Ten Tragic Days of 1913," which saw open battles between government and rebel soldiers in Mexico City, a rebel cannonball ripped through the tower and left it in shambles, evoking the Chinese who also felt the shocks and fury of the Mexican Revolution. (See figure 10.) Yet rather than leave it destroyed, the Chinese community dutifully raised funds for its reconstruction. Community leaders hired Mexican architect Carlos Gorbea to rebuild the tower, albeit with a modified design, and rededicated it in 1921, its base containing an inscription from "the Chinese residents in Mexico to celebrate the centenary of Mexican independence, 1821–1921." (See figure 11.) In the middle of the tower, there is an inscription of four Chinese characters—同聲相應 (tongsheng xiangying)—meaning "the same sounds continue to make echoes," which demonstrates "the [willingness] of the resident Chinese to share joys and sorrows with the Mexican people."[3] After the chaos of the armed phase of the Mexican Revolution, including the massacre of hundreds of Chinese in the city of Torreón in 1911, this commitment from the first wave of paisanos to live and work alongside Mexican neighbors in good times and bad is remarkable.

Far from remaining separate from Mexican society, paisanos and their descendants have indeed resonated with significant events in Mexico and across the Pacific Ocean. Although arriving Chinese workers and merchants established political and social associations similar to those enjoyed by other foreign communities in Mexico, this book has argued that in the long term these associations helped facilitate the integration of Chinese into Mexican society. As with other foreign communities, part of the explanation lies with Chinese Mexicans' long separation from China, during which paisanos began to adopt elements of Mexican culture.[4] Few were wealthy enough, like some Middle Eastern and German immigrants to Mexico, to maintain sole allegiance to their home country beyond the first generation.[5] A more important factor was that Chinese Mexicans did not remain passive but rather actively responded to changes in local, national, and international politics. In so doing, during moments of tension caused by revolutions, foreign invasions, and changes in government, Chinese Mexicans demonstrated numerous ways of belonging both to Mexico and to China. Today, like the Chinese Clock Tower and the cafés de chinos that continue to dot the capital, Chinese immigrants have become an integral part of Mexico's multicultural present.

This book has examined the ways in which Mexico's Chinese community has slowly integrated into Mexican society, in part by fulfilling its promise of sharing its joys and sorrows with the Mexican people. During the 1920s and 1930s, integration appeared impossible. As

FIGURE 10. The Chinese Clock Tower (El Reloj Chino) after it was damaged during the "Ten Tragic Days of 1913." Photo courtesy Fototeca Nacional INAH.

FIGURE 11. El Reloj Chino after it was reconstructed and rededicated in 1921. Photo courtesy Fototeca Nacional INAH.

demonstrated in chapters 1 and 2, anti-Chinese activists argued tirelessly for the expulsion of Chinese migrants from postrevolutionary Mexico, claiming that their presence was inconvenient and dangerous and that they ultimately would never fit in to the Mexican nation. During the anti-Chinese campaigns (1931–34), activists in the states of Sonora and Sinaloa went far beyond the law in expelling Chinese migrants from those two states. The resulting humanitarian crisis shocked observers in the United States and China, and scarred Chinese migrants in other areas of the country. In response, Chinese migrants had little choice but to strengthen their attachments to the Republic of China and to Chinese associations. The relationship between the Chinese embassy and Chinese Mexicans, forged during the anti-Chinese campaigns, would continue throughout much of the twentieth century.

The desire for greater stability encouraged *paisanos,* just a few years after the conclusion of the anti-Chinese campaigns, to donate time and money in support of the Republic of China during the Second World War. As demonstrated in chapter 3, rather than come to the aid of the Republic of China out of a sense of patriotism, Chinese Mexicans were mainly concerned about their vulnerability after the anti-Chinese campaigns. They believed that encouraging a strong Chinese government abroad would help promote a positive image of Chinese Mexicans at home, and guard against another anti-Chinese campaign. Rather than appealing to the ROC embassy to protect them, as they had done during the anti-Chinese movement, the donation drive demonstrates their increasing willingness to speak for themselves, undergirded by their increasing stability on Mexican soil. For the first time, these public demonstrations allowed them to speak directly to the Mexican people, and to present images of Chinese migrants radically different from those popularized by anti-Chinese activists. At the close of the Second World War, for example, victory celebrations deliberately incorporated prominent Mexican residents, politicians, and businesspeople, allowing members of the Chinese community to explain the meaning of the war as well as to present their sense of belonging to Mexican society.

Chinese Mexican public demonstrations were even more vigorous during the Cold War, which featured protests of the Economic and Cultural Exposition of the People's Republic of China and the annual pilgrimage to the Basílica de Nuestra Señora de Guadalupe, the focus of chapter 4. In addition to making statements of support for the Republic of China, these actions featured Chinese associations acting like other civic organizations in the country, demonstrating a sense of gratitude for their time in Mexico and embracing Mexican cultural symbols like the flag and the banner of the Virgin of Guadalupe.

In spite of the mutually beneficial relationship between Chinese Mexicans and the embassy of the Republic of China, the community did not simply follow the dictates of the embassy. Political attitudes, particularly attitudes about the development of mainland China, continued to matter. Crucial was obtaining the support of the Chee Kung Tong (later called the Min Zhi Dang), which had genuine reservations about the Guomindang's development of mainland China before 1949. Its hostile relationship with the Mexican branch of the Guomindang after the Tong Wars only made negotiations more difficult, meaning that, rather than dictate a settlement between them, the embassy of the Republic of China tried as delicately as possible to encourage the two sides to get along. During the Second World War, for example, the embassy saw itself forced to plead for the continued support of the Min Zhi Dang toward the donation effort. Even by the end of the Cold War, examined in chapter 5, the ROC embassy was eager to embarrass and shame individual Chinese Mexicans who had traveled to mainland China or who had embraced the People's Republic of China, but nevertheless was hesitant to antagonize the Min Zhi Dang, afraid that it would be pushed to embrace the Chinese Communists.

While the Chinese Clock Tower stood witness to Mexico's tumultuous twentieth century, toward the end of that century it was a testament to a time long since passed. By 1971, *paisanos* had lived long lives in Mexico, built small but thriving businesses, and established families in the country. That year, the embassy of the Republic of China closed permanently, and the relationship between Chinese Mexicans and the Republic of China ended abruptly. At the same time, associations like the ones that built and rebuilt the clock tower quickly suspended their activities. As a result, most Chinese associations founded by *paisanos* closed as their members quietly passed away. After 1971, the clock tower fell into disrepair, and Chinese association buildings turned into hollow shells. The old Guomindang building in Tapachula, for example, is currently only a facade—empty for decades, the roof having collapsed years ago. Proposals to renovate the old association buildings or use them for new purposes have languished.

Although there's an element of tragedy in the decline of these associations, it does not imply that they were insignificant or that they accomplished nothing. This book has endeavored to recover the history of the first wave of Chinese migrants after the anti-Chinese campaigns, and has argued that *paisanos* made a significant contribution to the eventual integration of immigrants in postrevolutionary Mexico, particularly during the Second World War and the Cold War.[6] As a result, it sheds additional light on Mexican postrevolutionary consolidation and stability, on changing notions of Mexican nationhood, and on the nature of Chinese transnational politics outside of the major areas of settlement in Southeast Asia and the United States. Chinese associations were in part victims of their own success at integrating into Mexican society, as second and subsequent generations did not feel pressured by domestic racism to maintain transpacific links to China. Overt racism against the Chinese has not disappeared, but the climate for Chinese immigrants, even new migrants, is far removed from the anti-Chinese campaigns of the early twentieth century. Although neither the Republic of China nor the initial generation of *paisanos* remain in Mexico, then, the impact of their presence continues to be felt among later generations of Chinese Mexicans. Miguel Ángel Osorio Chong, as Secretary of Gobernación, is likely the best-known descendant of this generation of *paisanos*. Rather than demonstrating how far the community has come, his rise demonstrates how barriers to mainstream success for immigrants to Mexico have gradually diminished. (Other examples include former president Vicente Fox, of Irish and Basque descent, and Mexican billionaire Carlos Slim Helú, of Lebanese ancestry.)[7]

As a result of new waves of Chinese migration to Mexico, discussed in chapter 6, the heterogeneity of the community of Chinese migrants has grown, and their ways of identifying with China and with their own identity have multiplied. Surprisingly, however, new waves of Chinese migration to Mexico and present-day Chinese–Mexican relations have mapped onto the patterns established by the Republic of China and by the Chinese associations of the twentieth century. Even the old clock tower, which remains standing, has not been exempt from this pattern. Rather than continuing to fall into disrepair, the clock was renovated in 2010 and rededicated once again to mark Mexico's bicentennial, this time from donations from *China Hoy* ("China Today"), a magazine from the People's Republic of China. The new renovation demonstrates the present-day coexistence of the children of earlier waves of Chinese migrants, indelibly marked by the anti-Chinese movement and the community's cooperation with the Republic of China, with newer waves of Chinese migrants who founded new associations under the encouragement of the ROC's rival, the People's Republic of China.

The arrival of new migrants seeking a better life across the Pacific Ocean represents a new challenge for Mexico and its people. New migratory waves have taken place amid increasing concerns about trade imbalances between China and Latin America, and fears of the repercussions that a rising China might have for the region. In this context, Chinese migrants and their ties to the People's Republic of China have been viewed with increasing alarm.[8] There is no shortage of Mexicans who continue to hold suspicions about the Chinese presence. In the course of this study, I encountered many people who, in large cities and small towns, lamented what they asserted to be the presence of too many Chinese in the country. The threat of a new eruption of xenophobia presents a substantial challenge to the Mexican government to ensure that the rights of immigrants are safeguarded and that Mexico does not repeat the grave mistakes of the past. Beyond the Mexican government, it will be up to everyday Mexicans to welcome new arrivals and, like the Chinese migrants of the past century, to be willing to share joys and sorrows into the twenty-first century.

Notes

INTRODUCTION

1. "Moxige fuzhuang biaoyan" [Mexican costume performance], October 20, 1961, Taiwan Digital Archives and E-Learning Joint Catalog, accessed September 15, 2015, http://catalog.digitalarchives.tw/item/00/31/9c/ob.html.

2. José Ángel Espinoza, *El problema chino en México* (México, DF, 1931), 33.

3. Erika Lee, *The Making of Asian America: A History* (New York: Simon & Schuster, 2015), 206. On the anti-Chinese movement in Mexico, see Robert Chao Romero, *The Chinese in Mexico, 1882–1940* (Tucson: University of Arizona Press, 2010); Grace Delgado, *Making the Chinese Mexican: Global Migration, Localism, and Exclusion in the U.S.–Mexican Borderlands* (Stanford, CA: Stanford University Press, 2012); Julia Maria Schiavone Camacho, *Chinese Mexicans: Transpacific Migration and the Search for a Homeland, 1910–1960* (Chapel Hill: University of North Carolina Press, 2012); and Elliott Young, *Alien Nation: Chinese Migration in the Americas from the Coolie Era through World War II* (Chapel Hill: University of North Carolina Press, 2014).

4. José Ángel Espinoza, *El ejemplo de Sonora* (México, DF, 1932), 102, 229–32.

5. Espinoza, *El ejemplo de Sonora*, 242.

6. José Vasconcelos, *La raza cósmica* (México, DF: Editorial Porrúa, 2010).

7. Espinoza, *El problema chino en México*, 108.

8. Schiavone Camacho, *Chinese Mexicans*, 4.

9. Jürgen Buchenau, *Tools of Progress: A German Merchant Family in Mexico City, 1865–Present* (Albuquerque: University of New Mexico Press, 2004), 7–8.

10. Chinese Mexicans largely hailed from Guangdong Province, but the anti-Chinese campaigns encouraged them to identify as Chinese. Similarly, Italians moved from regional attachments to national ones. See Michael Goebel, "Introduction: Reconceptualizing Diasporas and National Identities in Latin America

and the Caribbean, 1850–1950," in *Immigration and National Identities in Latin America,* ed. Nicola Foote and Michael Goebel (Gainesville: University Press of Florida, 2014), 15. Also see Nancy Foner, *In a New Land: A Comparative View of Immigration* (New York: New York University Press, 2005), 68–69.

11. Yen Le Espiritu, *Home Bound: Filipino American Lives across Cultures, Communities, and Countries* (Berkeley: University of California Press, 2003), 47.

12. Roger Waldinger, *The Cross-Border Connection: Immigrants, Emigrants, and Their Homelands* (Cambridge, MA: Harvard University Press, 2015), 84; Goebel, "Introduction," 6; Herbert J. Gans, "Toward a Reconciliation of 'Assimilation' and 'Pluralism': The Interplay of Acculturation and Ethnic Retention," *International Migration Review* 31, no. 4 (Winter 1997): 875–92.

13. This is similar to the case of Nisei in Brazil, who are often referred to as "*japonêses.*" Jeffrey Lesser, *A Discontented Diaspora: Japanese Brazilians and the Meanings of Ethnic Militancy, 1960–1980* (Durham, NC: Duke University Press, 2007), xix.

14. For an extended discussion of the word *paisano* in the context of Chinese communities, see Ernesto Martínez, "Border Chinese: Making Space and Forging Identity in Mexicali, Mexico" (PhD diss., Harvard University, 2008), 37–41. For examples of the use of the word, see Miguel Lisbona Guillén, *Allí donde lleguen las olas del mar: Pasado y presente de los chinos en Chiapas* (Chiapas: CONACULTA, 2014); and Julian Lim, "*Chinos* and *Paisanos:* Chinese Mexican Relations in the Borderlands," *Pacific Historical Review* 79, no. 1 (February 2010): 50–85. The word is also used in this sense in Spain's other former colonies. On the Philippines, see Richard Chu, *Chinese and Chinese Mestizos of Manila: Family, Identity, and Culture, 1860s–1930s* (Leiden: Brill, 2010). On Peru, see Humberto Rodríguez Pastor, "Perú: Presencia china e identidad nacional," in *Cuando oriente llegó a América: Contribuciones de inmigrantes chinos, japoneses y coreanos* (Washington, DC: Inter-American Development Bank, 2004), 126. *Pace* Martínez and Lim, the word is not used to denote native-born Chinese Mexicans, nor is it used by the Chinese community to refer to non-Chinese.

15. Buchenau, *Tools of Progress,* 8.

16. In this sense, the Chinese began to integrate at around the same time as the German and other foreign communities in Mexico. Buchenau, *Tools of Progress,* 6–8; Jürgen Buchenau, "The Limits of the Cosmic Race: Immigrant and Nation in Mexico, 1850–1950," in *Immigration and National Identities in Latin America,* ed. Nicola Foote and Michael Goebel (Gainesville: University Press of Florida, 2014), 85–87; also see Theresa Alfaro-Velcamp, *So Far from Allah, So Close to Mexico: Middle Eastern Immigrants in Modern Mexico* (Austin: University of Texas Press, 2007).

17. Lesser, *Discontented Diaspora,* xx.

18. Evelyn Hu-DeHart, "Voluntary Associations in a Predominantly Male Immigrant Community: The Chinese on the Northern Mexican Frontier, 1880–1930," in *Voluntary Organizations in the Chinese Diaspora,* ed. Kuhn Eng Kuah-Pearce and Evelyn Hu-DeHart (Hong Kong: Hong Kong University Press, 2006), 148–49.

19. Kathleen López, "In Search of Legitimacy: Chinese Immigrants and Latin American Nation Building," in *Immigration and National Identities in*

Latin America, ed. Nicola Foote and Michael Goebel (Gainesville: University Press of Florida, 2014), 183.

20. López, "In Search of Legitimacy," 183.

21. López, "In Search of Legitimacy," 192.

22. David FitzGerald and David Cook-Martín, *Culling the Masses: The Democratic Origins of Racist Immigration Policy in the Americas* (Cambridge, MA: Harvard University Press, 2014).

23. Wing Chung Ng, *The Chinese in Vancouver, 1945–80: The Pursuit of Identity and Power* (Vancouver, BC: UBC Press, 1999), 18; Ernest Koh, *Diaspora at War: The Chinese of Singapore between Empire and Nation, 1937–1945* (Leiden: Brill, 2013), 64.

24. Manying Ip, "Chinese Immigration to Australia and New Zealand: Government Policies and Race Relations," in *Routledge Handbook of the Chinese Diaspora,* ed. Chee-Beng Tan (London: Routledge, 2013), 163–165; Chu, *Chinese and Chinese Mestizos of Manila,* 403; Wing Chung Ng, "Becoming 'Chinese Canadian': The Genesis of a Cultural Category," in *The Last Half Century of Chinese Overseas,* ed. Elizabeth Sinn (Hong Kong: Hong Kong University Press, 1998), 205; Ching-hwang Yen, *The Chinese in Southeast Asia and Beyond: Socioeconomic and Political Dimensions* (Singapore: World Scientific Publishing, 2008), 23.

25. Ng, *Chinese in Vancouver,* 60–61; Isabelle Lausent-Herrera, "New Immigrants: A New Community? The Chinese Community in Peru in Complete Transformation," in *Routledge Handbook of the Chinese Diaspora,* ed. Chee-Beng Tan (London: Routledge, 2013), 375.

26. John Womack Jr., "The Spoils of the Mexican Revolution," *Foreign Affairs,* July 1970, cited in Louise Walker, *Waking from the Dream: Mexico's Middle Classes after 1968* (Stanford, CA: Stanford University Press, 2013), 4.

27. Buchenau, *Tools of Progress,* 141.

28. In Mexico, other foreign groups also "began to found chambers of commerce along national lines that (unlike individual entrepreneurs) could appeal for diplomatic protection." See Buchenau, "Limits of the Cosmic Race," 81; also see José Moya, "Immigrants and Associations: A Global and Historical Perspective," *Journal of Ethnic and Migration Studies* 31, no. 5 (September 2005): 838; and Delia Salazar Anaya, "Tres momentos de la inmigración internacional en México, 1880–1946," in *Extranjeros en México: Continuidades y aproximaciones,* ed. Ernesto Rodríguez Chávez (México, DF: Centro de Estudios Migratorios, Instituto Nacional de Migración, 2010), 76.

29. Walker, *Waking from the Dream,* 6.

30. Lorenzo Meyer, "Relaciones México-Estados Unidos: Arquitectura y montaje de las pautas de la guerra fría, 1945–1964," *Foro Internacional* 50, no. 2 (April–June 2010): 202–42; Mario Ojeda, *Alcances y límites de la política exterior de México* (México, DF: Colegio de México, 2011); Renata Keller, *Mexico's Cold War: Cuba, the United States, and the Legacy of the Mexican Revolution* (New York: Cambridge University Press, 2015), 9.

31. Jeanett Carrillo Magdaleno, *Mi nombre es Alicia Woong Castañeda* (Zapopan, Jalisco, Mexico: Editorial Amate, 2005); Manuel Lee Mancilla and Maricela González Félix, *Viaje al corazón de la península: Testimonio de Manuel*

Lee Mancilla (Mexicali, Baja California: Instituto de Cultura de Baja California, 2000); Monica Cinco Basurto, "China in Mexico: Yesterday's Encounter and Today's Discovery," in *Encounters: People of Asian Descent in the Americas,* ed. Roshni Rustomji-Kerns (Lanham, MD: Rowman & Littlefield, 1999).

CHAPTER 1

1. José Gómez Izquierdo, *El movimiento antichino en México: Problemas del racismo y del nacionalismo durante la Revolución Mexicana* (México, DF: Instituto Nacional de Antropología e Historia, 1991), 99; Gerardo Rénique, "Anti-Chinese Racism, Nationalism and State Formation in Post-Revolutionary Mexico, 1920s-1930s," in *Political Power and Social Theory*, vol. 14, ed. Diane E. Davis (Amsterdam: JAI, 2001), 93. A secret restriction on the entry of Chinese laborers existed as early as 1921, as the government sought a way to restrict Chinese migration while maintaining a positive relationship with China. Elliott Young, *Alien Nation: Chinese Migration in the Americas from the Coolie Era through World War II* (Chapel Hill: University of North Carolina Press, 2014), 207–11; David FitzGerald and David Cook-Martín, *Culling the Masses: The Democratic Origins of Racist Immigration Policy in the Americas* (Cambridge, MA: Harvard University Press, 2014), 241.

2. Henry Yu, "Mountains of Gold: Canada, North America, and the Cantonese Pacific," in *Routledge Handbook of the Chinese Diaspora*, ed. Chee-Beng Tan (New York: Routledge, 2013), 108–10; Ruth Mandujano López, "La migración interminable: Cantoneses en Manzanillo," *Legajos: Boletín del Archivo General de la Nación,* 7th ser., no. 1 (July–September 2009): 44–58.

3. Robert Chao Romero, *The Chinese in Mexico, 1882–1940* (Tucson: University of Arizona Press, 2010), 14–15, 27, 31. See also Lawrence Douglas Taylor Hansen, "The Chinese Six Companies of San Francisco and the Smuggling of Chinese Immigrants across the U.S.–Mexico Border, 1882–1930," *Journal of the Southwest* 48, no. 1 (Spring 2006): 37–61.

4. Romero, *Chinese in Mexico*, 5; Young, *Alien Nation*, 171–72.

5. Kennett Cott, "Mexican Diplomacy and the Chinese Issue, 1876–1910," *Hispanic American Historical Review* 67, no. 1 (February 1987): 63–85.

6. Pablo Yankelevich, "Corrupción y gestión migratoria en el México posrevolucionario," *Revista de Indias* 72, no. 255 (2012): 433–64.

7. Young, *Alien Nation*, 210; José Alfredo Gómez Estrada, *Gobierno y casinos: El origen de la riqueza de Abelardo L. Rodríguez* (Mexicali, Baja California: Instituto Mora, Universidad Autónoma de Baja California, 2002), 53.

8. Romero, *Chinese in Mexico*, 43, 46–47. See also Charles C. Cumberland, "The Sonora Chinese and the Mexican Revolution," *Hispanic American Historical Review* 40, no. 2 (May 1960): 191.

9. Catalina Velázquez Morales, "The Chinese Immigrants in Baja California: From the Cotton Fields to the City, 1920–1940," in *The Chinese in America: A History from Gold Mountain to the New Millennium,* ed. Susie Lan Cassel (Walnut Creek, CA: AltaMira Press, 2002), 402–5.

10. Chen Kwong Min, *Meizhou huaqiao tongjian* (New York: Meizhou Huaqiao Wenhuashe, 1950), 516–17, 521, 523, 534–35.

11. José Juan Cervera, *La gloria de la raza: Los chinos en Yucatán* (Mérida, Yucatán, Mexico: Instituto de Cultura de Yucatán, 2007), 79.

12. Yu Shouzhi (Yu Yuan-tse), "Moxige huaqiao dui zuguo kangzhan de gongxian," in *Huaqiao yu kangri zhanzheng* (Taipei: Huaqiao Xiehui Zonghui, 1999), 556–57; Romero, *Chinese in Mexico,* 191–95.

13. Evelyn Hu-DeHart, "Los chinos de Sonora, 1875 a 1930: La formación de una pequeña burguesía regional," in *Los inmigrantes en el mundo de los negocios, siglos XIX y XX,* ed. Rosa María Meyer and Delia Salazar Anaya (México, DF: CONACULTA-INAH, 2003), 118–19.

14. Young, *Alien Nation,* 250–54.

15. Evelyn Hu-DeHart, "Kang Youwei and the *Baohuanghui* in Mexico: When Two Nationalisms Collide" (unpublished manuscript). Also see Leo M. Dambourges Jacques, "The Chinese Massacre in Torreon (Coahuila) in 1911," *Arizona and the West* 16, no. 3 (Autumn 1974): 233–46; and Cumberland, "Sonora Chinese and the Mexican Revolution."

16. Young, *Alien Nation,* 77–78.

17. Romero, *Chinese in Mexico,* 58; Hu-DeHart, "Los chinos de Sonora," 116–17.

18. Romero, *Chinese in Mexico,* 1.

19. Hu-DeHart, "Los chinos de Sonora," 117. Before 1934, Mexican women assumed the nationality of their husbands at marriage, and thus could be counted as Chinese. However, the figure does not include Chinese men who naturalized as Mexicans, since they were counted as Mexican in the census. See Kif Augustine-Adams, "Making Mexico: Legal Nationality, Chinese Race, and the 1930 Population Census," *Law and History Review* 27, no. 1 (Spring 2009): 113–44.

20. Julia Maria Schiavone Camacho, *Chinese Mexicans: Transpacific Migration and the Search for a Homeland, 1910–1960* (Chapel Hill: University of North Carolina Press, 2012), 31–32.

21. Romero, *Chinese in Mexico,* 73–74.

22. The 1886 Law of Immigration and Naturalization granted citizenship to foreigners who had resided in the country for two years, as well as those who owned property in the country. Theresa Alfaro-Velcamp, *So Far from Allah, So Close to Mexico: Middle Eastern Immigrants in Modern Mexico* (Austin: University of Texas Press, 2007), 60; also see Susan Sanderson, Phil Sidel, and Harold Hims, "East Asians and Arabs in Mexico: A Study of Naturalized Citizens (1886–1931)," in *Asiatic Migrations in Latin America,* ed. Luz María Martinez Montiel (México, DF: Colegio de México, 1981).

23. Jürgen Buchenau, "The Limits of the Cosmic Race: Immigrant and Nation in Mexico, 1850–1950," in *Immigration and National Identities in Latin America,* ed. Nicola Foote and Michael Goebel (Gainesville: University Press of Florida, 2014), 75–76.

24. See Evelyn Hu-DeHart, "Voluntary Associations in a Predominantly Male Immigrant Community: The Chinese on the Northern Mexican Frontier, 1880–1930," in *Voluntary Organizations in the Chinese Diaspora,* ed. Khun Eng Kuah and Evelyn Hu-DeHart (Hong Kong: Hong Kong University Press, 2006).

25. Yu Shouzhi (Yu Yuan-tse), *Moxige huaqiao shihua* (Taipei: Haiwai Wenku Chubanshe, 1954), 13, 25.

26. Yucheng Qin, *The Diplomacy of Nationalism: The Six Companies and China's Policy towards Exclusion* (Honolulu: University of Hawaii Press, 2009), 9–10, 31.

27. Chen Kwong Min, *Meizhou huaqiao tongjian*, 514, 519; Eduardo Auyón Gerardo, *El dragón en el desierto: Los pioneros chinos en Mexicali* (Mexicali, Baja California: Instituto de Cultura de Baja California, 1991), 98.

28. Chen Kwong Min, *Meizhou huaqiao tongjian*, 507; Hu-DeHart, "Voluntary Associations," 149–50. Also see Feng Ziyou, *Huaqiao geming zuzhi shihua* (Taipei: Zhengzhong Shuju, 1958), 23–24.

29. Romero, *Chinese in Mexico*, 137; Chen Kuangmin, *Meizhou huaqiao tongjian*, 508.

30. FitzGerald and Cook-Martín, *Culling the Masses*, 226.

31. Chen Kwong Min, *Meizhou huaqiao tongjian*, 493–95; Wang Gungwu, *The Chinese Overseas: From Earthbound China to the Quest for Autonomy* (Cambridge, MA: Harvard University Press, 2000), 70.

32. Zhongyang weiyuanhui disanzu, *Zhongguo guomindang zai haiwai gedi dangbu shiliao chugao huibian* (Taipei: Zhongguo Guomindang Zhongyang Weiyuanhui Disanzu, 1961), 59, 67, 75, 79, 90; "Personalidad jurídica a la agrupación Partido Nacionalista Chino Kuo Ming Tang,'" March 21, 1927, Archivo General del Estado de Yucatán (hereafter AGEY), Fondo Congreso del Estado, Comisión de Gobernación, vol. 14, exp. 20, reg. 6130.

33. Him Mark Lai, "The Kuomintang in Chinese American Communities before World War II," in *Entry Denied: Exclusion and the Chinese Community in America, 1882–1943*, ed. Sucheng Chan (Philadelphia: Temple University Press, 1991) 183; Hu-DeHart, "Voluntary Associations," 151; Chen Kwong Min, *Meizhou huaqiao tongjian*, 504.

34. "Circular del Kuo Min Tang da a conocer su nuevo comité ejecutivo" *Chiapas* (Tapachula, Chiapas), January 19, 1930, front page, Centro Universitario de Información y Documentación, Universidad de Ciencias y Artes de Chiapas (hereafter CUID-UNICACH).

35. Archivo Plutarco Elías Calles Anexo—Fondo Plutarco Elías Calles, serie 12, exp. 2 leg. 7/11 inv. 1615, "Felicitaciones por entrega pacífica del poder: Estados."; Fernando Chi, exp., 36, inv. 1318. Both in Fidecomiso Archivo Plutarco Elías Calles y Fernando Torreblanca (hereafter FAPECFT).

36. Yu Shouzhi, "Moxige huaqiao dui zuguo kangzhan de gongxian, in *Huaqiao yu kangri zhanzheng* (Taipei: Huaqiao Xiehui Zonghui, 1999), 562–63.

37. Rénique, "Anti-Chinese Racism," 110.

38. Romero, *Chinese in Mexico*, 136–37.

39. Gómez Izquierdo, *El movimiento antichino en México*, 117; Velázquez Morales, "Diferencias políticas," 481.

40. Lisa Rose Mar, *Brokering Belonging: Chinese in Canada's Exclusion Era, 1885–1945* (New York: Oxford University Press, 2010), 61–63; Young, *Alien Nation*, 259–60; Velázquez Morales, "Diferencias políticas," 494–96.

41. Velázquez Morales, "Diferencias políticas," 490. As Stephen Craft notes, the warlord who controlled Beijing received diplomatic recognition. This would

explain why, as noted by Velázquez Morales and others, diplomatic envoys to Mexico before 1927 were hostile to the Guomindang. See Craft, *V. K. Wellington Koo and the Emergence of Modern China* (Lexington: University Press of Kentucky, 2004), 41.

42. Velázquez Morales, "Diferencias políticas," 495.

43. Yu Shouzhi, "Moxige huaqiao dui zuguo kangzhan de gongxian," 562–63.

44. Grace Peña Delgado, *Making the Chinese Mexican: Global Migration, Localism, and Exclusion in the U.S.–Mexico Borderlands* (Stanford, CA: Stanford University Press, 2012), 159–60.

45. Hu-DeHart, "Voluntary Associations," 152; Delgado, *Making the Chinese Mexican*, 168; Gómez Izquierdo, *El movimiento antichino en México*, 122.

46. Evelyn Hu-DeHart, "Indispensable Enemy or Convenient Scapegoat? A Critical Examination of Sinophobia in Latin America and the Caribbean, 1870s to 1930s," *Journal of Chinese Overseas* 5, no. 1 (2009): 81n16.

47. Lore Diana Kuehnert, "Pernicious Foreigners and Contested Compatriots: Mexican Newspaper Debates over Immigration, Emigration and Repatriation, 1928–1936" (PhD diss., University of California, Riverside, 2002), 154–60.

48. Velázquez Morales, "Diferencias políticas," 463–64.

49. Velázquez Morales, "Diferencias políticas," 486; Rénique, "Anti-Chinese Racism," 111; Romero, *Chinese in Mexico*, 139.

50. Rénique, "Anti-Chinese Racism," 111.

51. Rénique, "Anti-Chinese Racism," 114.

52. Catalina Velázquez Morales, "Xenofobia y racismo: Los comités antichinos en Sonora y Baja California, 1924–1936," *Meyibó*, no. 1, n.s. (November 2009): 43–81.

53. Gómez Izquierdo, *El movimiento antichino en México*, 88; Rénique, "Anti-Chinese Racism," 98–99.

54. Rénique, "Anti-Chinese Racism," 105.

55. Romero, *Chinese in Mexico*, 161; Rénique, "Anti-Chinese Racism," 111.

56. Dambourges Jacques, "Anti-Chinese Campaigns in Sonora," xii.

57. Hu-DeHart, "Indispensable Enemy or Convenient Scapegoat?" 81.

58. "Se comunica la parte considerativa de la sentencia dictada en el Amparo de Hip Lee y co-agraviados al C. Gobernador del Estado, Hermosillo," March 25, 1924, cited in Delgado, *Making the Chinese Mexican*, 179.

59. Rénique, "Anti-Chinese Racism," 104; "Apuntes relativos a las modificaciones que pueden introducirse al tratado de Amistad, comercio y navegación, existente entre México y la Rep. China" and "Acuerdo del Presidente Álvaro Obregón a la Secretaría de Relaciones Exteriores sin fecha," in *Chinos y antichinos en México: Documentos para su estudio,* ed. Humberto Monteón González and José Luis Trueba Lara (Guadalajara: Gobierno de Jalisco, Unidad Editorial, 1988), 61–63.

60. Delgado, *Making the Chinese Mexican*, 179.

61. The Mexican constitution of 1917 differentiates the rights of natural-born Mexicans from those of naturalized Mexicans. Yankelevich, "Nación y extranjería," 8–10.

62. "Ley de Extranjería y Naturalización Anotada por Armando C. Amador, Jefe de la Cancillería de Relaciones Exteriores," 1925, Archive of the Mexican Secretary of Foreign Relations (hereafter AHSRE) IV-338–1.

63. José Ángel Espinoza, *El problema chino en México* (México, DF, 1931), 131–35.

64. José Ángel Espinoza, *El ejemplo de Sonora* (México, DF, 1932), photograph insert opposite p. 144.

65. Governor José Ramón Valdez to Secretary of Gobernación, September 22, 1930, Archivo General de la Nación (hereafter AGN), Dirección General de Gobierno (hereafter DGG), 2.362.2 (7) 12.

66. Secretaría de Gobernación, February 28, 1931, AGN DGG 2.362.2 (7) 12.

67. Pablo Yankelevich, "El artículo 33 en cifras," in *¿Deseables o inconvenientes? Las fronteras de la extranjería en el México posrevolucionario* (México, DF: Bonilla Artigas Editores, 2011), 87–126.

68. These children were entitled to birthright citizenship as long as they renounced their Chinese citizenship after they turned eighteen years old. Although Espinoza lamented that these native-born Mexicans remained culturally Chinese, he did not propose stripping these children of their Mexican citizenship, nor did the anti-Chinese campaigns specifically target native-born children.

69. Robert Chao Romero, "'El destierro de los Chinos': Popular Perspectives on Chinese-Mexican Intermarriage in the Early Twentieth Century," *Aztlán: A Journal of Chicano Studies* 32, no. 1 (Spring 2007): 136–37. Cumberland, "Sonora Chinese and the Mexican Revolution," 199.

70. Kuehnert, "Pernicious Foreigners and Contested Compatriots," 147.

71. Daniela Gleizer, *Unwelcome Exiles: Mexico and the Jewish Refugees from Nazism, 1933–1945* (Leiden: Brill, 2014), 33–34, 37.

72. Delgado, *Making the Chinese Mexican,* 158.

73. Espinoza, *El problema chino en México,* 37. Rénique, "Anti-Chinese Racism," 93, 104.

74. Erika Lee, *The Making of Asian America: A History* (New York: Simon & Schuster, 2015), 106–7.

75. Alicia Gojman de Backal, *Camisas, escudos y desfiles militares: Los Dorados y el antisemitismo en México, 1934–1940* (México, DF: Fondo de Cultura Económica 2000), 167.

76. Lorenzo Meyer, Rafael Segovia, and Alejandra Lajous, *Los inicios de la institucionalización: La política del Maximato* (México, DF: Colegio de México, 1978), 9, 39; Tzvi Medin, *El minimato presidencial: Historia política del Maximato (1928–1935)* (México, DF: Ediciones Era, 1982), 41.

77. Rénique, "Anti-Chinese Racism," 104.

78. Buchenau, "Limits of the Cosmic Race," 80.

79. Part III, document 59, "Zhushun lingshiguan chengbao shunsheng paihua shi mo jiaoshe jingguo, qiaomin xiankuang ji banshi kunnan yuanyou" [Report from the consulate in Sonora on attempts to make representations in Sonora's anti-Chinese campaign from start to finish, current conditions of overseas nationals and reasons for the difficulties in handling affairs], October 29, 1931, in *Paihua shiliao huibian: Moxige,* ed. He Fengjiao (Taipei: Guoshiguan, 1991), 1:279–338; Gleizer, *Unwelcome Exiles,* 55.

80. Jürgen Buchenau, "From the *Caudillo* to Tata Lázaro: The *Maximato* in Perspective, 1928–1934," in *The Mexican Revolution: Conflict and Consolidation, 1910–1940,* ed. Douglas Richmond and Sam Haynes (College Station, TX: Texas A&M University Press, 2013), 145–46; Nora Hamilton, *The Limits of State Autonomy: Post-Revolutionary Mexico* (Princeton, NJ: Princeton University Press, 2014), 87.

81. Part III, document 40, "Zhumo shiguan chengbao moguo paihua ji qing mei diaoting zuijin qingxing" [Legation in Mexico reports on Mexico's anti-Chinese campaign and asks the United States to mediate most recent conditions], September 11, 1931, in He, *Paihua shiliao huibian: Moxige,* 1:241.

82. Part II, document 28, "Ma Jixiu dian moguo paihua jiaoshe shi" [Ma Jixiu telegram on the matter of making representations in Mexico's anti-Chinese campaign], January 6, 1931, in He, *Paihua shiliao huibian: Moxige,* 1:97–98.

83. Gómez Izquierdo, *El movimiento antichino en México,* 137.

84. Francisco S. Elías to Subsecretary of Foreign Relations, July 29, 1931, AHSRE III-297-26.

85. "Al Presidente Del Comité Ncta. Navojoa, Son," July 6, 1931, AHSRE III-297-26; "Memorandum," September 10, 1931, AHSRE III-297-26.

86. Alan Knight, "The Character and Consequences of the Great Depression in Mexico," in *The Great Depression in Latin America,* ed. Paulo Drinot and Alan Knight (Durham, NC: Duke University Press, 2014), 219; Medin, *El minimato presidencial,* 116; part III, document 59, "Zhushun lingshiguan chengbao," in He, *Paihua shiliao huibian: Moxige.*

87. Knight, "Great Depression in Mexico," 219; on the repatriation of Mexicans and Mexican Americans, see Francisco E. Balderrama and Raymond Rodríguez, *Decade of Betrayal: Mexican Repatriation in the 1930s* (Albuquerque: University of New Mexico Press, 1995).

88. Federación de Sindicatos y Uniones Obreras de Tijuana to the Secretary of Gobernación, April 1, 1932, AGN DGG 2.360 (30) 7; Dambourges Jacques, "Anti-Chinese Campaigns in Sonora," xii.

89. Federación de Sindicatos y Uniones Obreras de Tijuana to the Secretary of Gobernación, January 15, 1932, Instituto de Investigaciones Históricas, Universidad Autónoma de Baja California (hereafter IIH-UABC), Dirección General de Gobierno 25.1.

90. Cumberland, "Sonora Chinese and the Mexican Revolution," 202.

91. Kuehnert, "Pernicious Foreigners and Contested Compatriots," 83.

92. Part III, document 6, "Zhushun lingshiguan cheng shunsheng paihua yuanyin, jingguo ji jiaoshe qingxing" [Consulate in Sonora reports on reasons of anti-Chinese campaign in Sonora, result and negotiating conditions], July 28, 1931, in He, *Paihua shiliao huibian: Moxige,* 1:172–75; part III, document 59, "Zhushun lingshiguan chengbao," He, *Paihua shiliao huibian: Moxige.*

93. Part III, document 53, "Qiao mo nanhekebu zhenxiang gongsi baocheng gai gongsi sunshi ji yu paihuadang po dingzhi hetong" [Navojoa, Mexico, Chinese company Zhen Xiang reports company's losses and is forced to draw up a contract with anti-Chinese party], September 25, 1931, in He, *Paihua shiliao huibian: Moxige,* 1:262–64; Delgado, *Making the Chinese Mexican,* 184.

94. Part III, document 36, "Xingzhengyuan mishuchu han waijiaobu jiaoban zhumo zishadalengbu huaqiao tuantihui cheng qing kang moguo paihua" [Executive Yuan Office of the Secretary writes Ministry of Foreign Affairs to send along Mexico Mazatlán Chinese Association report asking to protest Mexico's anti-Chinese campaign], September 7, 1931, in He, *Paihua shiliao huibian: Moxige,* 1:232–34.

95. Romero, *Chinese in Mexico,* 189; Delgado, *Making the Chinese Mexican,* 157–58.

96. On strategic nationalism, see Schiavone Camacho, *Chinese Mexicans.*

97. Part II, document 14, attachment 2, "Zhongguo Guomindang zhumo zongzhibu tonggao huaqiao tuanjie yingfu paihua" [Central Branch of the Chinese Guomindang in Mexico notifies overseas Chinese to unite to deal with the anti-Chinese movement], October 2, 1930, in He, *Paihua shiliao huibian: Moxige,* 1:77–80.

98. Part III, document 1, "Zhumo shiguan chengbao shunsheng qiaoxing shixing gongli qingxing" [Legation in Mexico reports on Sonora forced enactment of Labor Law current conditions], July 9, 1931, in He, *Paihua shiliao huibian: Moxige,* 1:155–56; part III, document 5, "Zhumo shiguan chengbao Shun, Shan liangsheng paihua ji qi jiaoshe qingxing," [Legation in Mexico reports on the two states of Sonora and Sinaloa's anti-Chinese campaigns and other representations' current conditions], July 25, 1931; both in He, *Paihua shiliao huibian: Moxige,* 1:159–72; part III; document 6, "Zhushunsheng lingshiguan cheng," in He, *Paihua shiliao huibian: Moxige.* 172–76. Also see "Condiciones en Nogales, Sonora," "Condiciones en Ciudad Obregón, Sonora," and Alejandro Llánes to Chinese Minister to Mexico, n.d.; all in AHSRE III-297-26. Llánes includes receipts of wages paid to anti-Chinese activists on July 13, 14, 16, and 18.

99. Peng Yaoxiang to Governor of Sonora, n.d., copy as attachment to part III, document 59, "Zhushun lingshiguan chengbao," in He, *Paihua shiliao huibian: Moxige.*

100. Peng Yaoxiang to Governor of Sonora, July 22, 1931, copy as attachment to part III, document 59, "Zhushun lingshiguan chengbao," in He, *Paihua shiliao huibian: Moxige.*

101. Peng Yaoxiang to Governor of Sonora, n.d., copy as attachment to part III, document 59, "Zhushun lingshiguan chengbao," in He, *Paihua shiliao huibian: Moxige.*

102. Part III, document 13, "Xiong Chongzhi dian moguo paihua, jiaoshe jishou, qingshi duifu fangfa" [Xiong Chongzhi telegram Mexico anti-Chinese campaign, making representations thorny, ask for instructions on ways to handle], August 12, 1931, in He, *Paihua shiliao huibian: Moxige,* 1:198.

103. Part III, document 5, "Zhumo shiguan chengbao," in He, *Paihua shiliao huibian: Moxige.*

104. Part III, document 9, "Zhumo shiguan chengbao fensong zhumei shiguan moguo paihua qingxing jielüe" [Legation in Mexico reports on distributing to the embassy in the United States summary of Mexico's anti-Chinese campaign conditions], August 8, 1931, in He, *Paihua shiliao huibian: Moxige,* 1:177–96.

105. Part III, document 40, "Zhumo shiguan chengbao," in He, *Paihua shiliao huibian: Moxige.*

106. Part III, document 50, "Zhumo shiguan chengbao moguo paihua jinkuang ji gai guan jiaoshe qingxing" [Legation in Mexico reports Mexico anti-Chinese campaign current conditions and the conditions of the legation making representations], September 22, 1931, in He, *Paihua shiliao huibian: Moxige,* 1:256–59.

107. Peng Yaoxiang to Governor of Sonora, October 28, 1931, copy as attachment to part III, document 59, "Zhushun lingshiguan chengbao," in He, *Paihua shiliao huibian: Moxige;* part III, document 59, "Zhushun lingshiguan chengbao," in He, *Paihua shiliao huibian: Moxige;* Schiavone Camacho, *Chinese Mexicans,* 66–67.

108. Part III, document 62, "Zhumo shiguan cheng moguo paihua jinkuang ji gai guan xiang mozhengfu jiaoshe zhi qingxing" [Legation in Mexico reports on recent conditions of Mexico's anti-Chinese campaign and the conditions of the legation's representations before the Mexican government], November 20, 1931, in He, *Paihua shiliao huibian: Moxige* 1:339–41.

109. Part III, document 64, "Zhushun lingshiguan chengbao shunsheng paihua houguo" [Legation in Mexico reports on outcome of Sonora's anti-Chinese campaign], December 4, 1931, in He, *Paihua shiliao huibian: Moxige,* 1:352–54.

110. Chinese Minister in Mexico to Mexican Secretary of Foreign Relations, February 13, 1933, AHSRE III-297–26; part III, document 73, "Impuestos mensuales que pagan en este año varios comerciantes chinos en Sinaloa y los que les han sido asignados para el año de 1932," in He, *Paihua shiliao huibian: Moxige,* 1:371–74.

111. Chinese Minister in Mexico to Mexican Secretary of Foreign Relations, February 13, 1933; Chinese Minister in Mexico to Mexican Secretary of Foreign Relations, February 21, 1933. Both in AHSRE III-297–26.

112. Schiavone Camacho, *Chinese Mexicans,* 94.

113. Chinese Minister to Mexico to Secretary of Foreign Relations, February 20, 1932, AHSRE III-297–26.

114. Chinese Legation in Mexico to Secretary of Foreign Relations, August 25, 1932, AHSRE III-297–26.

115. Subsecretary of Gobernación to Secretary of Foreign Relations, October 7, 1932, AHSRE III-297–26. For more on an estimated two hundred Chinese Mexicans who remained in Sonora through the anti-Chinese campaigns, see Schiavone Camacho, *Chinese Mexicans,* 76–79.

116. Part III, document 62, "Zhumo shiguan cheng," in He, *Paihua shiliao huibian: Moxige;* Chinese Minister to Mexico to Mexican Secretary of Foreign Relations, November 30, 1931, AHSRE III-297–26.

117. "Mexico: Vamos!" *Time,* September 14, 1931, accessed September 19, 2009, http://www.time.com/time/magazine/article/0,9171,742223,00.html; Mexican Minister to Japan to Secretary of Foreign Relations, June 27, 1933, AHSRE III-297–26.

118. "Chinese from Mexico Arrive in Shanghai," AHSRE III-121–39.

119. Mauricio Fresco, Honorary Mexican Consul in Shanghai, to Secretary of Foreign Relations, May 10, 1933, AHSRE III-297–26.

120. "La revue de la presse chinoise: Le mouvement anti-chinois au Mexique," *Journal de Shanghai,* May 17, 1933, copy in AHSRE III-297–26.

121. "There Is a Difference," *St. Louis Globe Democrat,* March 8, 1933, copy in AHSRE III-297–26.

122. Archivo Plutarco Elías Calles, Elías, Francisco S., exp. 58, leg. 4/7, inv. 1722, FAPECFT.

123. Archivo Plutarco Elías Calles, Elías Calles Chacón, Rodolfo, exp. 4, leg. 13/24, inv. 1733, FAPECFT.

124. US Vice Consul in San Luis Potosí to Secretary of State, January 7, 1932, cited in Alfaro-Velcamp, *So Far from Allah,* 118.

125. Alfaro-Velcamp, *So Far from Allah,* 122.

126. Alfaro-Velcamp, *So Far from Allah,* 119.

127. Buchenau, "From the Caudillo to Tata Lázaro," 150.

128. Gleizer, *Unwelcome Exiles,* 29.

129. Mexican Secretary of Foreign Relations Puig Casauranc to Governor of Sinaloa Manuel Páez, May 15, 1933, AHSRE III-297–26.

130. Mexican Secretary of Foreign Relations Puig Casauranc to Governor of Sonora Rodolfo Calles, May 15, 1933, AHSRE III-297–26; Young, *Alien Nation,* 245.

CHAPTER 2

1. Secretary of Foreign Relations to Secretary of Gobernación, September 17, 1931; Provisional Governor of Nayarit, General Juventino Espinoza, to Secretary of Gobernación, October 3, 1931; Ramón Ley y Hermanos, Rosamorada, Nayarit, to State Government of Nayarit, September 8, 1931; Subsecretary of Foreign Relations José Vázquez Schiaffino to Secretary of Gobernación, December 9, 1931; all in AGN DGG 2.360 (15) 1.

2. Li Ying-Hui, *Huaqiao zhengce yu haiwai minzu zhuyi (1912–1949)* (Taipei: Guoshiguan, 1997), 220.

3. Charles C. Cumberland, "The Sonora Chinese and the Mexican Revolution," *Hispanic American Historical Review* 40, no. 2 (May 1960): 210.

4. Part II, document 35, "Zhumo shiguan cheng waijiaobu baogao banli moren paihua ji Yu yonghe deng sanshiren beibo huiguo an qingxing" [Legation in Mexico reports to Ministry of Foreign Affairs on handling Mexicans' anti-Chinese campaigns as well as Yu Yonghe and thirty others forced to return to China], December 18, 1930, in *Paihua shiliao huibian: Moxige,* ed. He Fengjiao (Taipei: Guoshiguan, 1991), 1: 103–7.

5. José Ángel Espinoza, *El problema chino en México* (México, DF, 1931), 179.

6. Espinoza, *El problema chino en México,* 179, 197, 233. Also see Catalina Velázquez Morales, "Xenofobia y racismo: Los comités antichinos de Sonora y Baja California, 1924–1936," *Meyibó* 1, n.s. (January–June 2010): 43–81.

7. Espinoza, *El problema chino en México,* 179–80.

8. Elliott Young, *Alien Nation: Chinese Migration in the Americas from the Coolie Era through World War II* (Chapel Hill: University of North Carolina Press, 2014), 220.

9. José Jorge Gómez Izquierdo, *El movimiento antichino en México (1871–1934): Problemas del racismo y del nacionalismo durante la Revolución Mexi-*

cana (México, DF: Instituto Nacional de Antropología e Historia, 1991), 151; AGN DGG 2.360 (3) 8002.

10. "Iniciativa del H. Ayuntamiento de Santa Ana, Estado de Sonora," Fondo Congreso del Estado, Sección Comisión de Trabajo, vol. 2, exp. 77, reg. 7544; "Los ayuntamientos de Nogales, Moctezuma y Santa Ana de Sonora, y Morelia de Michoacán proponen romper lazos de amistad con la nación China," Fondo Congreso del Estado, Sección Pleno del Congreso, vol. 13, exp. 18, reg. 6042; both in Archivo General del Estado de Yucatán (hereafter AGEY).

11. Chen Kwong Min, *Meizhou huaqiao tongjian* (New York: Meizhou Huaqiao Wenhuashe, 1950), 512.

12. Chen Kwong Min, *Meizhou huaqiao tongjian,* 502. There was an Anti-Chinese and Anti-Jewish League in Mexico City, but it appears not to have seriously threatened Chinese lives and businesses. AGN DGG 2.360 (29) 8105.

13. Chen Kwong Min, *Meizhou huaqiao tongjian,* 545.

14. Robert Chao Romero, *The Chinese in Mexico, 1882–1940* (Tucson: University of Arizona Press, 2010), 50–51; Grace Peña Delgado, *Making the Chinese Mexican: Global Migration, Localism, and Exclusion in the U.S.–Mexico Borderlands* (Stanford, CA: Stanford University Press, 2012), 36.

15. L. Ricardo Martínez Marín, "La migración china en el estado de Tamaulipas, 1900–1940" (MA thesis, UAM Iztapalapa, 1995), 44. See p. 54, table 5, for a breakdown of Chinese occupations according to the National Registry of Foreigners.

16. Evelyn Hu-DeHart, "Kang Youwei and the *Baohuanghui* in Mexico: When Two Nationalisms Collide" (unpublished manuscript); Chen Kwong Min, *Meizhou huaqiao tongjian,* 590.

17. Francisco Ramos Aguirre, *Los chinos del 14 y otros chinos: Crónica de Ciudad Victoria* (Ciudad Victoria, Tamaulipas, Mexico: Prograf, 2000), 11; US Consul in Tampico to US Secretary of State, "Political and Economic Report on the Tampico Consular District for the Month of January, 1943," U.S. Consulate, Tampico Classified General Records, 1938–1955, box 5, record group 84, US National Archives (hereafter USNA).

18. US Consul in Tampico to US Secretary of State, "Political and Economic Report."

19. Chen Kwong Min, *Meizhou huaqiao tongjian,* 510, 512.

20. Alan Knight, "The Character and Consequences of the Great Depression in Mexico," in *The Great Depression in Latin America,* ed. Paulo Drinot and Alan Knight (Durham, NC: Duke University Press, 2014), 226.

21. Part II, document 9, "Zhumo shiguan cheng waijiaobu cheng Kalishi ju bu hua an banli qingxing ji qita qiaowu" [Legation in Mexico reports to Ministry of Foreign Affairs on Villa Juárez detention of Chinese and other overseas Chinese affairs], October 6, 1930, in He, *Paihua shiliao huibian: Moxige,* 1:60–65.

22. "Informe de la comisión conferida en Villa Juárez, Tamps." October 10, 1930, AGN Dirección General de Investigaciones Políticas y Sociales (hereafter DGIPS), box 62, file 19.

23. Chen Kwong Min, *Meizhou huaqiao tongjian,* 511.

24. Part II, document 9, "Zhumo shiguan cheng," in He, *Paihua shiliao huibian: Moxige.*

25. Consul Chen to Secretary of Gobernación Carlos Riva Palacio, September 26, 1930, AGN DGG 2.362.2 (24) 42.

26. "Informe de la comisión conferida en Villa Juárez."

27. Guillermo Davis to Secretary of Gobernación Carlos Riva Palacio, September 30, 1930, AGN DGIPS box 62, file 19.

28. Chen Kwong Min, *Meizhou huaqiao tongjian*, 511.

29. Guillermo Davis to Secretary of Gobernación Carlos Riva Palacio, September 30, 1930, AGN DGIPS box 62, file 19.

30. Part II, document 3, "Xiong chongzhi dian waijiaobu yi yanzhong jiaoshe moguo paihua" [Xiong Chongzhi telegrams Ministry of Foreign Affairs as to serious negotiations on Mexico's anti-Chinese campaigns], September 27, 1930, in He, *Paihua shiliao huibian: Moxige*, 1:54.

31. Part II, document 50, "Zhumo shiguan chengbao ju bo an banli qingxing" [Legation in Mexico reports on handling matter of detaining and displacing (Chinese)], April 22, 1931, in He, *Paihua shiliao huibian: Moxige*, 1:138–44.

32. October 10, Ligas Diversas, exp. 10, leg. 6/16, inv. 3199, FAPECFT.

33. Part II, document 9, "Zhumo shiguan cheng," in He, *Paihua shiliao huibian: Moxige*.

34. Part II, document 50, "Zhumo shiguan chengbao," in He, *Paihua shiliao huibian: Moxige*, 1:138–44.

35. Jürgen Buchenau, *The Last Caudillo: Álvaro Obregón and the Mexican Revolution* (Malden, MA: Wiley-Blackwell, 2011), 145; Part II, document 9, "Zhumo shiguan cheng," in He, *Paihua shiliao huibian: Moxige*.

36. Part II, document 50, "Zhumo shiguan chengbao," in He, *Paihua shiliao huibian: Moxige*.

37. Part II, document 14, "Zhongguo Guomindang zhongyang zhixing weiyuanhui mishuchu han waijiaobu jiaoshe moguo paihua yijie daoxuan" [Secretariat of Executive Committee of China Guomindang writes to Ministry of Foreign Affairs to intercede in Mexico's anti-Chinese campaign so as to relieve distress], November 5, 1930, in He, *Paihua shiliao huibian: Moxige*, 1:75.

38. Part II, document 16, "Xiong chongzhi dian beiju huaqiao ji paihua an chuli qingxing" [Xiong Chongzhi Telegrams on condition of detained overseas Chinese and matter of handling anti-Chinese campaign], November 6, 1930, in He, *Paihua shiliao huibian: Moxige*, 1:80–81.

39. Part II, document 50, "Zhumo shiguan chengbao," in He, *Paihua shiliao huibian: Moxige*.

40. Part II, document 52, "Zhumo shiguan chengbao tansheng ju bu huaqiao ji jiaoshe qingxing" [Legation in Mexico reports Tamaulipas State detains overseas Chinese and conditions of intervention], June 1, 1931, in He, *Paihua shiliao huibian: Moxige*, 1:146–47; Encarnación González to Secretary of Gobernación, December 6, 1930, AGN DGG 2.362.2 (24) 42.

41. Part II, document 50, "Zhumo shiguan chengbao," in He, *Paihua shiliao huibian: Moxige*; part III, document 2, "Zhumo shiguan cheng banli moguo bo zhu huaqiao jiaoshe qingxing" [Legation in Mexico reports on handling negotiations on Mexico detaining and expelling overseas Chinese], July 14, 1931, in He, *Paihua shiliao huibian: Moxige*, 1:156–58.

42. Michael A. Ervin, "Marte R. Gómez of Tamaulipas: Governing Agrarian Revolution," in *State Governors in the Mexican Revolution, 1910–1952: Portraits in Conflict, Courage, and Corruption,* ed. Jürgen Buchenau and William H. Beezley (Lanham: Rowman & Littlefield, 2009), 132; US Consul in Tampico to US Secretary of State, "Political and Economic Report."

43. Eduardo Auyón Gerardo, *El dragón en el desierto: Los pioneros chinos en Mexicali* (Mexicali, Baja California, Mexico: Instituto de Cultura de Baja California, 1991), 50.

44. David Piñera Ramírez, ed., *Panorama histórico de Baja California* (Tijuana: Centro de Investigaciones Históricas UNAM-UABC, 1983), 465.

45. Catalina Velázquez Morales, "The Chinese Immigrants in Baja California: From the Cotton Fields to the City, 1920–1940," in *The Chinese in America: A History from Gold Mountain to the New Millennium,* ed. Susie Lan Cassel (Walnut Creek, CA, 2002), 408.

46. Ángela Moyano de Guevara and Jorge Martínez Zepeda, coords., *Visión histórica de Ensenada* (Mexicali, Baja California, Mexico: Centro de Investigaciones Históricas UNAM-UABC), 248.

47. Chen Kwong Min, *Meizhou huaqiao tongjian,* 615.

48. Marco Antonio Samaniego López, coord., *Breve Historia de Baja California* (Mexicali, Baja California: Universidad Autónoma de Baja California, 2006), 121.

49. Samaniego López, *Ensenada: Nuevas aportaciones,* 655–57.

50. Secretary of Gobernación Vasconcelos to Secretary of Foreign Relations Puig Casauranc, February 9, 1934, AGN DGG 2.360 (30) 7; Samaniego López, *Ensenada: Nuevas aportaciones,* 655–57.

51. J. Julio Dunn L., "La invasión china en Baja California," February 28, 1935. IIH-UABC, Lázaro Cárdenas 13.10.

52. Moyano de Guevara and Martínez Zepeda, *Visión histórica de Ensenada,* 248.

53. Dambourges Jacques, "Anti-Chinese Campaigns in Sonora," 259.

54. Comité Pro-Raza Rodolfo Elías Calles to Pascual Ortiz Rubio, August 8, 1932. IIH-UABC, Dirección General de Gobierno 25.1. Ortiz Rubio would cut off the entry of new Chinese immigrants to Baja California. Espinoza, *El problema chino en México,* 37.

55. Part IV, document 119, "Xinwenbao baodao moguo paihua yu'e" [Newspaper reports Mexico's anti-Chinese campaign worsening], April 3, 1934, in He, *Paihua shiliao huibian: Moxige,* 2:292; "Chinese Flee Mexican Drive," *Los Angeles Times,* February 23, 1934, 8.

56. Chen Kwong Min, *Meizhou huaqiao tongjian,* 545; part IV, document 104, "Zhu Moxige gongshiguan cheng waijiaobu jiaoshe xiajiasheng yuanshannadabu paihuadang baowei huaqiao shangdian qingxing" [Legation in Mexico reports to the Ministry of Foreign Affairs interceding in Ensenada, Baja California's anti-Chinese party surrounding overseas Chinese businesses], February 16, 1934, in He, *Paihua shiliao huibian: Moxige,* 2:263.

57. Part IV, document 108, "Zhu Moxige gongshi dian waijiaobu paihua jiaoshe jishou" [Legation in Mexico telegrams interceding in anti-Chinese

campaigns troublesome], February 23, 1934, in He, *Paihua shiliao huibian: Moxige,* 2:268.

58. Governor Agustín Olachea to Secretary of Gobernación, February 22, 1934, AGN DGG 2.360 (30) 7.

59. Part IV, document 104, "Zhu Moxige gongshiguan cheng," in He, *Paihua shiliao huibian: Moxige.*

60. Samaniego López, *Ensenada: Nuevas aportaciones,* 635.

61. Mexican Ambassador to the United States to the Mexican Secretary of Foreign Relations, April 9, 1934, AHSRE III-223–4.

62. "Chinese Flee Mexican Drive."

63. For example, "Moxige paihua yu'e" [Mexico's anti-Chinese situation worsening], *Xinwen Bao,* n.d., copy in Archives of the Ministry of Foreign Affairs, Academia Historica (Guoshiguan Xindian) (hereafter GSG), 020000037490A. Also see "Mo Ensainada cheng fasheng paihua" [Anti-Chinese movement erupts in Mexico's Ensenada], *Zhongyang Ribao,* February 24, 1934; and "Moxige: paihua xiangqing" [Mexico's anti-Chinese Movement: Detailed Conditions], *Xinwen Bao,* n.d.; copies in GSG 020000037491A.

64. Mexican Minister in China to Mexican Secretary of Foreign Relations, June 26, 1934, AHSRE III-223–4.

65. Governor Agustín Olachea to Secretary of Gobernación Eduardo Vasconcelos, February 18, 1934, IIH-UABC, fondo Dirección General de Gobierno 25.1.

66. Governor Agustín Olachea to Secretary of Gobernación Eduardo Vasconcelos, February 23, 1934, IIH-UABC, fondo Dirección General de Gobierno 25.1.

67. Part IV, document 109, "Zhu Moxige gongshiguan cheng waijiaobu mo waijiaobu fuyan xiajiasheng paihua rilie" [Legation in Mexico reports to the Ministry of Foreign Affairs Mexico's Secretary of Foreign Relations acting perfunctorily, Baja California anti-Chinese campaign more violent by the day], February 23, 1934, in He, *Paihua shiliao huibian: Moxige,* 2:268.

68. Part IV, document 116, "Zhu Moxige gongshiguan cheng waijiaobu xiajiasheng yuanshannadabu xiepo qiaoshang qianyue xianqili jingji jiaoshe qingxing" [Legation in Mexico reports to Ministry of Foreign Affairs on Ensenada Baja California forces Chinese businessmen to sign a contract giving them a time limit to leave the area and conditions of interceding], March 8, 1934, in He, *Paihua shiliao huibian: Moxige,* 2:276.

69. W.S. Wong [Chinese Minister Huang] to Foreign Relations Secretary Puig Casauranc, March 8, 1934, IIH-UABC, fondo Dirección General de Gobierno 25.1.

70. Secretary of Gobernación Vasconcelos to Secretary of Foreign Relations Puig Casauranc, March 14, 1934, AGN DGG 2.360 (30) 7.

71. Foreign Relations Secretary Puig Casauranc to Secretary of Gobernación Vasconcelos, March 9, 1934, IIH-UABC, Fondo Dirección General de Gobierno 25.1.

72. Secretary of Gobernación Eduardo Vasconcelos to Foreign Relations Secretary Puig Casauranc, March 14, 1934; Secretary of Gobernación Eduardo Vasconcelos to Foreign Relations Secretary Puig Casauranc, March 17, 1934. Both in IIH-UABC, fondo Dirección General de Gobierno 25.1.

73. President of the Regional PNR Héctor Migoni to Secretary of Gobernación Eduardo Vasconcelos, March 16, 1934, IIH-UABC, fondo Dirección General de Gobierno 25.1.

74. José Malok to Lic. Edmundo Guajardo, Secretaría of Gobernación, April 24, 1934, AGN DGG 2.360 (30) 7; part IV, document 131, "Zhu Moxige gongshiguan cheng waijiaobu xiajiasheng yuanshannadabu paihua fengchao yi qu hehuan" [Legation in Mexico reports to the Ministry of Foreign Affairs Ensenada, Baja California's anti-Chinese unrest relaxing], June 23, 1934, in He, *Paihua shiliao huibian: Moxige*, 2:327.

75. Foreign Relations Secretary Puig Casauranc to Secretary of Gobernación Eduardo Vasconcelos, April 20, 1934, IIH-UABC, fondo Dirección General de Gobierno 25.1.

76. Mexican Nationalist League, Mexicali, to President Lázaro Cárdenas, January 15, 1935, IIH-UABC Dirección General de Gobierno 9.62; José O. González, President Pro-Race Committee Mazatlán, Sinaloa to President Lázaro Cárdenas, March 7, 1935, IIH-UABC Lázaro Cárdenas 19.4; Letter from President of Nationalist Association, Temósachic, Chih. to President Cárdenas, March 12, 1935, IIH-UABC Dirección General de Gobierno 21.2.

77. "La expulsión de extranjeros pide la CROM," *La Opinión*, October 6, 1937; Oficial Mayor of the SRE to the Secretary of Gobernación, October 7, 1937; Oficial Mayor of the SRE to the Secretary of Gobernación, October 16, 1937; all in IIH-UABC Dirección General de Gobierno 25.6.

78. Chen Kwong Min, *Meizhou huaqiao tongjian*, 548; oral history of Manuel Chang, January 16, 1990, in Rossana Reyes Vega, "Los chinos del Soconusco: El surgimiento de una identidad étnica entre inmigrantes" (BA thesis, Escuela Nacional de Antropología e Historia, 1995), 127; Benjamín Lorenzana Cruz, "El comercio chino en la costa de Chiapas durante los años 1914–1920," in *Estado-nación en México: Independencia y revolución*, ed. Esaú Márquez Espinoza, Rafael de J. Araujo González, and María del Rocío Ortiz Herrera (Tuxtla Gutiérrez, Chiapas, Mexico: Universidad de Ciencias y Artes de Chiapas, 2011), 293.

79. Ma. Elena Tovar González, "Extranjeros en el soconusco," *Revista de Humanidades: Tecnológico de Monterrey* 8 (2000): 38–39.

80. Lorenzana Cruz, "El comercio chino," 292–94.

81. Chen Kwong Min, *Meizhou huaqiao tongjian*, 549.

82. Stephen E. Lewis, "Revolution without Resonance? Mexico's 'Fiesta of Bullets' and Its Aftermath in Chiapas, 1910–1940," in *The Mexican Revolution: Conflict and Consolidation, 1910–1940*, ed. Douglas Richmond and Sam Haynes (College Station: Texas A&M University Press, 2013), 161–62.

83. Lorenzana Cruz, "El comercio chino," 295–96, 300–302.

84. Lewis, "Revolution without Resonance?" 166.

85. Petition from Tapachula, Chiapas, to Secretary of Gobernación, May 15, 1930, AGN DGG 2.360 (5) 8007.

86. Part II, document 48, "Zhongguo guomindang zhongyang zhixing weiyuanhui qiaowu weiyuanhui ju moguo zhisheng zhonghua huagongshang tuantihui hanqing waijiaobu jiaoshe qu xiao mo paihua jiguan" [Executive Committee, Overseas Chinese Affairs Committee of China Guomindang according to

letter from Chiapas Mexico Zhonghua Gongsuo Tuantihui asking Ministry of Foreign Affairs to intercede to eliminate Mexico's anti-Chinese organization], February 28, 1931, in He, *Paihua shiliao huibian: Moxige*, 1:132–37.

87. "Fuera los chinos de nuestras poblaciones!!" n.d., AGN DGG 2.360 (5) 8007.

88. Governor of Chiapas Raymundo E. Enriquez to Subsecretary of Gobernación, August 1, 1929, AGN DGG 2.360 (5) 8007.

89. Mexican Anti-Chinese League of Tapachula to Secretary of Gobernación, October 21, 1930, AGN DGG 2.360 (5) 8007.

90. Mexican Anti-Chinese League of Tapachula, October 15, 1930, AGN DGG 2.360 (5) 8007; "Proyecto de acta constitutiva para la fundación de ligas nacionalistas," in José Espinoza, *El problema chino en México* (México, DF, 1931), 233–38. The Chiapas charter uses language that is much simpler than the sample charter, possibly pointing to differences in the level of education between the two chapters.

91. Part II, document 48, "Zhongguo Guomindang," in He, *Paihua shiliao huibian: Moxige;* "¡¡Chiapanecos Patriotas!!" "Campaña Anti-China," and "Ciudadano," n.d., AGN DGG 2.360 (5) 8007.

92. Extract from President of the Mexican Anti-Chinese League, Tapachula, Chiapas, to Secretary of Gobernación, January 21, 1931, AGN DGG 2.360 (5) 8007.

93. Part II, document 48, "Zhongguo Guomindang," in He, *Paihua shiliao huibian: Moxige.*

94. Part II, document 48, "Zhongguo Guomindang," in He, *Paihua shiliao huibian: Moxige;* Chinese Community in Mapastepec to Governor of Chiapas, November 10, 1930, AGN DGG 2.360 (5) 8007.

95. Part II, document 48, "Zhongguo Guomindang," in He, *Paihua shiliao huibian: Moxige.*

96. Cheng Kwong Min, *Meizhou huaqiao tongjian*, 549; Samuel Juan, Cámara China de Comercio y Agricultura, to Secretary of Gobernación, October 30, 1930, AGN DGG 2.360 (5) 8007. The Spanish name of the association was Cámara China de Comercio y Agricultura; the Chinese name was the Zhisheng Zhonghua Gongshang Tuantihui.

97. Samuel Juan, Cámara China de Comercio y Agricultura to President Pascual Ortiz Rubio, November 24, 1930, AGN DGG 2.360 (5) 8007.

98. Gran Logia "Valle de México," Mexico City, to Secretary of Gobernación, November 28, 1930, AGN DGG 2.360 (5) 8007; Chen Kwong Min, *Meizhou huaqiao tongjian*, 508.

99. National Revolutionary Block, Mexican Congress to Secretary of Gobernación, November 21, 1930, AGN DGG 2.360 (5) 8007.

100. Mexican Anti-Chinese League, December 22, 1930; Mexican Anti-Chinese League, December 26, 1930. Both in AGN DGG 2.360 (5) 8007.

101. Chiapas Governor Raymundo E. Enríquez to Secretary of Gobernación, November 19, 1931, AGN DGG 2.360 (5) 8007.

102. Extract from President of the Mexican Anti-Chinese League, Tapachula, Chiapas, to Secretary of Gobernación, January 21, 1931, AGN DGG 2.360 (5) 8007.

103. Subsecretary of Gobernación to Chief of Department of Gobernación, February 22, 1932, AGN DGG 2.360 (5) 8007.

104. Governor of Chiapas Raymundo E. Enríquez to Secretary of Gobernación, March 10, 1932, AGN DGG 2.360 (5) 8007.

105. Sub-Comité Anti-Chino to President Pascual Ortíz Rubio, January 8, 1931, AGN DGG 2.360 (5) 8007

106. For subsequent campaigns, see AGN DGG 2.360 (5) 8007 and AGN DGG 2.360 (5) 24732.

107. Evelyn Hu-DeHart, "Afterword: Brief Meditation on Diaspora Studies," *Modern Drama* 48, no. 2 (Summer 2005): 428–39; Maricela González Félix, *El proceso de aculturación de la población de origen chino en la ciudad de Mexicali* (Mexicali, Baja California: Universidad Autónoma de Baja California, Instituto de Investigaciones Sociales 1990).

108. Susan Sanderson, Phil Sidel, and Harold Hims, "East Asians and Arabs in Mexico: A Study of Naturalized Citizens," in *Asiatic Migrations in Latin America*, ed. Luz María Martinez Montiel (México, DF: Colegio de México, 1981).

109. "Report on Mexican Overseas Chinese Conditions, Business Affairs and Overseas Chinese Affairs," 136–137, June 30, 1943, Institute of Modern History, Academia Sinica (hereafter IMH) 501/0001.

110. Chinese Legation in Mexico to the Chinese Ministry of Foreign Affairs in Nanjing, "Moxige guoqing yu qiaoqing" [Current status of Mexico and Mexican overseas Chinese], June 30, 1943, IMH 501/0001.

111. Part IV, document 51, "Zhu Moxige gongshiguan cheng waijiaobu jiaoshe shansheng paihua shi" [Legation in Mexico reports to Ministry of Foreign Affairs on interceding in Sinaloa's anti-Chinese campaign], March 11, 1933, in He, *Paihua shiliao huibian: Moxige,* 2:114.

112. Part IV, document 126, "Zhu shunnala lingshiguan cheng waijiaobu huijing huaqiao xingmingbiao" [Consulate in Sonora reports to Ministry of Foreign Affairs on list of overseas Chinese returning to the area], June 8, 1934, in He, *Paihua shiliao huibian: Moxige* 2:308.

113. Reyes Vega, "Los chinos del Soconusco," 133–34.

114. "¡Alerta! Otra vez los chinos," attachment to part IV, document 127, "Zhu shunnala lingshiguan cheng waijiaobu paihuadang chundong daifa" [Consulate in Sonora reports to Ministry of Foreign Affairs on anti-Chinese party about to cause a disturbance), June 13, 1934, in He, *Paihua shiliao huibian: Moxige,* 2:310–12.

115. Part IV, document 139, "Qiaowu weiyuanhui han waijiaobu yu mo shang qia shou quan mo zhu hu lingshi qianzheng huzhao yibian qiaomin" [Overseas Chinese Affairs Committee writes Ministry of Foreign Affairs to make arrangements with Mexico to authorize Mexican consul in Shanghai to [issue] passport visa to facilitate expatriates], February 10, 1935, in He, *Paihua shiliao huibian: Moxige,* 2:336; AHSRE IV-396-5. The Chinese government would petition the Mexican Secretaría of Foreign Relations for years to establish a Mexican consulate in southern China.

116. See Julia María Schiavone Camacho, *Chinese Mexicans: Transpacific Migration and the Search for a Homeland, 1910–1960* (Chapel Hill: University of North Carolina Press, 2012).

117. Dr. Manuel Gamio, Chief of the Demographic Department, Secretaría de Gobernación, to Juan Sing, Coatzacoalcos, Veracruz, November 4, 1940. AGN Lázaro Cárdenas del Río (hereafter LCR) 546.6/80

118. Historical Archive of the National Institute of Migration (hereafter AHINM) 4–357–0–1936–2528. In accordance with the guidelines provided by the AHINM, all names provided using AHINM sources are pseudonyms.

119. AHINM 4–357–0–1936–2775.

120. Chinese Legation in Mexico to the Chinese Ministry of Foreign Affairs in Nanjing, "Moxige guoqing," IMH 501/0001. The report defines "old sojourners" as those overseas Chinese who had spent more than five years in Mexico. The 1937 quota system divided migrants into three regions: (1) the Americas, Spain, and Portugal, from which there was no limit; (2) other European countries and Japan, which had a yearly limit of five thousand; and (3) all other countries, which had a yearly limit of one hundred. In 1941, Japan's quota was revised down to one hundred.

121. AHINM 4–357–0–1932–108.

122. AHINM 4–357–0–1936–2745.

123. AHINM 4–357–0–1933–394; AHINM 4–357–0–1933–426.

124. Part IV, document 157, "Qiaowu weiyuanhui han xun waijiaobu guiqiao Huang hanrong kefou qingling huzhao fanmo yingsheng" [Overseas Chinese Affairs Commission writes Ministry of Foreign Affairs to inquire whether returned overseas Chinese Huang Hanrong could apply for a passport to return to Mexico to earn a living], October 1, 1936, in He, *Paihua shiliao huibian: Moxige*, 2:372.

125. "Report on Mexican Overseas Chinese Conditions," 129–35, IMH 501/0001. According to the legation report, those who wished to return to Mexico included Chinese husbands and fathers of Mexican women and children who were repatriated in 1937 and did not have the legal right to return to Mexico. See Julia Maria Schiavone Camacho, "Crossing Boundaries, Claiming a Homeland: The Mexican Chinese Transpacific Journey to Becoming Mexican, 1930s-1960s," *Pacific Historical Review* 78, no. 4 (November 2009): 545–77.

126. Part IV, document 149, "Qiaowu weiyuanhui ju zhongshanxian haiwai tongzhi she zhuan feng xi deng hanqing waijiaobu jiaoshe fanmo yingsheng" [Overseas Chinese Affairs Committee according to Zhongshan County overseas compatriot transmits Fengshan Xi and others writing to Ministry of Foreign Affairs asking to intercede in their returning to Mexico to make a living], November 15, 1935, in He, *Paihua shiliao huibian: Moxige*, 2:355; Part IV, document 153, "Qiaowu weiyuanhui hansong waijiaobu fengxi deng zhuce zhi guoji zhengmingshu deng wenjian," [Overseas Chinese Affairs Committee writes to Ministry of Foreign Affairs to send registration paperwork and proof of nationality of Feng Xi and others and other documents], March 16, 1936, in He, *Paihua shiliao huibian: Moxige*, 2:362.

127. On June 17, 1937, the Secretaría de Gobernación told one interested repatriate that "he would have to pay for himself . . . as our government doesn't have the budget to repatriate naturalized Mexicans and, further, as you know, the funds for the repatriation of Chinese are exclusively for the benefit of abandoned women and children of Mexican nationality" (AHINM 4–357–0–1936–2745). In 1960, the government of Adolfo López Mateos considered repatriat-

ing "nine such men in Macau and a few more in Hong Kong. With the exception of two, the men in Macau were now over the age of sixty" (Schiavone Camacho, "Crossing Boundaries, Claiming a Homeland," 573).

128. Schiavone Camacho, "Crossing Boundaries, Claiming a Homeland," 556; Gerardo Rénique, "Anti-Chinese Racism, Nationalism and State Formation in Post-Revolutionary Mexico, 1920s-1930s," in *Political Power and Social Theory*, vol. 14, ed. Diane E. Davis (Amsterdam: JAI, 2001), 135n79; Theresa Alfaro-Velcamp, *So Far from Allah, So Close to Mexico: Middle Eastern Immigrants in Modern Mexico* (Austin: University of Texas Press, 2007), 5; Maria Ota Mishima, *Destino México: Un estudio de las migraciones asiáticas a México, siglos XIX y XX* (México, DF: El Colegio de México, 1997), 13.

129. Kif Augustine-Adams, for example, suggests that information collected from the Chinese during the census was used against them during the anti-Chinese campaigns. See "Making Mexico: Legal Nationality, Chinese Race, and the 1930 Population Census," *Law & History Review* 27, no. 1 (2009): 122.

130. Many factors, in addition to their distrust of Mexican officials, discouraged Chinese migrants from registering. Those in Tampico cited a variety of reasons: the distance from the small hamlets where they resided to the consulate; their advanced age; their state of unemployment; their work in "irregular" occupations, such as gambling and the trade in narcotics; and their possession of dual citizenship. Report: "Conditions of huaqiao in the consular district of Tampico," in GSG 020000037168A.

131. In some cases, Mexican overseas Chinese associations even sent full lists of their members to central authorities in mainland China (see GSG 033000000379A.) Mexico City provides an example of how the embassies and consulates arrived at their estimates. Similar to other consular districts, the legation understood that many Chinese had not complied with the order to register for the National Registry of Foreigners. However, the legation knew that the vast majority of Chinese in the city had opened cafés and restaurants, and estimated a total of three hundred Chinese-owned cafés in the city in the early 1940s. Moreover, the consulate intervened and mediated during a labor dispute between the Chinese café owners and their workers when the workers attempted to form a union in 1941. They also knew of the presence and activities of overseas Chinese associations such as the Guomindang, the Chee Kung Tong, and anti-Japanese war-relief associations in the city. Finally, the legation negotiated on behalf of Chinese in Mexico City when a law was passed that targeted foreign nationals of allied countries. The regular interactions with the Chinese community allowed the legation to estimate just over twelve hundred Chinese residents in Mexico City in 1941. Report: "Mexican Legation 1941 General Report on Service to Overseas Chinese," in GSG 020000037168A, "Overseas Chinese Affairs in Mexico."

132. GSG 020000037168A, "Overseas Chinese Affairs in Mexico."

CHAPTER 3

1. Eiichiro Azuma, "Dancing with the Rising Sun: Strategic Alliances between Japanese Immigrants and Their 'Home' Government," in *The*

Transnational Politics of Asian Americans, ed. Christian Collet and Pei-te Lien (Philadelphia: Temple University Press, 2009); Max Paul Friedman, *Nazis and Good Neighbors: The United States Campaign against the Germans of Latin America in World War II* (Cambridge: Cambridge University Press, 2003); Jerry García, *Looking Like the Enemy: Japanese Mexicans, the Mexican State, and US Hegemony, 1897–1945* (Tucson: University of Arizona Press, 2014); Selfa Chew, *Uprooting Community: Japanese Mexicans, World War II, and the U.S.– Mexico Borderlands* (Tucson: University of Arizona Press, 2015).

2. Daniela Gleizer, *Unwelcome Exiles: Mexico and the Jewish Refugees from Nazism, 1933–1945* (Leiden: Brill, 2013), 54, 61–62.

3. Tzvi Medin, "La mexicanidad política y filosófica en el sexenio de Miguel Alemán, 1946–52," *Estudios Interdisciplinarios de América Latina y el Caribe* 1, no. 1 (1990); Monica A. Rankin, *¡México, la patria!: Propaganda and Production during World War II* (Lincoln: University of Nebraska Press, 2009), 5.

4. Gleizer, *Unwelcome Exiles,* 61–62.

5. "Shicha baogao [inspection report]" July 30, 1942, GSG 020000037168A.

6. Yu Shouzhi (Yu Yuan-tse), *Moxige huaqiao shihua* (Taipei: Haiwai Wenke Chubanshe, 1954), 15–16; Ling Lew, *Huaqiao renwuzhi / The Chinese in North America: A Guide to Their Life and Progress* (Los Angeles: Dongxi Wenhua Chubanshe, 1949), 291.

7. Chinese Legation in Mexico, Report to the Chinese Ministry of Foreign Affairs in Nanjing, "Moxige guoqing yu qiaoqing" [Current status of Mexico and Mexican overseas Chinese], n.d., IMH 501/0001.

8. Report: "Zhu Tanbigu lingshiguan xiaqu gaikuang baogao" [Consulate in Tampico reports on general situation within its jurisdiction], December 25, 1944, GSG 020000037168A. The statistics were skewed because few children of Chinese migrants were counted, even if the child was born of two Chinese parents.

9. Chen Kwong Min, *Meizhou huaqiao tongjian,* 522.

10. Chen Kwong Min, *Meizhou huaqiao tongjian,* 508, 514, 524, 543; "Zhu Tanbigu lingshiguan," December 25, 1944, GSG 020000037168A.

11. Ambassador to Mexico Chen Jie to Chinese Ministry of Foreign Affairs, n.d., GSG 020000037168A; ROC Embassy in Mexico to ROC Ministry of Foreign Affairs, July 24, 1943, GSG 020000037168A.

12. Chen Kwong Min, *Meizhou huaqiao tongjian,* 515; "Shicha Baogao," July 30, 1942, GSG 020000037168A; Chinese Vice-Consul in Mazatlán to Ministry of Foreign Affairs, December 31, 1947, GSG 020000037169A.

13. Yu Shouzhi (Yu Yuan-tse), "Moxige huaqiao dui zuguo kangzhan de gongxian," in *Huaqiao yu kangri zhanzheng* (Taipei: Huaqiao Xiehui Zonghui, 1999), 567.

14. "Moxige guoqing," n.d., IMH 501/0001; Cheng Tiangu, *Cheng tiangu huiyilu* (Taipei: Longwen Chubanshe, 1993), 2:448; "Shicha baogao," July 30, 1942, GSG 020000037168A.

15. The CKT incorporated an estimated four thousand members during the 1940s, or 33 percent of the Chinese population in the country. Chen Kwong Min, *Meizhou huaqiao tongjian,* 508.

16. Deng Chuanshan, "Zhongnan meizhou dangwu gaikuang ji gaishan yijian" [Party affairs conditions in Central and South America and suggestions for how to improve], KMT *te* 8/3.17, housed at National Taiwan University.

17. During the Northern Expedition (1926–28), armies loyal to the Nationalist government marched from Guangzhou to Beijing (Beiping), ending the dominance of local warlords and nominally unifying China under one government. As the army marched north, it incorporated defeated armies into its ranks. The expedition was interrupted in 1927 by intraparty struggles within the GMD. See Lloyd E. Eastman, "Nationalist China during the Nanking Decade" in Lloyd E. Eastman et al., *The Nationalist Era in China* (Cambridge and New York: Cambridge University Press, 1991), 1–3; Peter Gue Zarrow, *China in War and Revolution, 1895–1949* (London and New York: Routledge, 2005), 230–247.

18. Item 3, "Zhigongtang xuangua guoqi" [The Chee Kung Tong hanging the national flag], in "Zhu Moxige gongshiguan minguo sanshiyi nianfen qiaowu zongbaogao" [Overall report on overseas Chinese affairs from the Legation of the Republic of China in Mexico, 1942, Section on Overseas Chinese Affairs], n.d., GSG 020000037168A.

19. Chinese Minister to Mexico Y. S. Wong to Mexican Subsecretary of Foreign Relations José Ángel Ceniceros, October 4, 1935, AHSRE III-313-9.

20. Yu Shouzhi, "Moxige huaqiao dui zuguo kangzhan de gongxian," 561.

21. Item 2, "Mojing huaqiao gonghui yu mojing huashang fasheng jiufen ji susong zhi qingxing" [Mexico City's Overseas Chinese Labor Union's dispute with the Mexico City Chinese merchants and conditions of litigation], in "Zhu Moxige gongshiguan," n.d., GSG 020000037168A; Chinese Minister in Mexico Y. S. Wong to Eduardo Hay, Secretary of Foreign Relations, May 19, 1936, AHSRE III-160-11.

22. Item 2, "Mojing huaqiao gonghui."

23. Cheng, *Cheng tiangu huiyilu*, 2:445.

24. Part III, Document 46, "Xingzhengyuan mishuchu han waijiaobu banli Moguo qiaotuan cheng qi xiang mo, ri kangyi an" [Secretariat of Executive Yuan writes Ministry of Foreign Affairs to handle petition from Mexico Overseas Chinese Organization seeking protest before Mexico, Japan], n.d., in He, *Paihua shiliao huibian: Moxige*, 1:250–53.

25. Rana Mitter, *Forgotten Ally: China's World War II, 1937–1945* (Boston: Houghton Mifflin Harcourt, 2013), 63.

26. Zarrow, *China in War and Revolution*, 302–5; Li Ying-Hui, *Huaqiao zhengce yu haiwai minzu zhuyi (1912–1949) / The Origins of Overseas Chinese Nationalism, Vol. 1, 1912–1949* (Taipei: Guoshiguan, 1997), 219.

27. Iris Chang, *The Chinese in America: A Narrative History* (New York: Viking, 2003), 216–17.

28. Yu Shouzhi, "Moxige huaqiao dui zuguo kangzhan de gongxian," 576.

29. *Qiaosheng Yuekan*, no. 5 (July 1938): 6–8. The editorial used a Chinese idiom that can be translated in English as "Where can hair stand if the skin is gone?"

30. *Qiaosheng Yuekan*, no. 5 (July 1938): 7.

31. *Qiaosheng Yuekan,* no. 83 (June 1946): 9–13. Chen Kwong Min, *Meizhou huaqiao tongjian,* 574.

32. *Qiaosheng Yuekan,* no. 83 (June 1946): 11.

33. In the United States, "because these Chinese Americans consciously linked their struggle for survival in America to China's national salvation movement, they even began to develop a new consciousness of themselves as Chinese Americans." Renqiu Yu, *To Save China, to Save Ourselves: The Chinese Hand Laundry Alliance of New York* (Philadelphia: Temple University Press, 1992), 94. Also see K. Scott Wong, *Americans First: Chinese Americans and the Second World War* (Cambridge, MA: Harvard University Press, 2005); Karen T. Leong and Judy Tzu-Chun Wu, "Filling the Rice Bowls of China: Staging Humanitarian Relief during the Sino-Japanese War," and K. Scott Wong, "From Pariah to Paragon: Shifting Images of Chinese Americans during World War II," both in *Chinese Americans and the Politics of Race and Culture,* ed. Sucheng Chan and Madeline Y. Hsu (Philadelphia: Temple University Press, 2008); and Sue Fawn Chung, "Fighting for Their American Rights: A History of the Chinese American Citizens' Alliance," in *Claiming America: Constructing Chinese American Identities during the Exclusion Era,* ed. K. Scott Wong and Sucheng Chan (Philadelphia: Temple University Press, 1998).

34. War of Resistance Organization in the state of Chiapas, April 15, 1938, GSG 001000005449A.

35. This school, the Zhonghua Xuexiao, was founded in 1934. Prominent Chinese Mexicans, such as Lü Shifeng and Hu Erqin, served the school as either directors or teachers. The school received books and textbooks from China, held classes at the offices of the Zhonghua Shanghui, and solicited donations for school supplies. Since some Chinese Mexicans were not able to commute long distances to attend the school, it attracted only fifty students, and would shut its doors in 1946. Once dispatched to the school, Yu would almost certainly have taught Mandarin classes, since the Overseas Chinese Affairs Commission "decreed that all overseas Chinese education would include Mandarin." Chen Kwong Min, *Meizhou huaqiao tongjian,* 508; Eric C. Han, *Rise of a Japanese Chinatown: Yokohama, 1894–1972* (Cambridge, MA: Harvard University Asia Center, 2014), 122.

36. Yu Shouzhi, "Moxige huaqiao dui zuguo kangzhan de gongxian," 554.

37. Yu Shouzhi, "Moxige huaqiao dui zuguo kangzhan de gongxian," 563; Chen Kwong Min, *Meizhou huaqiao tongjian,* 565; "Moxige guoqing," June 30, 1943, IMH 501/0001; item 1, "Mojing Qiaowu Gaikuang" [Overall condition of Mexico City Chinese], in "Zhu Moxige Gongshiguan," n.d., GSG 020000037168A. In this chapter, I will refer to such organizations as "War of Resistance organizations."

38. Chinese legation in Mexico to Ministry of Foreign Affairs, May 15, 1942, IMH 560.1/0002. For more information on the War of Resistance organizations in the Mexican countryside, see Yu Shouzhi, "Moxige huaqiao dui zuguo kangzhan de gongxian," 569–71; Chen Kwong Min, *Meizhou huaqiao tongjian;* and Yu Shouzhi, *Moxige huaqiao shihua,* 21–22. For lists of members of War of Resistance committees, see Lümei Huaqiao Tongyi Yijuan Jiuguo Zonghui, *Qiqi kangzhan qizhounian jinian tekan* ([San Francisco?]: Gai Hui, 1946), 8–11.

39. *Qiaosheng Yuekan*, no. 1 (March 1938): 3.

40. Wu Genhua, *Moxige, guadimala huaqiao gaikuang* (Taipei: Zhengzhong Shuju, 1989), 43–44.

41. Yu Shouzhi, "Moxige huaqiao dui zuguo kangzhan de gongxian," 565; Chen Kwong Min, *Meizhou huaqiao tongjian,* 508.

42. Yu Shouzhi, "Moxige huaqiao dui zuguo kangzhan de gongxian," 565.

43. Yu Shouzhi, "Moxige huaqiao dui zuguo kangzhan de gongxian," 566–67. A list of those who donated to *Qiaosheng Yuekan* can be found at the back of each issue. Advertisers were mostly Chinese-owned restaurants and general stores, although the thriving business Chocolate Wong took out a full-page advertisement in every issue. Most ads were written in both Chinese and Spanish.

44. Him Mark Lai, "The Chinese Community Press in Hawaii," *Chinese America: History and Perspectives* 2010:101.

45. *Qiaosheng Yuekan*, no. 1 (March 1938): 7.

46. *Qiaosheng Yuekan*, no. 1 (March 1938): 3.

47. Rules for publication were placed in the last few pages of every issue of *Qiaosheng Yuekan,* for example, no. 2 (April 1938): 28.

48. For examples of donations from Chinese Mexicans, see Chiang Ming-Ching, *Documentary Collection on Donation (1926–1960)* (Taipei: Academia Historica, 1993), 2:1076–77; and *Shijiulu zongzhi huibu shouru kangri weilaojin baogaoshu* (Shanghai, 1932), no. 1, 379–80, 471–72, and no. 2, 77. For records of individual donations, see Lümei Huaqiao Tongyi Yijuan Jiuguo Zonghui, *Qiqi kangzhan qizhounian jinian tekan,* 89–99.

49. *Qiaosheng Yuekan*, nos. 10–11 (October–November 1939): 14. Early contributions among the Chinese in the United States took similar forms. See K. Wong, *Americans First,* 39; and Yong Chen, *Chinese San Francisco, 1850–1943: A Trans-Pacific Community* (Stanford, CA: Stanford University Press, 2000), 235.

50. For information about similar aviation drives in the United States, see H. Mark Lai, "The Kuomintang in Chinese American Communities before World War II," in *Entry Denied: Exclusion and the Chinese Community in America, 1882–1943,* ed. Sucheng Chan (Philadelphia: Temple University Press, 1991), 195.

51. Chang, *Chinese in America,* 217; item 4, "Hangkong jianshe xiehui Mojing zhishu zhihui chengli qingxing" [The establishment of the Mexico City branch Aviation Construction Association], in "Zhu Moxige gongshiguan," n.d., GSG 020000037168A.

52. Japanese Legation in Mexico, Memorandum, June 22, 1939, AHSRE III-407-24.

53. "Zhu Tanbigu lingshiguan," December 25, 1944, GSG 020000037168A; Zhongyang weiyuanhui disanzu, *Zhongguo guomindang zai haiwai gedi dangbu shiliao chugao huibian* (Taipei: Zhongguo Guomindang Zhongyang Weiyuanhui Disanzu, 1961), 68.

54. "Moxige guoqing," n.d., IMH 501/0001. For more on the Torreón aviation association, see *Qiaosheng Yuekan,* no. 68 (March 1945): 28–29.

55. Item 4, "The Establishment of the Mexico City General Aviation Association," in "Zhu Moxige gongshiguan," n.d., GSG 020000037168A.

56. *Qiaosheng Yuekan,* nos. 6–7 (August–September 1938): 18–19.

57. *Qiaosheng Yuekan,* no. 8 (October 1938): 16.

58. Yu Shouzhi, "Moxige huaqiao dui zuguo kangzhan de gongxian," 567–68.

59. Yu Shouzhi, "Moxige huaqiao dui zuguo kangzhan de gongxian," 567–68. For a description of one of these performances, see *Qiaosheng Yuekan,* no. 14 (May 1939): 17.

60. Yu Shouzhi, "Moxige huaqiao dui zuguo kangzhan de gongxian," 569–71; Liu Zongxun, *Huaqiao aiguo zidong juanxian* (Taipei: Qiaowu Weiyuanhui Qiaowu Yanjiushi, 1969), 86.

61. Cheng, *Cheng tiangu huiyilu,* 2:444–45.

62. *Qiaosheng Yuekan,* nos. 6–7 (August–September 1938): 20–21. Part of the reason that the Guomindang opted to attend was that Mexican leftists, including the CTM, had expressed sympathy with China's War of Resistance.

63. AHINM 4–209324; Chen Kwong Min, *Meizhou huaqiao tongjian,* 494; *Qiaosheng Yuekan,* no. 71 (July 1945): 47.

64. Even after the sinking of the Mexican oil tanker Potrero del Llano, public opinion was ambivalent about declaring war against the Axis powers. Although some leftists advocated for Mexico to enter the war, some prominent leftists, including Lázaro Cárdenas and Francisco Múgica, thought declaring war would be a mistake. Halbert Jones, *The War Has Brought Peace to Mexico: World War II and the Consolidation of the Post-Revolutionary State* (Albuquerque: University of New Mexico Press, 2014), 64, 74–75.

65. "Zhu Tanbigu lingshiguan," December 25, 1944, GSG 020000037168A.

66. Item 6, "Benguan xiang huaqiao xuanchuan gongzuo" [This legation's propaganda work toward overseas Chinese], in "Zhu Moxige Gongshiguan," n.d., GSG 020000037168A.

67. *Qiaosheng Yuekan,* nos. 10–11 (January–February 1939): 7–8. A similar "people's diplomacy" campaign was waged in the United States, seeking to obtain American support for China in the Second Sino-Japanese War. See R. Yu, *To Save China, to Save Ourselves,* 101.

68. Him Mark Lai, *Chinese American Transnational Politics* (Urbana: University of Illinois Press, 2010), 18.

69. Zarrow, *China in War and Revolution,* 310, 313.

70. Yu Shouzhi, "Moxige huaqiao dui zuguo kangzhan de gongxian," 564.

71. Chinese Legation in Mexico to Ministry of Foreign Affairs, May 15, 1942, IMH 560.1/0002.

72. For an example of one such donation, see Chee Kung Tong Branch in Tampico, Tamaulipas, November 26, 1938, GSG 001000005449A; and Chiang, *Documentary Collection on Donation,* 1077–83.

73. Item 12, "Xiajiasheng qiaotuan jiufen qingxing" [Dispute between Baja California overseas Chinese], in "Zhu Moxige gongshiguan," n.d., GSG 020000037168A.

74. Yu Shouzhi, "Moxige huaqiao dui zuguo kangzhan de gongxian," 574–75.

75. Cheng, *Cheng tiangu huiyilu,* 2:450–52.

76. Item 3, "Zhigongtang xuangua guoqi," in "Zhu Moxige gongshiguan," n.d., GSG 020000037168A; Yu Shouzhi, "Moxige huaqiao dui zuguo kangzhan de gongxian," 562–63.

77. Cheng, *Cheng tiangu huiyilu,* 2:449–50.

78. Chinese Legation in Mexico to Ministry of Foreign Affairs, May 15, 1942, IMH 560.1/0002; Yu Shouzhi, "Moxige huaqiao dui zuguo kangzhan de gongxian," 564; "Moxige guoqing," n.d., IMH 501/0001.

79. Alfonso Chong, Chee Kung Tong, to Ezequiel Padilla, Secretary of Foreign Relations, August 3, 1944, AHSRE III-5250–7.

80. Yu Shouzhi, "Moxige huaqiao dui zuguo kangzhan de gongxian," 571, 574–75; Yu Shouzhi, *Moxige huaqiao shihua,* 21; Liu, *Huaqiao aiguo zidong juanxian,* 86; Cai Renlong and Liang Guo, *Huaqiao kangri jiuguo shiliao xuanji* (Fuzhou: Zhonggong Fujiansheng Wei Dangshi Gongzuo Weiyuanhui: Zhongguo Huaqiao Lishi Xuehui, 1987), 618. The amount is less than a tenth of the $25 million that U.S. Chinese are estimated to have donated to the war. There are important factors that explain the discrepancy. First, the Chinese population in Mexico was about one-sixth of the Chinese population of the United States. Second, the average Chinese Mexican earned much less than his U.S. counterpart: Yu Shouzhi noted that the average worker's salary was only about 100 pesos per month, and Yu himself earned only 80 pesos a month (at the time, 3.6 Mexican pesos converted to one U.S. dollar). Lai, *Chinese American Transnational Politics,* 23.

81. Yu Shouzhi, "Moxige huaqiao dui zuguo kangzhan de gongxian," 576.

82. García, *Looking Like the Enemy,* 111–13. Although García asserts that this hysteria was driven by U.S. commentators, of interest is Cheng Tien-ku's memoirs, in which he asserts that his diplomatic staff discovered evidence of Japanese designs and presented them to U.S. and Mexican authorities. It's still unclear whether any of the accusations leveled by Cheng or U.S. observers have any basis in fact, and I share García's skepticism as to their likelihood. Cheng, *Cheng tiangu huiyilu,* 2:452–54.

83. García, *Looking Like the Enemy,* 144–45; Stephen R. Niblo, *Mexico in the 1940s: Modernity, Politics, and Corruption* (Wilmington, DE: Scholarly Resources, 1999), 119–20. According to Minister Cheng, Chinese Mexicans were offered the chance to operate Japanese-owned business, but could not pool the funds in time to take over these properties. Cheng, *Cheng tiangu huiyilu,* 2:454.

84. Stephen R. Niblo, *War, Diplomacy, and Development: The United States and Mexico, 1938–1954* (Wilmington, DE: Scholarly Resources, 1995), 78–80.

85. Diario Oficial, México, DF, November 25, 1942, copy in Chinese Consulate in Tampico to Ministry of Foreign Affairs, November 26, 1942, GSG 020000034442A.

86. Item 8, "Waiqiao zai Mo fu bingyi ji shou junshi xunlian qingxing" [Performing military service and training for expatriates in Mexico], in "Zhu Moxige gongshiguan," n.d., GSG 020000037168A.

87. Item 8, "Waiqiao zai Mo"; Eduardo Auyón Gerardo [Ouyang Min], *Moguo xiajiasheng huaqiao yange shilüe / Los chinos en Baja California ayer y hoy* (Hong Kong: Zhongshan Chubanshe, 1971), 47, 52.

88. Item 8, "Waiqiao zai Mo."

89. Item 9, "Zhousheng helishibu 'ORBE' xibao dengzai jishi anzhi gaibu dangbu xi wangpai hanjian zhi gaikuang" [Spanish-language newspaper *Orbe*

in Ciudad Juarez, Chihuahua, publishes a chronicle insinuating the city's local party branch as traitors], in "Zhu Moxige gongshiguan," n.d., GSG 020000037168A.

90. Chinese Ambassador Chen Jie to Chinese Ministry of Foreign Affairs, January 24, 1945, GSG 020000037168A.

91. Jones, *War Has Brought Peace to Mexico*, 104.

92. US Consul in Tampico, "Political and Economic Report on the Tampico Consular District for the Month of January, 1943," record group 84, Tampico Consulate Classified General Reports 1943, USNA.

93. Chinese Ambassador Chen Jie to Chinese Ministry of Foreign Affairs, January 24, 1945, GSG 020000037168A.

94. Wong, *Americans First*, 44.

95. Wong, *Americans First*, 104. In this respect, the comparison with Chinese in the United States is striking. The U.S. newspaper *China Daily News* declared that it "is founded by overseas Chinese in the United States. Among the overseas Chinese in this country, many have acquired U.S. citizenship. To them, to love and defend [their] motherland is a bound duty [*tianzhi*], and to be loyal to the United States is an obligation [*yiwu*]." No such sentiment existed in *Qiaosheng Yuekan*. See Renqiu Yu, "'Exercise Your Sacred Rights': The Experience of New York's Chinese Laundrymen in Practicing Democracy," in *Claiming America: Constructing Chinese American Identities during the Exclusion Era*, ed. K. Scott Wong and Sucheng Chang (Philadelphia: Temple University Press, 1998), 73.

96. Chinese Ambassador Chen Jie to Chinese Ministry of Foreign Affairs, January 24, 1945, GSG 020000037168A. Iris Chang estimates that fifteen to twenty thousand Chinese served in the U.S. military, "representing about 20 percent of the Chinese population in the continental United States." *Chinese in America*, 228. Chinese Canadians were barred from enlisting until 1944, but once that bar was lifted many nonetheless refused to enlist, citing racial discrimination and a lack of voting rights. According to Lisa Rose Mar, "less than 2 percent of the 30,000 Chinese in British Columbia served in the Canadian military." *Brokering Belonging: Chinese in Canada's Exclusion Era, 1885–1945* (New York: Oxford University Press, 2010), 126–30.

97. Wong, *Americans First*, 73.

98. Hans J. Van de Ven, *War and Nationalism in China, 1925–1945* (London and New York: Routledge Curzon, 2003), 2.

99. Wong, *Americans First*, 110.

100. Chen, *Chinese San Francisco, 1850–1943*, 254. Chinese exclusion acts were repealed in Canada (1947 and 1962), Australia (1958 and 1966), and New Zealand (1987). Philip A. Kuhn, *Chinese among Others: Emigration in Modern Times* (Lanham, MD: Rowman & Littlefield, 2008), 323.

101. Wong, *Americans First*, 110; 193–94.

102. Francisco Javier Haro, José Luis León, and Juan José Ramírez, *Historia de las relaciones internacionales de México, 1821–2010, vol. 6, Asia* (México, DF: Secretaría de Relaciones Exteriores, 2011), 182.

103. Manuel Ávila Camacho, third *informe de gobierno* (September 1943), in "Informes presidenciales Manuel Ávila Camacho" (Mexico City: Cámara de

Diputados [México], Dirección de Investigación y Análisis 2006), 242–43, accessed April 25, 2012, www.diputados.gob.mx/cedia/sia/re/RE-ISS-09-06-09 .pdf.

104. Haro, León, and Ramírez, *Historia de las relaciones internacionales de México*, 206.

105. Yu Shouzhi, *Moxige huaqiao shihua*, 9.

106. Chen Kwong Min, *Meizhou huaqiao tongjian*, 492.

107. Draft Treaty of Amity Between the Republic of China and the United States of Mexico, July 7, 1943, AHSRE III-5250–7.

108. Mexican Secretary of Foreign Relations Ezequiel Padilla to *oficialía mayor* of the SRE, July 13, 1943; Memorandum, September 11, 1943; both AHSRE III-5250–7.

109. "Zhuanti Baodao: Huaqiao zai Zhongnan Meizhou (shang)" [Special report: Overseas Chinese in Central and South America: Part 1], IMH 569/0002. A letter signed by twelve Chinese Mexicans in August 1945, for example, encouraged the Chinese government to renegotiate the recently signed treaty in light of China's victory in the Second World War. They specifically asked for more-liberal immigration provisions to allow new relatives to take over businesses operated by aging Chinese Mexicans. "Liuquan dahui congsu qianding zhongmo shangyue" [Sixth General Assembly as soon as possible sign China-Mexico treaty], KMT *fang* 003/3214, housed at National Taiwan University.

110. Cheng, *Cheng tiangu huiyilu*, 2:458–59.

111. "Moxige guoqing," n.d., IMH 501/0001; IMH 562.6/0001; document 146: Zhu mashadaleng fulingshiguan cheng waijiaobu fujing xiangban huaqiao zhuceshi [Vice-consul in Mazatlán reports to the Ministry of Foreign Affairs about traveling to Mexico City to assist processing overseas Chinese registrations], in He Fengjiao, *Paihua shiliao huibian: Moxige* (Taipei: Guoshiguan, 1991), 2:350–52.

112. Cheng, *Cheng tiangu huiyilu*, 2:466.

113. Yu Shouzhi, "Moxige huaqiao dui zuguo kangzhan de gongxian," 571–72. The spelling "Chiang Kai-shih" for Chiang Kai-shek (Jiang Jieshi) is in the original.

114. Yu Shouzhi, "Moxige huaqiao dui zuguo kangzhan de gongxian," 572–73.

115. *Qiaosheng Yuekan*, no. 74 (September 1945): 27–28.

116. US Consul in Mexicali, "Political and Economic Review for September 1945," Mexico Mexicali Consulate General Records 1945, box no. 44, record group 84, USNA; US Consul in Tijuana, "Monthly Economic Review—August 20—September 20, 1945," Mexico Mexicali Consulate General Records 1945, box no. 45, record group 84, USNA.

117. "¡Celebrarán la victoria!" *El apagón* (Tapachula, Chiapas), August 28, 1945, front page; "La col. china de esta ciudad celebró el triunfo aliado," *Crisol* (Tapachula, Chiapas), September 15, 1945, front page; both Centro Universitario de Información y Documentación, Universidad de Ciencias y Artes de Chiapas (hereafter CUID-UNICACH). Also see Miguel Lisbona Guillén, *Allí donde lleguen las olas del mar: Pasado y presente de los chinos en Chiapas* (Chiapas: CONACULTA, 2014), 155.

118. *Orientación* (Cacahoatán, Chiapas), September 15, 1945, p. 4, CUID-UNICACH.

119. *Qiaosheng Yuekan*, no. 74 (September 1945).

120. *Qiaosheng Yuekan*, no. 74 (September 1945): 30–31.

121. "La H. Colonia China" and "Jubilosa celebración del último aniversario del conflicto chino-japonés," *Crisol* (Cacahoatán, Chiapas), September 15, 1945, 4, 6, CUID-UNICACH.

122. *Qiaosheng Yuekan*, no. 74 (September 1945): 33–35.

123. Yu Shouzhi, "Moxige huaqiao dui zuguo kangzhan de gongxian," 571–72; Embassy of the United States in Mexico to Mexican Secretary of Foreign Relations, April 1, 1946, AHSRE III-750–1. For a report on the Chinese Navy's visit to Panama, see *Qiaosheng Yuekan*, no. 83 (June 1946): 28.

124. *Qiaosheng Yuekan*, no. 83 (June 1946): 11.

125. *Qiaosheng Yuekan*, no. 83 (June 1946): 12.

126. See Tatiana Seijas, *Asian Slaves in Colonial Mexico: From Chinos to Indians* (Cambridge: Cambridge University Press, 2014).

127. "El Saludo de China," *El Universal*, May 3, 1946, primera sección, 10.

128. "La bandera china"; "Cordial recibimiento tributado a la flota china en Acapulco," *Excélsior*, May 3, 1946, primera sección, 6.

129. "La bandera china de guerra ondea en paz sobre Acapulco," *El Universal*, May 3, 1946, primera sección, 1.

130. "Atareado día fue el de ayer para los militares visitantes," *Excélsior*, May 4, 1946, primera sección, 1.

131. "Desfilan por la Reforma los Bizarros Marinos Chinos," *Excélsior*, May 5, 1946, primera sección 1; "Desfile de los marinos chinos," *El Universal*, May 5, 1946, primera sección, 24.

132. "Cálido homenaje del gobierno y del pueblo de México al heroísmo chino," *El Universal*, May 5, 1946, primera sección, 1.

133. Yu Shouzhi, *Moxige huaqiao shihua*, 23.

134. Yu Shouzhi, "Moxige huaqiao dui zuguo kangzhan de gongxian," 577.

135. "Fang moxige Yu Shouzhi," April 14, 1969, KMT *yiban* 556.1/100.

CHAPTER 4

1. Jay Taylor, *The Generalissimo: Chiang Kai-shek and the Struggle for Modern China* (Cambridge, MA: Harvard University Press, 2009), 66, 341–42.

2. Yu Shouzhi, "Moxige huaqiao dui zuguo kangzhan de gongxian," in *Huaqiao yu kangri zhanzheng* (Taipei: Huaqiao Xiehui Zonghui, 1999), 573.

3. Renqiu Yu, *To Save China, to Save Ourselves: The Chinese Hand Laundry Alliance of New York* (Philadelphia: Temple University Press, 1992), 165–66.

4. Feng-Shan Ho, *Waijiao shengya sishinian* (Hong Kong: Zhongwen Daxue Chubanshe, 1990), 457.

5. See Robert F. Alegre, *Railroad Radicals in Cold War Mexico: Gender, Class, and Memory* (Lincoln: University of Nebraska Press, 2014); Celeste González de Bustamante, *"Muy Buenas Noches": Mexico, Television, and the Cold War* (Lincoln: University of Nebraska Press, 2012); and Rebecca Mina

Schreiber, *Cold War Exiles in Mexico: U.S. Dissidents and the Culture of Critical Resistance* (Minneapolis: University of Minnesota Press, 2009).

6. Lorenzo Meyer, "La guerra fría en el mundo periférico: El caso del régimen autoritario mexicano; La utilidad del anticomunismo discreto," in *Espejos de la guerra fría: México, América Central y el Caribe,* ed. Daniela Spenser (México, DF: CIESAS, 2004), 96–97.

7. For an analogous example concerning the triangular relationship between Mexico, the United States, and Cuba, see Eric Zolov, "¡Cuba sí, Yanquis no! The Sacking of the Instituto Cultural México-Norteamericano in Morelia, Michoacán, 1961," in *In from the Cold: Latin America's New Encounter with the Cold War,* ed. Gilbert M. Joseph and Daniela Spenser (Durham, NC: Duke University Press, 2008). Although tensions came to a head in the aftermath of the Cuban Revolution, they were certainly present after the Chinese Civil War and during the debate on recognition of the PRC.

8. Huping Ling, *Chinese Chicago: Race, Transnational Migration, and Community since 1870* (Stanford, CA: Stanford University Press, 2012), 229; Isabelle Lausent-Herrera, "New Immigrants: A New Community? The Chinese Community in Peru in Complete Transformation," in *Routledge Handbook of the Chinese Diaspora,* ed. Chee-Beng Tan (London: Routledge, 2013), 378.

9. Ching-Hwang Yen, *The Chinese in Southeast Asia and Beyond: Socioeconomic and Political Dimensions* (Singapore: World Scientific Publishing, 2008), 22; Wing Chung Ng, "Becoming 'Chinese Canadian': The Genesis of a Cultural Category," in *The Last Half Century of Chinese Overseas,* ed. Elizabeth Sinn (Hong Kong: Hong Kong University Press, 1998), 205; Manying Ip, "Chinese Immigration to Australia and New Zealand: Government Policies and Race Relations," in *Routledge Handbook of the Chinese Diaspora,* ed. Chee-Beng Tan (London: Routledge, 2013), 163; Richard Chu, *Chinese and Chinese Mestizos of Manila: Family, Identity, and Culture, 1860s–1930s* (Leiden: Brill, 2010), 403.

10. Joan S.H. Wang, "In the Name of Legitimacy: Taiwan and Overseas Chinese during the Cold War Era," *China Review* 11, no. 2 (Fall 2011): 66–67.

11. Wing Chung Ng, *The Chinese in Vancouver, 1945–80: The Pursuit of Identity and Power* (Vancouver, BC: UBC Press, 1999), 86.

12. Yu San Wang, "Foundation of the Republic of China's Foreign Policy," in *Foreign Policy of the Republic of China on Taiwan: An Unorthodox Approach,* ed. Yu San Wang (New York: Praeger, 1990), 6.

13. Donald Klein, "Formosa's Diplomatic World," *China Quarterly* 15 (July–September 1963), 50; Wang, "Republic of China's Foreign Policy," 2–3.

14. Klein, "Formosa's Diplomatic World," 45–50.

15. ROC Embassy in Mexico to Manuel Tello, Mexican Subsecretary of Foreign Relations, April 14, 1950, AHSRE 20-6-50.

16. "Moxige dianying daibiaotuan di jing," *Renmin Ribao,* August 13, 1959, 4.

17. US Embassy in Mexico City, "Recent Indications of Attempts to Orient Mexico towards the Afro-Asian Bloc," January 30, 1957, Central Decimal File 1956–1959 box 2590, record group 59, USNA.

18. Leonardo Ruilova, *China popular en América Latina* (Quito: Instituto Latinoamericano de Ciencias Sociales, 1978), 96.

19. Vicente Lombardo Toledano, *Victoria de la revolución china* (México, DF: Universidad Obrera de México, 1950); Daniela Spenser, "Vicente Lombardo Toledano envuelto en antagonismos internacionales," in *Revolución y exilio en la historia de México: Del amor de un historiador a su patria adoptiva; Homenaje a Friedrich Katz,* ed. Javier Dantan, Emilio Kourí, and Friedrich Katz (México, DF: Colegio de México; Chicago: Centro Katz de Estudios Mexicanos, 2010), 251–69; "Mao Zhuxi jiejian Moxige qian linshi zongtong," *Renmin Ribao,* October 6, 1960, front page.

20. Ministry of Foreign Affairs of the People's Republic of China (hereafter FMPRC) 111–00156–01.

21. "Memorandum of a Conversation, Los Pinos, August 12, 1959, 7 P.M.," in Foreign Relations of the United States, 1958–1960, vol. 5, American Republics, document 333, accessed August 16, 2012, https://history.state.gov/historicaldocuments/frus1958–60v05/d333.

22. The Estrada Doctrine, a pillar of Mexico's foreign policy, rejected the use of diplomatic recognition for political ends. Jürgen Buchenau, "Por una guerra fría más templada: México entre el cambio revolucionario y la reacción estadounidense en Guatemala y Cuba," in *Espejos de la guerra fría,* ed. Daniela Spenser (México, DF: CIESAS, 2004), 124.

23. "Moxige zai lianheguo de bufen qingkuang jieshao" [An introduction to a part of Mexico's situation in the United Nations], August 17, 1950, FMPRC 111–0002–05.

24. Pei Jianzhang, *Zhonghua renmin gongheguo waijiaoshi,* vol. 1 (Beijing: Shijie Zhishi, 1994), 352.

25. Jorge Octavio Fernández Montes, "Encuentros y desencuentros: México y la República Popular China antes del establecimiento de relaciones diplomáticas (1949–1972)," in *40 años de la relación entre México y China: Acuerdos, desencuentros y futuro,* ed. Enrique Dussel Peters (México, DF: Centro de Estudios China-México, Universidad Nacional Autónoma de México, 2012), 387–89; PRC Ambassador to Poland to Zhou Enlai, July 11, 1950; PRC Ambassador to Poland to Zhou Enlai, August 9, 1950; Zhou Enlai to PRC Ambassador to Poland, August 23, 1950, FMPRC 111–0002–04. See also Chen Jian, *Mao's China and the Cold War* (Chapel Hill: University of North Carolina Press, 2001).

26. "Interview Between Mr. Burrows, First Secretary of the U.S. Embassy in Mexico, and the Director General of the [Mexican] Diplomatic Service," February 6, 1950, AHSRE III-5430–4; Lorenzo Meyer, "Relaciones México-Estados Unidos: Arquitectura y montaje de las pautas de la guerra fría, 1945–1964," *Foro Internacional* 50, no. 2 (April–June 2010), 218–19.

27. George Ginsburgs and Arthur Stahnke, "Communist China's Trade Relations with Latin America," *Asian Survey* 10, no. 9 (September 1970), 803–19; Cecil Johnson, *Communist China and Latin America* (New York: Columbia University Press, 1970); Joseph J. Lee, "Communist China's Latin America Policy," *Asian Survey* 4, no. 11 (November 1964): 1123–34; William E. Ratliff, "Chinese Communist Cultural Diplomacy toward Latin America, 1949–1960," *Hispanic American Historical Review* 49, no. 1 (February 1969): 53–79.

28. Ginsburgs and Stahnke, "Communist China's Trade Relations with Latin America"; PRC Ambassador to Holland to PRC Ministry of Foreign

Affairs, March 8, 1956, FMPRC 111–0021–02. For more on abortive talks to establish commercial relations during the administration of Adolfo Ruiz Cortines, see Fernández Montes, "Encuentros y desencuentros," 389–91.

29. Francisco Javier Haro, José Luis León, and Juan José Ramírez, "Por si no nos volvemos a ver: Proceso de ruptura con Taiwán e inicio de una nueva etapa diplomática," in *Historia de las relaciones internacionales de México, 1821–2010*, ed. Mercedes de Vega, vol. 6, *Asia* (México, DF: Secretaría de Relaciones Exteriores, 2011), 225–26.

30. Mexico would appoint its ambassador to Japan as a dual ambassador to the Republic of China, which in effect meant that the Mexican ambassador to Japan spent almost no time on Taiwan. Haro, León, and Ramírez, "Por si no nos volvemos a ver," 6:223.

31. General Organization to Save Refugees from Mainland China to Anti-Communist Anti-Soviet National Salvation Support Organization of Mexicali, Mexico, February 21, 1953, IMH 561.2/0001. Other Chinese organizations also made donations to the anti-Communist cause, such as the Chinese Association in Tijuana and the Unión Fraternal China in Ciudad Juárez.

32. Klein, "Formosa's Diplomatic World," 45.

33. Klein, "Formosa's Diplomatic World," 46.

34. ROC Embassy in Mexico to ROC Ministry of Foreign Affairs Vice-Minister C. H. Shen, June 28, 1957, IMH 512.21/0012.

35. ROC Embassy in Mexico to ROC Ministry of Foreign Affairs, July 10, 1957, IMH 512.21/0012.

36. ROC Embassy in Mexico, August 21, 1957, IMH 512.21/0012.

37. Feng-Shan Ho and Monto Ho, *My Forty Years as a Diplomat* (Pittsburgh: Dorrance, 2010), 164.

38. Ho and Ho, *My Forty Years as a Diplomat*, 140.

39. Ho and Ho, *My Forty Years as a Diplomat*, 156–58.

40. Ho and Ho, *My Forty Years as a Diplomat*, 164–65.

41. Ho and Ho, *My Forty Years as a Diplomat*, 172, 174; Haro, León, and Ramírez, *Historia de las relaciones internacionales de México*, 6:226.

42. ROC Ambassador Feng-Shan Ho to Mexican Secretary of Foreign Relations José Gorostiza, May 2, 1964, AHSRE III-2990–30.

43. Embassy of the Republic of China to Mexican Secretary of Foreign Relations, October 14, 1964, AHSRE III-2990–30.

44. Ho and Ho, *My Forty Years as a Diplomat*, 167–68; Haro, León, and Ramírez, *Historia de las relaciones internacionales de México*, 6:226.

45. Ho and Ho, *My Forty Years as a Diplomat*, 170.

46. Ho and Ho, *My Forty Years as a Diplomat*, 171–72.

47. Julia Maria Schiavone Camacho, *Chinese Mexicans: Transpacific Migration and the Search for a Homeland, 1910–1960* (Chapel Hill: University of North Carolina Press, 2012), 14, 139–41.

48. Monica Cinco Basurto, "China in Mexico: Yesterday's Encounter and Today's Discovery," in *Encounters: People of Asian Descent in the Americas*, ed. Roshni Rustomji-Kerns (Lanham, MD: Rowman & Littlefield, 1999), 13–18.

49. Schiavone Camacho, *Chinese Mexicans*, 1.

50. Schiavone Camacho, *Chinese Mexicans,* 143.

51. Schiavone Camacho, *Chinese Mexicans,* 6.

52. Schiavone Camacho, *Chinese Mexicans,* 145.

53. Schiavone Camacho, *Chinese Mexicans,* 8.

54. Alberto Loyola, *Chino-mexicanos cautivos del comunismo: Su repatriación fue una gran proeza* (México, DF: Movimiento Continental Pro-Democracia Cristiana, 1961), 10, 15, 20–21, 23–25, 57–58.

55. Schiavone Camacho, *Chinese Mexicans,* 6.

56. "Homenaje de la Colonia China a la Guadalupana," *El Universal,* October 27, 1958, primera sección, 26; Ho and Ho, *My Forty Years as a Diplomat,* 178.

57. "Homenaje de la Colonia China a la Guadalupana." Capitalization in the prayer in original.

58. Ho and Ho, *My Forty Years as a Diplomat,* 178.

59. ROC Embassy in Mexico to ROC Ministry of Foreign Affairs, February 25, 1959, GSG 020000037171A; Pius XII, "Ad Apostolorum Principis: Encyclical Letter of Pope Pius XII on Communism and the Church in China," June 29, 1958, accessed September 13, 2012, www.vatican.va/holy_father/pius_xii/encyclicals/documents/hf_p-xii_enc_29061958_ad-apostolorum-principis_en.html, accessed September 13, 2012.

60. Roberto Blancarte, "Intransigence, Anticommunism, and Reconciliation: Church/State Relations in Transition," in *Dictablanda: Politics, Work, and Culture in Mexico, 1938–1968,* ed. Paul Gillingham and Benjamin T. Smith (Durham, NC: Duke University Press, 2014), 81.

61. "Homenaje de la Colonia China a la Guadalupana."

62. Feng-Shan Ho, *Waijiao shengya sishinian,* 415.

63. Ho and Ho, *My Forty Years as a Diplomat,* 184–86. During Ambassador Ho's tenure, Yu Bin visited Mexico City, where the Chinese community gave him an enthusiastic welcome.

64. "Los chinos residentes aquí oraron por que acabe el cautiverio de la China roja," *Excélsior,* October 28, 1963, found in GSG 020000024499A; Feng-Shan Ho, *Waijiao shengya sishinian,* 561–62.

65. "La colonia china en peregrinación," *El Universal,* October 31, 1960, primera sección, 13; "Homenaje de la colonia china a la Virgen," *El Universal,* October 30, 1961, primera sección, 7; "Oraron en la basílica los residentes chinos del D.F.," *El Universal,* October 26, 1964, segunda sección, 29; "Los chinos residentes aquí."

66. "Homenaje de la colonia china"; "Oraron en la basílica."

67. González de Bustamante, *"Muy Buenas Noches,"* 81.

68. *Jinri zhonghua minguo* (Taipei: Overseas Chinese Affairs Commission, 1963), 149, located in NSF box 24, "China General Gift Book to JFK From General Chiang Ching-Kuo," JFK Presidential Library.

69. ROC Embassy in Chile to ROC Ministry of Foreign Affairs, November 22, 1963; *"Zhonghua minguo renmin gongheguo jingji maoyi zhanlanhui* Exposición Económica y Comercial de la República Popular China," *El Mercurio* (Santiago, Chile), November 26, 1963; both GSG 020000024499A. A similar advertisement ran in the Mexico City daily *Excélsior,* December 3, 1963, found in AHSRE III-2899-3.

70. Ho and Ho, *My Forty Years as a Diplomat,* 193.

71. Zolov, "¡Cuba sí, Yanquis no!" 235.

72. ROC Embassy in Mexico to ROC Ministry of Foreign Affairs, September 26, 1963; ROC Embassy in Mexico to ROC Ministry of Foreign Affairs, October 9, 1963, GSG 020000024499A. One analysis of Salinas Lozano presented two possible readings of him: one asserted that he was a sympathizer of Lombardo Toledano's Partido Popular, while the other saw him "as a sharp opportunist without deep convictions." NSF box 141, "Mexico General 7/63–11/63," JFK Library.

73. Adolfo López Mateos, V Informe de Gobierno, in "Informes Presidenciales: Adolfo López Mateos," Servicio de Investigación y Análisis, Cámara de Diputados, 2006, accessed September 16, 2012, www.diputados.gob.mx/sedia/sia/re/RE-ISS-09–06–12.pdf. During his trip through Asia, López Mateos was asked about the position of the Mexican government toward the entry of the People's Republic of China into the United Nations. The president responded cautiously. "Mexico believes that one of the inherent rights of a nation is to have or not have diplomatic relations with another country," asserted López Mateos, "and Mexico maintains diplomatic relations with Nationalist China." *Discursos y pláticas del Licenciado Adolfo López Mateos en su gira por el oriente,* cited in Marisela Connelly, "Las relaciones de China y México en su contexto histórico," *Escenarios XXI* 1, nos. 5–6 (November–December 2010): 50–60.

74. "Mexico Bids for World Affairs Role," *Washington Post and Times-Herald,* September 2, 1963, A12.

75. ROC Embassy in Mexico to ROC Ministry of Foreign Affairs, February 12, 1963, GSG 020000024499A.

76. ROC Embassy in Mexico to ROC Ministry of Foreign Affairs, June 19, 1963, GSG 020000024499A.

77. ROC Embassy in Mexico to ROC Foreign Ministry, September 23, 1963, GSG 020000024499A.

78. "Mexico City to Get Chinese Exhibition," *New York Times,* November 17, 1963, 62; Ho and Ho, *My Forty Years as a Diplomat,* 192.

79. FMPRC 111–00477–06.

80. British Embassy in Mexico City, February 18, 1964, FO 371/174176, National Archives of the United Kingdom (hereafter UKNA).

81. "*Zhonghua renmin gongheguo jingji maoyi zhanlanhui* Exposición económica y comercial de la República Popular China" (program), copy in FO 371/174176, UKNA.

82. FMPRC 111–00477–06.

83. "*Zhonghua renmin gongheguo jingji maoyi zhanlanhui* Exposición Económica y Comercial de la República Popular China" (poster), AHSRE III-2899–3.

84. "La China Comunista no tiene qué exponer en materia industrial," *Novedades,* September 24, 1963, found in GSG 020000024499A.

85. ROC Embassy in Mexico to ROC Foreign Ministry, September 29, 1963, GSG 020000024499A.

86. ROC Embassy in Mexico to ROC Ministry of Foreign Affairs, October 4, 1963, GSG 020000024499A.

87. ROC Embassy in Mexico to ROC Ministry of Foreign Affairs, October 9, 1963; ROC Embassy in Mexico to ROC Ministry of Foreign Affairs, October 17, 1963; "Red China to Open Trade Fair in Mexico: Tons of Propaganda Brought In," *Miami Herald,* October 22, 1963; "10 toneladas de propaganda comunista llegan a Veracruz: Son destinadas a fomentar la infiltración roja en América," *Últimas noticias,* 2nd ed., October 16, 1963; all GSG 020000024499A.

88. ROC Embassy in Mexico to ROC Ministry of Foreign Affairs, November 14, 1963, GSG 020000024499A.

89. ROC Embassy in Mexico to ROC Ministry of Foreign Affairs, November 7, 1963, GSG 020000024499A.

90. ROC Embassy in Mexico to ROC Ministry of Foreign Affairs, October 4, 1963; ROC Embassy in Mexico to ROC Ministry of Foreign Affairs, December 2, 1963, both GSG 020000024499A.

91. ROC Embassy in Mexico to ROC Ministry of Foreign Affairs, November 8, 1963, GSG 020000024499A.

92. "Aniversario de la Independencia de la Gran República China," *El Fronterizo* (Ciudad Juárez, Chihuahua), October 10, 1963; H. Colonia China de Tampico to Mexican President Adolfo López Mateos, October 10, 1963; H. Colonia China in Tapachula, Chis. to President Adolfo López Mateos, October 10, 1963; Open letter from La Colonia China de la Ciudad de México to Mexican President Adolfo López Mateos, *Excélsior,* October 13, 1963; "La Exposición China, Paso Para Establecer Relaciones con México" *Novedades,* October 17, 1963; all GSG 020000024499A.

93. "Aniversario de la Independencia de la Gran República China," *El Fronterizo* (Ciudad Juárez, Chihuahua), October 10, 1963; H. Colonia China de Tampico to Mexican President Adolfo López Mateos, October 10, 1963; H. Colonia China in Tapachula, Chis. to President Adolfo López Mateos, October 10, 1963; Open letter from La Colonia China de la Ciudad de México to Mexican President Adolfo López Mateos, *Excélsior,* October 13, 1963; "La Exposición China, Paso Para Establecer Relaciones con México" *Novedades,* October 17, 1963; all GSG 020000024499A.

94. "Aniversario de la Independencia de la Gran República China," *El Fronterizo* (Ciudad Juárez, Chihuahua), October 10, 1963; H. Colonia China de Tampico to Mexican President Adolfo López Mateos, October 10, 1963; H. Colonia China in Tapachula, Chis. to President Adolfo López Mateos, October 10, 1963; Open letter from La Colonia China de la Ciudad de México to Mexican President Adolfo López Mateos, *Excélsior,* October 13, 1963; "La Exposición China, Paso Para Establecer Relaciones con México" *Novedades,* October 17, 1963; all in GSG 020000024499A.

95. "Red China Fair Here Protested" *News* (Mexico City), October 17, 1963; "Mexican Overseas Chinese Oppose the Chinese Communists Carrying out an Exposition," *China Tribune/Huamei Ribao* (New York), October 21, 1963; both GSG 020000024499A.

96. Report, "Chinese Communist Infiltration in Mexico," GSG 020000024499A.

97. "López Mateos Estuvo en la Exposición China: 'No Hay Duda Que Ha Progresado Este Pueblo' Dijo el Presidente," *Excélsior,* December 7, 1963, pri-

mera sección, 1; "Mexican President Tours Economic Exposition," *Xinhua,* December 7, 1963; "López Mateos Opens CPR Trade Exhibit," *Prensa Latina* (Havana), December 9, 1963; GSG 020000024499A.

98. "Inauguró Salinas Lozano la Muestra de China Roja," *Excélsior,* December 8, 1963, primera sección, 1; ROC Embassy in Brazil to ROC Foreign Ministry, January 3, 1964, GSG 020000024499A.

99. ROC Embassy in Mexico to ROC Ministry of Foreign Affairs, December 7, 1963, GSG 020000024499A

100. "Mexican Ex-President Cardenas Visited Communist Exhibition," *Xinhua,* December 10, 1963, GSG 020000024499A.

101. ROC Embassy in Mexico to ROC Foreign Ministry, December 27, 1963, GSG 020000024499A.

102. "'Trade' Mission: Peking's Wares in Mexico," *Christian Science Monitor,* December 19, 1963, found in AHSRE III-2899–3. Díaz Ordaz, by then a presidential candidate, gave the excuse that he needed to campaign outside of Mexico City.

103. Comité Anticomunista de la Colonia China de México, "Cuidado con las manos sangrientas de los comunistas chinos," *Excélsior,* December 7, 1963, copy in GSG 020000024499A; Feng-Shan Ho, *Waijiao shengya sishinian,* 564.

104. ROC Embassy in Mexico to ROC Foreign Ministry, December 18, 1963, GSG 020000024499A.

105. ROC Embassy in Mexico to ROC Foreign Ministry, December 18, 1963, GSG 020000024499A.

106. FMPRC 111–00477–06.

107. "Es aterradora la situación actual de la hambrienta China esclavizada," *La Extra,* December 8, 1963, copy in GSG 020000024499A.

108. "Infiltran propaganda comunista," n.d., copy in GSG 020000024499A.

109. ROC Embassy in Mexico to ROC Foreign Ministry, January 30, 1964, GSG 020000024499A; FMPRC 111–00477–06.

110. FMPRC 111–00477–06.

111. Feng-Shan Ho to ROC Ministry of Foreign Affairs, December 28, 1963, GSG 020000024499A.

112. "'64 Mexican Trade with Peking Said to Top $35 Million," *Washington Post and Times-Herald,* September 30, 1965. The 1963 trade was worth $3 million. Much of the 1964 trade was handled by Compensación Internacional, the Mexican company operated by Guillermo Nasser Quiñones.

113. Feng-Shan Ho to ROC Ministry of Foreign Affairs, December 22, 1963, GSG 020000024499A.

114. US Embassy in Mexico, "Communist Chinese Attempts to Establish a Presence in Mexico," Central Foreign Policy File, 1963, box 3862, USNA. The Mexican secretary of foreign relations told the British ambassador that Mexico would not recognize the People's Republic of China during the López Mateos administration. The British ambassador believed him, in part, because "Mexico's relations with the United States are too important." British embassy in Mexico City, February 11, 1964, FO 371/174159, UKNA.

115. "Memorandum for the President: Subject: Your Meeting with President Lopez Mateos," US Department of State, February 18, 1964, National Security

Archive, accessed November 15, 2015, http://nsarchive.gwu.edu/NSAEBB /NSAEBB83/us02.pdf.

116. "Mexico Prepares to Hail de Gaulle: Visit That Starts Tomorrow Seen as Good Beginning," *New York Times,* March 15, 1964, 26; Ho and Ho, *My Forty Years as a Diplomat,* 201; "Dicen en EU que México reconocerá a China Roja," *El Mexicano* (Mexicali), n.d., GSG 020000024499A.

117. In 1965, for example, Díaz Ordaz's Secretary of Foreign Relations emphatically denied that Mexico wished to establish relations with the People's Republic of China. US Embassy in Mexico City, May 1, 1965, Central Foreign Policy file 1964–1966, box 2039, USNA.

118. Johnson, *Communist China and Latin America,* 194.

119. "Subversion: Breath of the Dragon," *Time,* September 11, 1964, accessed September 21, 2012, www.time.com/time/magazine/article/0,9171, 830641,00.html.

120. Johnson, *Communist China and Latin America,* 18–19.

121. Ho and Ho, *My Forty Years as a Diplomat,* 200, 205.

122. Ho and Ho, *My Forty Years as a Diplomat,* 206–7.

CHAPTER 5

1. Lok C.D. Siu, *Memories of a Future Home: Diasporic Citizenship of Chinese in Panama* (Stanford, CA: Stanford University Press, 2005), 22.

2. Siu, *Memories of a Future Home,* 20.

3. Adam McKeown, "Conceptualizing Chinese Diasporas, 1842 to 1949," *Journal of Asian Studies* 58, no. 2 (May 1999): 329.

4. Meredith Oyen, "Communism, Containment and the Chinese Overseas," in *The Cold War in Asia: The Battle for Hearts and Minds,* ed. Yangwen Zheng, Hong Liu, and Michael Szonyi (Leiden: Brill, 2010), 66.

5. "Polliticking," *The News* (Mexico City), October 16, 1966; "Letters to the Editor," *The News* (Mexico City), October 28, 1966; both GSG 020000019053A.

6. Greg Grandin, *The Last Colonial Massacre: Latin America in the Cold War,* updated ed. (Chicago: University of Chicago Press, 2004), 17.

7. Him Mark Lai, *Chinese American Transnational Politics* (Urbana: University of Illinois Press, 2010), 5; Wing Chung Ng, *The Chinese In Vancouver, 1945–80: The Pursuit of Identity and Power* (Vancouver, BC: UBC Press, 1999), 86.

8. Embassy of the Republic of China in Mexico to ROC Ministry of Foreign Affairs, "Zhuanti Baogao: Feigong dui Moxige zhi shentou ji qi tongzhan huo-dong qingxing" [Special report: On the infiltration of Communist bandits in Mexico and its United Front activities], n.d., p. 1, GSG 020000024483A.

9. The People's Republic of China celebrates its National Day on October 1, when Chairman Mao proclaimed the People's Republic while overlooking Tiananmen Square; the Republic of China celebrates its National Day on October 10, in commemoration of the Wuchang uprising, which put an end to the Qing dynasty and helped give birth to the Chinese Republic.

10. Feng-Shan Ho and Monto Ho, *My Forty Years as a Diplomat* (Pittsburgh: Dorrance, 2010), 176.

11. ROC Ministry of Foreign Affairs to ROC Overseas Chinese Affairs Committee, May 26, 1964, GSG 020000025796A; ROC Embassy in Mexico to ROC Overseas Chinese Affairs Committee, July 1, 1965, GSG 020000025797A.

12. Wang Gungwu, *The Chinese Overseas: From Earthbound China to the Quest for Autonomy* (Cambridge, MA: Harvard University Press, 2000), 82.

13. Meredith Oyen, "Communism, Containment and the Chinese Overseas," in *The Cold War in Asia: The Battle for Hearts and Minds* (Leiden: Brill, 2010), 59.

14. Gloria Heyung Chun, "'To Become Still Better Americans': The Challenge of China Turning Communist," in *Of Orphans and Warriors: Inventing Chinese American Culture and Identity* (New Brunswick, NJ: Rutgers University Press, 2000), 75–76. To understand how Chinese communities in the United States were affected by the Cold War, see Xiaojian Zhao, *Remaking Chinese America: Immigration, Family, and Community* (New Brunswick, NJ: Rutgers University Press, 2002).

15. Wasana Wongsurawat, "From Yaowaraj to Plabplachai: The Thai State and Ethnic Chinese in Thailand during the Cold War," in *Dynamics of the Cold War in Asia: Ideology, Identity, and Culture,* ed. Tuong Vu and Wasana Wongsurawat (New York: Palgrave Macmillan, 2009), 179.

16. Lok C.D. Siu, *Memories of a Future Home: Diasporic Citizenship of Chinese in Panama (*Stanford, CA: Stanford University Press, 2005), 31.

17. Third area of the Guomindang to ROC Ministry of Foreign Affairs, February 5, 1951, GSG 020000037169A.

18. During the Second World War, the Republic of China consulate in San Francisco issued identification cards to Chinese immigrants and their descendants to distinguish them from Japanese and Japanese Americans. K. Scott Wong, *Americans First: Chinese Americans and the Second World War* (Philadelphia: Temple University Press, 2008), 80.

19. ROC Embassy in Mexico to ROC Ministry of Foreign Affairs, March 5, 1951, GSG 020000037169A.

20. Jaime M. Pensado, *Rebel Mexico: Student Unrest and Authoritarian Political Culture during the Long Sixties* (Stanford, CA: Stanford University Press 2013), 112.

21. Pensado, *Rebel Mexico,* 83.

22. Roberto Cuevas Pimienta, *La honorable colonia china en la república mexicana* (n.p.: Ediciones Rocío, 1957) 11, 41.

23. Cuevas Pimienta, *La honorable colonia china,* 5.

24. The Chee Kung Tong in 1947 reorganized globally into the Hongmen Min Zhi Dang. Chen Kwong Min, *Meizhou huaqiao tongjian* (New York: Meizhou Huaqiao Wenhuashe, 1950), 507.

25. Cuevas Pimienta, *La honorable colonia china,* 7.

26. Cuevas Pimienta, *La honorable colonia china,* 15, 51, 61, 106.

27. Cuevas Pimienta, *La honorable colonia china,* 43, 66.

28. Cuevas Pimienta, *La honorable colonia china,* 10, 23.

29. Of the biographies, almost all are of men born in Guangdong Province, meaning that the document also largely excludes Chinese Mexican children. Miguel Wongpec, however, was born in Mazatlán, Sinaloa, but at the age of

seven he was sent to Guangzhou, returning to Mexico twenty years later. Cuevas Pimienta, *La honorable colonia china*, 89.

30. Cuevas Pimienta, *La honorable colonia china*, 34, 72.

31. As Glen D. Peterson points out, PRC policy toward overseas Chinese overwhelmingly focused on mainland Chinese relatives of overseas Chinese (*qiaojuan*) and returned overseas Chinese (*guiqiao*) rather than overseas Chinese themselves. "Socialist China and the Huaqiao: The Transition to Socialism in the Overseas Chinese Areas of Rural Guangdong, 1949–1956," *Modern China* 14, no. 3 (July 1988): 309.

32. FMPRC 111–00086–01.

33. FMPRC 111–00304–01; Julia María Schiavone Camacho, *Chinese Mexicans: Transpacific Migration and the Search for a Homeland, 1910–1960* (Chapel Hill: University of North Carolina Press, 2012), 162.

34. Tan Xinmin to Executive Yuan, January 28, 1956, GSG 020000037170A.

35. Ham Cheem Jr. was alleged to have many aliases, including Tan Xiangbo, Tan Zhanweng, and Tan Xuanban. In some documents, "Cheem" is spelled "Cheen." ROC Embassy in Mexico to ROC Foreign Ministry, April 14, 1965, GSG 020000024482A.

36. ROC Embassy in Mexico to ROC Ministry of Foreign Affairs, October 8, 1955, GSG 020000037170A.

37. "Quedan los 'tongs' al descubierto: Fernando Chi Wi Ling, capturado a causa de una extraña denuncia," *Últimas Noticias de Excélsior,* December 3, 1955, primera sección, 1.

38. ROC Embassy in Mexico to ROC Ministry of Foreign Affairs, January 31, 1956, GSG 020000037170A.

39. Guomindang Central Committee to Ministry of Foreign Affairs, January 21, 1956, GSG 020000037170A.

40. ROC Embassy in Mexico to ROC Ministry of Foreign Affairs, December 12, 1955, GSG 020000037170A.

41. ROC Embassy in Mexico to ROC Ministry of Foreign Affairs, January 31, 1956, GSG 020000037170A.

42. Huang Yibin, "Lieju meinü zhiwai (Moxige hangxin)" [In addition to spirits and beautiful women (letter from Mexico)], December 20, 1963, *Xinwen Tiandi,* no. 777, copy in KMT *yiban* 586.422.

43. ROC Embassy in Mexico to ROC Ministry of Foreign Affairs, October 8, 1955, GSG 020000037170A. Also see ROC Embassy in Mexico, "Zhuanti baogao," n.d., GSG 020000024483A.

44. ROC Embassy in Mexico to ROC Ministry of Foreign Affairs, October 9, 1955; ROC Embassy in Mexico to ROC Ministry of Foreign Affairs, October 13, 1955; both GSG 020000037170A.

45. Feng-Shan Ho, *Waijiao shengya sishinian* (Hong Kong: Zhongwen Daxue Chubanshe, 1990), 461–63.

46. "Jack Anderson Article in 'Parade' on Communist Chinese Spy Ring in Mexico," Bureau of Inter-American Affairs, Entry #P2, Records Relating to Mexico, 1946–1975, container 16, record group 59, USNA.

47. Hal Hendrix, "Peking Has Spy Base in Mexico," July 9, 1964, copy in GSG 020000024482A.

48. ROC Embassy in Mexico to ROC Ministry of Foreign Affairs, August 26, 1965, GSG 020000024482A.

49. ROC Embassy in Mexico to ROC Ministry of Foreign Affairs, August 26, 1965, GSG 020000024482A.

50. "La China Popular no es lo que cuentan: Pepe Chong que estuvo allí, dice que hay orden, trabajo y alegría" (newspaper clipping), n.d., copy in GSG 020000024483A.

51. Third Group of the Central Authorities of the Guomindang to ROC Minister of Foreign Affairs Shen, December 28, 1965, GSG 020000024483A.

52. ROC Embassy in Mexico to ROC Ministry of Foreign Affairs, February 10, 1966, GSG 020000024483A.

53. ROC Embassy in Mexico to ROC Ministry of Foreign Affairs, April 14, 1965, GSG 020000024482A.

54. Fernando Gutiérrez Barrios, Captain of the DFS, "Actividades pro China Comunista en el estado de Baja California," n.d., AGN IPS 2958B.

55. "Washington Post Article—Parade Uncovers a Chinese Spy Ring in Mexico," Bureau of Inter-American Affairs, entry P2, Records Relating to Mexico, 1946–1975, container 16, record group 59, USNA.

56. ROC Embassy in Mexico to ROC Ministry of Foreign Affairs, October 6, 1964, GSG 020000024482A; ROC Embassy in Mexico to ROC Ministry of Foreign Affairs, October 23, 1965, GSG 020000024483.

57. ROC Embassy in Mexico, February 12, 1959, GSG 020000037171A.

58. Ho and Ho, *My Forty Years as a Diplomat,* 197.

59. FMPRC 111–00477–06; ROC Embassy in Mexico to ROC Ministry of Foreign Affairs, September 30, 1964, GSG 020000024482A.

60. ROC National Security Bureau to ROC Ministry of Foreign Affairs, November 17, 1965; ROC Embassy in Mexico to ROC Ministry of Foreign Affairs, September 15, 1965; both GSG 020000024483A; Mexico City Zhonghua Shanghui to ROC Overseas Chinese Affairs Commission, November 22, 1965, GSG 020000025797A.

61. Anderson, *Washington Exposé* (Washington DC: Public Affairs Press, 1967), 363.

62. Feng-Shan Ho, *Waijiao shengya sishinian,* 606, 624–25. The U.S. embassy confirmed that Anderson received his information from Ho. "Washington Post Article—Parade Uncovers a Chinese Spy Ring in Mexico," Bureau of Inter-American Affairs, entry P2, Records Relating to Mexico, 1946–1975, container 16, record group 59, USNA.

63. Anderson, *Washington Exposé,* 363.

64. Jack Anderson, "Parade Uncovers a Chinese Spy Ring: Just across the Border in Mexico, a Communist Headquarters Plots to Subvert the Empire," February 7, 1965, GSG 020000024482A; Jorge Octavio Fernández Montes, "Encuentros y desencuentros: México y la República Popular China antes del establecimiento de relaciones diplomáticas (1949–1972)," in *40 años de la relación entre México y China: Acuerdos, desencuentros y futuro,* ed. Enrique Dussel Peters (México, DF: Centro de Estudios China-México, Universidad Nacional Autónoma de México, 2012), 395–96.

65. Anderson, "Parade Uncovers a Chinese Spy Ring."

66. ROC Embassy in Mexico to ROC Ministry of Foreign Affairs, February 10, 1965, GSG 020000024482A.

67. Feng-Shan Ho, *Waijiao shengya sishinian*, 653.

68. ROC Embassy in Mexico to ROC Ministry of Foreign Affairs, February 10, 1965, GSG 020000024482A.

69. Ing. Alfonso Vilchis Alzate, "Tráfico de chinos, drogas y enervantes," *El Universal,* July 14, 1965, primera sección, 2.

70. Feng-Shan Ho, *Waijiao shengya sishinian*, 653; "Peiping Spy Ring Operating across US Border in Mexico," *China Post,* February 8, 1965, copy in GSG 020000024482A.

71. ROC Embassy in Mexico to ROC Ministry of Foreign Affairs, July 27, 1965, GSG 020000025796A.

72. ROC Embassy in Mexico to ROC Ministry of Foreign Affairs, February 25, 1966, GSG 020000024483A.

73. Report, "Summary of the Activities of the Chinese Communists in the Chinese Community in Mexico," ROC Ambassador Chen Chih-ping to Mexican Secretary of Foreign Relations Antonio Carrillo Flores, February 12, 1966, GSG 020000024483A.

74. ROC Embassy in Mexico to ROC Ministry of Foreign Affairs, February 25, 1966, GSG 020000024483A.

75. Manifiesto, Pablo Fong, March 17, 1965; Manifiesto Segundo, Pablo Fong, July 18, 1965; copies of both in GSG 020000024483A. Perhaps by mistake, the embassy's Chinese-language translation of Fong's declaration does not include the rationale behind his trip.

76. Manifiesto, Pablo Fong, March 17, 1965; Manifiesto Segundo, Pablo Fong, July 18, 1965; copies of both in GSG 020000024483A.

77. Manifiesto, Pablo Fong, March 17, 1965; Manifiesto Segundo, Pablo Fong, July 18, 1965; copies of both in GSG 020000024483A.

78. Feng-Shan Ho, *Waijiao shengya sishinian*, 651.

79. Jaime Pensado notes that in the aftermath of the 1968 massacre at the Plaza de Tres Culturas in Tlatelolco, several foreigners were deported for participating in Mexican politics. *Rebel Mexico,* 206.

80. Feng-Shan Ho, *Waijiao shengya sishinian*, 651.

81. On the boycott, see "Special report, '1965 Mexican overseas Chinese economic conditions,'" 8. Only a small quantity of products made in the People's Republic of China entered Mexico, including silk, ivory, evening wear, and tea. The boycott, begun in the early sixties, was encouraged by the ROC embassy in Mexico. For an example of Chinese Mexican trips to Taipei, see *Zhongyang Ribao/Central Daily News,* "Tour group of overseas Chinese in Mexico today fly to Hong Kong, return to Mexico," June 9, 1954, copy in KMT *yiban* 585.35; ROC Embassy in Mexico to Overseas Chinese Affairs Committee, "On the ninth return of Mexico overseas Chinese to China to celebrate National Day and the birthday of the President," September 26, 1966, GSG 020000025797A; "Canadian, Mexican, Cuban, Brazilian and other Chinese Groups Arrive in Taipei," *Gonglunbao* (Taiwan), October 7, 1957; "Overseas Chinese Leader Zhou Ruzhao Today Leaves Taiwan for Mexico," *Zhongyang Ribao/Central Daily News* (Taiwan), August 15, 1961; "Participate

in October Celebrations, Overseas Chinese Groups One by One Come Back [to China], Four Mexican Wives Follow Their Husbands Back to the Country," *Zhongyang Ribao/Central Daily News* (Taiwan), October 7, 1966; all Hong Kong Baptist University Overseas Chinese Clippings Database (hereafter HKBU).

82. ROC Embassy in Mexico to ROC Ministry of Foreign Affairs and Overseas Chinese Affairs Commission, September 26, 1966, GSG 020000025797A.

83. Report, "Summary of the Activities of the Chinese Communists," 2–3. The case of Francisco Chong Lung can illustrate how the ROC used its ability to issue travel documents to prevent Chinese from returning to East Asia. In September 1963, Chong Lung applied for a passport to visit Hong Kong and Macau, where he would meet with relatives from Guangdong Province. In the eyes of the embassy, however, Chong Lung was "an overseas Chinese deceived into returning to mainland China," and the embassy believed it had proof that Chong Lung collaborated with the Communists. The embassy refused his request and instructed the consulate in Mexicali to deny any requests from Chong Lung for travel documents. ROC Embassy in Mexico to ROC Ministry of Foreign Affairs, September 7, 1964, GSG 020000025796A.

84. "Recover the Mainland" Planning and Research Committee to Ministry of Foreign Affairs and Overseas Chinese Affairs Commission, copy of report from Mexican Representative to National Assembly of the Republic of China, Tan Xinmin, to the Committee, February 22, 1956, GSG 020000037170A.

85. Bao Jundi, ROC Ministry of Foreign Affairs, November 30, 1955, GSG 020000037170A.

86. Report, "On the Infiltration of Communist Bandits," 6.

87. Feng-Shan Ho, *Waijiao shengya sishinian*, 400.

88. Report, "On the Infiltration of Communist Bandits," 17–18.

89. Third Group of the Central Authorities of the Guomindang to First General Branch of the Guomindang in Mexico and Ambassador Feng-Shan Ho, May 22, 1964, GSG 020000025796A.

90. Mexico City Zhonghua Shanghui to ROC Overseas Chinese Affairs Commission, November 22, 1965, GSG 020000025797A.

91. Mexico City Zhonghua Shanghui to ROC Overseas Chinese Affairs Commission, November 22, 1965, GSG 020000025797A.

92. ROC Embassy in Mexico to ROC Ministry of Foreign Affairs, January 18, 1966, GSG 020000024483A.

93. ROC Embassy in Mexico to ROC Ministry of Foreign Affairs, January 18, 1966, GSG 020000024483A; ROC Embassy in Mexico to ROC Ministry of Foreign Affairs, September 11, 1959, GSG 020000037171A.

94. ROC Embassy in Mexico to ROC Ministry of Foreign Affairs, September 11, 1959, GSG 020000037171A.

95. ROC Embassy in Mexico to ROC Ministry of Foreign Affairs, January 18, 1966, GSG 020000024483A.

96. ROC Embassy in Mexico to ROC Ministry of Foreign Affairs, August 23, 1965, GSG 020000025796A.

97. ROC Embassy in Mexico to ROC Ministry of Foreign Affairs, October 4, 1966, GSG 020000025797A.

98. Third Group of the Central Authorities of the Guomindang to ROC Minister of Foreign Affairs Shen, February 25, 1966, GSG 020000024483A.

99. Report, "Summary of the Activities of the Chinese Communists, 1."

100. ROC Embassy in Mexico to ROC Ministry of Foreign Affairs, "Chengbao guanyu benguan daji gongfei zaimo huodong zhi qingxing you" [Report on the situation of this embassy attacking Communists' activities in Mexico], March 7, 1966, GSG 020000024483A.

101. Anderson, *Washington Exposé,* 366; Fernández Montes, "Encuentros y desencuentros," 395–96.

102. US Embassy in Mexico City to Department of State, "Mid-Point in the Diaz Ordaz Administration: A Political Assessment," Central Foreign Policy Files 1967–1969, box 2341, record group 59, USNA.

103. US Embassy in Mexico City to US Secretary of State, July 12, 1967, Central Foreign Policy Files 1967–1969, box 2343, record group 59, USNA.

104. ROC Embassy in Mexico, April 14, 1965, GSG 020000024482A.

105. AHSRE III-2990–30, cited in Fernández Montes, "Encuentros y desencuentros," 395.

106. ROC Ambassador to Mexico Chen Chih-ping to Mexican Secretary of Foreign Relations Antonio Carrillo Flores, July 5, 1967, AHSRE III-2990–30.

107. US Embassy in Mexico City to US Secretary of State, July 12, 1967, Central Foreign Policy Files 1967–1969, box 2343, record group 59, USNA.

108. José Rigoberto López, "Intentaban hacer de México una 'república socialista,'" *El Universal,* June 29, 1967, copy in AGN DGIPS 1678A.

109. Rigoberto Lorence, "Cada gobierno debe resolver cómo atacar las violaciones del orden y la subversión, dijo el canciller Carrillo Flores," *El Día,* August 2, 1967, copy in AGN DGIPS 1678A. According to Eric Zolov, "[e]stablishing a link between the Soviet Union and 'Communist-inspired agitators' was a well-established practice used by the Mexican government when it needed to justify political repression of dissidents." A similar logic seems to have taken hold in the repression of the distributors. "¡Cuba sí, Yanquis no! The Sacking of the Instituto Cultural México-Norteamericano in Morelia, Michoacán, 1961," in *In from the Cold: Latin America's New Encounter with the Cold War,* ed. Gilbert M. Joseph and Daniela Spenser, (Durham, NC: Duke University Press, 2008), p. 235.

110. US Embassy in Mexico City, Weeka no. 29, folder Pol 2–1 Mex, Central Foreign Policy Files 1967–1969, box 2338, record group 59, USNA.

111. "Alto a la represión," *Perspectiva Mundial,* July 1967, AGN DGIPS 1678A.

112. ROC Ambassador to Mexico Chen Chih-ping to Mexican Secretary of Foreign Relations Antonio Carrillo Flores, September 2, 1967, AHSRE III-2990–30.

113. Zhao, *Remaking Chinese America,* 2–3.

114. Chun, *Of Orphans and Warriors,* 75–76; Renqiu Yu, *To Save China, to Save Ourselves: The Chinese Hand Laundry Alliance of New York* (Philadelphia: Temple University Press, 1992), 185. After the Second World War, noted Chun, "citizenship was no guarantee against the infringement of civil rights" (76).

115. See Mae Ngai, "Legacies of Exclusion: Illegal Chinese Immigration during the Cold War Years," *Journal of American Ethnic History* 18, no. 1 (Fall 1998): 3–35.

116. Yu, *To Save China, to Save Ourselves*, 165.

CHAPTER 6

1. Similar demographic changes in the United States and Canada represented profound challenges for Chinese associations in those countries. See Him Mark Lai, "Historical Development of the Chinese Consolidated Benevolent Association / *Huiguan* System," in *Becoming Chinese American: A History of Communities and Institutions* (Walnut Creek, CA: AltaMira Press, 2004). On Canada, see Wing Chung Ng, "Collective Ritual and the Resilience of Traditional Organizations: A Case Study of Vancouver since the Second World War," in *The Chinese Diaspora: Selected Essays*, vol. 1, ed. Wang Ling-chi and Wang Gungwu (Singapore: Times Academic Press, 1998).

2. Monica Cinco Basurto, "Comunidades chinas en México: Actores, motivaciones e intereses" (forthcoming), 3.

3. ROC Embassy in Mexico to ROC Ministry of Foreign Affairs, December 13, 1966, GSG 020000025796A; ROC Embassy in Mexico to ROC Ministry of Foreign Affairs, January 5, 1967, GSG 020000025796A.

4. "Discurso pronunciado por el excelentísimo Señor Chih-Ping Chen, embajador de la República de China, con ocasión de la inauguración de la Exposición Cultural China en Mazatlán, Sin. el 21 de Julio de 1969"; "Más de mil años sellan los lazos de amistad entre China y México," *El Sol del Pacífico* (Mazatlán), July 22, 1969; "Extraordinario interés despierta la exposición de productos de China," *El Sol del Pacífico*, July 23, 1969; all GSG 020000016699A.

5. Francisco Javier Haro, José Luis León, and Juan José Ramírez, "Por si no nos volvemos a ver: Proceso de ruptura con Taiwán e inicio de una nueva etapa diplomática," in *Historia de las relaciones internacionales de México, 1821–2010*, ed. Mercedes de Vega, vol. 6, *Asia* (México, DF: Secretaría de Relaciones Exteriores, 2011), 229.

6. Haro, León, and Ramírez, "Por si no nos volvemos a ver," 6:231–32.

7. "Manuel Kong Chong" [pseud.] to Embassy of the ROC in Mexico, July 24, 1971; ROC Embassy in Mexico to ROC Foreign Ministry, July 28, 1971; both GSG 020000037304A.

8. ROC Consulate in Mexicali to Overseas Chinese Affairs Commission, August 3, 1971, GSG 020000037296A; Overseas Chinese Affairs Commission to Mexican Overseas Chinese General Organization, August 6, 1971, GSG 020000037304A.

9. Alexander Aviña, *Specters of Revolution: Peasant Guerrillas in the Cold War Mexican Countryside* (Oxford: Oxford University Press, 2014); Mario Ojeda, *Alcances y límites de la política exterior de México* (México, DF: Colegio de México, 2011), 203–4.

10. Romer Cornejo, "De la coincidencia diplomática a la competencia económica," in *40 años de la relación entre México y China: Acuerdos, desencuentros y futuro*, ed. Enrique Dussel Peters (México, DF: Universidad Nacional

Autónoma de México, Centro de Estudios China-México, 2012), 263–65; Hal Brands, *Latin America's Cold War* (Cambridge, MA: Harvard University Press, 2010), 134–35.

11. Haro, León, and Ramírez, "Por si no nos volvemos a ver," 6:232; "China Comunista Ingresó a la ONU: Terminante Derrota Sufrió EE. UU.," n.d., AGN Investigaciones Políticas y Sociales 1678A 2.

12. Jay Taylor, *The Generalissimo: Chiang Kai-shek and the Struggle for Modern China* (Cambridge, MA: Harvard University Press, 2009), 572.

13. "Normales Relaciones de México y China Nacionalista: Ping Chen," *El Sol de México*, November 10, 1971, AGN Investigaciones Políticas y Sociales 1678A 2.

14. US Ambassador to Mexico McBride to US Department of State, "Severance of Diplomatic Relations with Republic of China by Mexico," November 10, 1971, Subject Numeric Files 1970–73, box 2205, USNA.

15. Haro, León, and Ramírez, "Por si no nos volvemos a ver," 6:233.

16. US Ambassador to Mexico McBride to US Department of State, "Severance of Diplomatic Relations with Republic of China by Mexico," November 10, 1971, and "Expulsion of Republic of China Ambassador," November 11, 1971; both Subject Numeric Files 1970–73, box 2205, USNA.

17. US Ambassador to Mexico McBride to US Secretary of State, November 10, 1971; US Ambassador to Mexico McBride to US Secretary of State, November 11, 1971; US Ambassador to Mexico McBride to US Secretary of State, November 19, 1971; all record group 59, Subject Numeric Files 1970–73, box 2205, USNA.

18. "Press Release, Ministry of Foreign Affairs, Republic of China," November 17, 1971, IMH 505.1/0001

19. Consul Liu Tung-wei, "Liu zonglingshi dongwei gao lü mo xiajiasheng qiaobao shu" [Consul Liu Dongwei issues report on compatriots living in Baja California], November 17, 1971, IMH 501.11/88003. The consulate building, which had been donated by Chinese Mexican residents, reverted to Chinese associations after 1971. On its construction, see Fredy González, "We Won't Be Bullied Anymore: Chinese-Mexican Relations and the Chinese Community in Mexico, 1931–1971" (PhD diss., Yale University, 2013), 153–54.

20. Alejandro C. Manjarrez, "Cerraron el consulado chino," *La Voz de la Frontera*, November 18, 1971; "On Heels of U.N. Mexico Gives Nationalist Chinese 30 Days to Leave," *Imperial Valley Press*, November 18, 1971; both IMH 501.11/88003; "En el consulado de China Nacionalista, se reunieron los representantes de la colonia china de este estado para celebrar el último acto oficial en México de ésta representación diplomática," November 17, 1971, AGN Investigaciones Políticas y Sociales 1112A.

21. ROC Embassy in Mexico to ROC Ministry of Foreign Affairs, November 23, 1971, IMH 501.11/88003.

22. US Embassy in the Republic of China to US Department of State, January 27, 1972, Subject Numeric Files 1970–73, box 2205, record group 59, US National Archives.

23. US Embassy in Mexico to US Department of State, March 7, 1972, Subject Numeric Files 1970–73, box 2205, record group 59, US National Archives; Edu-

ardo Auyón Gerardo, *El dragón en el desierto: Los pioneros chinos en Mexicali* (Mexicali, Baja California: Instituto de Cultura de Baja California, 1991), 27.

24. Mariana Ming Sze Cheng Leung, interview with the author, July 23, 2009.

25. US Embassy in Mexico to US Department of State, March 7, 1972, Subject Numeric Files 1970–73, box 2205, record group 59, US National Archives.

26. Haro, León, and Ramírez, "Por si no nos volvemos a ver," 6:485–94. On the Republic of China's "economic and trade diplomacy," see Chen Jie, *Foreign Policy of the New Taiwan: Pragmatic Diplomacy in Southeast Asia* (Cheltenham, UK: Edward Elgar, 2002), chap. 3.

27. Beatriz Ramírez Camacho, "Los chinos en México: Esbozo de la comunidad de Tampico" (MA thesis, Universidad Nacional Autónoma de México, 1975), 84.

28. Exceptions include the online community "Inmigraciones Chinas a México" and Auyón Gerardo, *El dragón en el desierto*.

29. Instituto Nacional de Estadística y Geografía, VIII Censo General de Población 1960, www.inegi.org.mx/est/contenidos/proyectos/ccpv/cpv1960 /default.aspx; IX Censo General de Población 1970, www.inegi.org.mx/est /contenidos/proyectos/ccpv/cpv1970/default.aspx.

30. Republic of China Overseas Chinese Affairs Committee (Qiaowu Weiyuanhui), *Huaqiao jingji gaikuang* (Taipei: Qiaowu Weiyuanhui Disanchu, 1974), 299–301.

31. ROC Embassy in Mexico to ROC Overseas Chinese Affairs Committee, February 24, 1967, GSG 02000025797A.

32. ROC Embassy in Mexico to ROC Ministry of Foreign Affairs, October 18, 1966, GSG 020000025797A.

33. Record of ROC Embassy in Mexico First Talk on Party and Overseas Chinese Affairs, March 17, 1966, GSG 020000025796A.

34. ROC Consulate General in Mexicali to ROC Ministry of Foreign Affairs, n.d.; ROC Consulate General in Mexicali to ROC Ministry of Foreign Affairs, April 29, 1971; both GSG 020000037296A.

35. Miguel Lisbona Guillén, *Allí donde lleguen las olas del mar: Pasado y presente de los chinos en Chiapas* (Chiapas: CONACULTA, 2014), 40.

36. ROC Embassy in Mexico to ROC Ministry of Foreign Affairs, November 16, 1971, IMH 501.11/88003.

37. Lisbona Guillén, *Allí donde lleguen las olas del mar,* 152n95.

38. ROC Embassy in Mexico to ROC Ministry of Foreign Affairs, November 16, 1971, IMH 501.11/88003. Some Chinese Mexicans left the country when Mexico recognized the People's Republic of China, but most stayed "and continued to run their businesses." Republic of China Overseas Chinese Affairs Committee, *Huaqiao jingji gaikuang,* 299–301. On the formation of the Quanmo Huaqiao Zonghui, see González, "We Won't Be Bullied Anymore," 281–84.

39. Lisbona Guillén, *Allí donde lleguen las olas del mar,* 40; Jorge Fong, "China: La raíz negada," in *Asiáticos en la ciudad de México,* ed. Alfredo Romero et al. (México, DF: Instituto de Cultura de la Ciudad de México, 1999), 47.

40. ROC Embassy in Mexico to ROC Ministry of Foreign Affairs, December 4, 1971, IMH 501.11/88003.

244 | Notes to Chapter 6

41. Pei-te Lien and Dean P. Chen, "The Evolution of Taiwan's Policies toward the Political Participation of Citizens Abroad in Homeland Governance," in *Routledge Handbook of the Chinese Diaspora* ed. Chee-Beng Tan (London: Routledge, 2013), 43; See Chen Jie, *Foreign Policy of the New Taiwan*.

42. Weixiong Lü, "Moxige, eguaduoer huaren shetuan de xianzhuang" [Present conditions of overseas Chinese associations in Mexico and Ecuador], in *Haiwai huaren shehui xintoushi,* ed. Lü Weixiong (Guangzhou: Lingnan Meishu Chubanshe, 2005), 91.

43. Rebecca Lau, "Memories of Origins / Origins of Memories: The Collective Memory of the Chinese Community in Tapachula, Chiapas, Mexico" (MA thesis, University of British Columbia, 2003), 53.

44. Lisbona Guillén, *Allí donde lleguen las olas del mar,* 160–61.

45. Jeanett Carrillo Magdaleno, *Mi nombre es Alicia Woong Castañeda* (Zapopan, Jalisco, Mexico: Editorial Amate, 2005), 28.

46. "Relaciones diplomáticas entre México y China Roja," *El Universal,* February 15, 1972; "Las relaciones con China contribución a la paz del mundo," *El Día,* February 17, 1972; both AGN Investigaciones Políticas y Sociales 1678A 2.

47. "Promoveremos relaciones basados en el respeto mutuo: Hsiang-hui," *El Heraldo de México,* August 4, 1972, AGN Investigaciones Políticas y Sociales 1678A 2; "Diplomáticos de la República Popular China arribaron a ésta ciudad, acompañados del Sr. Guillermo Nasser Quiñones, e informaron que su viaje es con el fin de ver si su país puede hacer inversiones en el estado," August 24, 1972, AGN Investigaciones Políticas y Sociales 1622D; record group 59, Subject Numeric Files 1970–73, box 2186, USNA.

48. Haro, León, and Ramírez, "Por si no nos volvemos a ver," 6:235; US Embassy in Mexico to US Secretary of State, February 17, 1972; US Consulate in Mexicali to US Secretary of State, November 16, 1971; both Subject Numeric Files 1970–73, box 2186, record group 59, USNA.

49. Him Mark Lai, *Chinese American Transnational Politics* (Urbana: University of Illinois Press, 2010), 38; Wing Chung Ng, "Becoming 'Chinese Canadian': The Genesis of a Cultural Category," in Elizabeth Sinn, *The Last Half Century of Chinese Overseas* (Hong Kong: Hong Kong University Press, 1998), 210.

50. Lisbona Guillén, *Allí donde lleguen las olas del mar,* 46–47.

51. Taiwan Office for the Promotion of Commerce, Mexico City to ROC Ministry of Foreign Affairs, September 22, 1972, IMH 505.1/0001.

52. Auyón Gerardo, *El dragón en el desierto,* 77.

53. Taiwan Office for the Promotion of Commerce, Mexico City, to ROC Ministry of Foreign Affairs, September 22, 1972, IMH 505.1/0001

54. Calexico Consulate General to Ministry of Foreign Affairs, October 10, 1972; "Entusiasta recibimiento a las voleibolistas chinas," *La Voz de la Frontera,* October 7, 1972; both IMH 505.1/0001.

55. Auyón Gerardo, *El dragón en el desierto,* 75.

56. Feng Xiuwen, *Zhongmo guanxi: Lishi yu xianshi* (Beijing: Shehui Kexue Wenxian Chubanshe, 2007), 151.

57. Haro, León, and Ramírez, "Por si no nos volvemos a ver," 6:238.

58. Subsecretaría de Comercio Exterior, "Balanza comercial de México con China," accessed August 16, 2015, www.economia.gob.mx/comunidad-negocios/comercio-exterior/informacion-estadistica-y-arancelaria; Cornejo, "De la coincidencia diplomática," 263–76.

59. Sergio Ley López, "Algunas reflexiones sobre el futuro de la relación México-China," in 40 años de la relación entre México y China: Acuerdos, desencuentros y futuro, ed. Enrique Dussel Peters (México, DF: Centro de Estudios China-México, Universidad Nacional Autónoma de México, 2012), 60.

60. Enrique Dussel Peters, "Mexico-China: Profundas grietas," Reforma, February 26, 2015, accessed September 1, 2015, http://reforma.vlex.com.mx/vid/quo-vadis-mexico-china-558869402.

61. Ley López, "Algunas reflexiones sobre el futuro," 63.

62. Cinco Basurto, "Comunidades chinas en México, 11.

63. Fong, "China: La raíz negada," 47.

64. The 2012 pilgrimage was described as the fifty-second pilgrimage to the holy site, but because it has been conducted annually since 1958, the number would suggest that the pilgrimage was not carried out during three years.

65. Lisbona Guillén, Allí donde lleguen las olas del mar, 38–41.

66. Lisbona Guillén, Allí donde lleguen las olas del mar, 86–89, 158.

67. Cinco Basurto, "Comunidades chinas en México," 15–19.

68. Wing Chung Ng, The Chinese in Vancouver, 1945–80: The Pursuit of Identity and Power (Vancouver, BC: UBC Press, 1999), 107–8; Isabelle Lausent Herrera, "New Immigrants: A New Community? The Chinese Community in Peru in Complete Transformation," in Routledge Handbook of the Chinese Diaspora, ed. Chee-Beng Tan (London: Routledge, 2013), 375.

69. Gao Weinong, Lading meizhou huaqiao huaren yiminshi, shetuan yu wenhua huodong yuantiao (Guangzhou: Jinan Daxue Chubanshe, 2012), 78.

70. See Gao Shoujian, "Yu feifa yimin xiangyu zai moxige" [Meeting with illegal immigrants in Mexico], in Zhongguo waijiaoguan zai lading meizhou, ed. Li Tongcheng and Huang Shikang (Shanghai: Shanghai Renmin Chubanshe, 2001), 196–209; and Huang Shikang, Chushi lamei sanguo ganhuai (Shanghai: Dongfang Chuban Zhongxin, 2008), 94–97.

71. Mariana Ming Sze Cheng Leung, interview.

72. Ernesto Martínez, "Border Chinese: Making Space and Forging Identity in Mexicali, Mexico" (PhD diss., Harvard University, 2008), 69–72; Zhang Jinjiang, "Bainian bubian zhongguo xin: Moxige xibeibian cheng dihuana ji xing zhisi," Renmin Ribao, May 15, 2001.

73. Martínez, "Border Chinese," 58–61; Ernesto Rodríguez Chávez and Salvador Cobo, "Extranjeros residentes en México: Una aproximación cuantitativa con base en los registros administrativos del INM" (National Institute of Migration, 2012), 25, accessed September 1, 2015, http://www.politica migratoria.gob.mx/work/models/SEGOB/CEM/PDF/Estadisticas/Poblacion_Extranjera/ExtranjerosResMex.pdf.

74. "Hu Jintao fang moxige tisheng huaren diwei wei huashang chuang shangji," accessed September 1, 2015, http://news.sina.com.cn/o/2005–09–16/10556960682s.shtml.

75. Haro, León, and Ramírez, "Por si no nos volvemos a ver," 6:239–41.

76. Gao Weinong, *Lading meizhou huaqiao huaren yiminshi*, 78–79; Auyón Gerardo, *El dragón en el desierto*, 27.

77. Lü, "Moxige, eguaduoer huaren shetuan de xianzhuang," 87–92.

78. Lü, "Moxige, eguaduoer huaren shetuan de xianzhuang," 90.

79. Ximena Alba, "Fronteras de mercancía: El Chinatown de Mexicali, fachada de un barrio transnacional" (MA thesis, UAM Iztapalapa, 2008), 136–42, 146–49.

80. Feng Xiuwen, *Zhongmo guanxi*, 282–83; Jimmy Li, "La Cámara (general) de Empresarios Chinos en México," in *40 años de la relación entre México y China: Acuerdos, desencuentros y futuro*, ed. Enrique Dussel Peters (México, DF: Universidad Nacional Autónoma de México, Centro de Estudios China-México, 2012), 91–92.

81. Mohuatang.com; onemex.com; and chinomx.com; all accessed August 10, 2015.

82. On similar anti-Taiwanese independence and peaceful reunification organizations around the world, see Zhang Yinglong, "Cujin heping tongyi daye" [The great task of encouraging peaceful reunification], in *Huaqiao huaren yu xinzhongguo* (Guangzhou: Jinan Daxue Chubanshe, 2009), 377–93.

83. "Moxige huaren huaqiao chengli 'Zhongguo hetonghui,'" January 25, 2002, accessed January 19, 2013, http://hqhr.jnu.edu.cn/article.asp?newsid = 7586; also see *Moguo Qiaoxun* (Tijuana, Baja California), January 2009 and July 2009.

84. "Jianada Moxige huaren xiying xinchun," *Renmin Ribao*, February 15, 2002.

85. Lauren Gorfinkel, "Ideology and the Performance of Chineseness: Hong Kong Singers on the CCTV Stage," *Perfect Beat* 12, no. 2 (2011): 109; Nimrod Baranovitch, *China's New Voices: Popular Music, Ethnicity, Gender, and Politics, 1978–1997* (Berkeley: University of California Press, 2003), 233.

86. Live Yu-Sion, "The Sinwa of Reunion: Searching for a Chinese Identity in a Multicultural World," in *Beyond Chinatown: New Chinese Migration and the Global Expansion of China*, ed. Mette Thunø (Copenhagen: NIAS Press, 2005), 234.

87. Zhuang Guotu, "China's Policies on Overseas Chinese: Past and Present," in *Routledge Handbook of the Chinese Diaspora*, ed. Chee-Beng Tan (New York: Routledge, 2013), 38.

88. Philip A. Kuhn, *Chinese among Others: Emigration in Modern Times* (Lanham, MD: Rowman & Littlefield, 2008); Wanning Sun, "China's Rise and (Trans)National Connections: The Global Diasporic Chinese Mediasphere," in *Routledge Handbook of the Chinese Diaspora*, ed. Chee-Beng Tan (New York: Routledge, 2013), 443.

89. Zhang, "Bainian bubian zhongguo xin."

90. "'México, ejemplo de democracia' afirmó el gerente del Bco. de China en una reunión," *Excélsior*, March 14, 1972, copy in IMH 505.1/0001.

91. Zhang Dezhen and Guo Weicheng, "Lajiachang xu xiangqing ji Yang zhuxi huijian moxige huaqiao huayi daibiao," *Renmin Ribao*, May 18, 1990.

92. Zheng Weishu, "Cong lishi jiazu kan moxige huaqiao huaren de shengcun yu fazhan," in *Haiwai huaren shehui xintoushi*, ed. Lü Weixiong (Guangzhou:

Lingnan Meishu Chubanshe, 2005), 157–60; Feng, *Zhongmo guanxi*, 249–50; Supermercados Ley, "Nuestra Historia," accessed October 2, 2012, http://casaley.com.mx/2015/index.php/corporativo/empresa/historia.html.

93. "'Women shizhong renwei ziji shi huaren' moxige huaren shoufu Li Huawen chuxi 'haiwai zhongshanren' qidong yishi, qizi jiangshu chuangqi jiazu shi," *Nanfang Dushi Bao*, August 26, 2009.

94. "Moxige huaren shoufu fu guangdong zhongshan xungen chazu," accessed September 1, 2015, http://news.sina.com.cn/c/2005-07-09/10006392090s.shtml.

95. Ximena Alba, "Fronteras de la mercancía," 131.

96. Guo Weicheng, "Moxige huaqiao huaren qingzhu yangnian chunjie," *Renmin Ribao*, February 18, 1991.

97. Shen An, "Moxige qiaotuan huandu jiajie," *Renmin Ribao*, February 10, 1997.

98. Olga R. Rodriguez, "Chinese Mexicans Celebrate Repatriation to Mexico," accessed February 2, 2013, http://bigstory.ap.org/article/chinese-mexicans-celebrate-repatriation-mexico; CCTV Americas Now, "The Big Lusong," February 10, 2013, http://www.youtube.com/watch?v = wuDcWjtiZ4g; Canal Once, "Los que llegaron: Chinos," February 2, 2012, http://www.youtube.com/watch?v = uZqPiLrJ9As; Secretaría de Educación Pública, "Chinos en Mexicali: Ventana a mi comunidad," accessed August 16, 2015, https://youtu.be/mx9jLZDrkxc.

99. Quoted in Cinco Basurto, "Comunidades chinas en México," 18.

100. Gavin O'Toole, *The Reinvention of Mexico: National Ideology in a Neoliberal Era* (Liverpool: Liverpool University Press, 2010), 67–68; Jane Hindley, "Towards a Pluricultural Nation: The Limits of *Indigenismo* and Article 4," in *Dismantling the Mexican State?* ed. Rob Aitken, Nikki Craske, Gareth A. Jones, and David E. Stansfield (New York: St. Martin's Press, 1996), 235–36. For an example of how multicultural discourses provided an opening for Chinese communities in other parts of the hemisphere, see Ng, *Chinese in Vancouver*, 104–6.

101. Ximena Alba, "Fronteras de la mercancía," 131–32.

CONCLUSION

1. Jürgen Buchenau, *Tools of Progress: A German Merchant Family in Mexico City, 1865–Present* (Albuquerque: University of New Mexico Press, 2004), 193.

2. Theresa Alfaro-Velcamp, *So Far from Allah, So Close to Mexico: Middle Eastern Immigrants in Modern Mexico* (Austin: University of Texas Press, 2007), 151–52.

3. Xu Shicheng, "El Reloj Chino: Testimonio de la amistad sino-mexicana," *China Hoy*, September 13, 2010, accessed October 21, 2012, http://spanish.china.org.cn/specials/Mexico200/2010–09/13/content_20920574.htm.

4. Buchenau, *Tools of Progress*, 195.

5. Alfaro-Velcamp, *So Far from Allah*, 160; Buchenau, *Tools of Progress*, 196.

6. One study on immigration to Mexico during the second half of the twentieth century declined to study the Chinese because official statistics suggested

that there weren't many in the country. This might explain the absence of studies on Chinese Mexicans at midcentury. Mónica Palma Mora, *De tierras extrañas: Un estudio sobre la inmigración en México, 1950–1990* (México, DF: Instituto Nacional de Migración, 2006), 39–40.

7. Jürgen Buchenau, "The Limits of the Cosmic Race: Immigrant and Nation in Mexico, 1850–1950," in *Immigration and National Identities in Latin America,* ed. Nicola Foote and Michael Goebel (Gainesville: University Press of Florida, 2014), 66.

8. Kathleen López, "In Search of Legitimacy: Chinese Immigrants and Latin American Nation Building," in *Immigration and National Identities in Latin America,* ed. Nicola Foote and Michael Goebel (Gainesville: University Press of Florida, 2014), 200–201.

Bibliography

ARCHIVAL PRIMARY SOURCES
Mexico

Archivo Central Migratorio, National Institute of Migration (INM), Mexico City

Archivo General de la Nación (AGN), Mexico City

Archivo General de la Nación, Dirección General de Gobierno (hereafter AGN DGG), Mexico City

Archivo General de la Nación, Dirección General de Investigaciones Políticas y Sociales (AGN DGIPS), Mexico City

Archivo General del Estado de Yucatán (AGEY), Mérida

Archivo Histórico Genaro Estrada (AHSRE), Secretaría de Relaciones Exteriores, Mexico City

Archivo Histórico Municipal de Tampico, Tampico

Centro Universitario de Información y Documentación, Universidad de Ciencias y Artes de Chiapas (CUID-UNICACH), Tuxtla Gutiérrez

Fidecomiso Archivo Plutarco Elías Calles y Fernando Torreblanca (FAPECFT), Mexico City

Instituto de Investigaciones Históricas, Universidad Autónoma de Baja California (IIH-UABC), Tijuana

People's Republic of China

Hong Kong Baptist University Overseas Chinese Clippings Database (HKBU), Hong Kong

Ministry of Foreign Affairs of the People's Republic of China (FMPRC), Beijing

Republic of China (Taiwan)

Archives of the Ministry of Foreign Affairs, Academia Historica (Guoshiguan Xindian) (GSG), Taipei
Guomindang Archives (KMT), Taipei
Institute of Modern History, Academia Sinica (IMH), Taipei
National Taiwan University (NTU), Taipei
Taiwan Digital Archives

United Kingdom

United Kingdom National Archives (UKNA), Kew

United States

Foreign Broadcast Information Service (FBIS) Daily Reports
John F. Kennedy Presidential Library, Boston
National Security Archive, George Washington University
United States National Archives (USNA), Washington, DC

PUBLISHED AND ONLINE PRIMARY SOURCES

Ávila Camacho, Manuel. Third *informe de gobierno* (September 1943), in "Informes Presidenciales Manuel Ávila Camacho." Mexico City: Cámara de Diputados (México), Dirección de Investigación y Análisis, 2006. http://www.diputados.gob.mx/cedia/sia/re/RE-ISS-09-06-09.pdf.

Cárdenas, Lázaro. "Apuntes sobre México y China." In *México y China: Testimonios de amistad,* edited by Cecilia Garza Limón. México, D.F.: Secretaría de Relaciones Exteriores, 2001.

Carrillo Magdaleno, Jeanett. *Mi nombre es Alicia Woong Castañeda.* Zapopan, Jalisco, Mexico: Editorial Amate, 2005.

Cheng Tiangu. *Cheng tiangu huiyilu.* Taipei: Longwen Chubanshe, 1993.

Chiang Ming-Ching. *Documentary Collection on Donation (1926–1960).* 2 vols. Taipei: Academia Historica, 1993.

Cuevas Pimienta, Roberto. *La honorable colonia china en la república mexicana.* N.p.: Ediciones Rocío, 1957.

Espinoza, José Ángel. *El ejemplo de Sonora.* México, DF, 1932.

———. *El problema chino en México.* México, DF, 1931.

Foreign Relations of the United States, 1958–1960. Vol. 5, American Republics. Document 333, "Memorandum of a Conversation, Los Pinos, August 12, 1959, 7 P.M." Accessed August 16, 2012. http://www.history.state.gov/historicaldocuments/frus1958–60v05/d333.

He Fengjiao, ed. *Paihua shiliao huibian: Moxige.* Taipei: Guoshiguan, 1991.

Ho, Feng-Shan. *China verteidigt sich.* Vienna: M. Winkler, 1937.

———. *Waijiao shengya sishinian.* Hong Kong: Zhongwen Daxue Chubanshe, 1990.

Ho, Feng-Shan, and Monto Ho. *My Forty Years as a Diplomat.* Pittsburgh: Dorrance, 2010.

Huang Shikang. *Chushi lamei sanguo ganhuai.* Shanghai: Dongfang Chuban Zhongxin, 2008.

Instituto de Investigaciones Jurídicas, UNAM. "The Political Constitution of the United Mexican States." 2005. Accessed September 16, 2012. www .juridicas.unam.mx/infjur/leg/constmex/pdf/consting.pdf.

López Mateos, Adolfo. Fifth *informe de gobierno.* In "Informes Presidenciales: Adolfo López Mateos," Servicio de Investigación y Análisis, Cámara de Diputados, 2006. Accessed September 16, 2012. www.diputados.gob.mx /cedia/sia/re/RE-ISS-09-06-12.pdf.

Lümei Huaqiao Tongyi Yijuan Jiuguo Zonghui (China War Relief Association of America). *Qiqi kangzhan qizhounian jinian tekan.* [San Francisco?]: Gai Hui, 1946.

Monteón González, Humberto, and José Luis Trueba Lara, eds. *Chinos y antichinos en México: Documentos para su estudio.* Guadalajara: Gobierno de Jalisco, Unidad Editorial, 1988.

Pardinas, Felipe. *Relaciones diplomáticas entre México y China, 1898–1948.* México, DF: Secretaría de Relaciones Exteriores, 1982.

Pius XII. "Ad Apostolorum Principis: Encyclical Letter of Pope Pius XII on Communism and the Church in China." June 29, 1958. Accessed September 13, 2012. www.vatican.va/holy_father/pius_xii/encyclicals/documents/hf_p-xii_enc_29061958_ad-apostolorum-principis_en.html.

Shijiu lujun zongzhi huibu shouru kangri weilaojin baogaoshu. Shanghai, 1932.

Supermercados Ley, "Nuestra Historia." Accessed October 2, 2012. www .casaley.com.mx/index.php?option = com_content&view = article&id = 49&Itemid = 87.

Xu Shicheng, "El Reloj Chino: Testigo de la amistad sino-mexicana." *China Hoy,* September 13, 2010. Accessed October 21, 2012. http://spanish.china .org.cn/specials/Mexico200/2010–09/13/content_20920574.htm.

Yu Shouzhi (Yu Yuan-tse). "Moxige huaqiao dui zuguo kangzhan de gongxian." In *Huaqiao yu kangri zhanzheng.* Taipei: Huaqiao Xiehui Zonghui, 1999.

PERIODICALS

Excélsior, Mexico City
Los Angeles Times, Los Angeles
Moguo Qiaoxun, Tijuana
New York Times, New York
La Opinión, Los Angeles
Qiaosheng Yuekan, Mexico City
Reforma, Mexico City
Renmin Ribao, Beijing
Time
Últimas Noticias de Excélsior, Mexico City
El Universal, Mexico City
Washington Post, Washington, DC

SECONDARY SOURCES

Akashi, Yoji. *The Nanyang Chinese National Salvation Movement, 1937–1941.* Lawrence: Center for Asian Studies, University of Kansas, 1970.

Alba, Ximena. "Fronteras de mercancía: El Chinatown de Mexicali, fachada de un barrio transnacional." MA thesis, Universidad Autónoma Metropolitana, Unidad Iztapalapa, 2008.

Alegre, Robert F. *Railroad Radicals in Cold War Mexico: Gender, Class, and Memory.* Lincoln: University of Nebraska Press, 2014.

Alfaro-Velcamp, Theresa. *So Far from Allah, So Close to Mexico: Middle Eastern Immigrants in Modern Mexico.* Austin: University of Texas Press, 2007.

Anderson, Jack. *Washington Exposé.* Washington, DC: Public Affairs Press, 1967.

Anguiano Roch, Eugenio. "Relaciones México-China en su perspectiva histórica." In *China y México: Implicaciones de una nueva relación,* edited by Enrique Dussel Peters and Yolanda Trápaga Delfín. México, DF: Centro de Estudios China-México, Universidad Nacional Autónoma de México, 2007.

Armentrout Ma, L. Eve. *Revolutionaries, Monarchists, and Chinatowns: Chinese Politics in the Americas and the 1911 Revolution.* Honolulu: University of Hawaii Press, 1990.

August, Jack. "The Anti-Japanese Crusade in Arizona's Salt River Valley: 1934–35." *Arizona and the West* 21, no. 2 (Summer 1979): 113–36.

Augustine-Adams, Kif. "Making Mexico: Legal Nationality, Chinese Race, and the 1930 Population Census." *Law and History Review* 27, no. 1 (Spring 2009): 113–44.

Auyón Gerardo, Eduardo [Ouyang Min]. *El dragón en el desierto: Los pioneros chinos en Mexicali.* Mexicali, Baja California: Instituto de Cultura de Baja California, 1991.

———. *Moguo xiajiasheng huaqiao yange shilüe / Los chinos en Baja California ayer y hoy.* Hong Kong: Zhongshan Chubanshe, 1971.

Aviña, Alexander. *Specters of Revolution: Peasant Guerrillas in the Cold War Mexican Countryside.* Oxford: Oxford University Press, 2014.

Azuma, Eiichiro. "Dancing with the Rising Sun: Strategic Alliances between Japanese Immigrants and Their 'Home' Government." In *The Transnational Politics of Asian Americans,* edited by Christian Collet and Pei-te Lien. Philadelphia: Temple University Press, 2009.

Balderrama, Francisco E., and Raymond Rodríguez. *Decade of Betrayal: Mexican Repatriation in the 1930s.* Albuquerque: University of New Mexico Press, 1995.

Baranovitch, Nimrod. *China's New Voices: Popular Music, Ethnicity, Gender, and Politics, 1978–1997.* Berkeley: University of California Press, 2003.

Blaisdell, Lowell L. *The Desert Revolution: Baja California, 1911.* Madison: University of Wisconsin Press, 1962.

Blancarte, Roberto. "Intransigence, Anticommunism, and Reconciliation: Church/State Relations in Transition." In *Dictablanda: Politics, Work, and Culture in Mexico, 1938–1968,* edited by Paul Gillingham and Benjamin T. Smith. Durham, NC: Duke University Press, 2014.

Botton Beja, Flora. "La persecución de los chinos en México." *Estudios de Asia y África* 43, no. 2 (May-August 2008): 477–86.

Brands, Hal. *Latin America's Cold War.* Cambridge, MA: Harvard University Press, 2010.

Brooks, Charlotte. *Between Mao and McCarthy: Chinese American Politics in the Cold War Years.* Chicago: University of Chicago Press, 2015.

Bu Youfu. *Sihai guixin.* Hong Kong: Xinwen Tiandishe, 1957.

Buchenau, Jürgen. "From the *Caudillo* to Tata Lázaro: The *Maximato* in Perspective, 1928–1934." In *The Mexican Revolution: Conflict and Consolidation, 1910–1940,* edited by Douglas Richmond and Sam Haynes. College Station, TX: Texas A&M University Press, 2013.

———. *In the Shadow of the Giant: The Making of Mexico's Central America Policy, 1876–1930.* Tuscaloosa: University of Alabama Press, 1996.

———. *The Last Caudillo: Álvaro Obregón and the Mexican Revolution.* Malden, MA: Wiley-Blackwell, 2011.

———. "The Limits of the Cosmic Race: Immigrant and Nation in Mexico, 1850–1950." In *Immigration and National Identities in Latin America,* edited by Nicola Foote and Michael Goebel. Gainesville: University Press of Florida, 2014.

———. "Por una guerra fría más templada: México entre el cambio revolucionario y la reacción estadounidense en Guatemala y Cuba," In *Espejos de la guerra fría: México, América Central y el Caribe,* edited by Daniela Spenser. México, DF: CIESAS, 2004.

———. *Tools of Progress: A German Merchant Family in Mexico City, 1865–Present.* Albuquerque: University of New Mexico Press, 2004.

Cai Renlong and Liang Guo. *Huaqiao kangri jiuguo shiliao xuanji.* Fuzhou: Zhonggong Fujian Sheng Weidangshi Gongzuo Weiyuanhui: Zhongguo Huaqiao Lishi Xuehui, 1987.

Cardiel Marín, Rosario. "La migración china en el norte de Baja California, 1877–1949." In *Destino México: Un estudio de las migraciones asiáticas a México, siglos XIX y XX,* edited by Maria Ota Mishima. México, DF: Colegio de México, Centro de Estudios de Asia y África, 1997.

Castañón Cuadros, Carlos. *Las dos repúblicas: Una aproximación a la migración china hacia Torreón, 1924–1963.* Torreón, Coahuila, Mexico: Ediciones del R. Ayuntamiento de Torreón, 2004.

Cervera, José Juan. *La gloria de la raza: Los chinos en Yucatán.* Mérida, Yucatán, Mexico: Instituto de Cultura de Yucatán, 2007.

Chamberlin, Eugene Keith. "Mexican Colonization versus American Interests in Lower California." *Pacific Historical Review* 20, no. 1 (February 1951): 43–55.

Chan, K.C. "The Abrogation of British Extraterritoriality in China, 1942–43: A Study of Anglo-American-Chinese Relations." *Modern Asian Studies* 11, no. 2 (1977): 257–91.

Chang, Iris. *The Chinese in America: A Narrative History.* New York: Viking, 2003.

Chang, Jason. "Racial Alterity in the Mestizo Nation." *Journal of Asian American Studies* 14, no. 3 (October 2011): 331–59.

Chen, Yong. *Chinese San Francisco, 1850–1943: A Trans-Pacific Community.* Stanford, CA: Stanford University Press, 2000.

Chen Jian. *Mao's China and the Cold War.* Chapel Hill: University of North Carolina Press, 2001.

Chen Jie. *Foreign Policy of the New Taiwan: Pragmatic Diplomacy in Southeast Asia.* Cheltenham, UK: Edward Elgar, 2002.

Chen Kwong Min. *Meizhou huaqiao tongjian.* New York: Meizhou Huaqiao Wenhuashe, 1950.

Chew, Selfa. *Uprooting Community: Japanese Mexicans, World War II, and the U.S.–Mexico Borderlands.* Tucson: University of Arizona Press, 2015.

Chu, Richard. *Chinese and Chinese Mestizos of Manila: Family, Identity, and Culture, 1860s–1930s.* Leiden: Brill, 2010.

Chun, Gloria Heyung. "'To Become Still Better Americans': The Challenge of China Turning Communist." In *Of Orphans and Warriors: Inventing Chinese American Culture and Identity.* New Brunswick, NJ: Rutgers University Press, 2000.

Chung, Sue Fawn. "Fighting for Their American Rights: A History of the Chinese American Citizens' Alliance." In *Claiming America: Constructing Chinese American Identities during the Exclusion Era,* edited by K. Scott Wong and Sucheng Chan. Philadelphia: Temple University Press, 1998.

Cinco Basurto, Monica. "China in Mexico: Yesterday's Encounter and Today's Discovery." In *Encounters: People of Asian Descent in the Americas,* edited by Roshni Rustomji-Kerns. Lanham, MD: Rowman & Littlefield, 1999.

———. "Comunidades chinas en México: Actores, motivaciones e intereses." Forthcoming.

———. "La expulsión de chinos de los años treinta y la repatriación de chino mexicanos de 1960." MA thesis, Colegio de México, 2009.

Connelly, Marisela. "Las relaciones de China y México en su contexto histórico," *Escenarios XXI* 1, nos. 5–6 (November–December 2010): 50–60.

Connelly, Marisela, and Romer Cornejo. *China-América Latina: Génesis y desarrollo de sus relaciones.* México, DF: Colegio de México, 1992.

Cornejo, Romer. "De la coincidencia diplomática a la competencia económica." In *40 años de la relación entre México y China: Acuerdos, desencuentros y futuro,* edited by Enrique Dussel Peters. México, DF: Centro de Estudios China-México, Universidad Nacional Autónoma de México, 2012.

Cott, Kennett. "Mexican Diplomacy and the Chinese Issue, 1876–1910." *Hispanic American Historical Review* 67, no. 1 (February 1987): 63–85.

Craft, Stephen. *V.K. Wellington Koo and the Emergence of Modern China.* Lexington: University Press of Kentucky, 2004.

Craib, Raymond. *Chinese Immigrants in Porfirian Mexico: A Preliminary Study of Settlement, Economic Activity, and Anti-Chinese Sentiment.* Albuquerque: Latin American Institute, University of New Mexico, 1996.

Cumberland, Charles C. "The Sonora Chinese and the Mexican Revolution." *Hispanic American Historical Review* 40, no. 2 (May 1960): 191–211.

Curtis, James R. "Mexicali's Chinatown." *Geographical Review* 85, no. 3 (July 1995): 335–48.

Dambourges Jacques, Leo M. "The Anti-Chinese Campaigns in Sonora, Mexico, 1900–1911." PhD diss., University of Arizona, 1974.

———. "The Chinese Massacre in Torreon (Coahuila) in 1911." *Arizona and the West* 16, no. 3 (Autumn 1974): 233–46.

———. "Have Quick More Money than Mandarins: The Chinese in Sonora." *Journal of Arizona History* 17, no. 2 (Summer 1976): 201–18.

Dear, Michael, and Gustavo Leclerc, eds. *Postborder City: Cultural Spaces of Bajalta California.* New York: Routledge, 2003.

Delgado, Grace Peña. *Making the Chinese Mexican: Global Migration, Localism, and Exclusion in the U.S.–Mexican Borderlands.* Stanford, CA: Stanford University Press, 2012.

Duncan, Robert H. "The Chinese and the Economic Development of Northern Baja California, 1889–1929." *Hispanic American Historical Review* 74, no. 4 (November 1994): 615–47.

Eastman, Lloyd E. "Nationalist China during the Nanking Decade, 1927–1937." In *The Nationalist Era in China,* edited by Lloyd E. Eastman, Jerome Ch'en, Suzanne Pepper, and Lyman P. Van Slyke. Cambridge and New York: Cambridge University Press, 1991.

———. "Nationalist China during the Sino-Japanese War 1937–1945." In *The Cambridge History of China,* vol. 13, *Republican China, 1912–1949,* pt. 2., edited by John K. Fairbank and Albert Feuerwerker. Cambridge: Cambridge University Press, 1986.

Ervin, Michael A. "Marte R. Gómez of Tamaulipas: Governing Agrarian Revolution." In *State Governors in the Mexican Revolution, 1910–1952: Portraits in Conflict, Courage, and Corruption,* edited by Jürgen Buchenau and William H. Beezley. Lanham, MD: Rowman & Littlefield, 2009.

Espiritu, Yen Le. *Home Bound: Filipino American Lives across Cultures, Communities, and Countries.* Berkeley: University of California Press, 2003.

Fein, Seth. "Producing the Cold War in Mexico: The Public Limits of Covert Communications." In *In from the Cold: Latin America's New Encounter with the Cold War,* edited by Gilbert M. Joseph and Daniela Spenser. Durham, NC: Duke University Press, 2008.

Feng Xiuwen. *Zhongmo guanxi: Lishi yu xianshi.* Beijing: Shehui Kexue Wenxian Chubanshe, 2007.

Feng Ziyou. *Huaqiao geming zuzhi shihua.* Taipei: Zhengzhong Shuju, 1954.

Fernández Montes, Jorge Octavio. "Encuentros y desencuentros: México y la República Popular China antes del establecimiento de relaciones diplomáticas (1949–1972)." In *40 años de la relación entre México y China: Acuerdos, desencuentros y futuro,* edited by Enrique Dussel Peters. México, DF: Centro de Estudios China-México, Universidad Nacional Autónoma de México, 2012.

FitzGerald, David, and David Cook-Martín. *Culling the Masses: The Democratic Origins of Racist Immigration Policy in the Americas.* Cambridge, MA: Harvard University Press, 2014.

Fitzgerald, Stephen. *China and the Overseas Chinese: A Study of Peking's Changing Policy, 1949–1970.* Cambridge: Cambridge University Press, 1972.

Foner, Nancy. *In a New Land: A Comparative View of Immigration.* New York: New York University Press, 2005.

Fong, Jorge. "China: La raíz negada." In *Asiáticos en la ciudad de México,* edited by Alfredo Romero et al. México, DF: Instituto de Cultura de la Ciudad de México, 1999.

Foote, Nicola, and Michael Goebel, eds. *Immigration and National Identities in Latin America*. Gainesville: University Press of Florida, 2014.

Friedman, Max Paul. *Nazis and Good Neighbors: The United States Campaign against the Germans of Latin America in World War II*. Cambridge: Cambridge University Press, 2003.

Gans, Herbert J. "Toward a Reconciliation of 'Assimilation' and 'Pluralism': The Interplay of Acculturation and Ethnic Retention." *International Migration Review* 31, no. 4 (Winter 1997): 875–92.

Gao Shoujian. "Yu feifa yimin xiangyu zai moxige" [Meeting with illegal immigrants in Mexico]. In *Zhongguo waijiaoguan zai lading meizhou*, edited by Li Tongcheng and Huang Shikang. Shanghai: Shanghai Renmin Chubanshe, 2001.

Gao Weinong. *Lading meizhou huaqiao huaren yiminshi, shetuan yu wenhua huodong yuantiao*. Guangzhou: Jinan Daxue Chubanshe, 2012.

García, Jerry. *Looking Like the Enemy: Japanese Mexicans, the Mexican State, and US Hegemony, 1897–1945*. Tucson: University of Arizona Press, 2014.

Garza Elizondo, Humberto. *China y el tercer mundo: Teoría y práctica de la política exterior de Pequín, 1956–1966*. Colección Centro de Estudios Internacionales 13. México, DF: Colegio de México, 1973.

Ginsburgs, George, and Arthur Stahnke. "Communist China's Trade Relations with Latin America." *Asian Survey* 10, no. 9 (September 1970): 803–19.

Gleizer, Daniela. *Unwelcome Exiles: Mexico and the Jewish Refugees from Nazism, 1933–1945*. Leiden: Brill, 2014.

Goebel, Michael. "Introduction: Reconceptualizing Diasporas and National Identities in Latin America and the Caribbean, 1850–1950." In *Immigration and National Identities in Latin America*, edited by Nicola Foote and Michael Goebel. Gainesville: University Press of Florida, 2014.

Gojman de Backal, Alicia. *Camisas, escudos y desfiles militares: Los Dorados y el antisemitismo en México, 1934–1940*. México, DF: Fondo de Cultural Económica 2000.

———. "Minorías, estado y movimientos nacionalistas de clase media en México: Liga antichina y antijudía (siglo XX)." In *Judaica Latinoamericana Estudios Histórico-Sociales*. Jerusalem: Editorial Universitaria Magnes, Universidad Hebrea, 1988.

Gómez Estrada, José Alfredo. *Gobierno y casinos: El origen de la riqueza de Abelardo L. Rodríguez*. Mexicali, Baja California: Instituto Mora, Universidad Autónoma de Baja California, 2002.

Gómez Izquierdo, José. *El movimiento antichino en México: 1871–1934: Problemas del racismo y del nacionalismo durante la revolución mexicana*. México, DF: Instituto Nacional de Antropología e Historia, 1991.

Gong Xuesui. "Zhongnanmei (fu Moxige)." In *Zhongguo minzu haiwai fazhan zhuangkuang*. Shanghai: Dahua Shushe, 1929.

González, Fredy. "We Won't Be Bullied Anymore: Chinese-Mexican Relations and the Chinese Community in Mexico, 1931–1971." PhD diss., Yale University, 2013.

González de Bustamante, Celeste. *"Muy Buenas Noches": Mexico, Television, and the Cold War*. Lincoln: University of Nebraska Press, 2012.

González Félix, Maricela. *Desde la distancia del tiempo y la proximidad de mis sentimientos: Testimonio de Saúl Chong Martínez.* México, DF: Seminario de Cultura Mexicana, 2005.

———. "Fumaderos de opio: Una leyenda que usurpó a la historia." *Semidero de idea* 2 (n.d.).

———. *El proceso de aculturación de la población de origen chino en la ciudad de Mexicali.* Mexicali, Baja California: Universidad Autónoma de Baja California, Instituto de Investigaciones Sociales, 1990.

González Navarro, Moisés. *Los extranjeros en México y los mexicanos en el extranjero, 1821–1970.* México, DF: Colegio de México, 1994.

González Oropeza, Manuel. "La discriminación en México: El caso de los nacionales chinos." In *Cuadernos del Instituto de Investigaciones Jurídicas: La problemática del racismo en los umbrales del siglo XXI, VI Jornadas Lascasianas.* México, DF: Universidad Nacional Autónoma de México, Instituto de Investigaciones Jurídicas, 1997.

Gorfinkel, Lauren. "Ideology and the Performance of Chineseness: Hong Kong Singers on the CCTV Stage." *Perfect Beat* 12, no. 2 (2011): 107–28.

Grandin, Greg. *The Last Colonial Massacre: Latin America in the Cold War.* Updated ed. Chicago: University of Chicago Press, 2011.

Hamilton, Nora. *The Limits of State Autonomy: Post-Revolutionary Mexico.* Princeton, NJ: Princeton University Press, 2014.

Han, Eric C. *Rise of a Japanese Chinatown: Yokohama, 1894–1972.* Cambridge, MA: Harvard University Asia Center, 2014.

Hansen, Lawrence Douglas Taylor. "The Chinese Six Companies of San Francisco and the Smuggling of Chinese Immigrants across the U.S.–Mexico Border, 1882–1930." *Journal of the Southwest* 48, no. 1 (Spring 2006): 37–61.

Haro, Francisco Javier, José Luis León, and Juan José Ramírez. "Por si no nos volvemos a ver: Proceso de ruptura con Taiwán e inicio de una nueva etapa diplomática." In *Historia de las relaciones internacionales de México, 1821–2010,* edited by Mercedes de Vega. Vol. 6, *Asia.* México, DF: Secretaría de Relaciones Exteriores, 2011.

Hindley, Jane. "Towards a Pluricultural Nation: The Limits of *Indigenismo* and Article 4." In *Dismantling the Mexican State?* edited by Rob Aitken, Nikki Craske, Gareth A. Jones, and David E. Stansfield. New York: St. Martin's Press, 1996.

Hsu, Madeline Yuan-yin. *Dreaming of Gold, Dreaming of Home: Transnationalism and Migration between the United States and South China, 1882–1943.* Stanford, CA: Stanford University Press, 2000.

Hu-DeHart, Evelyn. "Afterword: Brief Meditation on Diaspora Studies." *Modern Drama* 48, no. 2 (Summer 2005): 428–39.

———. "The Chinese of Baja California Norte." In *Proceedings of the Pacific Coast Council on Latin American Studies.* Vol. 12, *Baja California and the North Mexican Frontier.* San Diego, CA: San Diego State University Press, 1986.

———. "Los chinos de Sonora, 1875 a 1930: La formación de una pequeña burguesía regional." In *Los inmigrantes en el mundo de los negocios, siglos*

XIX y XX, edited by Rosa María Meyer and Delia Salazar Anaya. México, DF: CONACULTA-INAH, 2003.

———. "Concluding Commentary: On Migration, Diasporas and Transnationalism in Asian American History." *Journal of Asian American Studies* 8 (October 2005): 309–12.

———. "Immigrants to a Developing Society: The Chinese in Northern Mexico." *Journal of Arizona History* 21 (Autumn 1980): 49–86.

———. "Indispensable Enemy or Convenient Scapegoat? A Critical Examination of Sinophobia in Latin America and the Caribbean, 1870s to 1930s." In *The Chinese in Latin America and the Caribbean,* edited by Walton Look Lai and Chee Beng Tan. Leiden: Brill, 2010.

———. "Kang Youwei and the *Baohuanghui* in Mexico: When Two Nationalisms Collide." Unpublished manuscript.

———. "Opium and Social Control: Coolies on the Plantations of Peru and Cuba." *Journal of Chinese Overseas* 1, no. 2 (November 2005): 169–83.

———. "Racism and Anti-Chinese Persecution in Sonora, Mexico, 1876–1932." *Amerasia* 9, no. 2 (Fall/Winter 1982): 1–27.

———. "Voluntary Associations in a Predominantly Male Immigrant Community: The Chinese on the Northern Mexican Frontier, 1880–1930." In *Voluntary Organizations in the Chinese Diaspora,* edited by Kuhn Eng Kuah-Pearce and Evelyn Hu-DeHart. Hong Kong: Hong Kong University Press, 2006.

Ip, Manying. "Chinese Immigration to Australia and New Zealand: Government Policies and Race Relations." In *Routledge Handbook of the Chinese Diaspora,* edited by Chee-Beng Tan. London: Routledge, 2013.

Johnson, Cecil. *Communist China and Latin America.* New York: Columbia University Press, 1970.

Jones, Halbert. *The War Has Brought Peace to Mexico: World War II and the Consolidation of the Post-Revolutionary State.* Albuquerque: University of New Mexico Press, 2014.

Keller, Renata. *Mexico's Cold War: Cuba, the United States, and the Legacy of the Mexican Revolution.* New York: Cambridge University Press, 2015.

Klein, Donald. "Formosa's Diplomatic World." *China Quarterly* 15 (July–September 1963): 45–50.

Knight, Alan. "The Character and Consequences of the Great Depression in Mexico." In *The Great Depression in Latin America,* edited by Paulo Drinot and Alan Knight. Durham, NC: Duke University Press, 2014.

———. *The Mexican Revolution.* Vol. 2, *Counter-Revolution and Reconstruction.* New York: Cambridge University Press, 1986.

Koh, Ernest. *Diaspora at War: The Chinese of Singapore between Empire and Nation, 1937–1945.* Leiden: Brill, 2013.

Kuehnert, Lore Diana. "Pernicious Foreigners and Contested Compatriots: Mexican Newspaper Debates over Immigration, Emigration and Repatriation, 1928–1936." PhD diss., University of California, Riverside, 2002.

Kuhn, Philip A. *Chinese among Others: Emigration in Modern Times.* Lanham, MD: Rowman & Littlefield, 2008.

Lai, Him Mark. *Chinese American Transnational Politics.* Urbana: University of Illinois Press, 2010.

———. "The Chinese Community Press in Hawaii." In "The Hawaii Chinese: Their Experience and Identities over Two Centuries." Special issue, *Chinese America: History & Perspectives* 2010.

———. "Historical Development of the Chinese Consolidated Benevolent Association / *Huiguan* System." In *Becoming Chinese American: A History of Communities and Institutions*. Walnut Creek, CA: AltaMira Press, 2004.

———. "The Kuomintang in Chinese American Communities before World War II." In *Entry Denied: Exclusion and the Chinese Community in America, 1882–1943*, edited by Sucheng Chan. Philadelphia: Temple University Press, 1991.

Lai, Him Mark, Russell C. Leong, and Jean Pang Yip. *A History Reclaimed: An Annotated Bibliography of Chinese Language Materials on the Chinese of America*. Los Angeles: UCLA Asian American Studies Center, 1986.

Lau, Rebecca. "Memories of Origins / Origins of Memories: The Collective Memory of the Chinese Community in Tapachula, Chiapas, Mexico." MA thesis, University of British Columbia, 2003.

Lausent-Herrera, Isabelle. "New Immigrants: A New Community? The Chinese Community in Peru in Complete Transformation." In *Routledge Handbook of the Chinese Diaspora,* edited by Chee-Beng Tan. London: Routledge, 2013.

Lee, Erika. *At America's Gates: Chinese Immigration during the Exclusion Era, 1882–1943*. Chapel Hill: University of North Carolina Press, 2003.

———. *The Making of Asian America: A History*. New York: Simon & Schuster, 2015.

Lee, Joseph J. "Communist China's Latin American Policy" *Asian Survey:* 4, no. 11 (November 1964): 1123–34.

Leong Karen T., and Judy Tzu-Chun Wu. "Filling the Rice Bowls of China: Staging Humanitarian Relief during the Sino-Japanese War." In *Chinese Americans and the Politics of Race and Culture,* edited by Sucheng Chan and Madeline Y. Hsu. Philadelphia: Temple University Press, 2008.

Lesser, Jeffrey. *A Discontented Diaspora: Japanese Brazilians and the Meanings of Ethnic Militancy, 1960–1980*. Durham, NC: Duke University Press, 2007.

———. *Negotiating National Identity: Immigrants, Minorities, and the Struggle for Ethnicity in Brazil*. Durham, NC: Duke University Press, 1999.

Lew, Ling. *Huaqiao renwu zhi / The Chinese of North America: A Guide to Their Life and Progress*. Los Angeles: Dongxi Wenhua Chubanshe, 1949.

Lewis, Stephen E. "Revolution without Resonance? Mexico's 'Fiesta of Bullets' and Its Aftermath in Chiapas, 1910–1940." In *The Mexican Revolution: Conflict and Consolidation, 1910–1940*, edited by Douglas Richmond and Sam Haynes. College Station: Texas A&M University Press, 2013.

Ley López, Sergio. "Algunas reflexiones sobre el futuro de la relación México-China." In *40 años de la relación entre México y China: Acuerdos, desencuentros y futuro,* edited by Enrique Dussel Peters. México, DF: Centro de Estudios China-México, Universidad Nacional Autónoma de México, 2012.

Li, Jimmy. "La Cámara (general) de Empresarios Chinos en México." In *40 años de la relación entre México y China: Acuerdos, desencuentros y futuro,* edited by Enrique Dussel Peters. México, DF: Centro de Estudios China-México, Universidad Nacional Autónoma de México, 2012.

Li Ying-Hui. *Huaqiao zhengce yu haiwai minzu zhuyi (1912–1949) / The origins of overseas Chinese nationalism, vol. 1, 1912–1949*. Taipei: Guoshiguan, 1997.

Lien, Pei-te, and Dean P. Chen. "The Evolution of Taiwan's Policies toward the Political Participation of Citizens Abroad in Homeland Governance." In *Routledge Handbook of the Chinese Diaspora*, edited by Chee-Beng Tan. London: Routledge, 2013.

Lim, Julian. "*Chinos* and *Paisanos:* Chinese Mexican Relations in the Borderlands." *Pacific Historical Review* 79, no. 1 (February 2010): 50–85.

Lin Chou, Diego. *Chile y China: Inmigración y relaciones bilaterales, 1845–1970*. Santiago, Chile: Pontifica Universidad Católica de Chile, Instituto de Historia, 2004.

Ling, Huping. *Chinese Chicago: Race, Transnational Migration, and Community since 1870*. Stanford, CA: Stanford University Press, 2012.

Lisbona Guillén, Miguel. *Allí donde lleguen las olas del mar: Pasado y presente de los chinos en Chiapas*. Chiapas: CONACULTA, 2014.

Liu Zongxun. *Huaqiao aiguo zidong juanxian*. Taipei: Qiaowu Weiyuanhui Qiaowu Yanjiu Shi, 1969.

Lombardo Toledano, Vicente. *Victoria de la revolución china*. México, DF: Universidad Obrera de México, 1950.

López, Kathleen. *Chinese Cubans: A Transnational History*. Chapel Hill: University of North Carolina Press, 2013.

———. "In Search of Legitimacy: Chinese Immigrants and Latin American Nation Building." In *Immigration and National Identities in Latin America*, edited by Nicola Foote and Michael Goebel. Gainesville: University Press of Florida, 2014.

Lorenzana Cruz, Benjamín. "El comercio chino en la costa de Chiapas durante los años 1914–1920." In *Estado-nación en México: Independencia y revolución*, edited by Esaú Márquez Espinoza, Rafael de J. Araujo González, and María del Rocío Ortiz Herrera. Tuxtla Gutiérrez, Chiapas, Mexico: Universidad de Ciencias y Artes de Chiapas, 2011.

Loyola, Alberto Antonio. *Chino-mexicanos cautivos del comunismo: Su repatriación fue una gran proeza*. México, DF: Movimiento Continental Pro-Democracia Cristiana, 1961.

Lü, Weixiong. "Moxige, eguaduoer huaren shetuan de xianzhuang." In *Haiwai huaren shehui xintoushi*, edited by Lü Weixiong. Guangzhou: Lingnan Meishu Chubanshe, 2005.

Mancilla, Manuel Lee, and Maricela González Félix. *Viaje al corazón de la península: Testimonio de Manuel Lee Mancilla*. Mexicali, Baja California: Instituto de Cultura de Baja California, 2000.

Mandujano López, Ruth. "La migración interminable: Cantoneses en Manzanillo." *Legajos*, no. 1 (July–September 2009): 44–58.

Mar, Lisa Rose. *Brokering Belonging: Chinese in Canada's Exclusion Era, 1885–1945*. New York: Oxford University Press, 2010.

Martínez, Ernesto. "Border Chinese: Making Space and Forging Identity in Mexicali, Mexico." PhD diss., Harvard University, 2008.

Martínez Marín, L. Ricardo. "La migración china en el estado de Tamaulipas, 1900–1940." MA thesis, Universidad Autónoma Metropolitana, Unidad Iztapalapa, 1995.

McCullough, Kenneth Bruce. "America's Back Door: Indirect International Immigration via Mexico to the United States from 1875 to 1940." PhD diss., Texas A&M University, 1992.

McKeown, Adam. "Conceptualizing Chinese Diasporas, 1842 to 1949." *Journal of Asian Studies* 58, no. 2 (May 1999): 306–37.

Medin, Tzvi. "La mexicanidad política y filosófica en el sexenio de Miguel Alemán, 1946–1952." *Estudios Interdisciplinarios de América Latina y el Caribe* 1, no. 1 (1990). Accessed January 2, 2017. http://eial.tau.ac.il/index.php /eial/article/view/1308/1334.

———. *El minimato presidencial: Historia política del Maximato (1928–1935)*. México, DF: Ediciones Era, 1982.

Meyer, Lorenzo. "La guerra fría en el mundo periférico: El caso del régimen autoritario mexicano; La utilidad del anticomunismo discreto." In *Espejos de la guerra fría: México, América Central y el Caribe,* edited by Daniela Spenser. México, DF: CIESAS, 2004.

———. "Relaciones México–Estados Unidos: Arquitectura y montaje de las pautas de la guerra fría, 1945–1964." *Foro Internacional* 50, no. 2 (April–June 2010): 202–42.

Meyer, Lorenzo, Rafael Segovia, and Alejandra Lajous. *Los inicios de la institucionalización: La política del Maximato.* México, DF: Colegio de México, 1978.

Millán Alarid, Alfredo. *Sinaloa, territorio promisorio: Migraciones japonesa y china.* Culiacán, Sinaloa, Mexico: Fundación Noroeste Topolobampo y la Cuenca del Pacífico; Universidad Autónoma de Sinaloa, 1998.

Ming Zhenhua, *Zhonggong dui lading meizhou de shentou.* Taipei: Haiwai Chubanshe, 1959.

Mitter, Rana. *Forgotten Ally: China's World War II, 1937–1945.* Boston: Houghton Mifflin Harcourt, 2013.

Moya, José. "Immigrants and Associations: A Global and Historical Perspective." *Journal of Ethnic and Migration Studies* 31, no. 5 (September 2005): 833–64.

Moyano de Guevara, Ángela, and Jorge Martínez Zepeda, coords. *Visión histórica de Ensenada.* Mexicali, Baja California: Centro de Investigaciones Históricas UABC, 1982.

Ng, Wing Chung. "Becoming 'Chinese Canadian': The Genesis of a Cultural Category." In *The Last Half Century of Chinese Overseas,* edited by Elizabeth Sinn. Hong Kong: Hong Kong University Press, 1998.

———. *The Chinese in Vancouver, 1945–80: The Pursuit of Identity and Power.* Vancouver, BC: UBC Press, 1999.

———. "Collective Ritual and the Resilience of Traditional Organizations: A Case Study of Vancouver since the Second World War." In *The Chinese Diaspora: Selected Essays,* vol. 1, edited by Wang Ling-chi and Wang Gungwu. Singapore: Times Academic Press, 1998.

Ngai, Mae M. "Legacies of Exclusion: Illegal Chinese Immigration during the Cold War Years." *Journal of American Ethnic History* 18, no. 1 (Fall 1998): 3–35.

Niblo, Stephen R. *Mexico in the 1940s: Modernity, Politics, and Corruption.* Wilmington, DE: Scholarly Resources, 1999.

———. *War, Diplomacy, and Development: The United States and Mexico, 1938–1954.* Wilmington, DE: Scholarly Resources, 1995.

Ojeda, Mario. *Alcances y límites de la política exterior de México.* México, DF: Colegio de México, 2011.

O'Toole, Gavin. *The Reinvention of Mexico: National Ideology in a Neoliberal Era.* Liverpool: Liverpool University Press, 2010.

Oyen, Meredith. "Allies, Enemies, and Aliens: Migration and U.S.-Chinese Relations, 1940–1965." PhD diss., Georgetown University, 2007.

———. "Communism, Containment and the Chinese Overseas." In *The Cold War in Asia: The Battle for Hearts and Minds,* edited by Yangwen Zheng, Hong Liu, and Michael Szonyi. Leiden: Brill, 2010.

Palma Mora, Mónica. "De la simpatía a la antipatía: La actitud oficial ante la inmigración, 1908–1990." *Historias* 56 (September–December 2003): 63–76.

———. *De tierras extrañas: Un estudio sobre la inmigración en México, 1950–1990.* México, DF: Instituto Nacional de Migración, 2006.

Pei Jianzhang. *Zhonghua renmin gongheguo waijiao shi.* Vol. 1. Beijing: Shijie Zhishi, 1994.

Pensado, Jaime M. *Rebel Mexico: Student Unrest and Authoritarian Political Culture during the Long Sixties.* Stanford, CA: Stanford University Press, 2013.

Peterson, Glen D. "Socialist China and the Huaqiao: The Transition to Socialism in the Overseas Chinese Areas of Rural Guangdong, 1949–1956," *Modern China* 14, no. 3 (July 1988): 309–35.

Piñera Ramírez, David, ed. *Panorama histórico de Baja California.* Tijuana: Centro de Investigaciones Históricas UNAM-UABC, 1983.

Portes Gil, Emilio. *China: El fenómeno social, político, económico y cultural más extraordinario de todos los tiempos.* México, DF: Editorial Diana, 1961.

Qin, Yucheng. *The Diplomacy of Nationalism: The Six Companies and China's Policy towards Exclusion.* Honolulu: University of Hawaii Press, 2009.

Rae, Ian, and Morgen Witzel. *The Overseas Chinese of South East Asia: History, Culture, Business.* Basingstoke, UK: Palgrave Macmillan, 2008.

Ramírez Camacho, Beatriz. "Los chinos en México: Esbozo de la comunidad de Tampico." MA thesis, Universidad Nacional Autónoma de México, 1975.

Ramos Aguirre, Francisco. *Los chinos del 14 y otros chinos: Crónica de Ciudad Victoria.* Ciudad Victoria, Tamaulipas, Mexico: Prograf, 2000.

Rankin, Monica A. *¡México, la patria!: Propaganda and Production during World War II.* Lincoln: University of Nebraska Press, 2009.

Ratliff, William E. "Chinese Communist Cultural Diplomacy toward Latin America, 1949–1960." *Hispanic American Historical Review* 49, no. 1 (February 1969): 53–79.

Rénique, Gerardo. "Anti-Chinese Racism, Nationalism and State Formation in Post-Revolutionary Mexico, 1920s–1930s." In *Political Power and Social Theory,* vol. 14, edited by Diane E. Davis, 89–137. Amsterdam: JAI, 2001.

Republic of China Overseas Chinese Affairs Committee (Qiaowu Weiyuanhui). *Huaqiao jingji gaikuang*. Taipei: Qiaowu Weiyuanhui Disanchu, 1974.

Reyes Vega, Rossana. "Los chinos del Soconusco: El surgimiento de una identidad étnica entre inmigrantes." BA thesis, Escuela Nacional de Antropología e Historia, 1995.

Rodríguez Pastor, Humberto. "Perú: Presencia china e identidad nacional." In *Cuando oriente llegó a América: Contribuciones de inmigrantes chinos, japoneses y coreanos*. Washington, DC: Inter-American Development Bank, 2004.

Romero, Alfredo, et al., eds. *Asiáticos en la ciudad de México*. México, D.F.: Instituto de Cultura de la Ciudad de México, 1999.

Romero, Robert Chao. *The Chinese in Mexico, 1882–1940*. Tucson: University of Arizona Press, 2010.

———. "'El destierro de los chinos': Popular Perspectives on Chinese-Mexican Intermarriage in the Early Twentieth Century." *Aztlán: A Journal of Chicano Studies* 32, no. 1 (Spring 2007): 113–44.

Rothwell, Matthew Daniel. "Transpacific Revolutionaries: The Chinese Revolution in Latin America." PhD diss., University of Illinois at Chicago, 2003.

Ruilova, Leonardo. *China popular en América Latina*. Quito: Instituto Latinoamericano de Ciencias Sociales, 1978.

Salazar Anaya, Delia "Tres momentos de la inmigración internacional en México, 1880–1946." In *Extranjeros en México: Continuidades y nuevas aproximaciones*, edited by Ernesto Rodríguez Chávez. México, DF: Centro de Estudios Migratorios, Instituto Nacional de Migración, 2010.

———, ed. *Xenofobia y xenofilia en la historia de México siglos XIX y XX: Homenaje a Moisés González Navarro*. México, DF: SEGOB, INM, 2006.

Samaniego López, Marco Antonio, ed. *Breve historia de Baja California*. Mexicali, Baja California: Universidad Autónoma de Baja California, 2006.

———, ed. *Ensenada: Nuevas aportaciones para su historia*. Mexicali, Baja California: Instituto de Investigaciones Históricas, Universidad Autónoma de Baja California, 1999.

Sanderson Susan, Phil Sidel, and Harold Hims. "East Asians and Arabs in Mexico: A Study of Naturalized Citizens (1886–1931)." In *Asiatic Migrations in Latin America*, edited by Luz María Martinez Montiel. México, DF: Colegio de México, 1981.

Schiavone Camacho, Julia Maria. *Chinese Mexicans: Transpacific Migration and the Search for a Homeland, 1910–1960*. Chapel Hill: University of North Carolina Press, 2012.

———. "Crossing Boundaries, Claiming a Homeland: The Mexican Chinese Transpacific Journey to Becoming Mexican, 1930s-1960s." *Pacific Historical Review* 78, no. 4 (November 2009): 545–77.

Schmitt, Karl M. *Communism in Mexico: A Study in Political Frustration*. Austin: University of Texas Press, 1965.

Schreiber, Rebecca Mina. *Cold War Exiles in Mexico: U.S. Dissidents and the Culture of Critical Resistance*. Minneapolis: University of Minnesota Press, 2009.

Schuler, Friedrich. *Mexico between Hitler and Roosevelt: Mexican Foreign Relations in the Age of Lázaro Cárdenas, 1934–1940*. Albuquerque: University of New Mexico Press, 1998.

Seijas, Tatiana. *Asian Slaves in Colonial Mexico: From Chinos to Indians.* Cambridge: Cambridge University Press, 2014.

Sha Ding. *Zhongguo he lading meizhou guanxi jianshi.* Zhengzhou: Henan Renmin Chubanshe, 1986.

Siu, Lok C. D. *Memories of a Future Home: Diasporic Citizenship of Chinese in Panama.* Stanford, CA: Stanford University Press, 2005.

———. "Queen of the Chinese Colony: Gender, Nation, and Belonging in Diaspora." *Anthropological Quarterly* 78, no. 3 (Summer 2005): 511–42.

Slack, Edward R., Jr. "Sinifying New Spain: Cathay's Influence on Colonial Mexico via the Nao de China." In *The Chinese in Latin America and the Caribbean,* edited by Walton Look Lai and Tan Chee-Beng, 7–34. Leiden: Brill, 2010.

Spenser, Daniela. *The Impossible Triangle: Mexico, Soviet Russia, and the United States in the 1920s.* Durham, NC: Duke University Press, 1999.

———. "Vicente Lombardo Toledano envuelto en antagonismos internacionales." In *Revolución y exilio en la historia de México: Del amor de un historiador a su patria adoptiva; Homenaje a Friedrich Katz,* edited by Javier Dantan, Emilio Kourí, and Friedrich Katz. México, DF: Colegio de México; Chicago: Centro Katz de Estudios Mexicanos, 2010.

Sun, Wanning. "China's Rise and (Trans)National Connections: The Global Diasporic Chinese Mediasphere." In *Routledge Handbook of the Chinese Diaspora,* edited by Chee-Beng Tan. New York: Routledge, 2013.

Taylor, Jay. *The Generalissimo: Chiang Kai-shek and the Struggle for Modern China.* Cambridge, MA: Harvard University Press, 2009.

Tovar González, Ma. Elena. "Extranjeros en el soconusco." *Revista de humanidades: Tecnológico de Monterrey* 8 (2000): 29–43.

Treviño Rangel, Javier, and Pablo Hammeken. "Racismo y nación: Comunidades imaginadas en México." *Estudios sociológicos* 26, no. 78 (September–December 1978): 669–94.

Trueba Lara, José. *Los chinos en Sonora: Una historia olvidada.* Hermosillo, Sonora, Mexico: Instituto de Investigaciones Históricas Universidad de Sonora, 1990.

Van de Ven, Hans J. *War and Nationalism in China, 1925–1945.* London and New York: Routledge Curzon, 2003.

Vasconcelos, José. *La raza cósmica.* México, DF: Editorial Porrúa, 2010.

Velázquez Morales, Catalina. "The Chinese Immigrants in Baja California: From the Cotton Fields to the City, 1920–1940." In *The Chinese in America: A History from Gold Mountain to the New Millennium,* edited by Susie Lan Cassel. Walnut Creek, CA: AltaMira Press, 2002.

———. "Diferencias políticas entre los inmigrantes chinos del noroeste de México (1920–1930): El caso de Francisco L. Yuen." *Historia Mexicana* 55, no. 2 (October–December 2005): 461–512.

———. *Los inmigrantes chinos en Baja California, 1920–1937.* Mexicali, Baja California: Universidad Autónoma de Baja California, 2001.

———. "Xenofobia y racismo: Los comités antichinos en Sonora y Baja California, 1924–1936." *Meyibó,* no. 1, n.s. (November 2009): 43–81.

Waldinger, Roger. *The Cross-Border Connection: Immigrants, Emigrants, and Their Homelands*. Cambridge, MA: Harvard University Press, 2015.

Walker, Louise. *Waking from the Dream: Mexico's Middle Classes after 1968*. Stanford, CA: Stanford University Press, 2013.

Wang, Joan S.H. "In the Name of Legitimacy: Taiwan and Overseas Chinese during the Cold War Era." *China Review* 11, no. 2 (Fall 2011): 65–90.

Wang, Yu San, ed. *Foreign Policy of the Republic of China on Taiwan: An Unorthodox Approach*. New York: Praeger, 1990.

———. "Foundation of the Republic of China's Foreign Policy." In *Foreign Policy of the Republic of China on Taiwan: An Unorthodox Approach*, edited by Yu San Wang. New York: Praeger, 1990.

Wang Gungwu. *The Chinese Overseas: From Earthbound China to the Quest for Autonomy*. Cambridge, MA: Harvard University Press, 2000.

———. "The Status of Overseas Chinese Studies." In *The Chinese Diaspora: Selected Essays*, vol. 1, edited by Wang Ling-chi and Wang Gungwu. Singapore: Times Academic Press, 1998.

Wong, K. Scott. *Americans First: Chinese Americans and the Second World War*. Cambridge, MA: Harvard University Press, 2005.

———. "From Pariah to Paragon: Shifting Images of Chinese Americans during World War II." In *Chinese Americans and the Politics of Race and Culture*, edited by Sucheng Chan and Madeline Y. Hsu, 153–72. Philadelphia: Temple University Press, 2008.

Wongsurawat, Wasana. "From Yaowaraj to Plabplachai: The Thai State and Ethnic Chinese in Thailand during the Cold War." In *Dynamics of the Cold War in Asia: Ideology, Identity and Culture*, edited by Tuong Vu and Wasana Wongsurawat. New York: Palgrave Macmillan, 2009.

Wu, Genhua. *Moxige, guadimala huaqiao gaikuang*. Taipei: Zhengzhong Shuju, 1989.

Xue Dianzeng. *Baohu qiaomin lun*. Shanghai: Shangwu Yinshuguan, 1937.

Yankelevich, Pablo. "El artículo 33 en cifras." In *¿Deseables o inconvenientes? Las fronteras de la extranjería en el México posrevolucionario*. México, DF: Bonilla Artigas Editores, 2011.

———. "Corrupción y gestión migratoria en el México posrevolucionario." *Revista de Indias* 72, no. 255 (2012): 433–64.

———. "Extranjeros indeseables en México (1911–1940): Una aproximación cuantitativa a la aplicación del artículo 33 constitucional." *Historia Mexicana* 53, no. 3 (January–March 2004): 693–744.

———. "Mexico for the Mexicans: Immigration, National Sovereignty, and the Promotion of Mestizaje." *Americas* 68, no. 3 (January 2012): 405–36.

———. "Nación y extranjería en el México revolucionario." *Cuicuilco* 11, no. 31 (May–August 2004): 1–29.

Yen, Ching-hwang. *The Chinese in Southeast Asia and Beyond: Socioeconomic and Political Dimensions*. Singapore: World Scientific Publishing, 2008.

Young, Elliott. *Alien Nation: Chinese Migration in the Americas from the Coolie Era through World War II*. Chapel Hill: University of North Carolina Press, 2014.

Yu, Henry. "Mountains of Gold: Canada, North America, and the Cantonese Pacific." in *Routledge Handbook of the Chinese Diaspora,* edited by Chee-Beng Tan. New York: Routledge, 2013.

Yu, Renqiu. *To Save China, to Save Ourselves: The Chinese Hand Laundry Alliance of New York.* Philadelphia: Temple University Press, 1992.

Yu Shouzhi (Yu Yuan-tse). *Moxige huaqiao shihua.* Taipei: Haiwai Wenke Chubanshe, 1954.

Yu-Sion, Live. "The Sinwa of Reunion: Searching for a Chinese Identity in a Multicultural World." In *Beyond Chinatown: New Chinese Migration and the Global Expansion of China,* edited by Mette Thunø. Copenhagen: NIAS Press, 2005.

Yun, Lisa. *The Coolie Speaks: Chinese Indentured Laborers and African Slaves in Cuba.* Philadelphia: Temple University Press, 2008.

Zarrow, Peter Gue. *China in War and Revolution, 1895–1949.* London and New York: Routledge, 2005.

Zhang Yinglong. "Cujin heping tongyi daye" [The great task of encouraging peaceful reunification]. In *Huaqiao huaren yu xinzhongguo,* edited by Zhang Yinglong. Guangzhou: Jinan Daxue Chubanshe, 2009.

Zhao, Xiaojian. *Remaking Chinese America: Immigration, Family, and Community, 1940–1965.* New Brunswick, NJ: Rutgers University Press, 2002.

Zheng Weishu. "Cong lishi jiazu kan moxige huaqiao huaren de shengcun yu fazhan." In *Haiwai huaren shehui xintoushi,* edited by Lü Weixiong. Guangzhou: Lingnan Meishu Chubanshe, 2005.

Zhongyang Weiyuanhui Disanzu. *Zhongguo guomindang zai haiwai gedi dangbu shiliao chugao huibian.* Taipei: Zhongguo Guomindang Zhongyang Weiyuanhui Disanzu, 1961.

Zhuang Guotu. "China's Policies on Overseas Chinese: Past and Present." In *Routledge Handbook of the Chinese Diaspora,* edited by Chee-Beng Tan. New York: Routledge, 2013.

Zolov, Eric. "¡Cuba sí, Yanquis no! The Sacking of the Instituto Cultural México-Norteamericano in Morelia, Michoacán, 1961." In *In from the Cold: Latin America's New Encounter with the Cold War,* edited by Gilbert M. Joseph and Daniela Spenser. Durham, NC: Duke University Press, 2008.

Index

Page numbers in italic refer to illustrations.